Scalable And Applications in Kotlin

*Write and maintain large
Android application code bases*

Myles Bennett

www.bpbonline.com

First Edition 2025

Copyright © BPB Publications, India

ISBN: 978-93-65899-276

All Rights Reserved. No part of this publication may be reproduced, distributed or transmitted in any form or by any means or stored in a database or retrieval system, without the prior written permission of the publisher with the exception to the program listings which may be entered, stored and executed in a computer system, but they can not be reproduced by the means of publication, photocopy, recording, or by any electronic and mechanical means.

LIMITS OF LIABILITY AND DISCLAIMER OF WARRANTY

The information contained in this book is true to correct and the best of author's and publisher's knowledge. The author has made every effort to ensure the accuracy of these publications, but publisher cannot be held responsible for any loss or damage arising from any information in this book.

All trademarks referred to in the book are acknowledged as properties of their respective owners but BPB Publications cannot guarantee the accuracy of this information.

To View Complete
BPB Publications Catalogue
Scan the QR Code:

www.bpbonline.com

Dedicated to

My wife and business partner

Heather

and

My daughter **Aimi**

About the Author

Myles Bennett has been working as an Android developer for more than 13 years, and has worked in mobile development for further 10 years as a Symbian developer. Having graduated with a Bachelor of Engineering degree in 1995, he has worked for many high profile clients such as Samsung, Warner Bros Discovery and Sky, to name a few. In his capacity as a contractor throughout his career, he has been in the unique position to gain exposure to a huge variety of different working environments. He is therefore extremely qualified to say what works and what does not work in terms of large software development projects. As a passionate Kotlin professional, he is currently diversifying into other areas where Kotlin is making an impact. This includes full stack development, serverless provisioning and cross platform implementation.

About the Reviewers

- **Awais Zaka** is a seasoned software developer with more than 20 years of industry experience. He has contributed to various sectors, including media/broadcast, telecommunications, and transport, collaborating with companies like NBCUniversal, Sky, Discovery, O2, BBC, and Samsung. He has also created and released his own apps across multiple platforms. Awais lives in London with his wife and three children. In his free time, he enjoys cycling, playing badminton, and reading.

- **Zaid Kamil** is a Google-certified Android app developer and a professional coding trainer who has been developing and teaching how to make Android apps for over a decade. He is the Training Head at Digipodium, a leading IT training institute in India, where he mentors and guides hundreds of students and professionals in various domains of technology. He has a rich portfolio of projects in both Java and Kotlin, using Android and various third-party libraries and APIs. He is also skilled in the areas of Data Science, AI, Cloud services and Web development, and holds multiple certifications from IBM and Microsoft in Python. He has a keen interest in designing and implementing machine learning models to analyze data and improve business operations. He has worked with cross-functional teams to design and deploy AI solutions for various domains. Zaid Kamil is passionate about learning new skills and technology. He constantly updates himself with the latest trends and developments in the tech industry. He also likes to explore new tools and frameworks that can enhance his coding abilities. He believes that learning is a lifelong process and one should never stop growing and improving.

- **Ayomitide Odunyemi** is currently a Principal Engineer at Rad and CTO of Loger, with 8 years of experience in developing and scaling enterprise applications in domains such as Fintech, Edutech, Blockchain, AI, and Proptech, with a track record delivering 27+ production applications scaling to millions of users.

Acknowledgement

I want to express my deepest gratitude to my family for their unwavering support and encouragement throughout this book's writing, especially my wife Heather and my daughter Aimi.

I am also grateful to BPB Publications for their guidance and expertise in bringing this book to fruition. It was a long journey of revising this book, with valuable participation and collaboration of reviewers, technical experts, and editors.

I would particularly like to acknowledge the valuable contributions of my colleague, Awais Zaka, whose reviews of the last few chapters helped push this book over the line.

Finally, I would like to thank all the readers who have taken an interest in my book and for their support in making it a reality. Your encouragement has been invaluable.

Preface

This book introduces the reader to Kotlin and Jetpack Compose for novice or intermediate Android app developers. It proceeds to build upon this foundation, proposing ideologies and methods valuable to even seasoned professionals.

Modern technology in the mobile space is advancing at an ever increasing rate. Mobile applications in turn are becoming more and more complex with multiple features and user journeys. The subsequent code-bases can quickly become unmanageable if not organized correctly. Typical symptoms of this can be seen when adding or fixing one thing breaks another, or when two developers are unable to work on seperate features without overwriting or conflicting with each others code.

There are many established development paradigms in place to address these issues, such as clean-code architecture, test-driven development, layering, model-view-intent, etc., all of which will be covered here, bridging the gap between the theory and practical application in an Android development environment.

The initial chapters will help all the readers who need to know about Kotlin, Jetpack compose and introduce feature orientated project organization. Continuing chapters chart the history of presentation layer architecture leading to working implementations of MVI and Unit-directional Flow using Kotlin and Jetpack Compose. Further chapters introduce cross platform development as a means of seperation of concerns. The readers will also learn the fine details of unit and automation testing with continous integration.

Chapter 1: Introduction to Kotlin for Android – discusses the finer aspects of Kotlin that makes it stand out from other languages and why it is a great choice for Android development. From nullable and built-in lambda types through to asynchronous implementations with Coroutines and everything in between, this chapter provides the foundation for all the concepts discussed in the entire book.

Chapter 2: Breaking Down App Code with Separation of Concerns - details the breakdown of app code by introducing **separation of concerns (SoC)**. The entire foundation for this book is based on this concept. This chapter also has a brief look at its benefits, examines the concept at a high level and discusses the aspects of the Kotlin language that facilitate its implementation.

Chapter 3: Feature-Oriented Development in Android - continues the theme of SoC, this chapter discusses the high-level method of splitting an app into conceptual features and how this helps contribute to code quality. It examines the origins of the Feature concept and provides an example in the form of a case study.

Chapter 4: Clean Code Architecture - looks at the recommended way of further subdividing those features into modules representing different layers of CCA. It will describe the original CCA concept in depth and then present a very similar arrangement adapted specifically for Android, combining it with Data-Domain-Presentation layering.

Chapter 5: Cross-Platform App Development - covers the topic of cross-platform development and how it relates to large project development. Over the years, there have been several attempts to unify the development of iOS and Android apps using cross-platform environments. These attempts have largely failed. This chapter looks briefly at those platforms, why they failed and discusses the half-way-house of cross-platform development, **Kotlin Multi-mobile (KMM)**, and how it can be used in a clean code arrangement for pattern enforcement as well as cross-platform compatibility.

Chapter 6: Dependency Injection - explains the concept and looks at the basic **Dependency Injection (DI)** techniques, their benefits, and the popular open-source libraries for implementing it. It also explains why it is vital for clean code and Test-driven Development. Further, this chapter provides some code samples, with and without the libraries.

Chapter 7: Introduction to Jetpack Compose - the modern UI toolkit for building native Android apps. The subsequent chapters rely on some rudimentary knowledge of Jetpack Compose. This chapter provides some basic concepts for those unfamiliar with Compose.

Chapter 8: Presentation Layer Evolution in Compose - presents the Uni-directional Flow presentation architecture suited for the latest development paradigms in Android. In doing so, it charts the journey that led to this arrangement by examining each of the popular architectures that went before.

Chapter 9: Test-Driven Development with Mocking Libraries for Android - Test-Driven Development is a software development methodology that emphasizes writing tests before writing the actual code for a software component. This chapter describes the technique in detail and introduces the popular open-source mocking libraries used in its execution.

Chapter 10: Kotlin DSL and Multimodule Apps - describes how to create a project from scratch using Kotlin DSL, suggests a strategy for a module hierarchy and examines an approach to maintain consistent dependency versioning across modules.

Chapter 11: Creating the Module Hierarchy - introduces a simple method for creating module hierarchies and suggests an approach in line with solutions highlighted elsewhere in this book.

Chapter 12: Networking and APIs in Kotlin - examines use cases for and aspects of networking in Android. By the end of this chapter, the readers will understand the concepts of APIs (in particular, RESTful APIs), caching and authentication. This chapter provides a worked example of a network call using the clean-code architecture and test-driven development concepts introduced elsewhere in the book.

Chapter 13: Creating UI with Jetpack Compose - continuing from *Chapter 7, Introduction to Kotlin*, this chapter examines four important high-level aspects of Jetpack Compose, namely, Themes, The Scaffold, Navigation and Animation, that help structure the code and provides a smooth experience to the user. By the end of this chapter, the user will have a solid foundation in the application of these features and have some ideas for their use in a multiplatform environment.

Chapter 14: Debugging in Kotlin - explores the powerful debugging capabilities integrated within Android Studio. It will demonstrate how to utilize breakpoints, watch variables, and logcat to monitor application behavior and identify issues. This chapter will also cover advanced topics such as memory profiling, analyzing thread performance, and leveraging Kotlin-specific debugging tools.

Chapter 15: Test Automation - focuses on automation testing in Kotlin with Jetpack Compose, providing the essential knowledge and tools to create reliable and maintainable test suites for applications. A range of topics will be covered, from setting up a testing environment and writing basic UI tests to more advanced techniques such as testing state management, handling asynchronous operations, and integrating testing into a continuous integration pipeline.

Chapter 16: Building and Distributing Applications - discusses the process of building and distributing Android apps, exploring the essential steps and best practices to bring ideas to life and share them with the world. By the end of this chapter, the reader will have gained insight into creating and uploading an APK to Google Play Store or Amazon App Store.

Code Bundle and Coloured Images

Please follow the link to download the
Code Bundle and the *Coloured Images* of the book:

https://rebrand.ly/rx7hy1h

The code bundle for the book is also hosted on GitHub at
https://github.com/bpbpublications/Scalable-Android-Applications-in-Kotlin.
In case there's an update to the code, it will be updated on the existing GitHub repository.

We have code bundles from our rich catalogue of books and videos available at **https://github.com/bpbpublications**. Check them out!

Errata

We take immense pride in our work at BPB Publications and follow best practices to ensure the accuracy of our content to provide with an indulging reading experience to our subscribers. Our readers are our mirrors, and we use their inputs to reflect and improve upon human errors, if any, that may have occurred during the publishing processes involved. To let us maintain the quality and help us reach out to any readers who might be having difficulties due to any unforeseen errors, please write to us at :

errata@bpbonline.com

Your support, suggestions and feedbacks are highly appreciated by the BPB Publications' Family.

Did you know that BPB offers eBook versions of every book published, with PDF and ePub files available? You can upgrade to the eBook version at www.bpbonline.com and as a print book customer, you are entitled to a discount on the eBook copy. Get in touch with us at :

business@bpbonline.com for more details.

At **www.bpbonline.com**, you can also read a collection of free technical articles, sign up for a range of free newsletters, and receive exclusive discounts and offers on BPB books and eBooks.

Piracy

If you come across any illegal copies of our works in any form on the internet, we would be grateful if you would provide us with the location address or website name. Please contact us at **business@bpbonline.com** with a link to the material.

If you are interested in becoming an author

If there is a topic that you have expertise in, and you are interested in either writing or contributing to a book, please visit **www.bpbonline.com**. We have worked with thousands of developers and tech professionals, just like you, to help them share their insights with the global tech community. You can make a general application, apply for a specific hot topic that we are recruiting an author for, or submit your own idea.

Reviews

Please leave a review. Once you have read and used this book, why not leave a review on the site that you purchased it from? Potential readers can then see and use your unbiased opinion to make purchase decisions. We at BPB can understand what you think about our products, and our authors can see your feedback on their book. Thank you!

For more information about BPB, please visit **www.bpbonline.com**.

Join our book's Discord space

Join the book's Discord Workspace for Latest updates, Offers, Tech happenings around the world, New Release and Sessions with the Authors:

https://discord.bpbonline.com

Table of Contents

1. Introduction to Kotlin for Android 1
Introduction 1
Structure 2
Objectives 2
The reason why Kotlin is a great choice for Android development 2
Key differences between Kotlin and Java 3
    Null safety 3
    Type inference 5
    Functional programming 6
        Immutability 6
        First-class functions and variables 7
        Lambdas 7
    Extension functions 9
    Scoping functions 10
    Built-in collection class extensions 12
    Getters and setters 13
    One-line functions 15
    Delegation 15
    Lazy initialization 18
    No more type erasure 19
    Named and default parameters 20
    Companion objects 21
    Internal scope 22
    Coroutines 23
    Flows and StateFlows 23
        Flows 24
        StateFlows 24

Conclusion	25
Points to remember	26
Questions	26

2. Breaking Down App Code with Separation of Concerns ... 27

Introduction	27
Structure	27
Objectives	28
Benefits of SoC	28
Kotlin code constructs facilitating SoC	29
SOLID principles	30
Single Responsibility Principle	*30*
Open/Closed Principle	*32*
Liskov Substitution Principle	*34*
Interface Segregation Principle	*35*
Dependency Inversion Principle	*37*
Conclusion	38
Points to remember	39
Questions	39

3. Feature-Oriented Development in Android ... 41

Introduction	41
Structure	41
Objectives	42
Understanding feature module	42
Concept origins	42
Granularity of features	43
Identifying features	44
User journeys	45
Case study	45
Conclusion	51
Points to remember	52
Questions	52

4. Clean Code Architecture 53

Introduction 53
Structure 53
Objectives 54
The ubiquitous CCA onion diagram 54
Domain-data-presentation layering 55
Combined CCA/layering for Android 56
Domain layer 57
    Domain entities 57
    Use cases 59
Data layer 61
    Repositories 62
    Data sources 63
Presentation layer 64
Flow of control 65
Infrastructure layer 69
Conclusion 70
Points to remember 70
Questions 70

5. Cross-Platform App Development 71

Introduction 71
Structure 71
Objectives 72
Cross-platform development overview 72
    Disadvantages of cross-platform development 74
Xamarin 75
    Disadvantages of Xamarin 76
Ionic 78
    Disadvantages of Ionic 79
React Native 80
    Disadvantages of React Native 82

Flutter	83
Disadvantages of Flutter	*84*
Compose Multiplatform	85
Disadvantages of Compose Multiplatform	*86*
Common failures	87
Kotlin multi-mobile	88
Disadvantages of KMM	*89*
Conclusion	92
Points to remember	92
Questions	92

6. Dependency Injection 93

Introduction	93
Structure	93
Objectives	94
Overview of Dependency Injection	94
Setter/method injection	95
Constructor injection	96
Interface injection	96
Field injection	98
Injection frameworks	99
Hilt injection framework	*101*
History of Hilt	*101*
Working with Hilt	*102*
Setting up Hilt	*103*
Koin injection framework	*106*
History of Koin	*106*
Working with Koin	*107*
Pros and cons of Hilt and Koin	109
Hilt pros	*109*
Hilt cons	*109*
Koin pros	*109*

Koin cons 110
Conclusion 110
Points to remember 111
Questions 111

7. Introduction to Jetpack Compose 113
Introduction 113
Structure 113
Objectives 114
Overview of Jetpack Compose 114
Advantages over traditional views 115
Getting started with Jetpack Compose 116
Some commonly used composables 119
Modifiers 125
Scoped custom composables 128
State management primitives 130
Conclusion 134
Points to remember 135
Questions 135

8. Presentation Layer Evolution in Compose 137
Introduction 137
Structure 137
Objectives 138
Summary of presentation architecture evolution 138
Model-View-Controller 139
Model-View-Presenter 141
Model-View-ViewModel 144
LiveData 145
Data binding 147
Model-View-Intent 149
Key concepts and summary of MVI 151
Implementing MVI with Jetpack Compose 152

  UDF base ViewModel: First pass 152
  Implementing view in Jetpack compose 154
  UDF base ViewModel: Second pass 156
  Using the side effect in the controller 158
  UDF base ViewModel: Third pass 162
 Disadvantage of the UDF/MVI pattern 165
 Conclusion 165
 Points to remember 165
 Questions 166

9. Test-Driven Development with Mocking Libraries for Android 167
 Introduction 167
 Structure 167
 Objectives 168
 The TDD cycle 168
 Advantages of TDD 168
 Historical obstacles to TDD 169
 The bowling game example 170
 Dependency injection and TDD 174
 Mocking libraries 175
  Mockito 177
  MockK 177
 Disadvantages of mocking libraries 179
 Test driving Kotlin flows and StateFlows 179
  Problems associated with test-driving flows 179
  kotlinx-coroutines-test and dispatchers 181
  Turbine mocking library 183
 Test driving a UDF ViewModel 185
 Advanced flow testing scenarios 188
 Conclusion 189
 Points to remember 190
 Questions 190

10. Kotlin DSL and Multimodule Apps 191

Introduction 191
Structure 191
Objectives 192
Definition of DSL 192
Advantages of Kotlin DSL for build scripts 192
Multimodule project creation 193
The buildSrc module 195
    Steps for creating the buildSrc module *196*
Version catalogs 200
Updating and adding to the Version Catalog 203
Recommended IDE settings 206
    Optimizing imports on-the-fly *206*
    Project structure suggestions *207*
Conclusion 207
Points to remember 207
Questions 208

11. Creating the Module Hierarchy 209

Introduction 209
Structure 209
Objectives 210
Creating a feature presentation module 210
Creating data and domain modules 213
Binding data to domain 218
    Koin DI *219*
    Hilt DI *222*
        KAPT *223*
        KSP *225*
        Key considerations *227*
Splitting out UI from presentation 228
Creating an infrastructure (common) module 230

Conclusion 231
Points to remember 231
Questions 232

12. Networking and APIs in Kotlin 233
Introduction 233
Structure 233
Objectives 234
Networking in Android 234
Definition of an API 235
    Key aspects of APIs 236
    Common types of APIs 237
RESTful APIs 238
Networking libraries 239
    Android framework (java.net) 240
    OkHttp 241
    Volley 243
    Retrofit 244
    Ktor 245
Authentication and security 246
    API keys 246
    OAuth tokens 247
Data module setup 248
    Build script updates 248
Data classes 250
Test-driving the network call 251
    MockEngine 252
    Use-case input port 253
    The first test 255
Caching 258
    Http caching 259
    Custom caching 259

Test-driving the use cases	260
DI module binding	264
Hilt	264
Koin	265
Conclusion	266
Points to remember	266
Questions	267

13. Creating UI with Jetpack Compose 269

Introduction	269
Structure	269
Objectives	270
Themes	270
Color scheme	272
Typography	273
Fonts	274
FontFamily	275
TextStyle	276
Typography	276
Shapes	277
The Scaffold	279
TopAppBar()	282
BottomAppBar()	284
DrawerContent()	285
Fab()	285
SnackHost()	286
Scaffold()	287
Navigation	288
The Navigation component (legacy)	288
Navigation Compose	290
Navigation Compose with parameters	292
Navigation Compose with Scaffold	296

	Navigating in and out of the Scaffold 297
	Animation 300
	AnimationSpec 300
	AnimatedVisibility 302
	Transition animations 303
	Multiplatform considerations 305
	Conclusion 306
	Points to remember 307
	Questions 307
14.	**Debugging in Kotlin** **309**
	Introduction 309
	Structure 309
	Objectives 310
	Android device bridge 310
	Breakpoints 311
	Conditional breakpoints 313
	Exception breakpoints 313
	Set an exception breakpoint 314
	Watch expressions 315
	Evaluate expression 316
	Profiling tools 316
	Logcat logging 319
	Timber 321
	Other considerations 323
	Conclusion 323
	Points to remember 323
	Questions 324
15.	**Test Automation** **325**
	Introduction 325
	Structure 325
	Objectives 326

Espresso 326

Compose tree 327

ComposeTestRule.. 329

Finders, Matchers and Asserters... 330

    Finders.. 330

    Matchers... 330

    Asserters 331

The Robot Pattern 331

    Advantages of the Robot pattern 337

Code coverage 338

Continuous integration 339

Conclusion 340

Points to remember 340

Questions.. 341

16. Building and Distributing Applications 343

Introduction 343

Structure 343

Objectives 344

Preparing to release an Android app 344

    Setting version information 344

    Android Application Package... 345

    Android app bundle... 345

    Keystore 346

    Creating a keystore with Android Studio.. 347

    Creating a keystore on the Command Line 349

    Configuring building and signing in Gradle 351

    Building and signing on CI.. 352

    Build flavors 356

Distribution portals... 357

Google Play store 358

    Create Developer account 358

Releasing an app on Google Play store 359
   Finish setting up your application 359
   Internal/closed testing 361
      Adding countries (closed only) 361
      Adding testers 361
      Creating new release 361
      Send the release to Google for review (Closed only) 364
      Pre-registration 364
   Apply for production 364
   Production application process 365
Amazon App store 365
   Creating Developer Account 365
   Releasing an app on Amazon App Store 366
Conclusion 373
Points to remember 374
Questions 374
Index **375-386**

CHAPTER 1
Introduction to Kotlin for Android

Introduction

This book describes how to build, from scratch, large, multi-feature apps using Kotlin and Jetpack Compose. It achieves this by combining modern paradigms and techniques, all of which will be described here.

Existing commercial Android code tends not to employ a scalable framework suitable for these types of applications. An important reason for this is that these projects are usually *grown* from one of the Android Studio new project wizards.

All these wizards are designed to showcase certain app features in a **Hello World** fashion. They typically produce code with a single module, **app**, containing a single Activity and perhaps a Fragment with XML layouts and Android Views. They do not present any kind of scalable structure.

What typically happens with large applications that start in this way is that over time, different developers come and go, usually bolting on the popular paradigm at the time. The resulting code becomes *Frankenstein's* Monster; a tangle of fragile spaghetti code that is very difficult to read, likely to break with any changes and that screams out to be rewritten. Too often though, clients are reluctant to do this as the existing code already represents a significant investment.

Throughout his book, we examine how built-in Kotlin features help to address this by breaking up the code in a recognizable fashion making initial creation, maintenance and updating quicker and easier whilst retaining quality.

Firstly though, this chapter examines the differences between Kotlin and Java and discusses why it is a great choice for Android development.

Structure

This chapter covers the following topics:

- The reason why Kotlin is a great choice for Android development
- Key differences between Kotlin and Java

Objectives

By the end of this chapter, not only will the answer to why Kotlin is a great language for Android be apparent, you will also be introduced to the key concepts of the Kotlin language that make it distinct from other languages. In particular, you will become familiar with functional programming, null safety, extension, and scoping functions, asynchronous programming with coroutines, and much more.

The reason why Kotlin is a great choice for Android development

Kotlin is a modern, open-source programming language that is designed to be concise, expressive, and safe. It has quickly gained popularity in the Android development community, as it offers a number of benefits over Java, the traditional language used for Android development.

Here are some of the reasons why Kotlin is a great choice for Android development:

- **Interoperability with Java**: Kotlin is designed to be fully interoperable with Java, which means that existing Java code can be easily integrated into Kotlin projects and vice versa. This makes it easy for developers who are already familiar with Java to start using Kotlin without having to learn a completely new language.

- **Concise and expressive syntax**: Kotlin has a clean and concise syntax that makes it easy to read and write. It also supports several modern programming features such as lambdas, extension functions, and operator overloading that can make code more expressive and concise.

- **Increased productivity**: Kotlin's concise syntax, powerful features, and strong type system can help increase developer productivity. It can reduce the amount of boilerplate code that developers need to write and can make it easier to refactor code and catch errors early. Kotlin's other language features, such as extension functions and data classes, can help developers write code more quickly and efficiently. This can lead to increased productivity and faster development time.

- **Enhanced performance**: Kotlin's performance is at par with Java, and in some cases, it can even outperform it. This is due to Kotlin's efficient bytecode, which is optimized for performance.
- **Improved code safety**: Kotlin has several features that can help improve code safety, such as null safety, type inference, and data classes. These features can help prevent common runtime errors and make it easier to write code that is more robust and maintainable. One of the most significant problems with Java is the potential for null pointer exceptions, which can cause crashes and other issues in Android apps. Kotlin provides null safety features that help developers avoid these issues and write safer code.
- **Extension functions and properties**: Kotlin allows developers to extend existing classes with new functions and properties without having to create new subclasses. This makes it easy to add new features to existing code without having to modify the original code.
- **Coroutines**: Java has historically relied on third-party solutions and plugins to deal with asynchronous code and background tasks. Android initially provided its own solution in the form of `AsyncTask`. Later, `RxJava` became popular but could be difficult to use due to its chained interface pattern. A value spawned in the first part of the chain would become unavailable in a later part of the chain making complex tasks messy to write. Kotlin provides built-in support for coroutines, which makes it easier to write asynchronous code. This can be especially useful in Android development, where asynchronous operations are common.
- **Android Studio support**: Kotlin is fully supported in Android Studio, which is the primary development environment for Android development. This means that developers can take advantage of Kotlin's features and benefits within a familiar and powerful development environment.

Kotlin is a great choice for Android development due to its concise syntax, interoperability with Java, null safety, enhanced performance, and improved productivity. The adoption rate by developers has already made Kotlin and Android synonymous (despite Kotlin also being picked up for backend development now).

Key differences between Kotlin and Java

Whilst there are many differences between Kotlin and Java, in this section we will describe the features of Kotlin that have been found as the most useful in comparison to Java. It is by no means a comprehensive examination of the Kotlin language. There are plenty of existing texts dedicated to that.

Null safety

This is a key feature of Kotlin that helps prevent null pointer exceptions at runtime. In Kotlin, null safety is achieved through a combination of nullable and non-null types, safe call operator, and null coalescing, that is, Kotlin provides more advanced type inference capabilities compared to Java. Kotlin's compiler can deduce types based on initializers, expressions, and other context, reducing the need for explicit type declarations. This contributes to more concise and readable code. Java's type inference is more limited, primarily focused on simplifying the usage of generics with the diamond operator..

In Kotlin, every variable has a type, that can either be nullable or non-null. A nullable type is denoted by the **?** symbol at the end of the type, while a non-null type does not have the **?** symbol. For example, **String?** Is a nullable type, while **String** is a non-null type.

When a variable is declared as nullable, the compiler forces the developer to handle the possibility of the variable being null. This means that the developer has to use a safe call operator **?.** or elvis operator **?:** to avoid a **NullPointerException** at runtime.

The safe call operator **?.** is used to safely access properties or methods on nullable variables. If the variable is null, the expression will return null, instead of throwing a **NullPointerException**. For example:

```
1. val str: String? = null
2. val length = str?.length
```

The elvis operator **?:** is used to provide a default value for a nullable variable if it is null. For example:

```
1. val str: String? = null
2. val length = str?.length ?: 0 // will be 0 if str is null
```

The equivalent Java code would look like this:

```
1. if (str != null) { // not null
2.     length = str.length();
3. } else {
4.     length = 0;
5. }
```

This becomes extremely powerful when mapping complex data from backend APIs where all fields are nullable. Consider this (somewhat contrived) example given an object received of type **DetailResponse**:

```
1. data class DetailResponse(
2.     val website: Website? = null
3. )
4.
5. data class Website(
6.     val uri: Uri? = null
7. )
```

```
8.
9. data class Uri(
10.     val url: String? = null
11. )
```

In the instance where you were only interested in the final URL string, then the mapping would look like this:

```
1. data class DetailDomain (val url: String)
2.
3. fun responseToDomain(detailResponse: DetailResponse?):DetailDomain {
4.     return DetailDomain(detailResponse?.website?.uri?.url ?: "")
5. }
```

In fact, Kotlin provides an extended function to replace the elvis operator just for strings, **orEmpty()**, so the return statement could look like this:

```
1.     return DetailDomain(detailResponse?.website?.uri?.url.orEmpty())
```

Kotlin also provides a non-null assertion operator **!!** which tells the compiler that a nullable variable is not null. This can be useful in certain situations, but should be used with caution, as it can still result in a **NullPointerException** at runtime if the variable is actually null. In fact, we would only recommend its use in unit tests (more on this later). There is a reason it is a double-exclamation mark – to draw attention to it in code reviews.

Type inference

Type inference in Kotlin and Java refers to the ability of the compiler to automatically determine the type of a variable or expression based on the context. However, there are some differences in how type inference is handled in Kotlin compared to Java.

In Java, type inference was introduced in Java 8 with the introduction of the diamond operator (**<>**) for generics. The primary purpose of type inference in Java is to simplify the usage of generics. For example:

```
1. List<Integer> numbers = new ArrayList<>();
2. // Type inference with diamond operator
```

In this Java code, the diamond operator (**<>**) allows the type **Integer** to be inferred based on the declaration of **numbers** on the left-hand side.

The Java type inference is more limited compared to Kotlin. Java still requires explicit type declarations in most cases, and the compiler's ability to infer types is more restricted than in Kotlin. In Kotlin, the compiler has more powerful type inference capabilities, which allows it to deduce the type of a variable based on its initializer or its usage. This means that you can omit explicit type declarations in many cases, reducing verbosity and making the code more concise. For example:

```
1. val name = "John" // Compiler infers the type as String
2. val age = 25 // Compiler infers the type as Int
3. val numbers = listOf(1, 2, 3) // Infers the type List<Int>
```

In the above Kotlin code, the compiler can infer the types of **name**, **age**, and **numbers** based on their initial values. You do not need to explicitly specify the types, as the compiler can determine them automatically. Kotlin provides more advanced type inference capabilities compared to Java. Kotlin's compiler can deduce types based on initializers, expressions, and other context, reducing the need for explicit type declarations. This contributes to more concise and readable code. Java's type inference is more limited, primarily focused on simplifying the usage of generics with the diamond operator.

Functional programming

Java was an evolution of languages that have gone before, in particular C and C++. Functional programming is a programming paradigm that emphasizes the use of functions to create software and C was certainly that. It used the concepts of pointers and references to pass functions as parameters to other functions. Classes were introduced to C++ when **Object Oriented Programming (OOP)** became popular but since C++ was just an extension of C, all functional programming capabilities were still available. Java was then developed, focusing completely on the OOP paradigm. Any Java code written had to be inside a class. Java fixed many common problems faced by C++ developers but, in doing so, lost most of the more convenient functional programming features, such as passing functions as parameters.

Immutability

Kotlin and Java handle immutability in slightly different ways. Here is a comparison of how immutability is approached in Kotlin compared to Java.

In Kotlin, immutability is supported through the use of the **val** keyword, which is used to declare read-only variables as opposed to the **var** keyword for full mutability. Once assigned, the value of a **val** cannot be changed. Immutability is enforced by the compiler, preventing reassignments or modifications to **val** variables. For example:

```
1. var name1 = "Jane" // mutable - can be reassigned
2. val name2 = "John" // immutable - can *not* be reassigned
```

In this example, the name variable is declared as a read-only **val**. Its value is assigned as **John** and cannot be changed afterward. If an attempt is made to reassign a value to name, a compilation error will occur. The closest equivalent in Java would look like this:

```
1. final String name = "John";
```

In this Java example, the name variable is declared as **final**, making it read-only. Once assigned, the value cannot be changed. However, it is important to note that the object referenced by name could still be mutable, and its internal state could be modified. Java provides no inherent protection against mutating the state of an object.

In contrast, Kotlin promotes immutability not only through read-only variables (**val**) but also by providing immutable collections as the default. Kotlin's standard library offers various immutable collection classes, such as **listOf**, **setOf**, and **mapOf**, which do not allow modifications after creation. This encourages the use of immutable collections, reducing the risk of unintentional modification of collections. Kotlin provides stronger support for immutability through its **val** keyword and default immutability for collections. Java relies on the **final** keyword for read-only variables but does not enforce immutability for objects.

First-class functions and variables

The first thing to note on this topic is that, like with C, functions and values do not have to be part of a class. They can be declared in any file, including a file that contains one or more classes.

Another major difference between Java and Kotlin is that in Java there is a one-to-one relationship between a file and a public class. There is no such restriction in Kotlin. You can easily write something like the following:

```
1.  val myInt = 1
2.  fun myfun(input: Int) {
3.      // do something
4.  }
5.
6.  class MyClass() {
7.      val myFloat = 0.0
8.
9.      fun myClassFun(){
10.         // do something else
11.     }
12. }
```

In this case, **myInt** and **myFun** would have global scope.

Lambdas

A lambda (also known as a lambda function, anonymous function, or function literal) is a way to define a small, anonymous function without a name. It is a function that can be created on-the-fly and passed as an argument to other functions or stored in variables. Lambdas were only introduced into Java in version 8:

```
1.  List<Integer> nums = Arrays.asList(1, 2, 3, 4, 5);
2.  List<Integer> evenNums = nums.stream()
```

```
3.          .filter(n -> n % 2 == 0)
4.          .collect(Collectors.toList());
```

In this Java example, we use the Stream API to filter out the even numbers from a list. We create a stream from the list of numbers, **nums** using the **stream()** method. Then, we chain the filter method, which takes a lambda expression:

n -> n % 2 == 0 as an argument to filter out the even numbers. Finally, we collect the filtered numbers into a new list using the **collect** method.

The Kotlin alternative is somewhat more concise:

```
1. val nums = listOf(1, 2, 3, 4, 5)
2. val evenNums = nums.filter { it % 2 == 0 }
```

In this Kotlin example, we use the filter function along with a lambda expression to filter out the even numbers. The lambda expression

{ it % 2 == 0 } takes a single parameter, it (implicitly declared), and returns true if the number is even. The result, **evenNums**, will contain the filtered list of even numbers.

I should point out here that the implied **"it"** name can be overridden for something more readable if required. For example:

```
1. val evenNums = nums.filter { num -> num % 2 == 0 }
```

This goes for all lambdas that supply the implied **"it"** parameter name. Note that the built-in filter function does not need function parenthesis **()** because its lambda parameter is the last (and only) parameter. Because of this, it is good practice when writing your own functions to put the lambda parameter at the end of the parameter list.

Key differences:

- **Syntax**: The syntax of lambdas in Kotlin is more concise. In Kotlin, the parameter is implicitly declared, if not explicitly named. In Java, you need to explicitly declare the parameter.
- **Type inference**: Kotlin performs better type inference for lambdas. In Kotlin, the type of the lambda parameter inferred is based on the context, so you do not need to explicitly declare the type. In Java, you must specify the type of the lambda parameter explicitly.
- **Stream API**: In Kotlin, you can directly use higher-order functions like filter, map, and so on, without the need for a separate API. In Java, to work with collections, you often need to use the Stream API (introduced in Java 8) to achieve similar functionality as Kotlin.
- **Nullability handling**: Kotlin's null safety features seamlessly integrate with lambdas. If a lambda parameter is expected to be nullable, Kotlin's null safety rules apply, and you can safely handle nullability within the lambda expression.

Kotlin's lambda syntax and type inference makes the code more concise and readable. It eliminates some of the boilerplate code required in Java when working with lambdas, especially in combination with collections.

Extension functions

Extension functions are a powerful feature in Kotlin that allows developers to add new functions to existing classes, including third-party classes, without modifying their source code. These functions can be called as if they were regular member functions of the class.

In Kotlin, extension functions are defined outside the class they extend, using the following syntax:

```
1. fun MyClass.functionName() {
2.     // Function implementation
3. }
```

For example:

```
1. fun String.addExclamationMark(): String {
2.     return "$this!"
3. }
4.
5. fun myFun() {
6.     val text = "Hello"
7.     val modifiedText = text.addExclamationMark()
8.     println(modifiedText) // Output: Hello!
9. }
```

Here, we define an extension function **addExclamationMark()** for the String class. The extension function appends an exclamation mark to the given string. Inside the extension function, this refers to the instance of the class being extended, which, in this case, is the string itself.

In the **myFun()** function, we create a text variable of type **String** with the value **"Hello"**. We then call the extension function **addExclamationMark()** on the text variable, which results in the modified string **Hello!**.

Extension functions can be defined for classes, interfaces, and nullable types. They provide a way to extend the functionality of existing types and promote code reusability and readability.

It is worth noting that extension functions do not actually modify the original class or create new subclasses. They are purely syntactic sugar provided by the Kotlin language, allowing the function to be called as if it were a member function of the extended class.

Caution should be exercised when creating extension functions not to over-pollute the namespace of the extended class. In the above example, **addExclamationMark()** would be available globally and would appear as an auto-complete option in Android Studio wherever String was used. It is often better to make the extension function private to the scope of the calling function, either at first-class level or within a regular class:

```
1. private fun String.addExclamationMark(): String {
2.     return "$this!"
3. }
```

There is nothing to compare this to in Java. If you wanted to extend a third-party class in Java, you would have to do so by creating a new class (**String2** in this case) using extends from **String**. If the third-party class was final, you could not even do that.

Scoping functions

Scoping functions in Kotlin are first-order functions that allow for more concise and expressive code by providing a temporary scope for executing operations on an object. They provide a way to work with an object within a specific context without the need for repetitive object references.

There are five of these scoping functions in Kotlin, one of which (in my opinion) is redundant and works differently to the rest so we tend to avoid it. They are **let**, **run**, **apply**, **also**, and **with**.

- **let**: Executes a block of code on a non-null object and returns the result of the last expression within the block. The implicitly declared **it** parameter passed to the lambda is provided as the non-null object in the block. It is most useful for executing a lambda on non-null objects.

  ```
  1. val bar = getFoo()?.let {
  2.     it.toBar()
  3. }
  ```

  Introducing an expression as a variable in local scope:

  ```
  1. (…complicated_expression…).let {
  2.     doSomethingWith(it)
  3. }
  ```

- **run**: Similar to **let**, the non-null object is provided in the block as the scope (or the optional this). It can be more concise than **let** in the circumstances where the **it** value would otherwise be referred to several times before returning a value.

  ```
  1. data class Person(
  2.     val name: String, val surname: String, val address: String
  3. )
  ```

```
4.
5. val totalLength = person?.run {
6.     name.length + surname.length + address.length
7. } ?: 0
```

- **apply**: Executes a block of code on an object and returns the object itself. It is often used for initializing properties of an object. The scope of the block is the object, as with **run**.

```
1. val person = Person().apply {
2.     name = "John"
3.     age = 25
4.     // Other property initialisations
5. }
```

- **also**: Similar to **apply**, returning the object itself, the non-null object is referred to by the implicitly declared **it**, as with **let**. It is useful for performing additional actions on an object within a chain of operations or when it is more concise for the scope in the block to be that of the containing class or function.

```
1. val length = str?.also {
2.     // Perform additional actions on nullable 'str'
3.     print("Length of '$it' is ${it.length}")
4. }?.length
```

let, **run**, **apply** and **also** can all be used with a preceding safe call operator **?.** with nullable instances. In that case, the block is only executed on the condition of non-null otherwise a null value is returned to any assignment.

- **with**: Executes a block of code with an object as the receiver (that is, no need to specify the object name repeatedly).

```
1. with(person) {
2.     name = "John"
3.     age = 25
4.     // Other operations on 'person'
5. }
```

It is exactly the same as **run** except it is inconsistently not an extension so you might as well use **run** or **apply** in its place.

In Java, there are no direct equivalents to Kotlin's scoping functions. However, Java provides alternatives that can achieve similar results. For example, using an anonymous inner class.

```
1. String str = ...;
2. if (str != null) {
3.     Integer length = new Function<String, Integer>() {
```

```
4.      @Override
5.      public Integer apply(String s) {
6.          // Perform operations on non-null 'str'
7.          return s.length();
8.      }
9.  }.apply(str);
10. }
```

Using lambda expressions and functional interfaces (Java 8+):

```
1. String str = …;
2. Optional<Integer> length = Optional.ofNullable(str).map(s -> {
3.     // Perform operations on nullable 'str'
4.     return s.length();
5. });
```

While these Java alternatives achieve similar results, they are typically more verbose and require the use of additional constructs, such as functional interfaces or explicit null checks.

Built-in collection class extensions

Kotlin provides a set of useful extension functions for working with collections. These extension functions enhance the functionality of the standard collection classes and allow for more concise and expressive code. Here are some commonly used Kotlin collection class extensions:

- **map**: Transforms each element of a collection and returns a new collection with the transformed elements.
    ```
    1. val numbers = listOf(1, 2, 3, 4, 5)
    2. val squaredNumbers = numbers.map { it * it }
    3. // squaredNumbers: [1, 4, 9, 16, 25]
    ```
- **filter**: Returns a new collection containing only the elements that satisfy the given predicate:
    ```
    1. val numbers = listOf(1, 2, 3, 4, 5)
    2. val evenNumbers = numbers.filter { it % 2 == 0 }
    3. // evenNumbers: [2, 4]
    ```
- **sorted**: Returns a new collection with elements sorted in natural ascending order or according to a provided comparator:
    ```
    1. val numbers = listOf(5, 3, 1, 4, 2)
    2. val sortedNumbers = numbers.sorted()
    3. // sortedNumbers: [1, 2, 3, 4, 5]
    ```

These are just a few examples of the many extension functions available for Kotlin collections. Kotlin's collection class extensions provide several advantages over the equivalent operations in Java:

- **Concise and readable code**: Kotlin's collection class extensions allow for more concise and expressive code. The use of higher-order functions and lambda expressions simplifies common collection operations, reducing the need for explicit loops and boilerplate code. This leads to more readable and compact code compared to their Java counterparts.
- **Null safety**: Kotlin's collection class extensions are designed to handle nullable elements effectively. For example, when using functions like map or filter, Kotlin automatically handles null elements in the collection, ensuring safe execution and preventing null pointer exceptions. In Java, handling null elements requires additional null checks, making the code more verbose and error prone.
- **Immutable collections by default**: Kotlin's collection class extensions promote immutability by default. The standard library provides immutable versions of collection classes, such as `listOf`, `setOf`, and `mapOf`, which do not allow modifications after creation. This reduces the risk of accidental modification of collections and encourages functional programming practices.
- **Enhanced functional programming support**: Kotlin's collection class extensions align well with functional programming principles. They support operations like `map`, `filter`, `reduce`, and `groupBy`, which are common in functional programming paradigms. This allows developers to write more declarative and functional-style code, leading to a code that is easier to reason about, test, and maintain.
- **Improved type inference**: Kotlin's type inference capabilities make it easier to work with collections. The compiler can often infer the type of collection elements, reducing the need for explicit type declarations. This improves code readability and reduces verbosity compared to Java, where explicit type declarations are often necessary.

Getters and setters

In Kotlin, the syntax for defining getters and setters for properties is more concise and flexible compared to Java. Kotlin provides a simplified syntax using property accessors.

In Java, when defining a class with a property, you typically need to manually write getter and setter methods for each property. For example:

```
1. public class Person {
2.     private String name;
3. 
4.     public String getName() {
5.         return name;
6.     }
7. 
```

```
8.    public void setName(String newname) {
9.        this.name = newname;
10.   }
11. }
```

In Kotlin, you can define a property directly in the class body, and Kotlin automatically generates the default getter and setter for you. The syntax for defining a property in Kotlin is as follows:

```
1. class Person {
2.     var name = ""
3. }
```

In the above Kotlin code, **name** is a property of the **Person** class with an inferred type of String. By default, Kotlin generates a getter and setter for the **name** property.

You can also customize the behavior of the getter and setter by explicitly defining them. In Kotlin, you use property accessors to define the behavior of the getter and setter.

```
1. class Person {
2.     var name: String = ""
3.         get() {
4.             // Custom getter logic
5.             return field
6.         }
7.         set(value) {
8.             // Custom setter logic
9.             field = value
10.        }
11. }
```

In the example above, we have overridden the default getter and setter for the **name** property. Inside the custom getter and setter, you can provide your own logic, manipulate the property, or perform additional operations.

Kotlin also provides a more concise syntax for read-only properties (where only a getter is needed) and mutable properties with a private setter:

```
1. class Person {
2.     val age: Int = 25   // Read-only property, default getter
3.
4.     var email: String = ""
5.         private set // Mutable property, private setter
6. }
```

One-line functions

Simple one-line functions can be declared with an assignment as opposed to a scope with a **return** statement.

```
1. fun square(num: Int) = num * num
```

This can also be useful for reducing code topology (excessive indentation from nested scopes), for example:

```
1. fun customMap(list: List<Int>) = list.map {
2.     // custom mapping
3. }
```

Compare this with the indentation produced by a regular **return** statement:

```
1. fun customMap(list: List<Int>): List<Unit>  {
2.     return list.map {
3.         // custom mapping
4.     }
5. }
```

Delegation

Delegation is a programming pattern where an object delegates certain responsibilities or method calls to another object. It allows for code reuse and composition while maintaining a clear separation of concerns.

Kotlin provides the **by** keyword that allows you to delegate the implementation of an interface to another object without explicitly implementing each method. Here is an example:

```
1. interface Calculator {
2.     fun add(a: Int, b: Int): Int
3.     fun subtract(a: Int, b: Int): Int
4. }
5.
6. class BasicCalculator : Calculator {
7.     override fun add(a: Int, b: Int): Int = a + b
8.     override fun subtract(a: Int, b: Int): Int = a - b
9. }
10.
11. class CalculatorWithLogging(
12.     private val calculator: Calculator
```

```
13. ) : Calculator by calculator {
14.
15.     override fun add(a: Int, b: Int): Int = calculator.add(a,
    b).also {
16.         println("Adding $a and $b = $it")
17.     }
18. }
```

An object of type **CalculatorWithLogging** would then be able to directly call both the **add** and **subtract** methods with extra logging on the **add** method:

```
1. fun main() {
2.     val basicCalculator = BasicCalculator()
3.     val calculatorWithLogging =
   CalculatorWithLogging(basicCalculator)
4.
5.     calculatorWithLogging.add(5, 3)
6.     calculatorWithLogging.subtract(10, 7)
7. }
```

To achieve the same thing in Java, the **CalculatorWithLogging** class would need to override all of the methods specified by **Calculator**, not just **add**:

```
1.  class CalculatorWithLogging implements Calculator {
2.      private Calculator calculator;
3.
4.      public CalculatorWithLogging(Calculator calculator) {
5.          this.calculator = calculator;
6.      }
7.
8.      @Override
9.      public int add(int a, int b) {
10.         int result = calculator.add(a, b);
11.         System.out.println("Adding " + a + " and " + b + " = " +
    result);
12.         return result;
13.     }
14.
15.     @Override
16.     public int subtract(int a, int b) {
17.         return calculator.subtract(a, b);
18.     }
19. }
```

Kotlin supports both interface delegation, as shown above, and property delegation. Property delegation is a powerful feature in Kotlin that allows for the automatic generation of boilerplate code for properties, such as getters and setters, by delegating their implementation to another object or class.

```
1. class Example {
2.     var myValue: String by MyDelegate()
3. }
4.
5. class MyDelegate {
6.     operator fun getValue(
7.         thisRef: Any?,
8.         property: KProperty<*>
9.     ): String {
10.        // Custom logic for property get
11.        return "Custom value"
12.    }
13.
14.    operator fun setValue(
15.        thisRef: Any?,
16.        property: KProperty<*>,
17.        value: String
18.    ) { // Custom logic for property set
19.        println("Setting value: $value")
20.    }
21. }
```

From the above example, you can invoke the setter and getter respectively with this:

```
1. var e = Example().apply { myValue = "x" }
2. val f = e.myValue
```

- value is the value being set - **x** in this case.
- **thisRef** is the property's parent object, in this case an anonymous instance of **Example**. Had **myValue** been a first-class field (no parent class) then, **thisRef** would have been null. This may be useful if the delegated setter needs data or methods from the parent object in order to initialize the value.
- **property** is a reflected object containing information about the field to be set, like type (**String** in this case) and name (**myValue** in this case). Mostly, this is only useful for logging and debugging.

Kotlin provides property delegators returned by built-in first-order functions, such as **lazy**.

Lazy initialization

Lazy initialization refers to the technique of deferring the creation or initialization of an object until it is needed. This can help improve performance by avoiding unnecessary initialization when the object might not be used.

In Java, lazy initialization typically involves manually implementing a check-and-create pattern using a volatile field and a synchronized block or a lock object.

```
1.  class MyClass {
2.      private volatile ExpensiveObject expensiveObject;
3.
4.      public ExpensiveObject getExpensiveObject() {
5.          if (expensiveObject == null) {
6.              synchronized (this) {
7.                  if (expensiveObject == null) {
8.                      expensiveObject = new ExpensiveObject();
9.                  }
10.             }
11.         }
12.         return expensiveObject;
13.     }
14. }
```

In the above Java example, the **getExpensiveObject()** method checks if the **expensiveObject** field is null. If it is null, it enters a synchronized block to ensure thread safety and then initializes the object.

In Kotlin, lazy initialization is built into the language with the help of delegated properties. Kotlin provides a lazy function that allows you to declare a property as lazy and define its initialization using a lambda expression.

```
1.  class MyClass {
2.      val expensiveObject by lazy { ExpensiveObject() }
3.  }
```

In the Kotlin example, the **expensiveObject** property is declared as **lazy**, and its initialization is defined using a lambda expression:

`{ ExpensiveObject() }`

The **lazy** function ensures that the lambda expression is only executed when the property is accessed for the first time. The result is stored and returned on subsequent accesses.

The Kotlin **lazy** property is thread-safe by default, ensuring that the initialization code is executed only once, even in multi-threaded scenarios. It provides a concise and thread-safe way to implement lazy initialization without the need for explicit synchronization.

Using lazy initialization in Kotlin allows you to defer the expensive object creation until it is needed, which can help improve performance and resource usage in certain scenarios. It is especially useful in Android **Activity** and **Fragment** overrides that have member values set to inflated views. With Java these value declaration and assignment would be typically separated with the assignment happening in the **onCreate**/**onViewCreated** methods. Not only does the lazy property allow declaration and assignment to be together, but it ensures the assignment would not happen if the value is never accessed.

```
1. private val imageView by lazy {
2.     findViewById<ImageView>(R.id.image_view)
3. }
```

No more type erasure

Kotlin introduces a construct that overcomes the issue of type erasure. Java type erasure is a process in which the type information of generic types is removed (or erased) during compilation. This means that the type parameters used in generic classes and methods are not available at runtime. The **Java Virtual Machine (JVM)** does not retain specific type information for generic types.

During compilation, Java generics are used to provide compile-time type safety and allow for generic code to be written. However, at runtime, the JVM treats generic types as their raw types or objects, without the ability to distinguish between different type parameters. This was done to maintain backward compatibility with code that had been written prior to the introduction of generics that only happened in Java 5.

For example, the following Java code:

```
1. List<String> list = new ArrayList<>();
2. list.add("Hello");
3. String value = list.get(0);
```

It is transformed into the following code at compile time:

```
1. List list = new ArrayList();
2. list.add("Hello");
3. String value = (String) list.get(0);
```

As you can see, the generic type **List<String>** is replaced with the raw type **List**, and an explicit cast is added (and needed) when retrieving the element from the list. The type parameter **String** is erased, and the JVM treats the list as a raw **List** type.

Java developers are likely to come across this when trying to write anything remotely clever using generic classes with the following compilation warning at some point:

Type safety: The method <method>(Object) belongs to the raw type <class>. References to generic type <class> should be parameterized.

In most cases this ends up getting patched with

```
1. @SuppressWarnings("unchecked")
```

Unlike Java, Kotlin retains generic type information at runtime through a feature called type reification. Type reification allows you to access and manipulate generic type information at runtime, providing more flexibility and safety when working with generics. This is achieved by adding the **reified** modifier to a type parameter in a function.

```
1. inline fun <reified T> printType() {
2.     println(T::class.simpleName)
3. }
4.
5. printType<String>()
```

This will output **String** at runtime, demonstrating that the generic type **T** is retained and accessible.

Kotlin's type reification allows for more advanced generic operations, such as checking the type of a generic parameter, creating new instances of generic types using reflection, or passing generic types as arguments. It enables the development of more robust and flexible generic-based code.

Named and default parameters

Named and default parameters are language features in Kotlin that provide flexibility when defining and calling functions or constructors. They allow you to specify default values for function parameters and provide named arguments when invoking functions. Kotlin allows you to define default values for function parameters directly in the function declaration. When calling the function, you can omit the arguments for parameters that have default values, and those will be used instead:

```
1. fun greet(name: String = "Guest") {
2.     println("Hello, $name!")
3. }
4. greet()         // Output: Hello, Guest!
5. greet("John")   // Output: Hello, John!
```

In Java, these features are not available natively and alternative approaches must be used to achieve similar behavior. You would need to define overloaded versions of the function to do this.

```
1. void greet() {
2.     greet("Guest");
```

```
3. }
4.
5. void greet(String name) {
6.     System.out.println("Hello, " + name + "!");
7. }
8.
9. greet();             // Output: Hello, Guest!
10. greet("John");      // Output: Hello, John!
```

Kotlin allows you to specify function arguments by name during function calls. This means you can provide arguments in any order by specifying the parameter names explicitly.

```
1. fun greet(name: String, age: Int) {
2.     println("Hello, $name! You are $age years old.")
3. }
4.
5. // Output: Hello, John! You are 30 years old.
6. greet(age = 30, name = "John")
7. greet(name = "John", age = 30)   // Output same as above
```

In Java, named parameters are not available. Function arguments must be provided in the order they are defined in the function signature, which can be less readable, especially for functions with many parameters.

Companion objects

In my opinion, probably the only feature in Kotlin that adds any verbosity over Java is that of the replacement construct for Java's **static** keyword; Companion objects. Java uses statics to provide global access to functions and values scoped to a particular class. A typical application of this is for a factory function.

```
1. public class IntContainer {
2.     private int value;
3.
4.     private IntContainer(int value) {
5.         this.value = value;
6.     }
7.
8.     public int getValue() {
9.         return value;
10.     }
```

```
11.
12.     public static IntContainer intContainerFactory(int value) {
13.         return new IntContainer(value);
14.     }
15. }
```

As the constructor is private, the only way to get an instance of **IntContainer** is via its static factory function **intContainerFactory**:

```
1. val container = IntContainer.intContainerFactory(3)
```

The equivalent container class in Kotlin would look like this:

```
1. class IntContainer private constructor(val value: Int) {
2.
3.     companion object {
4.
5.         fun intContainerFactory(value: Int): IntContainer {
6.             return IntContainer(value)
7.         }
8.     }
9. }
```

Anything that would have **static** status within the namespace of a Kotlin class would be inside the one companion object scope. This is also the place to define any constants associated with the class.

Internal scope

Anyone familiar with Java will also be familiar with access scopes, namely **public**, **protected** and **private**.

- By way of a reminder, classes, class functions or class members specified as **public** are accessible anywhere within the scope of the application.
- **protected** is only accessible within the scope of the parent class or class that extends the parent.
- **private** is only accessible within the immediate parent class.

Both Java and Kotlin have these scopes with the same meanings, but each language has one extra scope. Java has **package** scope and Kotlin has **internal** scope.

Any class, class function or class member in Java that specifies package scope effectively has **public** scope, but only to code within the same package or code folder. Package scope is the Java default so if you do not specify anything, it is package scope.

Kotlin was designed to be a *modular* language. Packages within a module are there simply for organizing code and have no bearing on accessibility. Kotlin has no package scope.

Instead, it has **internal** scope. Any class, function, or value, first-class or otherwise, with **internal** scope is effectively **public** to any code in any package *but only within the same module*. It is a feature that is leveraged heavily in the practical section of this book.

Coroutines

Kotlin coroutines are a language feature that allows for efficient and sequential asynchronous programming in Kotlin. They provide a way to write asynchronous code that looks like regular sequential code, making it easier to understand, read, and maintain.

```kotlin
1.  suspend fun doTask(): String {
2.      delay(1000) // Simulate some asynchronous task
3.      return "Task completed"
4.  }
5.
6.  fun myFun() {
7.      println("Start")
8.
9.      GlobalScope.launch {
10.         val result = doTask()
11.         println(result)
12.     }
13.
14.     Thread.sleep(3000) // Wait for coroutines to complete
15.     println("End")
16. }
```

The **suspend** keyword indicates that the associated method is a coroutine and must be run within a coroutine scope, that is, on a separate thread. In this case, that scope is supplied by **GlobalScope.launch {…}**. In Android, there are built-in first-order extension functions that supply coroutine scopes in the places where they are needed: - **lifecycleScope** for **Activitys** and **viewModelScope** for **ViewModels**.

Flows and StateFlows

Kotlin **Flow** and **StateFlow** objects are part of Kotlin's standard library and provide an elegant and powerful way to handle asynchronous and reactive programming. They are designed to simplify working with asynchronous streams of data while leveraging the strengths of Kotlin's language features and coroutines. There is nothing like this supplied as standard with Java.

Flows

- Flows are a representation of a sequence of values emitted over time asynchronously. They are designed to replace `RxJava` Observables and `LiveData` for asynchronous programming in Kotlin.
- They use Kotlin coroutines under the hood to achieve concurrency and structured concurrency, making them highly compatible with Kotlin's coroutine ecosystem.
- Flows support various operators similar to those in `RxJava`, allowing you to transform, combine, and manipulate streams of data.
- They provide built-in support for handling backpressure, which helps control the rate of emitting values to avoid overwhelming consumers.
- Flows are *cold* data streams: They only emit values when they are actively collected by subscribers and those subscribers receive the entire sequence of values from the start.
- Example of creating a simple Flow:

```
1.  fun createFlow(): Flow<Int> = flow {
2.      for (i in 1..5) {
3.          delay(100)
4.          emit(i)
5.      }
6.  }
7.
8.  // Collect and print the emitted values
9.  fun main() = runBlocking {
10.     createFlow().collect { value ->
11.         println(value)
12.     }
13. }
```

Here, the `main` function starts to collect values from `createFlow()` and receives the first value after 100 milliseconds which it then prints. It then receives and prints the subsequent four values before completing.

StateFlows

- StateFlows are a specialized type of Flow designed to represent a mutable state over time. They provide a way to model and observe state changes in a reactive manner.
- They maintain a state value that can be updated, and they emit the current state and subsequent changes to subscribers.

- StateFlows are often used in UI components to observe and react to changes in the application's state.
- StateFlows are *hot* streams: They emit values continuously, whether there are subscribers or not. Subscribers can join and leave the stream at any time, and they will receive values that were emitted while they were active subscribers. In other words., they will not receive any values that were emitted before they subscribed.
- Due to their *hot* nature, StateFlows need to have an initial state assigned on creation.
- Example of creating and observing a StateFlow:

```
1.   data class AppState(val counter: Int)
2.
3.   fun main() = runBlocking {
4.       val stateFlow = MutableStateFlow(AppState(counter = 0))
5.
6.       val job = launch {
7.           stateFlow.collect { state ->
8.               println("Counter: ${state.counter}")
9.           }
10.      }
11.
12.      delay(1000)
13.      stateFlow.value = AppState(counter = 1)
14.      delay(1000)
15.      stateFlow.value = AppState(counter = 2)
16.
17.      job.cancel()
18.  }
```

In this example, a mutable **StateFlow** is created and set with an initial state value of **AppState(0)**. This is immediately picked up and printed when the **StateFlow** starts to be collected. Subsequently, two new states are printed out at one second intervals.

Conclusion

This chapter covered why Kotlin is a great choice for Android development and presented a handful of the language's features in comparison to Java.

The next chapter delves into the concept of Separation of Concerns providing Kotlin code snippets to illustrate some of the more important methods.

Points to remember

- Kotlin has full interoperability with Java so Kotlin classes can be added to legacy Java projects.
- Kotlin has precise and expressive syntax.
- Kotlin can out-perform Java due to its efficient byte-code generation.
- Kotlin provides improved code safety with null safety, type inference, and data classes.
- Kotlin has asynchronous operations built-in with Coroutines.
- Kotlin is fully supported in Android Studio.

Questions

1. How do you declare a lambda parameter and what would be the best position for it in a function's parameter list?
2. How would you write an extension function?
3. What are the four most useful scoping functions and how do they differ from one another?
4. How would you sort a Kotlin list?
5. How would you write a templatized function in Kotlin to avoid type erasure?
6. What is `internal` scope?

Join our book's Discord space

Join the book's Discord Workspace for Latest updates, Offers, Tech happenings around the world, New Release and Sessions with the Authors:

https://discord.bpbonline.com

CHAPTER 2
Breaking Down App Code with Separation of Concerns

Introduction

To avoid an app evolving into a disorderly tangle, there are several established methods for breaking up code into manageable, independent entities. This chapter further details the breakdown of app code by introducing **separation of concerns (SoC)**. In fact, the entire foundation for this book is based on this concept.

SoC is a software design principle that aims to separate a system into distinct and independent parts, with each part handling a specific concern or responsibility. The goal is to modularize the system, organizing code and functionality in a way that promotes maintainability, readability, and reusability.

In this chapter, we will also have a brief look at the benefits of SoC, examine the concept at a high level, and discuss the aspects of the Kotlin language that facilitate its implementation.

Structure

This chapter covers the following topics:

- Benefits of SoC
- Kotlin code constructs facilitating SoC
- SOLID principles

Objectives

In this chapter, you will gain a deep understanding of SoC and its significance in software development. The tangible benefits of implementing SoC will be explored, such as improved code maintainability, scalability, and testability. By the end of this chapter, you will understand various Kotlin language structures and features that inherently support and facilitate SoC, providing practical knowledge on leveraging these tools in projects. Additionally, you will be introduced to the SOLID principles, a set of design guidelines that align closely with the goals of SoC, helping to create more robust and flexible software architectures. By the end of this chapter, you will be able to effectively apply SoC principles in Kotlin, ensuring cleaner, more efficient codebases that are easier to manage and evolve.

Benefits of SoC

The benefits of applying SoC in software development are:

- **Modularity and organization:** SoC helps in breaking down a complex system into smaller, manageable modules. Each module focuses on a specific aspect of the system, making it easier to understand and maintain. It promotes code organization, allowing developers to work on specific parts of the system without affecting unrelated components.

- **Readability and maintainability:** By separating concerns, code becomes more readable and understandable. It improves the clarity and reduces the complexity of individual modules, making it easier for developers to comprehend and modify the code. Changes or updates to one concern have minimal impact on other parts of the system, enabling easier maintenance and reducing the risk of unintended side effects.

- **Reusability:** Separating concerns allows for greater code reusability. Modules that are focused on specific concerns can be reused in different parts of the system or even in other projects. This promotes code sharing, reduces duplication, and increases development efficiency.

- **Testing and debugging:** SoC facilitates effective testing and debugging. With well-defined and isolated concerns, writing unit tests and performing focused testing on specific modules becomes easier. Issues or defects can be isolated to a particular concern, making identifying and fixing problems easier.

- **Collaboration and parallel development:** Separating concerns enables parallel development and collaboration among multiple developers or teams. Different concerns can be assigned to different individuals or teams, allowing them to work independently without interfering with each other's work. This promotes productivity and scalability in large-scale projects.

- **Flexibility and extensibility:** SoC provides a flexible and extensible architecture. When new requirements or features need to be added, it is easier to identify the relevant modules and make the necessary changes without impacting the entire system. New concerns can be introduced, existing concerns can be modified or extended, and the system can adapt to evolving needs more effectively.

Kotlin code constructs facilitating SoC

The problems associated with spaghetti code is nothing new. Coding language after coding language has come and gone incorporating features designed to address the problem. One of the outstanding aspects of Kotlin is that it has picked up the best features from these languages and added a few new ones. They are described as follows:

- **Packages**: Kotlin allows you to organize code into packages, which provide a way to group related classes, functions, and other components. Packages promote SoC by providing a clear organizational structure, making it easier to locate and manage code related to specific concerns.
- **Functions and methods**: Kotlin's functions and methods promote SoC by allowing you to write small, focused units of code that perform specific tasks. By breaking down functionality into smaller functions, you can separate concerns and make code more modular, readable, and maintainable.
- **Classes and objects**: Kotlin's classes and objects allow for the encapsulation of related data and behavior. By defining classes that have a single responsibility, you can separate concerns and achieve better modularity. Kotlin's support for object-oriented programming principles, such as inheritance, polymorphism, and interfaces, further supports SoC by allowing for clear separation and abstraction of responsibilities.
- **Extension functions**: Kotlin's extension functions enable you to add functionality to existing classes without modifying their source code. This promotes SoC by allowing you to extend the behavior of classes without introducing unrelated concerns. Extension functions can be defined separately, keeping the code for each concern isolated and organized.
- **Nullable types and null safety**: Kotlin's built-in null safety features help separate the concern of nullability handling from other aspects of the code. By distinguishing nullable types from non-nullable types, Kotlin promotes SoC by providing a clear indication of where null values can be expected. This helps in writing code that is more robust and avoids null pointer exceptions.
- **Coroutines**: Kotlin's coroutines facilitate SoC by allowing you to write asynchronous code sequentially and structured. Coroutines provide a way to handle asynchronous tasks without introducing complex call-backs or blocking operations. Coroutines promote readability and separation of concerns by writing asynchronous code that looks like regular sequential code.
- **Data classes**: Kotlin's data classes provide a concise way to define classes that hold data. Data classes automatically generate useful methods like `equals()`,

`hashCode()`, and `toString()`, allowing you to separate the concern of data modeling from other aspects of the system.

- **Property delegation**: Kotlin's property delegation allows you to separate property access and modification concerns. By delegating the implementation of property behavior to separate classes, you can keep the code focused on specific concerns while providing reusable and customizable behavior.
- **Functional programming**: Functional programming paradigms, such as immutability, pure functions, and higher-order functions, also contribute to SoC. By focusing on composing functions and avoiding side effects, functional programming helps build small, composable, and reusable modules, which leads to a clearer separation of concerns.
- **Interfaces**: Kotlin extends Java's interface capability by allowing member declarations as well as function signatures. This contributes to SoC by enhancing the abstraction possibilities allowing for better decoupling of different parts of a system.
- **Modularization**: By dispensing with package scope and introducing the `internal` keyword, Kotlin encourages the use of self-contained modules to enable SoC at a higher level than packages.

The features discussed above are building blocks for achieving SoC. Building blocks, however, are not enough without some sort of plan or set of principles to guide their usage.

SOLID principles

SOLID principles were proposed by *Robert C. Martin* in the year 2000. They are a set of five design principles that aim to help software developers create more maintainable, flexible, and scalable software. While these principles don't directly mention SoC, they are closely related to SoC and often used in combination with it to achieve the goal of better software design.

The principles are:

- **Single Responsibility Principle (SRP)**
- **Open/Closed Principle (OCP)**
- **Liskov Substitution Principle (LSP)**
- **Interface Segregation Principle (ISP)**
- **Dependency Inversion Principle (DIP)**

Single Responsibility Principle

A class or module should have only one reason to change, meaning it should have a single responsibility or concern. By adhering to SRP, you ensure that each class is focused on one concern or task. This separation of responsibilities helps to maintain a clear distinction between different concerns in your codebase. Here is a class that violates SRP:

```
1.  class Customer {
2.      var name: String = ""
3.      var email: String = ""
4.
5.      fun save() {
6.          // Code to save the customer to a database
7.      }
8.
9.      fun sendEmail() {
10.         // Code to send an email to the customer
11.     }
12.
13.     fun calculateDiscount() {
14.         // Code to calculate the discount for the customer
15.     }
16. }
```

In the above-mentioned example, the **Customer** class has multiple responsibilities. It not only stores customer data but also handles saving the customer to a database, sending emails, and calculating discounts. This violates SRP because the class has more than one reason to change.

A better approach to adhere to SRP would be to separate the responsibilities into separate classes. For example:

```
1.  data class Customer (
2.      val name: String = ""
3.      val email: String = ""
4.  )
5.
6.  class CustomerRepository {
7.      fun save(customer: Customer) {
8.          // Code to save the customer to a database
9.      }
10. }
11.
12. class EmailService {
```

```
13.     fun sendEmail(to: String, message: String) {
14.         // Code to send an email
15.     }
16. }
17.
18. class DiscountCalculator {
19.     fun calculateDiscount(customer: Customer) {
20.         // Code to calculate the discount for the customer
21.     }
22. }
```

In this revised design, the **Customer** class is responsible for storing customer data only. The **CustomerRepository** class handles the database operations, the **EmailService** class handles email sending, and the **DiscountCalculator** class is responsible for calculating discounts. Each class has a single responsibility, making the code more maintainable, testable and flexible. Also, notice that **Customer** is now a pure data class.

This is a very low-level example. In any system you can argue that there would be a hierarchy of responsibilities. After all, something must be calling **calculateDiscount**, and so on. What is the responsibility of the caller? This responsibility hierarchy goes all the way up to **MainActivity**. The idea to take away from this is that any code file should have only one reason to change, so you should try to organize your code accordingly. SRP is the foundation principle behind most of the recommendations in this book.

Open/Closed Principle

Software entities (classes, modules, functions) should be open for extension but closed for modification, allowing for new functionality to be added without modifying existing code. This principle promotes the creation of extension points (for example, interfaces, abstract classes) that allow you to add new functionality without modifying existing code. It encourages the separation of concerns by enabling you to extend the system's behavior without altering its core components.

The following is a class that violates OCP:

```
1. class Shape(val type: String) {
2.     fun calculateArea(): Double {
3.         return when (type) {
4.             "circle" -> {
5.                 // Code to calculate the area of a circle
6.             }
7.             "rectangle" -> {
```

```
8.              // Code to calculate the area of a rectangle
9.          }
10.         "triangle" -> {
11.             // Code to calculate the area of a triangle
12.         }
13.         else -> throw IllegalArgumentException("Unsupported shape")
14.     }
15. }
16. }
```

In the preceding example, the **Shape** class has a method **calculateArea()** that calculates the area based on the type of shape. The violation of the OCP occurs when a new shape, such as a square, needs to be added. To support the square, the code within the **Shape** class needs to be modified, violating the principle of being closed for modification.

A better approach to adhere to the OCP would be to use abstraction and inheritance. For example:

```
1. interface Shape {
2.     fun calculateArea(): Double
3. }
4.
5. class Circle() : Shape {
6.     override fun calculateArea(): Double {
7.         // Code to calculate the area of a circle
8.     }
9. }
10.
11. class Rectangle() : Shape {
12.     override fun calculateArea(): Double {
13.         // Code to calculate the area of a rectangle
14.     }
15. }
16.
17. class Triangle() : Shape {
18.     override fun calculateArea(): Double {
19.         // Code to calculate the area of a triangle
20.     }
21. }
```

With this revised design, the `Shape` class is now an interface and serves as a base for specific shape implementations like `Circle`, `Rectangle` and `Triangle`. Each shape class implements the `calculateArea()` method according to its specific formula. If a new shape, such as a square, needs to be added, it can simply implement the `Shape` class and provide its own definition of the `calculateArea()` method. This way, the code is open for extension (adding new shapes) but closed for modification (existing code does not need to be changed), adhering to OCP. The principle facilitates SoC by allowing developers to extend the behavior of a program without modifying the existing code. By using interfaces instead of inheritance, the polymorphic OCP enables loose coupling, further promoting SoC and improving maintainability.

Liskov Substitution Principle

The Liskov Substitution Principle is named after *Barbara Liskov*, a computer scientist who introduced this concept in 1987. The principle states that subtypes must be substitutable for their base types without affecting the correctness of the program. In other words, objects of derived classes should be able to replace objects of their base classes without breaking the behavior of the program.

This principle helps ensure that derived classes adhere to the same contracts and interfaces as base classes. By maintaining this consistency, you separate the concerns of the base class from those of the derived class, allowing for interchangeable usage.

By way of an example, the following code violates LSP:

```
1. open class Rectangle(var width: Int, var height: Int) {
2.     open fun area(): Int {
3.         return width * height
4.     }
5. }
6.
7. class Square(side: Int) : Rectangle(side, side) {
8.     override fun area(): Int {
9.         return side * side
10.    }
11. }
```

In this example, the `Square` class extends the `Rectangle` class. According to the LSP, subtypes should be substitutable for their base types without affecting the correctness of the program. However, in this case, the behavior of the `Square` class violates the expected behavior of the `Rectangle` class.

The issue arises because a square's sides are expected to be equal, whereas a rectangle's sides can be different. By overriding the `area()` method in the `Square` class and calculating the area based on a single side length, the behavior of the **Square** class differs from that of the **Rectangle** class.

To correct the LSP violation, we can rethink the class hierarchy and avoid the inheritance relationship between **Rectangle** and **Square**:

```
1.  interface Shape {
2.      fun area(): Int
3.  }
4.
5.  class Rectangle(val width: Int, val height: Int) : Shape {
6.      override fun area(): Int {
7.          return width * height
8.      }
9.  }
10.
11. class Square(val side: Int) : Shape {
12.     override fun area(): Int {
13.         return side * side
14.     }
15. }
```

In this corrected version, both **Rectangle** and **Square** inherit from a common **Shape** interface. They each have their area calculation methods without violating LSP. The **Shape** interface serves as a shared base type for both shapes but does not enforce a specific behavior, allowing each subclass to define its unique characteristics and behavior.

You can see from above that although OCP and LSP address different coding mistakes, they have similar solutions.

By adhering to LSP, developers can design systems with clear SoC where objects can be used interchangeably based on their shared behavior defined by base types.

Interface Segregation Principle

Clients should not be forced to depend on interfaces they do not use. Instead of having large, monolithic interfaces, it is better to define smaller, focused interfaces. This principle encourages the creation of smaller, more focused interfaces that contain only the methods relevant to a particular concern. By following ISP, you prevent clients from being burdened with methods they don't need, which contributes to a cleaner separation of concerns.

Consider the following ISP violation:

```
1.  interface Printer {
2.      fun printDocument(document: String)
```

```kotlin
3.     fun scanDocument(document: String)
4.     fun faxDocument(document: String)
5. }
6.
7. class SimplePrinter : Printer {
8.     override fun printDocument(document: String) {
9.         // Code to print the document
10.    }
11.
12.    override fun scanDocument(document: String) {
13.        // Code to scan the document
14.    }
15.
16.    override fun faxDocument(document: String) {
17.        // Code to fax the document
18.    }
19. }
```

In this example, the **Printer** interface defines three methods: **printDocument**, **scanDocument**, and **faxDocument**. However, not all classes implementing the **Printer** interface may need to support all these methods.

The **SimplePrinter** class implements the **Printer** interface, but it may not require the functionality of scanning or faxing documents. This violates ISP because the **Printer** interface is too broad and forces the implementation of methods that are not needed in all classes.

To address this violation, we can split the **Printer** interface into smaller, more focused interfaces:

```kotlin
1. interface Printer {
2.     fun printDocument(document: String)
3. }
4.
5. interface Scanner {
6.     fun scanDocument(document: String)
7. }
8.
9. interface FaxMachine {
10.    fun faxDocument(document: String)
```

```
11.  }
12.
13.  class SimplePrinter : Printer {
14.      override fun printDocument(document: String) {
15.          // Code to print the document
16.      }
17.  }
```

In the above revised design, the responsibilities are separated into three interfaces: **Printer**, **Scanner**, and **FaxMachine**. The **SimplePrinter** class now only implements the **Printer** interface, as it does not need to support scanning or faxing functionality. Other classes can implement the additional interfaces as per their specific requirements. This segregation of interfaces allows clients to depend only on the interfaces they need, promoting a more focused and flexible design that adheres to ISP.

By following ISP, interfaces are tailored to provide only the necessary methods required by each client, enabling a more focused and cohesive SoC.

Dependency Inversion Principle

High-level modules should not depend on low-level modules, but both should depend on abstractions. Abstractions should not depend on details; details should depend on abstractions. By relying on abstractions, you separate the high-level, policy-related concerns from low-level, implementation-related concerns. This separation allows for flexibility in substituting different implementations without affecting the higher-level code.

Consider the following DIP violation:

```
1.  class EmailService {
2.      fun sendEmail(to: String, subject: String, body: String) {
3.          // Code to send an email
4.      }
5.  }
6.
7.  class NotificationService(private val emailService: EmailService) {
8.      fun sendNotification(to: String, message: String) {
9.          val subject = "Notification"
10.         val body = "Message: $message"
11.         emailService.sendEmail(to, subject, body)
12.     }
13. }
```

In this example, the **NotificationService** depends directly on the concrete implementation of the **EmailService**. This violates DIP because the high-level **NotificationService** class depends on a low-level implementation detail, which makes it tightly coupled to the **EmailService** class.

To correct this violation and adhere to DIP, we can introduce an abstraction in the form of an interface or abstract class:

```
1.  interface NotificationService {
2.      fun sendNotification(to: String, message: String)
3.  }
4.
5.  class EmailNotificationService(
6.      private val emailService: EmailService
7.  ) : NotificationService {
8.      override fun sendNotification(to: String, message: String) {
9.          val subject = "Notification"
10.         val body = "Message: $message"
11.         emailService.sendEmail(to, subject, body)
12.     }
13. }
14.
15. class EmailService {
16.     fun sendEmail(to: String, subject: String, body: String) {
17.         // Code to send an email
18.     }
19. }
```

In this revised design, the **NotificationService** now depends on the **NotificationService** interface instead of the concrete **EmailService** implementation. The **EmailNotificationService** class implements the **NotificationService** interface and delegates the email sending functionality to the **EmailService**. This allows for dependency inversion, where the higher-level module (**NotificationService**) depends on an abstraction (**NotificationService** interface) rather than on a concrete implementation.

By introducing an abstraction and depending on it rather than concrete implementations, we achieve loose coupling between modules, achieve a better SoC, adhere to DIP, and improve the codebase's flexibility, testability, and maintainability.

Conclusion

SoC is a vital concept for the design and implementation of any system. Without it, a code base will descend into an unmanageable tangle over a short span of time – even during development. By employing SoC techniques, a code base can be easier to test, debug, and add more functionality over time. The Kotlin language inherits all of the SoC facilitating features of Java and adds more such as functional programming, enhanced interface capabilities, delegation, data classes, and coroutines, amongst others.

In this chapter, we also discussed Uncle Bob's SOLID principles and provided some Kotlin code examples of each, showing how they can be used to achieve SoC.

The next chapter shows how the SoC concept can be extended to a higher order of code organization.

Points to remember

- SoC is a software design principle that aims to separate a system into distinct and independent parts, with each part handling a specific concern or responsibility.
- The Kotlin language draws on the best of previous coding languages to provide better constructs for achieving SoC.
- SOLID principles, first proposed by Robert C. Martin, offer a set of rules to follow when writing code that facilitates SoC.

Questions

1. What is SoC?
2. Why is SoC a vital aspect of code development?
3. What features does Kotlin provide that make it easier to achieve SoC?
4. What does the acronym *SOLID* stand for?
5. What does each of the SOLID principles teach us about achieving SoC in our code base?

Join our book's Discord space

Join the book's Discord Workspace for Latest updates, Offers, Tech happenings around the world, New Release and Sessions with the Authors:

https://discord.bpbonline.com

CHAPTER 3
Feature-Oriented Development in Android

Introduction

As previously stated, as new requirements are added during the lifetime of an application, the code base will expand. We need to find a way to control that expansion to avoid our code base becoming an unmanageable, tangled, tightly-coupled mess (or spaghetti code as it is better known). We already discussed how **separation of concerns** (**SoC**) can conceptually tackle this issue and subsequent chapters will look at how this is implemented at the code level.

Continuing the theme of SoC, this chapter discusses the high-level method of splitting an app into conceptual features and how this helps to contribute to code quality. It will examine the origins of the Feature concept and provide an example in the form of a case study.

Structure

This chapter covers the following topics:
- Understanding feature module
- Concept origins
- Granularity of features
- Identifying features

- User journeys
- Case study

Objectives

By the end of this chapter, you should understand the concept of a *feature* and be able to apply the *user journey* paradigm to your app's requirement specifications. You will also consider how your code might be organized to facilitate feature modules.

Understanding feature module

Feature-oriented development (FOD) is an approach to software development that focuses on organizing and building applications based on distinct features or functionalities. In the context of Android development, feature-oriented development involves structuring an Android application's codebase, resources, and other components around specific features.

In traditional application development, the codebase is typically organized based on layers such as activities, fragments, models, utilities, and so on. However, the codebase is organized based on the application's features or user stories in feature-oriented development. Each feature is treated as a self-contained module or component with its own set of code, resources, dependencies, and configuration. A **feature** module is a feature code that has been organized and isolated into a software module.

Concept origins

The concept of feature-oriented development originated from the software product line engineering field. Software product line engineering focuses on developing a family of software products that share common features and can be efficiently customized or configured to meet specific requirements.

FOD emerged as a way to address the challenges of developing and managing complex software systems with varying features and functionalities. It provides a systematic approach to organizing and building software applications based on their distinct features.

The concepts and principles of FOD draw inspiration from various software engineering disciplines, including modular programming, component-based development, and object-oriented design. FOD extends these principles by emphasizing the organization of software around features and their dependencies.

The earliest references to FOD can be found in academic research papers and publications on software product line engineering, which date back to the 1990s. Over the years, FOD has gained recognition as an effective approach for developing software systems focusing on modularity, reusability, and customization.

FOD principles and practices have been applied in various domains, including enterprise software, embedded systems, web applications, and mobile development. In the context of Android development, FOD has been embraced as an approach to structuring and managing applications with modular features using concepts such as dynamic feature modules, modular architecture patterns, and dependency management.

While FOD originated from the software product line engineering discipline, it has evolved and found practical applications in various software development contexts.

Granularity of features

The granularity of features refers to the level of detail or the size of individual features in our application. It determines how finely you break down your application's functionality into distinct features or modules.

Features can be of varying sizes and complexity. They can range from small, specific functionalities to larger, more comprehensive components. The granularity of features determines how narrowly or broadly you define the scope of each feature.

A fine-grained or more granular approach means breaking the functionality into smaller, focused features. Each feature represents a specific task or functionality of the application. For example, in a social media app, features such as user registration, post creation, commenting, or friend requests could be defined at a granular level.

On the other hand, a coarse-grained or less granular approach means grouping related functionality into larger features. Each feature encompasses multiple tasks or functionalities that are closely related. For example, a larger feature in the social media app could be user profile management, which includes registration, profile editing, and password recovery functionalities.

The granularity of features depends on various factors, including the complexity of your application, the level of modularity desired, the development team's capabilities, and the specific requirements of your project.

Finding the right balance in feature granularity is important. Too fine-grained features may result in excessive fragmentation and increased overhead in managing and maintaining many small features. On the other hand, if features are too coarse-grained, it can make the codebase and modules less focused and harder to understand and maintain.

It is essential to strike a balance based on the specific needs of your application, considering factors like the level of reuse, modularity, development effort, and the ability to deliver and iterate on features effectively. The granularity of features can be adjusted and refined as you gain more insights during the development process and receive feedback from users and stakeholders.

Remember that the granularity of features can vary depending on the complexity of your app and the desired level of modularity. It is important to strike a balance between breaking down the app into manageable features while avoiding excessive fragmentation that might hinder development and maintenance.

By carefully analyzing user requirements, breaking down functionality, prioritizing features, and considering complexity and interdependencies, you can effectively identify features for FOD in your Android app.

Identifying features

Deciding what constitutes a feature in your Android app for FOD requires careful analysis and consideration of your application's functionality and user requirements. Here are some steps you can follow to determine the features of FOD. In the case of very large projects, normally, most of these steps would have been carried out by members of the team specializing in their respective fields, such as system architecture, design, etc.:

- **Identify user requirements**: Start by understanding the requirements and expectations of your target users. Conduct user research, gather feedback, and analyze user personas to identify your app's essential functionalities and features. Consider the user tasks, goals, and needs that your app aims to address.
- **Break down functionality**: Analyze your app's functionality and break it down into distinct units or capabilities. Consider the different tasks or actions that users can perform within your app. Each of these tasks or actions can potentially be considered as a feature.
- **Prioritize features**: Once you have identified the potential features, prioritize them based on their importance and impact on the overall user experience. Determine which features are essential for the core functionality of your app and which ones can be considered secondary or optional.
- **Evaluate complexity and interdependencies**: Assess the complexity and interdependencies of each feature. Consider the level of effort and resources required to develop and maintain each feature. Identify features that are independent and can be developed in isolation, as well as features that have dependencies on each other.
- **Consider business goals**: Consider your app's business goals and strategies. Consider features that align with your business objectives and can provide value to your users. Prioritize features that can contribute to user engagement, retention, or monetization.
- **Iterative approach**: Feature identification is not a one-time process. It evolves as your app grows and user needs change. Adopt an iterative approach and consider user, stakeholder, and analytics feedback to refine and prioritize features continuously.

This last point is especially important to app developers. To facilitate an iterative approach to feature identification, the architecture of your app needs to be such that it is relatively easy to refactor code to combine or split features. The practical sections of this book will suggest such an architecture.

User journeys

A popular way to detect features in your app is by identifying distinct user journeys. A user journey refers to the path or series of steps a user takes within an application to accomplish a specific task or reach a particular goal. It represents the sequence of interactions and screens a user navigates through while using the app.

A user journey encompasses the entire flow of interactions, starting from the initial entry point of the app to the final desired outcome. It includes various stages, such as onboarding, user registration or authentication, accessing different features or screens, performing actions, and achieving the intended result.

The user journey typically considers the following aspects:

- **Entry point**: The starting point where the user launches the app or accesses a specific feature.
- **Navigation**: The flow of screens and interactions that guide the user through the app. It includes navigating between screens, accessing menus, interacting with buttons or controls, and transitioning to different views or activities.
- **Interactions**: The user's interactions within the app, such as inputting data, selecting options, submitting forms, performing actions, or consuming content.
- **Feedback and notifications**: Providing appropriate feedback to the user during the journey, including success messages, error notifications, progress indicators, or any other relevant feedback to guide the user through the process.
- **Completion and result**: The desired outcome or goal the user intends to achieve by following the user journey. This could be completing a purchase, submitting a form, viewing information, or any other defined objective.

Understanding the user journey is crucial in app development as it helps design a seamless and intuitive user experience. By analyzing the user journey, developers and designers can identify potential pain points, improve the flow, streamline interactions, and ensure that users can accomplish their tasks efficiently and effectively.

User journey mapping techniques, such as creating flowcharts, storyboards, or visual representations, can be used to visualize and document the user journey. These visual representations provide a holistic view of the app's flow and aid in identifying areas for improvement, optimizing the user experience and aligning the app's functionality with user needs and expectations.

Case study

As hinted up to this point, we cannot tell you definitively how to divide your specific application into features. This has to be dependent on what your app does and the dynamics of the team working on it. We can, however, describe a case where the split worked reasonably well.

A multi-feature app was recently developed by a small team within a software agency. The app served as a multipurpose utility for visitors to a small country and was commissioned by that country's government. At the time, the country hosted a large international sports tournament. The app was intended to provide everything the visiting sports fan would need during (and immediately before) their visit. Due to the risk of copyright infringement, this section describes an arrangement inspired by that app rather than the app itself. It was broken down into the following features based on distinct user journeys similar to these:

- **Splash**: A sporting tournament artistic logo displayed on the screen for three seconds or for as long as it takes to load and cache app data from the backend, whichever is longer.
- **Onboarding**: This refers to the process of guiding and familiarizing new users with the app's features, functionality, and user interface. It is the initial experience users go through when they launch the app for the first time. It usually looks like the following figure:

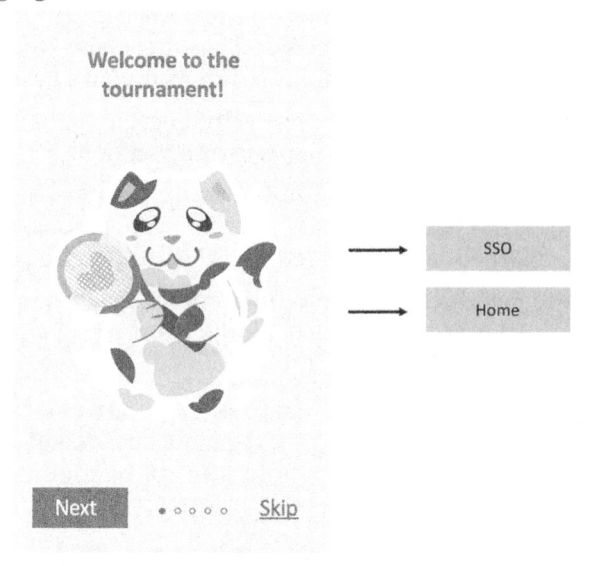

Figure 3.1: Onboarding journey

They typically use a view-pager arrangement with both swipe and button paging with an option to skip. Although one of the purposes of the onboarding screens is to familiarize the user with the interface, there are Play Store submission protocols that state that onboarding screens must not have app screenshots. Instead, any images in the onboarding pages must be flat, clip-art style graphics.

With this app, every page on the onboarding screens would advertise each feature. The final page optionally allows the user to jump to the single sign-on feature or to continue straight on to the home page (itself a feature).

As with all app onboarding journeys, it is only displayed on the first run from an install.

- **Single Sign-On (SSO)**: This is an authentication mechanism that allows users to access multiple systems, applications, or services with a single set of login credentials. With SSO, users can authenticate once and gain access to various resources without re-entering their credentials for each separate system or application.

  The primary goal of SSO is to simplify the user experience by eliminating the need for multiple usernames and passwords. It improves convenience, productivity, and security by reducing the burden of managing and remembering multiple login credentials. From a user's point of view, it provides a one-button registration or login to an app avoiding the tedium of filling in forms.

  Instead of the application handling the authentication process itself, it delegates this responsibility to an **Identity Provider** (**IdP**). The IdP is a trusted system that authenticates the user's credentials.

  The app used only two IdPs for the Android app: Google and Facebook. This is illustrated in the following figure:

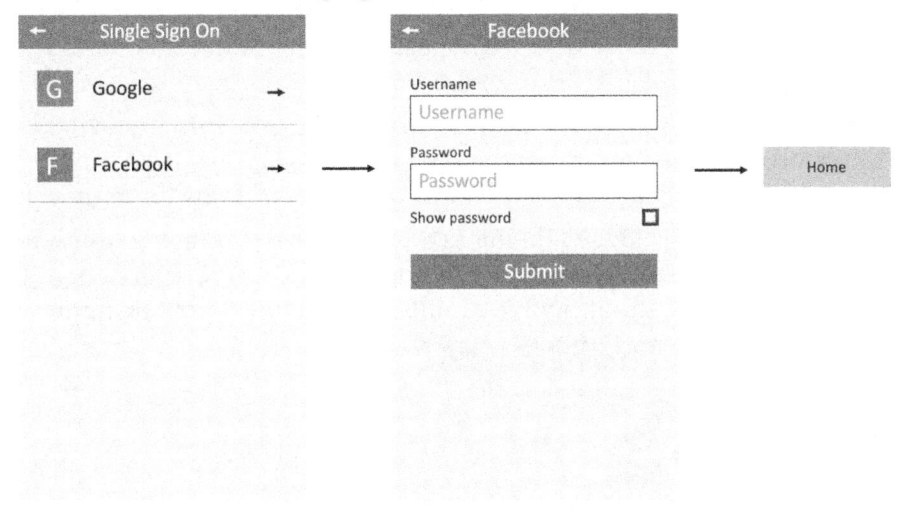

  Figure 3.2: SSO journey

  Figure 3.2 shows the possible SSO journey when selecting **Facebook**. These two IdPs were selected because they were the ones most likely to be already signed in. In this case, the username/password screen would not be presented.

  The SSO feature is accessible from the onboarding and profile features (if not logged in).

- **Home**: This is the normal initial landing screen (except on the first install) after the splash screen. This can be considered a feature navigation hub. Take a look at the following figure:

48 ■ *Scalable Android Applications in Kotlin*

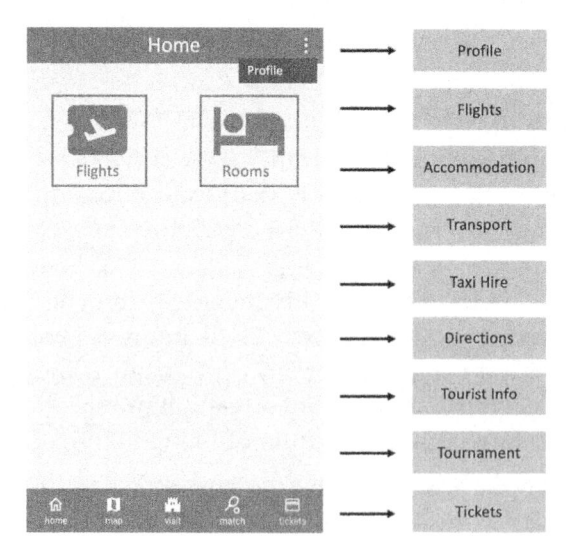

Figure 3.3: Home hub

- The **Flights** and **Accommodation** (**Rooms**) feature launch **Calls-To-Action** (**CTA**s) are only visible when the user is outside the host country. Once inside, the view changes to local info, such as tournament updates and CTAs for launching the Public Transport and Taxi Hire features.

- The **Direction** (map), **Tourist Info** (visit), **Tournament Info** (match), and **Tickets** features are each launched via the bottom navigation bar. The profile feature is launched via the **kebab** menu (the three vertical dots in the top-right corner).

- **Profile**: If the user is logged in, this is a simple form displaying user info gleaned from the SSO call, such as name, email address, and so on, with options to change each of these fields. Profile journey is illustrated in the following figure:

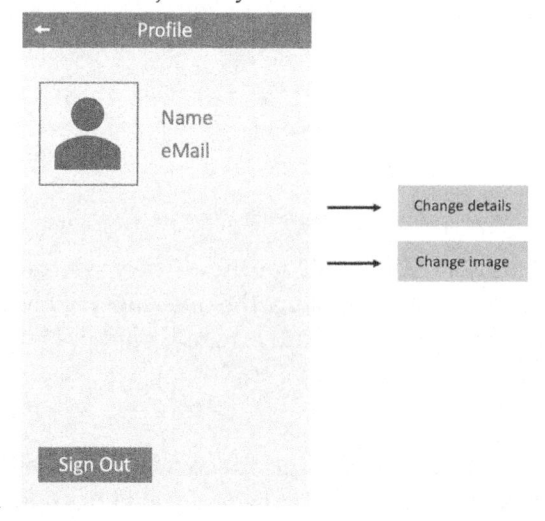

Figure 3.4: Profile journey

- If the user is not logged in, a **Please Login** message is displayed with a CTA to launch the SSO journey.
- **Flights**: This set of screens for booking flights to the tournament host country is a customized version of the host country's national airline booking site.
- **Accommodation**: This is a journey for booking accommodation for the tournament. Residents and large hotel chains were able to advertise rooms here in a list-style arrangement due to the oversubscription at the time. Look at the following figure:

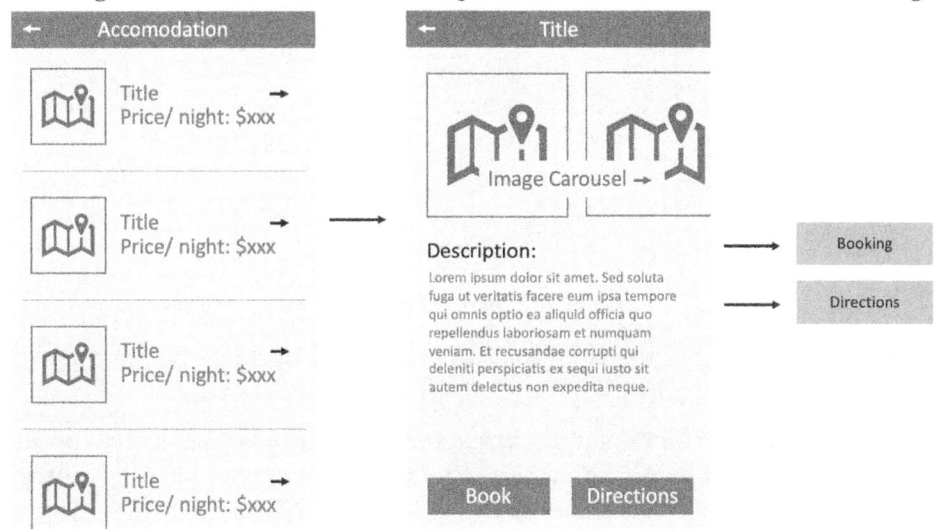

Figure 3.5: Accommodation journey

The journey included a detailed screen for each entry with further images and a CTA for launching the Map feature preconfigured to center on the accommodation's geolocation.

- **Tournament info**: Real-time updated information on past, current, and upcoming tournament matches. The tournament journey screen is shown in the following figure:

50 ■ *Scalable Android Applications in Kotlin*

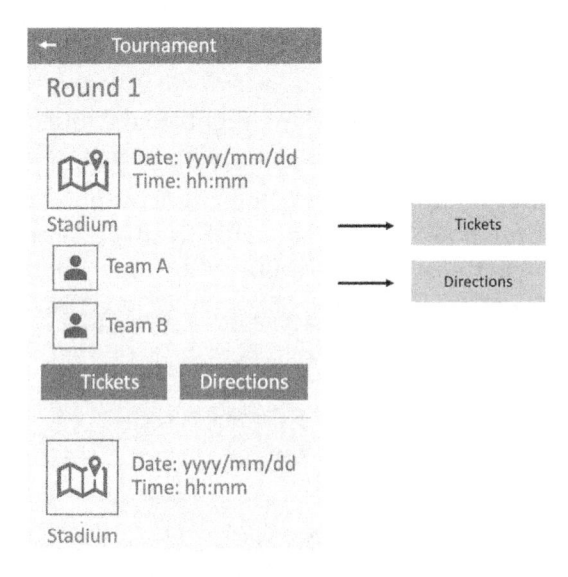

Figure 3.6: Tournament journey

The tournament was a knock-out competition, so information regarding who was matched against who was updated against back-end services.

- **Tickets**: A journey for booking tournament match tickets. Each entry conditionally included a CTA for launching the map feature pre-configured to center on the relevant stadium's geolocation. As with the tournament info, information regarding who was matched against who was updated against back-end services.
- **Tourism info**: A list of tourist attractions fetched from back-end services with images and a short description. Take a look at the following figure:

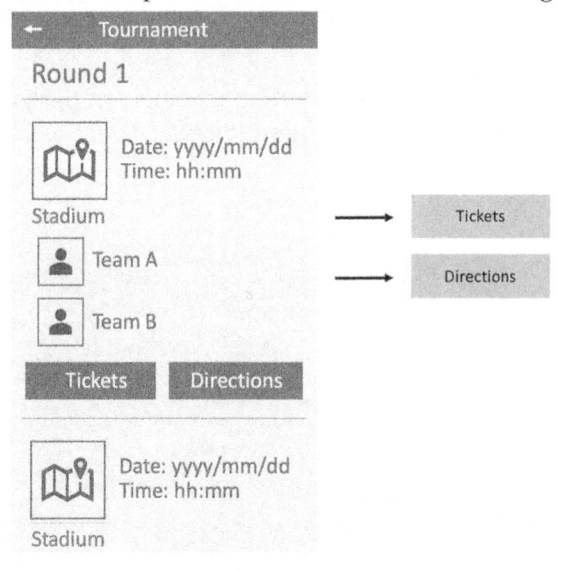

Figure 3.7: Tourism Journey

The journey includes a detail screen for each entry with further images and a CTA for launching the map feature preconfigured to center on the attraction's geolocation.

- **Map/ Directions**: The landing page for this feature is a map rendered from the Google Maps API and reskinned with the tournament app's theme colors and customized location icons, including bespoke miniature images for each of the stadiums. If launched from the home screen, if the user is in the tournament country, then the map is centered on the user's location; otherwise, the map is centered on the country's capital. Take a look at the following figure:

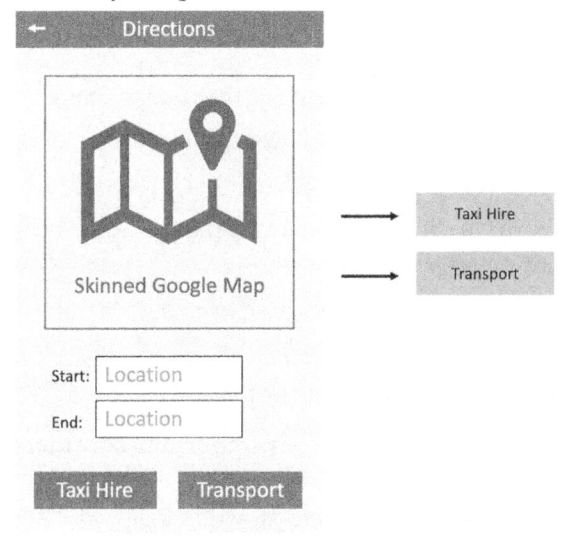

Figure 3.8: Directions journey

Like Google Maps, the user can enter a destination and get directions based on public transport, taxi, or by walking (default), which would be rendered on the map accordingly. At this point, CTAs would be available to launch the public transport or Taxi Hire features preconfigured with the start and finish locations.

- **Public Transport**: Provides route and timetable information on the country's public transport system, given start and destination locations.
- **Taxi Hire**: Taxi drivers registered with this app can receive instructions and fares directly from the user. The drivers have their own drivers' app on their phones that broadcasts their location to a central server. The app then uses these locations to provide a list of the nearest drivers to the user's start location.

Conclusion

In this chapter, we introduced the concept of features and feature modules, exploring rules for and ways of splitting an app into features. Finally, a case study closely based on a real-life app was described, promoting user journeys to identify features.

The practicalities of how to write features in code will be discussed throughout this book. For example, in *Chapter 11, Creating the Module Hierarchy*, we examine how to create a module hierarchy that accommodates features, and in *Chapter 12, Networking and APIs in Kotlin*, and *Chapter 13, Creating UI with Jetpack Compose*, we demonstrate the development of those modules with a simple, practical example.

Before doing that, however, there are several foundation concepts that need attention. Starting with the next chapter, we will learn how to go about organizing a feature's code by examining Clean Code Architecture and its specific application to Android architecture.

Points to remember

- Breaking an app into Features begins at the design stage.
- Apply the *user journey* paradigm to identify features.
- Create separate modules in your code for each feature.
- Where possible, look to previous examples where features were successfully implemented for precedent.

Questions

1. What steps can you follow to identify features?
2. What is granularity and why is it an important consideration when identifying features?
3. What aspects does a user journey typically consider?

Join our book's Discord space

Join the book's Discord Workspace for Latest updates, Offers, Tech happenings around the world, New Release and Sessions with the Authors:

https://discord.bpbonline.com

Chapter 4
Clean Code Architecture

Introduction

Further continuing the theme of Separation of Concerns, this chapter examines the concept of **Clean Code Architecture** (**CCA**), as proposed by *Robert C. Martin*, and its contribution to breaking a feature into entities that can be developed in parallel.

Clean code architecture, also known as Clean Architecture or Onion Architecture, provides a way to structure and organize code, emphasizing the **separation of concerns** (**SoC**) and the independence of different layers within an application. It consists of several layers, including the data layer, domain layer, and presentation layer (also known as the user interface layer).

Structure

This chapter covers the following topics:

- The ubiquitous CCA onion diagram
- Domain-Data-Presentation layering
- Combined CCA/layering for Android
- Domain layer
- Data layer

- Presentation layer
- Flow of control
- Infrastructure layer

Objectives

Previously we discussed breaking down an app's requirements into features and advised that each feature be developed in its own module. In this chapter, we will look at the recommended way of further subdividing those features into modules representing the different layers of CCA. By the end of this chapter, you will understand the original CCA concept in depth and then present a very similar arrangement adapted specifically for Android.

The ubiquitous CCA onion diagram

Figure 4.1 comes directly from *Robert C. Martin*'s site at **blog.cleancoder.com**:

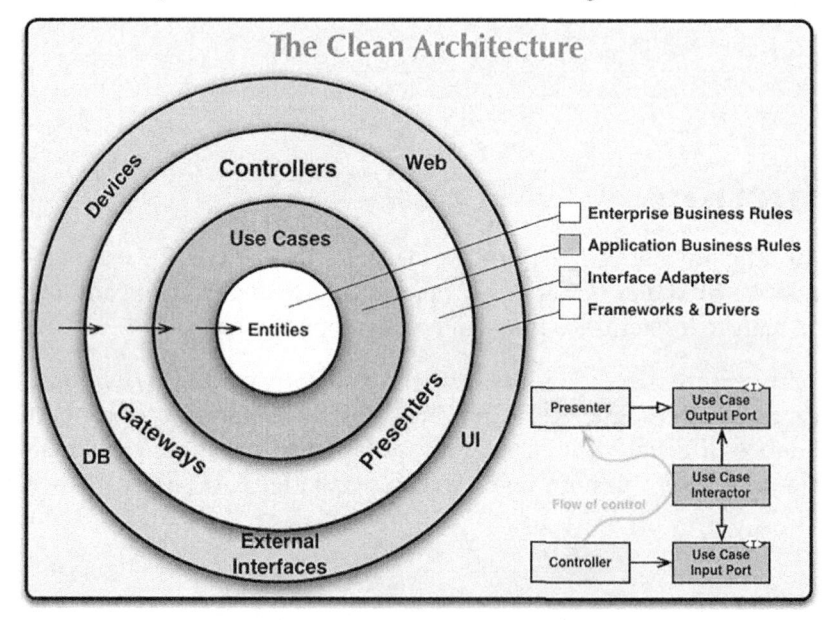

Figure 4.1: The original CCA onion diagram

The key principle behind CCA is the dependency rule, which states that dependencies should always point inward. This is indicated by the horizontal arrows pointing inwards on the left of *Figure 4.1*. This means that outer layers (such as the presentation layer) should depend on inner layers (such as the domain layer), but the inner layers should not have any direct knowledge of the outer layers. This rule helps enforce SoC and maintain a high level of modularity and testability.

The different elements in the concentric circles are described as follows:

- **Entities**: Entities represent the core business objects or concepts of the application. They encapsulate the business logic and contain the state and behavior relevant to the domain. Entities are typically independent of any specific framework or technology.
- **Use cases**: Use cases, also known as Interactors, define the application-specific workflows or behaviors. They encapsulate the application's business rules and orchestrate the interaction between entities, data sources, and other components. Use cases operate on inputs received from controllers and produce outputs for presentation or data manipulation.
- **Controllers**: Controllers handle the communication between the user interface and the underlying layers of the application. They receive input from the user, interpret it, and coordinate the execution of relevant use cases. Controllers are responsible for input validation, managing the flow of business logic, and updating the user interface based on the outcomes.
- **Presenters**: Presenters transform the data received from use cases into a format suitable for presentation. They prepare the data to be displayed by the user interface components and decouple the presentation logic from the business logic.
- **Gateways**: Gateways provide an interface for accessing and manipulating external data sources or systems. They abstract the specific details of data storage or retrieval, allowing the application to work with data through a unified interface. Gateways may include databases, network services, file systems, or other external data sources.
- **Frameworks and drivers**: This layer comprises frameworks, libraries, and tools that facilitate communication with the outside world. It includes web frameworks, database frameworks, user interface frameworks, and other technologies specific to the platform or infrastructure being used.
- **External interfaces**: External interfaces define the boundaries between the application and the external world. They include user interfaces, web APIs, messaging interfaces, or any other means of communication with external systems or users.

Domain-data-presentation layering

The data, domain, and presentation layer paradigm is a concept commonly associated with software architecture and design, particularly in the context of developing applications. It is not attributed to a specific individual or source but has evolved as a best practice over time in the field of software engineering. This paradigm helps organize and structure software systems into distinct layers, each with its own responsibilities and concerns.

Here is a brief overview of each layer in this paradigm:

- **Data layer**: This layer is responsible for managing data storage and retrieval. It includes databases, file systems, or any other data storage mechanism. The primary focus of the data layer is to ensure data integrity, reliability, and efficient data access.
- **Domain layer (also known as business logic layer)**: The domain layer contains the core business logic and rules of an application. It encapsulates the application's behavior and defines how data is processed and manipulated. It often includes classes and functions that represent the business entities and operations.
- **Presentation layer**: The presentation layer is the user interface of the application. It's responsible for displaying data to users and collecting input from them. This layer includes user interfaces, such as web pages, mobile app screens, or desktop application interfaces.

The purpose of separating these layers is to promote modularity, maintainability, and scalability in software systems. By isolating each layer's responsibilities, developers can make changes or updates to one layer without significantly impacting the others. This separation also enhances collaboration among development teams, as different teams can focus on different layers of the application.

The data, domain, and presentation layer paradigm are closely related to the more general concept of layered architecture, which has been a fundamental principle in software engineering for many years. It has its roots in various software engineering principles, including SoC and the **model-view-controller** (**MVC**) architectural pattern, among others.

While there may not be a single origin or specific source associated with this paradigm, it has become a widely accepted and practiced approach in software development due to its effectiveness in building maintainable and scalable applications. Different software development methodologies and frameworks also often recommend or enforce this SoC as a best practice.

It should also be noted, however, that domain-data-presentation layering is only recommended for small apps or features that are implemented in their own modules, as is described here. With large, complex apps that are modularized purely on this basis, the benefits of layering are lost. In this instance, a change to a single requirement generally leads to changes across all modules.

Furthermore, despite popular misconception, whilst layering is considered an architecture and its deployment can lead to cleaner code, it is not part of the official CCA as described in the previous section.

Combined CCA/layering for Android

Figure 4.1 is an excellent catch-all arrangement for every kind of system. This highly generalized arrangement, however, means that it is open to interpretation when applied to a specific system. In *Figure 4.2*, we map the elements depicted in *Figure 4.1* to the more familiar Android features and superimpose layering, effectively combining the two architectures.

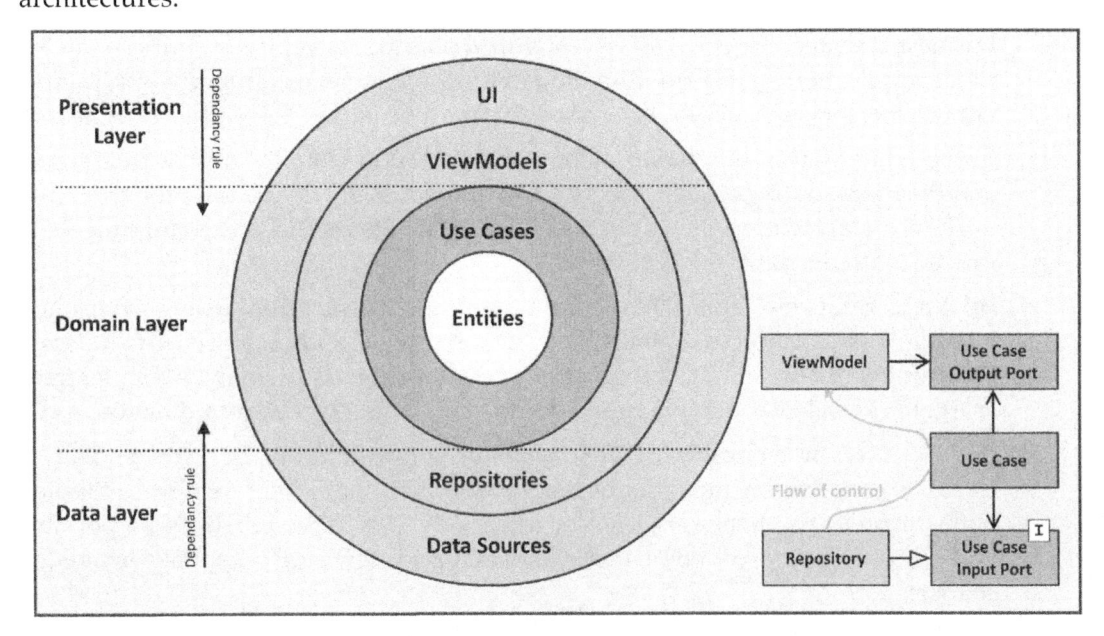

Figure 4.2: CCA for Android

Domain layer

The domain layer, also known as the business logic layer or domain model, is a key component in software development that represents the core business concepts, rules, and behaviors of an application. Its primary purpose is to capture and express the business rules and processes of the problem domain in a way that is independent of technical details and infrastructure. As such, it represents the heart of the application.

As depicted in *Figure 4.2*, the domain layer will host use cases and domain entities:

Domain entities

Domain entities are the core building blocks of the application's business logic. They represent the key concepts, objects, or entities central to the domain or problem domain being addressed by the software.

Domain entities encapsulate both the state (data) and behavior (methods) specific to the business domain. They are independent of external concerns such as frameworks, databases, or user interfaces. The primary focus of Domain Entities is to model and implement the business rules, validations, and behaviors that govern the application.

Here are some characteristics of domain entities:

- **Business-centric**: Domain entities are defined based on the understanding of the business domain. They represent real-world objects, concepts, or entities relevant to the application's problem domain. For example, in an e-commerce application, entities like **Product**, **Order**, or **Customer** would be part of the domain entities.
- **Encapsulate state and behavior**: Domain entities encapsulate both the data (state) and the methods (behavior) associated with them. They define the properties and attributes representing the entity's state and provide methods to manipulate and interact with the data.
- **Business rules and invariants**: Domain entities enforce the business rules and invariants specific to the domain. They ensure the data stays consistent and valid according to the defined rules. For example, an **Order** entity may have rules such as total price calculation, inventory checks, or validation of required fields.
- **Independent of technical details**: Domain entities should be independent of technical concerns or implementation details. They should not be tightly coupled with frameworks, databases, or user interfaces. This allows them to be portable and reusable across different parts of the application and potential technology changes.
- **Testable in isolation**: Domain entities can be easily tested by focusing on their behavior and state. Unit tests can be written to validate the behavior and ensure that the entities adhere to the defined business rules.

Although domain entities are officially defined as containing both data and methods, in practice, it's challenging to find cases where the methods in data entities don't belong in a use case. To avoid violating the **Single Responsibility Principle (SRP)**, data entities are often kept as pure data classes. Whether or not a data entity needs to encapsulate methods needs to be determined on a case-by-case basis. It may be a scenario where common behavior on a data entity needs only to be shared amongst two or more use cases. in that case, those methods on the data entity should have `internal` access scope. Otherwise, if there is a reason for that behavior to be used in the presentation layer then the access scope can be left as public.

For example:

```
1.  data class ProductEntity(
2.      val id: String,
3.      val name: String,
4.      val price: Double,
5.      val quantity: Int
6.  ) {
7.      internal fun increaseQuantity(amount: Int): ProductEntity {
8.          require(amount > 0) { "Amount must be positive" }
```

```
 9.         return copy(quantity = quantity + amount)
10.     }
11.
12.     internal fun decreaseQuantity(amount: Int): ProductEntity {
13.         require(amount > 0) { "Amount must be positive" }
14.         require(amount <= quantity) { "Insufficient quantity" }
15.         return copy(quantity = quantity - amount)
16.     }
17. }
```

In this example, we have a **ProductEntity** representing a product in an e-commerce system. It has properties such as **id**, **name**, **price**, and **quantity**, which define its state.

The **ProductEntity** also provides behavior through methods like **increaseQuantity** and **decreaseQuantity**. These methods manipulate the **quantity** property based on certain rules and validations. For instance, **increaseQuantity** allows increasing the quantity by a positive amount, and **decreaseQuantity** decreases the quantity while ensuring it does not go below zero.

The **ProductEntity** encapsulates the state (data) and the behavior (methods) specific to a product in the e-commerce domain. It can be used to enforce business rules, perform validations, and maintain the consistency of product data.

Note: The data modifier in Kotlin is used to automatically generate common methods like **toString**, **equals**, and **copy** based on the properties defined in the primary constructor.

Also note that the methods **increaseQuantity** and **decreaseQuantity** are marked as internal. We do not want to expose these methods to the presentation layer since we need to keep that layer as thin as possible. Only use cases, which are implemented in the same module, will have access to these behaviors.

Use cases

A use case represents a specific business operation or a user-driven action within an application. It encapsulates the logic and behavior required to fulfill a particular user goal or accomplish a specific task.

Use cases contain the core business rules and processes of the application. They serve as a bridge between the outer layers (such as the presentation layer and data layer) and the innermost Domain Layer.

Here are some key characteristics of a use case:

- **Represents a user goal**: A use case focuses on fulfilling a specific user goal or providing value to the end user. It represents a meaningful and cohesive unit of functionality from the user's perspective.

- **Encapsulates business logic**: A use case contains the business logic necessary to orchestrate the data flow and coordinate interactions between different application components. It may involve multiple entities, services, and repositories to achieve its objective.
- **Independent of external details**: A use case should be independent of the specific technology, frameworks, or external systems used in the application. It operates on the domain entities and interacts with the necessary components through interfaces or abstractions.
- **Driven by inputs and outputs**: A use case receives input data, such as user input or external data, and produces outputs, such as updated entities or response messages. It may involve validation, transformation, and other processing steps to handle the inputs and generate the desired outputs.
- **Testable in isolation**: Use cases can be easily tested in isolation, without dependencies on external resources or frameworks. This allows for effective unit testing and ensures that the business logic is functioning correctly.

Here is an example of a use case in Kotlin:

```kotlin
class AddToCartUseCase(
    private val cartRepository: CartRepository,
    private val productRepository: ProductRepository
) {

    suspend operator fun invoke(
        productId: String,
        quantity: Int
    ): Result<Response> {
        val product = productRepository.getProductById(productId)
        val cart = cartRepository.getCart()
        // Perform business logic and update the cart
        val updatedCart = cart.addItem(product, quantity)
        return cartRepository.updateCart(updatedCart)
    }
}
```

In this example, we have an **AddToCartUseCase** that represents a use case of adding a product to the shopping cart in an e-commerce application.

The **AddToCartUseCase** takes two dependencies: **cartRepository** and **productRepository**. These dependencies are interfaces or abstractions that provide access to the necessary data for performing the use case.

The **invoke** operator is the entry point for executing the use case. It takes the **productId** and **quantity** as input parameters. Inside the method, the use case retrieves the product information from the **productRepository** based on the provided **productId**. It also fetches the current state of the cart from the **cartRepository**.

The use case then performs the business logic, such as validating the quantity or applying any additional rules. In this case, it adds the product to the cart with the specified quantity. Finally, the updated cart is passed to the **cartRepository** to persist the changes.

The use case encapsulates the logic required to handle the specific user action of adding a product to the cart. It orchestrates the interaction between the repositories, performs any necessary validations or transformations, and ensures the consistency of the data.

Note: The use of the invoke operator. This allows an object of the use case to be called like a function. Since use cases should only have one method, this is preferable to having redundant member function names such as execute:

```
1. GlobalScope.launch {
2.     val addToCartUseCase = AddToCartUseCase(cartRepo, productRepo)
3.     addToCartUseCase("productId", 3).onFailure { /* Do something */ }
4. }
```

The invoke operator is marked with suspend in this case so the call above would need to be within a coroutine scope.

Data layer

The data layer is responsible for managing the persistence and storage of data within an application. It provides an abstraction over the underlying data storage technology (such as a database) and offers methods to interact with the data. The data layer typically includes functionality for data retrieval, manipulation, and storage. It ensures data integrity and handles the complexities of interacting with the storage system.

Figure 4.3 depicts the data layer including real-world resources:

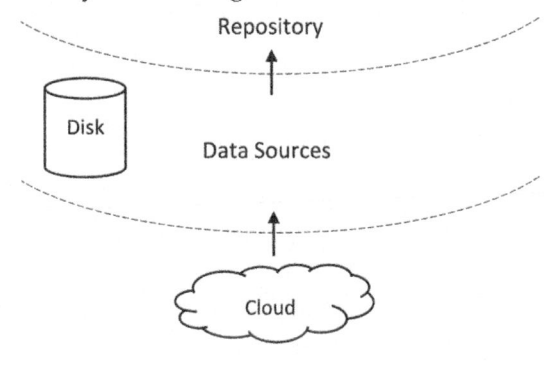

Figure 4.3: Data layer

The data layer implements the repository (specified in the domain layer). It defines the external data sources.

Repositories

Repositories provide an abstraction over the data layer and encapsulate the logic for data access. They act as an intermediary between the domain model layers and data mapping, providing a clean and standardized way to retrieve and store data. Repositories offer methods for querying, saving, and updating data entities. They abstract the underlying data storage details and provide a consistent interface to work with data. Client objects declaratively build queries and send them to the repositories for answers. Repositories separate and clearly define the dependency between the data allocation, the work and or domain mapping. Here are some key aspects and responsibilities of repositories in the data layer:

- **Data access abstraction**: Repositories abstract away the specific details of data access and storage technologies, providing a consistent and simplified interface for accessing and manipulating data. They define methods and operations that enable the application to perform common data operations, such as retrieving, storing, updating, and deleting data entities.

- **Encapsulation of data access logic**: Repositories encapsulate the implementation of data access logic, hiding the complexities of querying the data storage system and mapping the retrieved data to application-specific data structures. They provide a higher-level interface that shields the application from the intricacies of the underlying data storage implementation.

- **Data retrieval and persistence**: Repositories handle the retrieval and persistence of data entities. They encapsulate the queries or commands required to interact with the data storage system and provide methods to perform **Create, Read, Update, Delete** (**CRUD**) operations on data entities.

- **Querying and filtering**: Repositories often provide methods for querying and filtering data based on specific criteria. They enable the application to retrieve subsets of data based on conditions, such as searching for specific records or filtering by certain attributes.

- **Unit of work**: Repositories can also play a role in managing a unit of work, which represents a logical group of related data operations that need to be performed together. They ensure that changes to multiple entities within a unit of work are treated atomically, either all succeeding or all failing, to maintain data consistency.

Repositories are typically designed to align with the domain entities and concepts of the application's problem domain. They provide a clean separation between the application's business logic layer (or domain layer) and the details of data access and storage, promoting modularity, testability, and maintainability of the application.

Data sources

Data sources refer to the components responsible for providing access to external data or external systems. They serve as interfaces or gateways for interacting with external entities, such as databases, network services, file systems, or any other form of data storage or retrieval mechanism. They abstract the specific details and implementation of these external systems, allowing the rest of the application to work with data in a unified and technology-agnostic manner.

Here are a few key points about data sources in CCA:

- **Abstraction**: Data sources provide abstractions and interfaces that define how the application can interact with the external systems or data sources. They encapsulate the specific technical details and provide a consistent API for accessing and manipulating data.
- **Interface segregation**: Data sources adhere to the **Interface Segregation Principle (ISP)** by exposing only the methods and operations relevant to the specific data access needs of the application. This ensures that clients of the data sources are not burdened with unnecessary or unrelated functionality.
- **Dependency inversion**: Data sources depend on abstractions or interfaces defined within the domain layer or the application's core. This enables the **Dependency Inversion Principle (DIP)**, allowing the domain layer to define the necessary contracts and the Data Layer to implement them.
- **Persistence and retrieval**: Data sources handle the tasks of persisting data to external systems (such as writing to a database) and retrieving data from those systems (such as querying a web service). They may involve operations like CRUD, data mapping, serialization, and de-serialization.
- **Caching and synchronization**: Data sources may also be responsible for implementing caching mechanisms or handling data synchronization between the external systems and the application's internal state. This helps improve performance, reduce network traffic, and ensure data consistency.

Here is a typical data source interface:

```
1. interface ProductDataSource {
2.     suspend fun getProductById(productId: String): Product
3.     suspend fun saveProduct(product: Product)
4.     suspend fun deleteProduct(productId: String)
5.     // Other methods for data manipulation and retrieval
6. }
```

In this example, we have a **ProductDataSource** interface that represents a data source responsible for managing product-related data. The interface defines several methods that define the operations that can be performed on the product data.

The `getProductById` method retrieves a `Product` entity based on the provided `productId`. The `saveProduct` method is responsible for persisting or updating a `Product` entity in the data source. The `deleteProduct` method deletes a product with the specified `productId` from the data source.

The interface serves as a contract or abstraction for interacting with the product data. The actual implementation of the `ProductDataSource` interface would be provided by a specific data source class, such as a database repository, a network API client, or a file system manager.

By defining the data source operations in an interface, the application's core and higher-level components can depend on the abstraction rather than concrete implementations. This allows for easier testing, decoupling from specific data storage technologies, and enables the flexibility to switch between different data sources or implementations without affecting the consuming components.

Presentation layer

The presentation layer, also known as the **user interface** (UI) layer or the presentation tier, is a component within the software architecture that focuses on presenting information to users and receiving user input. It is responsible for delivering a user-friendly and visually appealing interface that enables users to interact with the application. The presentation layer should be kept as thin as possible, delegating most of the application logic to the domain layer.

The primary purpose of the presentation layer is to facilitate the communication and interaction between users and the underlying system. It takes care of the visual representation of data, user input validation, and providing appropriate feedback to the user. The presentation layer is concerned with the look, feel, and usability of the application.

Here are some key characteristics and responsibilities of the presentation layer:

- **User interface:** The presentation layer is responsible for creating and managing the user interface components, such as screens, forms, buttons, menus, and widgets. It defines how the application's data and functionality are presented to the user and how the user interacts with the system.
- **User input handling:** The presentation layer captures and validates user input, ensuring that the entered data meets the specified requirements. It performs input validation and handles user actions, such as button clicks, form submissions, and menu selections.
- **User experience (UX):** The presentation layer plays a vital role in designing and delivering a positive user experience. It focuses on factors such as visual design, layout, navigation, responsiveness, and accessibility to create an intuitive and engaging user interface.

- **Presentation logic:** The presentation layer may contain presentation-specific logic that is responsible for tasks like data formatting, localization, and rendering data in the appropriate visual representation for the user. In modern Android applications, this logic will be defined in the **ViewModel** classes.

In Android, the UI has been supplied by **Activity**, **Fragment** and **View** objects. Most recently this arrangement has been replaced by Jetpack Compose. In the future, this may be replaced by something else especially as much of the Jetpack Compose implementation is currently experimental. It is important, then, that the UI and **ViewModel** objects be properly separated with the dependency rule as shown in *Figures 4.1* and *4.2*. There will be more on this in *Chapter 8, Presentation Layer Evolution in Compose*.

Flow of control

This section looks at how the three layers fit together. In particular, it concentrates on the bottom-left corner of the CCA diagram in *Figure 4.2* as shown in *Figure 4.4*:

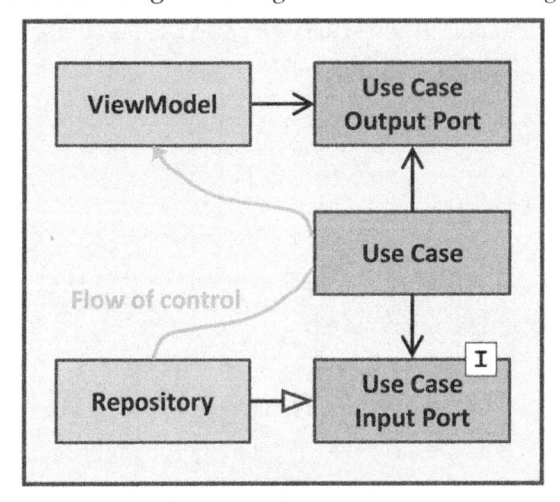

Figure 4.4: Android flow control

Robert C. Martin's original CCA diagram in *Figure 4.1* depicts the flow of control from a *Controller* to a *Presenter*. This is not applicable in the Android scenario because the Android equivalent of these paradigms are both in the same layer, so there is no boundary to cross. Hence the flow of control in the Android version is from the repository implementation in the Data Layer to the **ViewModel** in the presentation layer, via the domain layer use case, that is, the **ViewModel** gets its data from the repository via the use case.

The different colors indicate layer and module boundaries. The use case input port is an interface. Traditionally the output port had also been an interface but this is no longer the case This will be discussed shortly. Given standard UML nomenclature, the repository will provide concrete implementations of the input port interfaces and the **ViewModel** will use the output port result of the use case. Finally, the **ViewModel** and use case classes have associations with input and output ports respectively. This association will always be via constructor parameters. This will be expanded on in *Chapter 12, Networking and APIs in Kotlin*.

As previously mentioned, the output port was traditionally defined as an interface. For example, taking another look at the previous **AddToCartUseCase** example, the following would have been considered a use case output port:

```
1. interface AddToCartUseCaseOutputPort {
2.     fun onSuccess(response: Response)
3.     fun onFailure(error: Throwable)
4. }
```

The **ViewModel** or presenter would implement this interface locally and pass an instance to the use case, effectively creating a callback on success or failure of the network call. This pattern was so common, however, that the developers of Kotlin created the **Result** class in the core library that does exactly the same thing. Instead of implementing an interface, the **ViewModel** provides lambdas to the result of the use case instead, for example:

```
1. class CartViewModel(
2.     private val addToCartUseCase: AddToCartUseCase
3.     // ...
4. ) : ViewModel() {
5.     // ...
6.     private fun onAddToCartEvent(prodId: String, qty: Int) =
7.         viewModelScope.launch {
8.             addToCartUseCase(prodId, qty)
9.                 .onSuccess { /* trigger some ui */ }
10.                .onFailure { /* trigger another ui */ }
11.        }
12. }
```

Result is the use case output port and is not an interface. It is a templatized class with companion factories. The use case input port (repository) implementations would typically use these factories to create a network call response.

The following are use case input port examples:

```
1. interface CartRepository {
2.     fun getCart(): Cart
3.     fun updateCart(updatedCart: Any): Result<Response> =
4.         Result.success(object : Response{})
5. }
6.
```

```
7. interface ProductRepository {
8.     fun getProductById(productId: String)
9. }
```

The **updateCart** method has a defaulted response that demonstrates a **Result** companion factory, **success**. This is for demonstrating the companion only. It is not normal to provide input port defaults.

In addition, it is common to enforce interface segregation and expose the use case itself as an interface:

```
1. interface AddToCartUseCase {
2.     suspend operator fun invoke(
3.         productId: String,
4.         quantity: Int
5.     ): Result<Response>
6. }
7.
8. internal class AddToCartUseCaseImpl(
9.     private val cartRepository: CartRepository,
10.    private val productRepository: ProductRepository
11. ) : AddToCartUseCase {
12.
13.     override suspend operator fun invoke(
14.         productId: String,
15.         quantity: Int
16.     ): Result<Response> {
17.         ...
18.     }
19. }
```

The preceding ports and implementation (apart from the **ViewModel**) are all written in the domain layer. As well as affecting Dependency Inversion (see above, DIP, and *Chapter 2, Breaking Down App Code with Separation of Concerns*), this approach is the preferred vehicle for writing unit tests. When injecting interfaces in this way, you do not necessarily have to rely on object mocking libraries, you can provide any kind of dummy implementation that suits the test. This will be discussed at length in *Chapter 9, Test-Driven Development with Mocking Libraries for Android*.

The data layer would define an implementation of a use case output port, in this case, the **ProductRepository** interface:

```
1. internal class ProductRepositoryImpl(
2.     private val dataSource: ProductDataSource
3. ): ProductRepository {
4.     override fun getProductById(productId: String): Product {
5.         ...
6.     }
7. }
```

Note: In this case, `ProductDataSource` is an interface and therefore becomes a Repository input port in a similar fashion to the use case input port, creating dependency inversion between the data sources and the repository. This is useful to maintain in case there is ever a decision to swap out data source libraries and to better facilitate unit testing, as with `AddToCartUseCaseImpl`.

The `Impl` class name postfix in `AddToCartUseCaseImpl`, and `ProductRepositoryImpl` for that matter, is an unfortunate naming convention that is difficult to get away from. In episode two of his Clean Coders videos, *Robert C. Martin* devotes almost all of the forty minutes on naming conventions where he quite correctly says that interface names should be generic and their implementations should be specific. He gives examples like `Account` (abstract, generic) and `SavingsAccount` (concrete, specific). This is for the situation where there could be several implementations of the abstract class such as `CurrentAccount`. He does not say anything about naming conventions where the interface exists purely to affect dependency inversion. In other words, a one-to-one relationship where the implementation is not a specialization of the interface. Since he specifically condemns the `I` prefix for interfaces (for example `IAccount` instead of `Account`), we are left with this `Impl` postfix for implementations instead.

In many current in-house app projects, it is common to see `Impl` concrete use case classes like `AddToCartUseCaseImpl` given public access and then used directly for injection binding. This is a mistake and an indication of an error in the code structure. Furthermore, the only time you will ever see classes from well-written third-party libraries with the `Impl` postfix is in the debugger. For that reason, we recommend making `Impl` classes like this internal and using a first-class public factory function defined alongside it for the purposes of injection:

```
1. fun addToCartUseCaseImpl(
2.     cartRepo: CartRepository,
3.     productRepo: ProductRepository
4. ) : AddToCartUseCase = AddToCartUseCaseImpl(cartRepo, productRepo)
```

Even better, a companion function on the interface itself:

```
1. interface AddToCartUseCase {
2.     suspend operator fun invoke(
3.         productId: String,
```

```
4.         quantity: Int
5.     ): Result<Response>
6.
7.     companion object {
8.         fun impl (
9.             cartRepo: CartRepository,
10.            prodRepo: ProductRepository
11.        ): AddToCartUseCase =  AddToCartUseCaseImpl (
12.            cartRepo, prodRepo
13.        )
14.    }
15. }
```

If **AddToCartUseCase** and **AddToCartUseCaseImpl** are defined in the same file then the visibility of the latter could even be reduced from **internal** to **private**.

Infrastructure layer

Many sources will quote a fourth layer to CCA. This is indicated in *Figure 4.1* and *Figure 4.2* as the outermost concentric circle: that of the infrastructure layer. The infrastructure layer represents the outermost layer of the architecture. It is responsible for handling the technical implementation details and external dependencies required to run the application. The infrastructure layer interacts with external systems, frameworks, libraries, and devices.

Here are some key aspects of the infrastructure layer in CCA:

- **External interfaces**: The infrastructure layer provides implementations for the interfaces defined in the inner layers of the architecture. For example, it may implement the data access interfaces defined in the data layer or the UI interfaces defined in the presentation layer.
- **Frameworks and libraries**: The infrastructure layer incorporates third-party frameworks, libraries, and tools that support the application's functionality. This includes technologies for networking, databases, file systems, authentication, logging, and other infrastructure concerns.
- **Device and platform interaction**: The infrastructure layer handles the interaction with the underlying hardware, operating system, and platform-specific features. It provides the necessary abstractions and adapters to communicate with device sensors, peripherals, system services, or platform-specific APIs.
- **External services**: The infrastructure layer integrates with external services such as databases, web services, cloud platforms, message queues, or any other external systems required by the application. It encapsulates the details of interacting with these services and provides the necessary adapters or connectors.

- **Cross-cutting concerns**: The infrastructure layer addresses cross-cutting concerns such as logging, error handling, caching, security, and performance optimizations. It encapsulates the technical aspects that are not specific to a particular business rule or use case but affect the overall behavior and quality of the application.
- **Testing utilities**: The infrastructure layer may provide test doubles, stubs, or mock implementations for the interfaces defined in the inner layers, enabling the testing of the application in isolation from external dependencies.

In summary then, from an Android point of view, the infrastructure layer will include things like Retrofit, Room DB, common code, and the Android OS itself.

Conclusion

In this chapter, we discussed Clean Code Architecture along with Domain-Data-Presentation layering and demonstrated how, at a high level, they can be applied to Android. It gave some practical examples of how the Flow of Control between the layers can be achieved by implementing Dependency Inversion. You may have noticed that since the domain layer defines the repository interfaces, and since both the presentation layer and data layer are both dependent on the domain layer, then the presentation layer will have access to the repository interfaces. On the surface, this may seem redundant, but remember that the presentation layer in Android can supply a data source in the form of the `SharedPreferences` supplied by Android OS infrastructure. For that reason, the presentation layer needs to have the option of being able to inject its implementation of a repository into the use cases.

In the next chapter, we will discuss dependency injection and how it can be used to achieve our hybrid CCA arrangement. Firstly though, the next chapter will delve into the concept of cross-platform development and how it can be used to further enforce SoC.

Points to remember

- Domain-Data-Presentation layering is not officially Clean Code Architecture.
- Feature modules can be broken down into data, domain and presentation modules.
- Domain-Data-Presentation layering should not be used at app level – unless it is a single-feature, single module app and is never going to implement any further features (we would suggest that to make any app future-proof, you should always create at least one feature module).
- It is important to correctly establish the flow of control between layers using use case input and output ports.

Questions

1. What is a use case?
2. How many methods should a use case define?
3. Give an example of use case input and output ports.

CHAPTER 5
Cross-Platform App Development

Introduction

Before moving on to Dependency Injection, in this chapter, we will cover the topic of cross-platform development and how it relates to large project development.

Over the years, there have been several attempts to unify the development of iOS and Android apps using cross-platform environments. These attempts have largely failed. This chapter looks briefly at those platforms, why they failed, and discusses the half-way-house of cross-platform development, **Kotlin Multi-mobile** (**KMM**), and how it can be used in a clean code arrangement for pattern enforcement and cross-platform compatibility.

Structure

This chapter covers the following topics:

- Cross-platform development overview
- Xamarin
- Ionic
- React Native
- Flutter
- Compose multiplatform
- Common failures
- Kotlin multi-mobile

Objectives

By the end of this chapter, you will understand the state of affairs with respect to cross-platform development by examining each of the technologies currently available. Ultimately, we will lead into Kotlin multi-mobile and demonstrate how this technology can enforce SoC by restricting code development of non-presentation layers to pure Kotlin.

Cross-platform development overview

Cross-platform mobile development refers to the practice of creating mobile applications that can run on multiple platforms, such as iOS and Android, using a single codebase. It involves using frameworks, tools, and programming languages that allow developers to write code once and deploy it across multiple platforms rather than developing separate applications for each platform.

Without a cross-platform arrangement, development of multiple platforms would typically follow this paradigm:

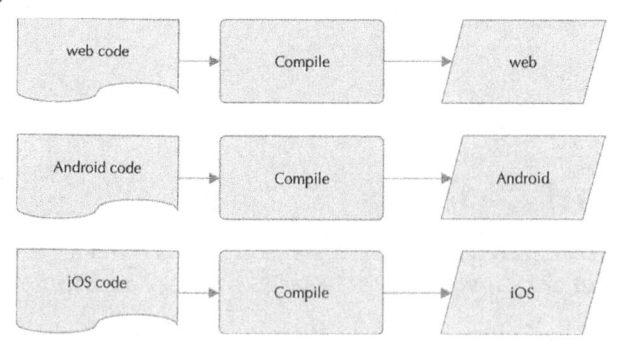

Figure 5.1: Separate platform development

Each platform is developed in isolation. By contrast, cross-platform development consolidates the coding effort:

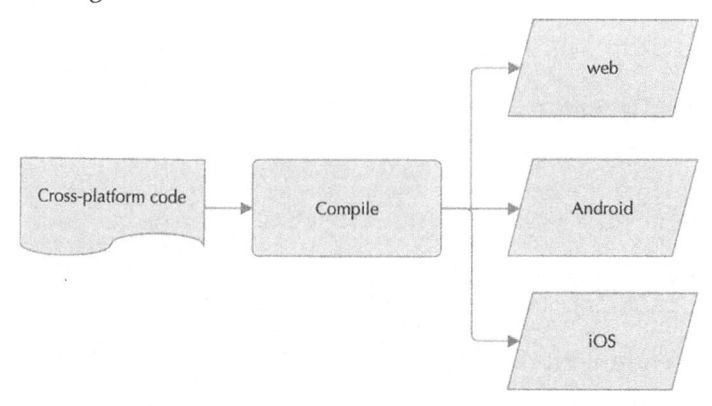

Figure 5.2: Cross-platform development

Here are some key aspects *promised* by cross-platform mobile development:

- **Shared codebase**: With cross-platform development, a significant portion of the codebase is shared across different platforms. This allows developers to write the logic, data models, and business rules once and reuse them across multiple platforms, reducing development effort and improving code maintainability.
- **Platform abstraction**: Cross-platform frameworks provide abstractions and APIs that allow developers to access platform-specific functionalities, such as UI components, sensors, or device capabilities, in a unified manner. This allows developers to leverage platform features while writing code that works across different platforms.
- **Write once, deploy anywhere**: Cross-platform development enables developers to write the code once and deploy it on multiple platforms, such as iOS, Android, and even web platforms. This promises to significantly reduce the time and cost of developing and maintaining separate codebases for each platform.

  In fact, in large projects code is not written once. App development is an iterative process with regular releases. Analytic feedback from users of the app will often drive changes and new features. Iterative development is essential for large projects because it helps to ensure that customers are satisfied with the final product. By delivering working software at the end of each iteration, customers can see how the product is progressing and provide feedback. This feedback can be used to improve the product in subsequent iterations.
- **Code sharing and reusability**: By sharing a significant portion of the codebase, developers can achieve higher code reusability (all platforms reuse the same code). Changes or updates made to the shared codebase can be quickly reflected across all platforms, simplifying the maintenance process. This promise becomes a burden on large projects. Code sharing and reusability can make code more complex and difficult to understand. This is because code that is shared between different parts of a project needs to be designed in a way that is flexible and reusable, which can add complexity. It can also increase the cost of maintaining a software project. This is because changes to shared code need to be carefully considered to avoid breaking other parts of the project. Additionally, reused code may need to be modified to fit the specific needs of the project, which can be time-consuming and expensive. We will discuss this further when we examine Kotlin multi-mobile later in this chapter.
- **Development efficiency**: Cross-platform development promises to improve development efficiency as developers can work on a single codebase, avoiding the need to switch between different development environments, tools, and languages for each platform.
- **Consistent user experience**: Cross-platform frameworks often provide tools and libraries that help in creating a consistent user experience across different platforms. This allows developers to maintain a consistent look and feel, behavior, and functionality of the application regardless of the platform.

- **Rapid prototyping and iteration**: Cross-platform development can facilitate rapid prototyping and iteration cycles, as changes and updates can be quickly applied across multiple platforms. This can be particularly beneficial for start-ups or small projects with tight time constraints.

Some popular cross-platform frameworks for mobile development include React Native, Flutter, Xamarin, and Ionic. These frameworks provide the necessary tools and abstractions to create cross-platform applications with varying degrees of code sharing and platform compatibility.

Disadvantages of cross-platform development

While cross-platform development offers several advantages, it also has some potential disadvantages. Here are a few disadvantages:

- **Performance limitations**: Cross-platform frameworks often introduce an additional layer of abstraction, which impacts performance compared to native development. The performance difference may be more noticeable in applications that require intensive graphics rendering or complex calculations. Native Android code has consistently outperformed cross-platform code in benchmarks. For example, in the Geekbench 5 benchmark, native Android code outperformed cross-platform code by an average of 15% on single-core tests and 20% on multi-core tests.

- **Limited access to platform-specific features**: Cross-platform frameworks aim to provide a unified set of features and APIs that work across multiple platforms. However, they may not offer access to all platform-specific features or capabilities. They tend to cover only the more popular features, or they introduce their own. If your application heavily relies on certain platform-specific functionalities, you may face limitations or require additional workarounds.

- **Learning curve**: Adopting a cross-platform framework may require developers to learn new tools, languages, and frameworks. This learning curve can slow down the initial development process and potentially impact the productivity of the team, especially if they are already familiar with native development.

- **Framework limitations**: Cross-platform frameworks may have limitations or inconsistencies compared to native development. These limitations can range from incomplete support for certain platform features to differences in UI rendering, device compatibility, or debugging tools. It is important to carefully evaluate the capabilities and limitations of the chosen framework by considering what your app does, how it does it and if the platform can achieve it.

- **Customization challenges**: As cross-platform frameworks provide a unified codebase, customizing the user interface to match the platform-specific design guidelines or requirements may be challenging. This can result in compromises in the UI/UX design and may require additional effort to achieve the desired platform-specific look and feel. This is due to differences in recommended UI guidelines between platforms.

- **Dependency on third-party frameworks**: Cross-platform development often relies on third-party frameworks or libraries. This introduces a level of dependency on these external tools, which may have their own lifecycle, updates, and potential compatibility issues. Keeping up with the updates and ensuring compatibility can be an additional challenge.

  In truth, this is not a limitation specific to cross platform development. One of the problems currently with native android development using Jetpack Compose is that of balancing the version of Compose to the version of Kotlin. Both can be considered third party frameworks for all intents and purposes.

- **Debugging and tooling**: The debugging and development tooling for cross-platform frameworks may not be as fully comprehensive or feature-rich as those available for native development. This can impact the development process, troubleshooting, and overall productivity. One of the biggest limitations of cross-platform development tools is that they may not provide the same level of visibility into native code as native development tools. This can make it difficult to debug problems that are occurring in the native code layer. For example, a cross-platform debugger may not be able to step through native code or set breakpoints in native functions. This can make it difficult to identify and fix the root cause of a bug. This lack of visibility can increase debugging time, reduce code quality and increase development costs.

Xamarin

Xamarin is a cross-platform development framework that allows developers to build native mobile applications using C# and .NET. It enables code sharing across multiple platforms, including iOS, Android, and Windows, while providing access to platform-specific APIs and functionalities.

Figure 5.3: Xamarin logo (Source: wikipedia.org)

Here are some key aspects of Xamarin:

- **C# and .NET**: Xamarin use the C# programming language and the .NET framework, providing a familiar and powerful development environment for Microsoft Windows developers. C# is a statically typed, object-oriented language that offers a wide range of language features and libraries, making it suitable for building robust and scalable applications.

- **Native performance**: Xamarin allows developers to write code in C# and .NET, which is then compiled to native code for each target platform. This results in high-performance applications that closely match the performance of native apps developed using platform-specific languages like Swift for iOS and Java/Kotlin for Android.
- **Code sharing**: Xamarin promotes code sharing between platforms by utilizing a shared codebase written in C#. Developers can share a significant portion of the business logic, data access layers, and utility classes across different platforms. This reduces development effort and improves code maintainability.
- **Access to platform-specific APIs**: Xamarin provides bindings to platform-specific APIs, allowing developers to access native functionalities, such as camera, GPS, sensors, and device-specific features. This enables developers to create applications that fully leverage the capabilities of each platform.
- **Xamarin.Forms**: Xamarin.Forms is a UI framework within Xamarin that enables developers to build a single, shared user interface using XAML markup. Xamarin.Forms allows for rapid UI development with a common codebase, while still providing the flexibility to customize the UI for each platform if needed.
- **Visual Studio Integration**: Xamarin integrates seamlessly with Microsoft's Visual Studio IDE, providing a comprehensive development environment with powerful debugging, profiling, and testing tools. Developers can utilize familiar tools and workflows for building, testing, and deploying Xamarin applications.
- **Xamarin.Essentials**: Xamarin.Essentials is a library that provides a set of cross-platform APIs for common functionalities, such as connectivity, device information, geolocation, and more. It simplifies accessing device-specific capabilities by providing a unified API that works across platforms.

It is worth noting that while Xamarin allows for cross-platform development, there are still platform-specific considerations and UI customization required to provide a native user experience on each platform. Xamarin is a powerful choice for organizations that already have a significant investment in the .NET ecosystem and want to leverage their existing codebase and expertise to develop cross-platform mobile applications.

Disadvantages of Xamarin

While Xamarin offers several advantages for cross-platform mobile development, it also has some limitations and disadvantages to consider:

- **Learning curve**: Xamarin requires developers to learn C# and the Xamarin framework. Java, Kotlin, and C# share similarities as they are all part of the C-style language family, so the learning curve for C# syntax may not be so steep for those with Java or Kotlin expertise. However, each language has its own set of features and capabilities. Learning C# involves understanding these unique features, such as **language-integrated query** (**LINQ**), for example. Additionally, understanding the concepts of native development for each target platform is still necessary.

- **Size of application**: Xamarin applications tend to have larger file sizes compared to native apps or applications built with other frameworks. This is because Xamarin requires a runtime environment to be bundled with the application, resulting in increased download and installation times.

  The exact difference in file size can vary depending on the complexity of the application, but it is typically in the range of 20% to 50% larger than a native app. For example, a simple Xamarin app might be 5MB in size, while a native app for the same platform might be only 4MB. A more complex Xamarin app could be 50MB or more, while a native app for the same platform might be only 30MB. This difference in size may be of concern with apps that are distributed over the internet or that are deployed to devices with limited storage.

- **Performance**: Although Xamarin allows developers to build native-like applications, it adds an additional layer of abstraction between the code and the target platform. This can sometimes lead to slightly reduced performance compared to fully native applications. However, with careful optimization and leveraging platform-specific features, the impact on performance can be minimized.

- **Community and Ecosystem**: Xamarin's active community is not as large as some other cross-platform frameworks like React Native or Flutter. This means there may be fewer community-driven libraries, resources, and support available. However, Xamarin is backed by Microsoft, which provides official documentation, tutorials, and support.

- **Cost**: Xamarin has both free and commercial licensing options. The free version, Xamarin Community, provides most of the core features, but certain advanced features and tools require a paid subscription. The cost of licensing and additional tools may be a factor to consider, particularly for small or independent developers. For example, the Professional option, at the time of writing, was $499 per year and included some Enterprise-level support, cross-platform desktop development and additional tools such as the profiler and the VS editor.

  The more expensive Enterprise option, again, at the time of writing, was $2999 per year and included cross-platform cloud development, production environment support and more advanced development tools. There are several more licensing options available depending upon the size of the team and the platforms used, the details of which are beyond the scope of this book.

- **Platform-specific limitations**: Although Xamarin offers platform-specific bindings and APIs, there might be certain platform-specific features or functionalities that are not readily available or require additional workarounds. This can be a limitation if your application heavily relies on such features.

- **Development cycle**: Xamarin applications typically have a longer development cycle compared to frameworks that utilize hot reloading or instant preview features. This is because Xamarin requires a compilation step, which can increase the time it takes to see the changes made in the code.

Ionic

Ionic is an open-source framework for building cross-platform mobile applications using web technologies such as HTML, CSS, and JavaScript. It allows developers to create native-like applications that run on multiple platforms, including iOS, Android, and the web, using a single codebase.

Figure 5.4: Ionic logo (Source: wikimedia.org)

Here are some key aspects of Ionic:

- **Web technologies**: Ionic leverages web technologies, primarily HTML, CSS, and JavaScript, to build mobile applications. Developers can use familiar web development tools, frameworks, and libraries to create the user interface and application logic.
- **Cordova integration**: Ionic integrates with Apache Cordova, a platform that enables access to native device features using web technologies. This allows developers to access native functionalities, such as camera, contacts, geolocation, and more, through JavaScript APIs.
- **UI components and theming**: Ionic provides a library of pre-designed UI components, called Ionic components, that follow the design guidelines of various platforms. These components enable developers to create a visually appealing and consistent user interface across different platforms. Ionic also offers theming capabilities, allowing developers to customize the look and feel of the application.
- **Cross-platform compatibility**: Ionic applications are built using web technologies and packaged as native applications using Cordova. This allows the same codebase to be used across multiple platforms, reducing development effort and maintenance costs.
- **Angular integration**: Ionic is tightly integrated with Angular, a JavaScript framework for building web applications. Angular provides a robust structure and development patterns, making it easier to develop complex applications with Ionic. However, it is important to note that while Ionic has a strong association with Angular, it can also be used with other JavaScript frameworks like React or Vue.js.
- **Performance optimization**: Ionic is designed to provide good performance on mobile devices. It uses hardware-accelerated CSS transitions and animations

to deliver smooth user experiences. Additionally, Ionic applications can take advantage of native optimization techniques provided by Cordova to ensure optimal performance.

Several benchmark studies have compared the performance of Ionic, React Native, and Flutter. The results of these studies have been mixed, with each framework showing strengths and weaknesses in different areas. However, overall, Ionic's performance is generally considered to be on par with React Native and Flutter. Several factors can affect the performance of Ionic apps such as the complexity of the app, the use of native plugins and the device itself.

Developer tools: Ionic offers a **Command-Line Interface (CLI)** tool that simplifies the development and deployment process. The CLI provides a range of features, including project scaffolding, code generation, live-reload for rapid development, and building and packaging the application for different platforms.

- **Ionic capacitor**: Capacitor is a modern alternative to Cordova that is developed and maintained by the Ionic team. It provides a more flexible and extensible approach to accessing native features and APIs. Capacitor supports both Ionic and non-Ionic projects, allowing developers to choose between the two based on their specific requirements.
- **Ionic Appflow**: Ionic Appflow is a cloud-based mobile app development and deployment platform. It provides services such as automated builds, app distribution, native binary management, and live updates. It streamlines the app development lifecycle and simplifies collaboration among team members. Ionic Appflow offers a variety of pricing plans, including a free plan for individual developers. The paid plans start at $419 per month (at the time of writing) and include features such as unlimited native builds, live updates, and automations.

While Ionic enables cross-platform development, there are limitations and platform-specific considerations, particularly when it comes to accessing advanced native features or achieving pixel-perfect UI on each platform.

Disadvantages of Ionic

Ionic, as a cross-platform mobile development framework, offers various benefits, but it also has some limitations and disadvantages to consider:

- **Performance**: Ionic uses web technologies (HTML, CSS, and JavaScript) to build mobile applications, which inherently introduces a performance overhead compared to fully native applications. While Ionic has made significant improvements in performance over time, it will still not match the native performance achieved by frameworks like React Native or Flutter, especially for complex or graphics-intensive applications. Ionic requires plugins and third-party packages.
- **Limited native functionality**: Ionic relies on web views and plugins to access native device features. Although there is a wide range of plugins available to

bridge the gap between web and native functionality, not all platform-specific features may be supported or available as plugins. In some cases, you may need to build custom plugins or use platform-specific code to access certain capabilities, which can increase development time and effort.

- **User Interface (UI) customization**: Ionic provides a set of pre-designed UI components and themes, which can be customized to fit the application's branding. However, compared to fully native frameworks, the degree of UI customization and adherence to platform-specific design guidelines may be somewhat limited. Achieving pixel-perfect UI matching across different platforms may require additional effort.

- **Limited Access to Device APIs**: Although Ionic provides access to a wide range of device APIs through plugins, there may still be certain low-level or specialized, niche APIs that are not readily available. If your application heavily relies on such APIs, you may need to build custom plugins or consider other frameworks that provide deeper access to native APIs.

- **Dependency on web technologies**: Ionic uses web technologies, which means developers must have proficiency in HTML, CSS, and JavaScript. If your development team is not familiar with these technologies or prefers a different programming language, there may be a learning curve and potential challenges in adopting Ionic.

- **Community and ecosystem**: The Ionic community is not as extensive as some other cross-platform frameworks like React Native or Flutter. This will result in fewer available community-driven plugins, libraries, and resources.

- **App store approval**: Since Ionic apps are not fully native, there might be additional scrutiny during the app store approval process. Some app stores may have stricter guidelines or requirements for hybrid or web-based applications, which could potentially lead to challenges in getting the app published. Ionic apps cross-platform nature can sometimes lead to issues with the app's native feel or performance, which may not meet the app store's quality standards. Similar challenges may arise with the use of WebView's and third-party plugins which can introduce security vulnerabilities or compatibility issues.

React Native

React Native is an open-source framework for building cross-platform mobile applications using JavaScript and React. It allows developers to create native mobile apps that run on iOS and Android platforms using a single codebase.

Figure 5.5: *React Native logo (Source: testrigor.com)*

Here are some key aspects of React Native:

- **JavaScript and React**: React Native utilizes JavaScript, a popular programming language, and React, a JavaScript library for building user interfaces. React follows a component-based approach, where the UI is divided into reusable components. This enables developers to build rich and interactive mobile applications.
- **Native components**: React Native provides a set of pre-built components that map to native UI components on both iOS and Android platforms. These components are written in platform-specific languages like Objective-C, Swift, and Java, and are rendered natively, resulting in high-performance user interfaces that closely resemble native apps. React supplies components very similar to those provided by native Android, such as view, text, image, so on, and, like native Android, these components can be customized by supplying various property arguments.
- **Code reusability**: With React Native, developers can write a single codebase that can be shared across multiple platforms. This allows for significant code reuse and reduces the need for maintaining separate codebases for each platform. However, platform-specific code can still be written when necessary to access device-specific APIs or implement platform-specific functionality.
- **Hot reloading**: React Native provides a feature called **hot reloading**, which allows developers to see the changes they make in the code immediately reflected in the app while it is running. These speeds up the development process and make it easier to iterate and test UI changes in real-time.
- **Native API access**: React Native provides a bridge that allows JavaScript code to interact with platform-specific APIs and functionalities. Additionally, if a specific feature is not available through the provided APIs, developers can create custom native modules to extend the functionality of their app.
- **Third-party libraries and community support**: React Native has an ecosystem of third-party libraries and tools created by the community. These libraries offer ready-made solutions for common functionalities, UI components, and integrations with various services.
- **Performance**: React Native achieves good performance by rendering components using native UI controls. It leverages the device's GPU for rendering, resulting in smooth animations and interactions. However, for compute-intensive tasks such as Cryptography, React Native may still need to rely on native code or third-party libraries.
- **Developer efficiency**: React Native emphasizes developer efficiency by allowing rapid development with its declarative syntax, component reusability, and hot reloading feature. It also provides tools like React Native CLI and Expo, which streamline the development process and enable easy project setup, testing, and building.

It is important to note that while React Native offers cross-platform development, there are instances where platform-specific customization or optimization is required to achieve a truly native user experience. React Native is well-suited for applications that prioritize code sharing and development speed, particularly when UI responsiveness and performance are not the primary concerns.

Disadvantages of React Native

Disadvantages of React Native are:

- **Performance**: React Native aims to provide near-native performance. For example, JetBrains Benchmark registers React code at 94% performant as compared to Android native code whereas JSPerf registered React at 85%. However, there are instances where it falls short compared to fully native development. Performance issues can arise when dealing with complex animations, heavy computations, or when relying on certain platform-specific features that are not readily available in React Native. In such cases, developers may need to write custom native code or use third-party libraries to optimize performance.
- **Platform-specific limitations**: Although React Native provides access to a wide range of native device functionalities through its bridge mechanism, there are still certain platform-specific features or APIs that are not yet supported. This will require developers to write custom native code or use third-party libraries to bridge the gap, which can increase development complexity.
- **Learning curve**: While React Native allows developers to leverage their existing JavaScript skills, there is still a learning curve associated with the framework itself, its ecosystem, and the React paradigm. Developers who are not familiar with JavaScript or the React ecosystem may need some time to ramp up their skills and adapt to the React Native way of building applications.
- **Dependency on native modules**: In some cases, to access specific device features or functionality that is not readily available in React Native, developers need to build custom native modules. This requires knowledge of native development languages (Objective-C/Swift for iOS, Java/Kotlin for Android) and can introduce complexity and potential maintenance overhead.
- **UI customization and native look-and-feel**: While React Native provides a set of pre-built UI components, achieving pixel-perfect UI matching across different platforms or adhering to platform-specific design guidelines requires additional effort. Customizing UI components beyond what is provided out-of-the-box will involve writing additional CSS or leveraging third-party libraries.
- **Community and ecosystem**: While there are many available libraries and resources, there will be instances where certain niche functionalities or solutions are not readily available or lack robust community support.
- **Tooling and debugging**: While React Native has improved its tooling and debugging capabilities, there are still cases where the development experience is not as seamless as native development. Issues related to debugging, hot

reloading, and IDE integrations may arise, requiring additional troubleshooting and workarounds.

Flutter

Flutter is an open-source UI framework developed by Google for building natively compiled applications for mobile, web, and desktop platforms. It allows developers to create visually appealing, high-performance applications using a single codebase written in the Dart programming language.

Figure 5.6: Flutter logo (Source: wikimedia.org)

Here are some key aspects of Flutter:

- **Dart programming language**: Flutter uses Dart as its primary programming language. Dart is an object-oriented language with a syntax similar to languages like Java and JavaScript. It offers features such as a **just-in-time (JIT)** compiler for fast development cycles and an **ahead-of-time (AOT)** compiler for producing efficient and performant native code.
- **Widget-based UI development**: Flutter follows a reactive and component-based approach to building user interfaces. It uses a rich set of pre-designed and customizable UI components called widgets. These widgets can be combined to create complex UI layouts, and their state can be updated dynamically to reflect changes in the application.
- **Hot reload**: Flutter provides a powerful Hot Reload feature, allowing developers to see the changes they make in the code immediately reflected in the running app. This enables fast iteration and experimentation, making it easier to fine-tune the UI and quickly fix issues.
- **Fast and native performance**: Flutter apps are compiled into native code, enabling them to deliver high-performance experiences on multiple platforms. Flutter's rendering engine, called Skia, leverages the GPU to achieve smooth animations and transitions. Additionally, Flutter apps can access platform-specific features and APIs through a set of comprehensive and well-maintained plugins.
- **Cross-platform development**: Flutter allows developers to create applications for multiple platforms from a single codebase. It supports iOS, Android, web, and desktop platforms (Windows, macOS, and Linux). This capability eliminates the need for separate development teams or codebases for different platforms, resulting in faster development cycles and code reuse.
- **Material Design and Cupertino Widgets**: Flutter provides both Material Design widgets (for Android-like UI) and Cupertino widgets (for iOS-like UI), allowing

developers to create platform-specific experiences or customize the UI to fit their brand identity.

- **Strong community and ecosystem**: Flutter has a rapidly growing community of developers, which contributes to a rich ecosystem of packages and plugins. These packages offer ready-made solutions for various functionalities, integrations with services, and UI components. The community actively shares knowledge, resources, and libraries, making it easier to learn and accelerate development.
- **Developer tools**: Flutter comes with a comprehensive set of developer tools, including a CLI for project setup and management, a debugging tool called Flutter DevTools for inspecting and profiling apps, and integration with popular IDEs like Visual Studio Code and Android Studio.

Flutter has gained significant popularity for its ability to deliver beautiful and performant apps across multiple platforms. It is widely used by developers and organizations to build mobile apps, but its capabilities for web and desktop development are also expanding. With frequent updates and community support, Flutter continues to evolve as a powerful framework for creating cross-platform applications with stunning user interfaces and excellent performance.

Disadvantages of Flutter

Flutter, as a cross-platform mobile development framework, has gained popularity for its fast development, high-performance, and native-like user interfaces. However, it also has some limitations and disadvantages to consider:

- **Limited native functionality**: Although Flutter provides a wide range of built-in widgets and libraries, there may be certain platform-specific features or native APIs that are not readily available. In such cases, developers may need to write platform-specific code using platform channels or rely on third-party packages to access specific device capabilities.
- **Large app size**: Flutter applications tend to have larger file sizes compared to fully native applications. This is because Flutter includes a self-contained runtime and framework within the app package. While Flutter has made efforts to optimize app size, it may still be a concern, particularly for apps with strict size limitations or in regions with slow internet speeds.
- **Limited maturity of some packages**: While Flutter has a growing ecosystem of packages and libraries, not all of them may have reached the same level of maturity or stability. Some packages may be less maintained or lack extensive documentation. This can require additional effort in evaluating and finding reliable packages for specific functionalities.
- **Platform-specific differences**: While Flutter aims to provide a consistent user interface across platforms, there may still be slight differences in UI rendering and behavior, especially when it comes to platform-specific design guidelines or

animations. Developers need to pay attention to these platform nuances to ensure a native-like experience.

- **Learning curve**: Flutter uses Dart as its programming language, which may require developers to learn a new language if they are not already familiar with it. Although Dart is relatively easy to pick up, developers with a background in other languages may need some time to become proficient in Dart and its associated ecosystem.
- **Limited community and third-party support**: While Flutter has a growing community, it may not be as extensive as some other frameworks like React Native. This can lead to a smaller pool of available resources, tutorials, and third-party libraries compared to more mature ecosystems. However, the Flutter community is vibrant and continuously growing.
- **Limited accessibility support**: Flutter has made improvements in accessibility features, but it may not offer the same level of accessibility support as some native platforms. Developers need to ensure they test and implement appropriate accessibility features to ensure their apps are accessible to all users.

Compose Multiplatform

Compose Multiplatform is an extension of Jetpack Compose, a modern UI toolkit for building native Android user interfaces. Compose Multiplatform aims to bring the power and simplicity of Jetpack Compose to other platforms, allowing developers to build user interfaces that can be shared across multiple platforms, such as Android, iOS, desktop, and web.

Figure 5.7: Compose Multiplatform logo (Source: adapted from dev.to)

Here are some key aspects of Compose Multiplatform:

- **Shared UI code**: Compose Multiplatform allows developers to write UI code using Jetpack Compose, a declarative UI framework that simplifies the process of building user interfaces. With Compose Multiplatform, you can write the UI code once using Kotlin and share it across different platforms. This enables a consistent and efficient development experience for multiple platforms.
- **Platform-specific adaptations**: While the UI code is shared, Compose Multiplatform provides mechanisms to adapt the UI to the specifics of each platform. This includes platform-specific components, layout adjustments, and platform-specific behaviors. Platform-specific adaptations can be implemented using platform-

specific modules or libraries, allowing you to leverage the unique capabilities and conventions of each platform.

- **Composable functions**: Compose Multiplatform is based on the concept of composable functions, which are functions that describe the UI and its behavior in a declarative manner. Composable functions are written using Kotlin and allow you to build UI components by composing smaller reusable functions. This makes it easier to create complex UIs and promotes code reuse.
- **Gradle plugin**: Compose Multiplatform integrates with the Gradle build system and provides a plugin to set up and manage multiplatform projects. The plugin handles the compilation, packaging, and distribution of the shared UI code and platform-specific artifacts. It streamlines the process of generating platform-specific code and bindings.
- **Interoperability**: Compose Multiplatform ensures interoperability between the shared UI code and the platform-specific adaptations. It provides mechanisms to call into platform-specific APIs, handle platform-specific events and input, and access platform-specific features. This enables developers to utilize platform-specific capabilities while maintaining code sharing and consistency.
- **Ecosystem and tooling**: Compose Multiplatform benefits from the existing Kotlin and Jetpack Compose ecosystem and tooling. This includes libraries, frameworks, developer tools, and a supportive community. The ecosystem provides a rich set of resources and extensions to enhance the development experience and expand the capabilities of Compose Multiplatform.

Compose Multiplatform is an emerging technology that aims to simplify the process of building cross-platform UIs using Jetpack Compose. It brings the benefits of code sharing, consistent development experience, and reduced development effort to multiple platforms. However, it is worth noting that Compose Multiplatform is still in its early stages, and the availability of platform-specific adaptations and tooling may vary across platforms.

Disadvantages of Compose Multiplatform

While Compose Multiplatform offers several advantages for building cross-platform user interfaces, it also has some limitations and considerations to keep in mind:

- **Platform support**: Compose Multiplatform is a relatively new technology, and platform support may be limited compared to mature cross-platform frameworks. While it aims to support multiple platforms, the availability and maturity of platform-specific adaptations may vary. Some platforms may have fewer resources, community support, and third-party libraries compared to more established frameworks.
- **Learning curve**: Adopting Compose Multiplatform requires developers to learn and understand both Jetpack Compose and the specific concepts and APIs of Compose Multiplatform. This can involve learning Kotlin, declarative UI patterns,

composable functions, and the intricacies of platform-specific adaptations. The learning curve may be steeper for developers who are not already familiar with Jetpack Compose.

- **Platform-specific adjustments**: While Compose Multiplatform allows for code sharing, platform-specific adaptations are still necessary to account for differences in UI conventions, layout, and behavior across platforms. Implementing these adaptations may require writing platform-specific code or leveraging platform-specific libraries, which can introduce additional complexity and potential inconsistencies.
- **Ecosystem maturity**: Compose Multiplatform is part of the larger Kotlin and Jetpack Compose ecosystem, which is evolving but may not yet have the same level of maturity, stability, and breadth of resources as established frameworks. Some libraries, tools, and community support may still be in early stages, which can impact productivity and the availability of solutions for specific use cases.
- **Performance considerations**: Compose Multiplatform introduces an additional layer of abstraction to achieve cross-platform compatibility. While efforts are made to optimize performance, the performance characteristics may differ from native platform development. Careful consideration and profiling may be required to ensure optimal performance across platforms.
- **Interoperability challenges**: Ensuring smooth interoperability between the shared UI code and platform-specific adaptations can be challenging. Handling platform-specific APIs, events, and input, and accessing platform-specific features may require additional effort and careful design. Managing platform-specific dependencies and ensuring compatibility can also pose challenges.
- **Tooling and developer experience**: While Compose Multiplatform benefits from the existing Kotlin and Jetpack Compose tooling, the tooling specific to Compose Multiplatform may still be evolving. IDE support, build systems, and debugging capabilities may not be as comprehensive or mature as those available for traditional platform-specific development.

Common failures

All the technologies mentioned so far suffer from issues with platform-specific adaptations. In other words, for example, if you want to have slightly different user controls to comply with the separate UI guidelines for each of Android and iOS, you will have to write native code anyway, which defeats the purpose of having the cross-platform code in the first place. Furthermore, the *bridging* code required to achieve this in most cases will add to the complexity of the code overall and makes it difficult to apply some of the CCA architecture previously discussed.

Apart from the learning curve and performance hit that affects almost all the technologies discussed so far, the main reason why big corporations are ditching cross-platform for their large, multi-feature apps is because of the cost of maintenance. On the surface, this would seem to run contrary to the promises of cross-platform development. Those promises to assume that any bugs found whilst testing on one platform will manifest on all platforms. Sadly, this is rarely the case. In accordance with proper **Quality Assurance (QA)** procedures, large corporations will have release and bug-fix procedures that will include extensive manual testing to accompany any automated instrumentation testing. A change to cross-platform code to address an issue in one platform will have to be tested across all platforms since that change will affect all platforms. Furthermore, a change to common code to fix one platform will often break another platform. It was the extra QA costs incurred by this that prompted at least one multi-national to clone their code repositories for each of the platforms. At this point, the cross-platform code just adds unnecessary complexity.

Ideally, a cross-platform arrangement should allow the sharing of code between platforms that is truly common (such as everything in the domain and data layers) but not provide common UI infrastructure. KMM was developed with this in mind.

Kotlin multi-mobile

The KMM working logic can be represented like this:

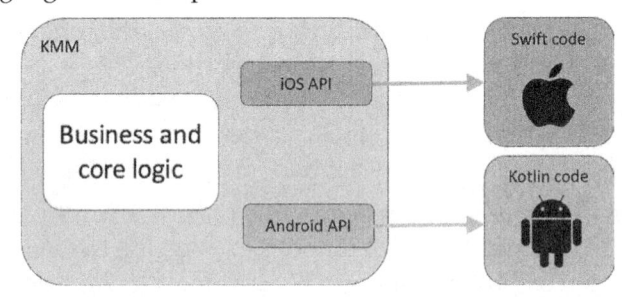

Figure 5.8: *KMM working logic (Apple logo source: cleanpng.com, Android logo source: flaticon.com)*

Here are some key aspects of KMM:

- **Shared code**: With KMM, you can write shared code using the Kotlin programming language. This includes business logic, data processing, networking, and other common functionalities that don't have platform-specific dependencies. The shared code is written once and can be used on both Android and iOS platforms.
- **Platform-specific code**: While majority of the code is shared, KMM also allows writing platform-specific code for each target platform. This enables developers to incorporate platform-specific UI components, access platform-specific APIs, and handle other platform-specific functionalities. Platform-specific code is written using the respective platform's native language and APIs (Kotlin for Android and Swift for iOS). Whilst this feature is available, it should be used sparingly or not at all otherwise it defeats the purpose of cross platform shared code.

- **Code sharing**: KMM facilitates code sharing by providing a common API surface between the shared code and the platform-specific code. This allows the shared code to be easily consumed and used by the platform-specific code. Developers can define shared interfaces and contracts that are implemented by the platform-specific code, enabling seamless communication between the shared and platform-specific layers.
- **Gradle plugin**: KMM integrates with the Gradle build system, making it easy to set up and manage multiplatform projects. The KMM plugin handles the compilation, packaging, and distribution of the shared code and platform-specific artifacts. It automates the process of generating the necessary bindings and bridges between Kotlin and the native platform languages.
- **Interoperability**: KMM ensures interoperability between the shared Kotlin code and the platform-specific code. It provides mechanisms for calling platform-specific APIs, handling call-backs and events, and accessing platform-specific features. This allows developers to leverage the full capabilities of each platform while maintaining code sharing and consistency.
- **Ecosystem and tooling**: KMM benefit from the existing Kotlin ecosystem and tooling, including the rich set of libraries, frameworks, and developer tools available for Kotlin. It also provides tooling support within popular IDEs like Android Studio and IntelliJ IDEA, making it convenient for developers to work with KMM projects.

KMM offers significant advantages in terms of code sharing, reduced development effort, and faster time-to-market for mobile applications. However, it is important to consider the specific requirements and constraints of your project to determine if KMM is the right choice. It is particularly well-suited for applications with a substantial amount of shared business logic or data processing logic that can be written in Kotlin and shared across platforms.

Disadvantages of KMM

While KMM offers numerous advantages for cross-platform mobile development, it also has some limitations and considerations to keep in mind:

- **Platform-specific dependencies**: KMM is designed to share business logic and non-platform-specific code, but there may be cases where you need to utilize platform-specific libraries or APIs. Incorporating platform-specific dependencies in shared code requires careful consideration and potentially writing platform-specific wrappers or interfaces, which can add complexity to the project.
- **Limited iOS framework Access**: While KMM allows sharing code between Android and iOS, it doesn't provide direct access to all iOS frameworks and APIs. Interfacing with platform-specific frameworks may require writing platform-specific code or leveraging existing inter-operational solutions like Kotlin Native's

interoperability with Objective-C/Swift. This is another good reason to restrict KMM development to Domain and Data layer code.

- **Development and debugging workflow**: The development and debugging workflow for KMM projects can be more involved compared to traditional platform-specific development. Setting up the project, managing dependencies, and troubleshooting platform-specific issues may require extra effort and familiarity with both Kotlin and the native platform languages.
- **Tooling and ecosystem maturity**: While KMM benefits from the Kotlin ecosystem and existing tooling, it is still a relatively new technology. Some libraries and tooling that are readily available for traditional platform-specific development may not have comprehensive KMM support or may still be evolving. This can result in limited options and a smaller ecosystem compared to mature cross-platform frameworks.
- **Learning curve**: Adopting KMM may require developers to learn and understand the specific workflows, best practices, and limitations of the technology. It can involve learning Kotlin Multiplatform concepts, understanding the interop with native platforms, and adapting to the specific build and deployment processes.
- **Team skills and expertise**: Building a KMM project requires developers with expertise in both Kotlin and the native platform languages (Swift/Objective-C for iOS). Finding developers with experience in both can be a challenge, and additional training or upskilling may be required for team members who are primarily proficient in only one of the languages.
- **Maintenance and upkeep**: While KMM aims to provide code sharing benefits, it also introduces an additional layer of complexity in managing and maintaining a shared codebase. As the project evolves and platform-specific requirements change, maintaining the shared code and ensuring compatibility across platforms may require ongoing effort and coordination.

KMM has its place in the CCA architecture, namely the domain and data layers and most of the points listed above relate to issues that arise when you try to use it for something else that is, the presentation layer. The learning curve issue is valid. What tends to happen is that iOS developers will wait for Android developers to write an entire feature, including UI, before starting the feature themselves. This means that iOS will lag behind Android in any project by at least one feature. A good solution to this is to employ the pair-programming technique with one iOS and one Android developer working on the same domain/data layer code at the same time with the iOS developer driving a single workstation. Doing this will provide the following added benefits:

- **Improved code quality**: With two sets of eyes on the code, pair programming helps catch bugs, logic errors, and code smells more effectively. It encourages continuous code review and feedback, resulting in higher-quality code.
- **Knowledge sharing**: Pair programming facilitates knowledge sharing between team members. Junior developers can learn from more experienced developers

by observing their thought process, problem-solving techniques, and coding practices. It also promotes cross-functional collaboration and reduces knowledge silos (knowledge hoarded by one group or individual) within the team.

- **Reduced time and effort**: Although pair programming involves two developers, it often results in faster development compared to individual programming. The combined efforts of the pair lead to quicker problem-solving, reduced debugging time, and increased productivity.
- **Enhanced learning and skill development**: Pair programming provides an opportunity for continuous learning and skill development. Developers can learn new techniques, programming patterns, and best practices from each other. It also promotes better understanding of the codebase and the underlying system.
- **Increased collaboration and communication**: Pair programming encourages frequent and effective communication between developers. It facilitates discussions, brainstorming sessions, and knowledge exchange in real-time, leading to better decision-making and shared understanding of the codebase.
- **Continuous feedback and peer review**: In pair programming, feedback is immediate and continuous. Developers can provide instant feedback to each other, fostering a culture of constructive criticism and learning. This feedback loop helps identify and address issues early, leading to better code design and fewer defects.
- **Reduced risk and improved problem solving**: Pair programming mitigates the risk of introducing critical bugs or making poor design decisions. Two minds working together can approach problems from different perspectives, leading to more robust solutions and reduced rework in the long run.
- **Team bonding and morale**: Pair programming promotes a collaborative and supportive environment within the development team. It builds trust, encourages teamwork, and boosts morale. Developers feel more engaged, motivated, and accountable for the success of the project.
- **Improved code reviews**: With pair programming, the need for formal code reviews is reduced as the code is reviewed in real-time. This leads to more thorough and timely code reviews, ensuring that code quality standards are maintained.
- **Reduced knowledge Silo**: Pair programming helps spread knowledge and expertise across the team, reducing the reliance on specific individuals for critical tasks. It minimizes the impact of team members leaving or being unavailable, ensuring continuity and resilience within the team.

Restricting the code sharing to the domain and data layers should largely eliminate the issue described previously of increased QA effort. Given the clear boundary between the domain and presentation layers, bugs identified on one platform and not on another are extremely likely to be down to the offending platform's processing of the domain layer output. Regardless, if the bug can be fixed in the platform's presentation layer, then there will be no need to test the other platforms since the other platforms code will not have changed.

Even if you only intend to develop for Android without any cross-platform support, the domain and data layers are, by definition, meant to be platform independent. Using KMM for these layers will provide pattern enforcement for this paradigm with the added flexibility of any possible future use for cross-platform.

Conclusion

Full cross-platform solutions are popular with companies that have skills in non-mobile technologies that need to write mobile apps. For example, Windows developers would be at home with Xamarin whilst web developers may be more familiar with Ionic or React. However, organizations that maintain large code bases are falling out of favor with cross-platform development due to extra QA costs. KMM offers a half-way house solution by providing cross-platform for just the parts of the application that really are common, that is, the data models and business logic found in the Data and Domain layers.

Even if you do not intend to develop cross-platform, writing your Domain and Data layers with KMM helps to enforce their platform independence.

In the next chapter, we will continue the CCA paradigm by examining one of the practical implementations of SoC, namely Dependency Injection.

Points to remember

- There are several cross-platform mobile development environments that leverage different coding languages.
- They tend to be used by companies to save money in the short term on development of apps with brief life spans.
- KMM offers a half-way house solution by providing cross-platform for just the parts of the application that really are common.
- KMM in combination with pair-programming can spread the knowledge of Kotlin and promote team coordination.

Questions

1. What are the common failures of full cross-platform solutions?
2. Why does KMM mitigate those failures?
3. How could KMM promote cross-platform coordination?

CHAPTER 6
Dependency Injection

Introduction

One of the lower-level methods for achieving **Separation of Concerns** (**SoC**) is that of **Dependency Injection** (**DI**). This chapter explains the concept of basic DI techniques, their benefits, and the popular open-source libraries for implementing it. It also explains why it is vital for clean code and Test-driven Development and provides some code samples with and without the libraries.

Structure

This chapter covers the following topics:
- Overview of Dependency Injection
- Setter/method injection
- Constructor injection
- Interface injection
- Field injection
- Injection frameworks
- Pros and cons of Hilt vs. Koin

Objectives

By the end of this chapter, you will be able to understand the importance of DI in achieving clean code. It will describe the means provided by Kotlin language for DI and discuss the two most popular libraries for managing dependencies.

Overview of Dependency Injection

Dependency Injection is a software design pattern that allows the dependencies of an object to be provided externally rather than created or managed by the object itself. It promotes loose coupling and modular design by decoupling the creation and use of objects.

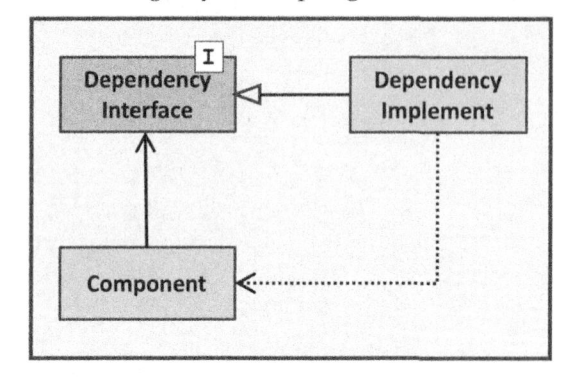

Figure 6.1: Dependency Injection overview

In DI, the dependencies of an object are *injected* into it, typically through constructor parameters, method parameters, or setters. The responsibility of creating and providing these dependencies lies with an external entity, often called the *dependency injector* or container.

The main benefits of DI include:

- **Decoupling**: DI helps decouple the dependencies from the objects that use them. This allows for easier maintenance, testing, and modifications, as changes to one object's dependencies do not directly impact other objects.
- **Testability**: By providing dependencies through injection, it becomes easier to mock or substitute dependencies during unit testing. This enables more effective testing of individual components in isolation. Examples of this will be detailed in a later chapter.
- **Reusability**: With DI, dependencies can be shared and reused across multiple objects. This reduces code duplication and promotes modular design.
- **Flexibility**: DI enables the configuration of dependencies at runtime. This allows for easy swapping of different implementations of dependencies without modifying the consuming code.

- **Scalability**: By externalizing the management of dependencies, DI supports scalable architectures. It becomes easier to introduce new dependencies or modify existing ones without significant changes to the codebase.

There are different approaches to implementing Dependency Injection, including setter injection, interface injection, and constructor injection. DI frameworks and containers, such as Hilt and Koin, provide automated ways to manage and inject dependencies based on configuration.

Setter/method injection

Here is an example of setter/method dependency injection:

```
1.  class UserService {
2.      private var userRepository: UserRepository? = null
3.
4.      fun setUserRepository(userRepository: UserRepository) {
5.          this.userRepository = userRepository
6.      }
7.
8.      fun getUserById(id: String): User = userRepository?.getUserById(id)
9.              ?: throw IllegalStateException("UserRepository not set")
10. }
```

In this example, **UserService** delegates the responsibility of fetching the user-by-id to an instance of **UserRepository**. **UserService**, therefore, has a dependency on **UserRepository**. Instead of directly creating an instance of **UserRepository** within **UserService**, we provide a setter method **setUserRepository**, to inject the dependency from outside.

To use this code, you would create an instance of **UserService** and inject the **UserRepository** dependency using the setter method:

```
1.  val userRepository = UserRepository()
2.  val userService = UserService()
3.  userService.setUserRepository(userRepository)
4.
5.  val user = userService.getUserById("123")
```

Using setter injection, we can provide different extensions of **UserRepository** to **UserService** at runtime, making it more flexible and allowing easy testing and swapping of dependencies. The problem with this approach is that there is no pattern enforcement. Nothing can stop a developer from creating an instance of **UserService** and calling **getUserById** without first setting the user repository, save for a run-time **IllegalStateException** crash.

Constructor injection

Here is a similar example using constructor injection:

```
1. class UserRepository(private val dataSource: DataSource) {
2.     fun getUserById(id: String): User {
3.         TODO("Implementation of fetching user from the data source")
4.     }
5. }
6.
7. class UserService(private val userRepository: UserRepository) {
8.     fun getUserById(id: String): User {
9.         return userRepository.getUserById(id)
10.    }
11. }
```

In this example, the **UserRepository** class depends on a **DataSource** to fetch user data. Instead of using a setter, we pass the **DataSource** dependency through the constructor of **UserRepository**.

Similarly, the **UserService** class depends on the **UserRepository**. Again, we pass the **UserRepository** dependency through the constructor of **UserService**.

To use this code, you would create instances of **DataSource**, **UserRepository**, and **UserService**, and provide the necessary dependencies:

```
1. val dataSource = SomeDataSource()
2. val userRepository = UserRepository(dataSource)
3. val userService = UserService(userRepository)
4.
5. val user = userService.getUserById("123")
```

By using constructor injection, we ensure that all required dependencies are provided when creating instances of classes. This promotes better encapsulation, testability, and allows for easier substitution of dependencies.

Interface injection

Interface injection uses either of the previous two methods, except that the dependency passed in is an interface. This is particularly powerful when combined with constructor injection:

```kotlin
1. interface UserRepository {
2.     fun getUserById(id: String): User
3. }
4.
5. class UserService(private val userRepository: UserRepository) {
6.     fun getUserById(id: String): User {
7.         return userRepository.getUserById(id)
8.     }
9. }
```

In this example, **UserService** depends on the **UserRepository** interface. Instead of using a setter or a constructor that takes a concrete class, we pass an implementation of **UserRepository** through the constructor of **UserService**.

To use this code, you would create an instance of **UserRepository** and pass it to the **UserService** constructor:

```kotlin
1.  class InMemoryUserRepository : UserRepository {
2.      private val users = mapOf(
3.          "1" to User("1", "John"),
4.          "2" to User("2", "Jane")
5.      )
6.
7.      override fun getUserById(id: String): User =
8.          users[id] ?: throw IllegalArgumentException("User not found")
9.  }
10.
11. val userRepository = InMemoryUserRepository()
12. val userService = UserService(userRepository)
13.
14. val user = userService.getUserById("1")
```

In this example, **InMemoryUserRepository** implements **UserRepository**, and it is an instance of **InMemoryUserRepository** that is injected into **UserService**. We could easily have created a different implementation of **UserRepository** (say, **DiskUserRepository**, for example) and injected that instead.

By using interface injection, we achieve loose coupling between **UserService** and **UserRepository**. This allows us to easily swap different implementations of **UserRepository** as long as they implement the **UserRepository** interface, making the code more modular and testable. It is this combination of interface with constructor injection that is particularly suited to CCA with regard to use case ports.

Field injection

Field injection is a form of DI where the dependencies are directly injected into the fields (properties) of a class. In field injection, the dependency is typically annotated with an injection annotation, and the injection framework assigns the dependency to the corresponding field.

Here is an example of field injection in Kotlin using the `javax.inject.Inject` annotation:

```
1.  class UserService {
2.      @Inject
3.      lateinit var userRepository: UserRepository
4.
5.      // ...
6.  }
```

In this example, the **UserService** class has a **userRepository** field marked with the **@Inject** annotation. The injection framework, such as Dagger or Hilt, will automatically assign an instance of **UserRepository** to this field when creating an instance of **UserService**.

To enable field injection, you need to configure the injection framework to process the injection annotations and perform the injection at runtime. This typically involves setting up the framework and creating an injector or a component that handles the injection process.

For example, given the code above, in the Dagger DI framework, there would need to be **@Binds**, **@Provides**, or similar annotated code that the compiler would use to map the actual instance of **userRepository**:

```
1.  @Module
2.  class MyModule {
3.      @Provides
4.      fun getUserRepository(
5.          injectObject: InMemoryUserRepository
6.      ): UserRepository {
7.          return injectObject
8.      }
9.  }
```

It is worth noting that while field injection can be convenient and concise, it has some potential drawbacks. It tightly couples the class to the injection framework, making it less portable and harder to test in isolation. Field injection can also make it more difficult to reason about the dependencies of a class since they are not explicitly defined in the constructor or method parameters.

As a best practice, it is generally recommended to prefer constructor injection or method injection over field injection whenever possible, as they provide better control over dependencies, improve testability, and promote clearer code. Field injection should be used judiciously and in cases where it genuinely simplifies the code and does not introduce unnecessary coupling.

Traditionally, in Android, field injection has only been needed in objects that are generated by the Android OS, such as **Activity** and **Fragment** objects. In these cases, it is not possible to use method or constructor injection. With the introduction of the **ViewModel** arrangement, the need for field injection has been largely eliminated – except for the injection of the **ViewModel** object itself. **ViewModel** derivatives support the use of constructor/ interface injection, and it is these objects that will be coordinating the business objects from the Domain layer, leaving **Activity**, **Fragment**, or **Composable** objects to deal with rendering UI. Due to the singleton-like nature of **ViewModel** objects, Android provides its own injection method without the need for any third-party injection frameworks (although it is still cleaner to use them). Furthermore, with Jetpack Compose navigation, the injection of **ViewModel** objects can be accomplished by method injection. More on this is discussed in later chapters.

Injection frameworks

There are several injection frameworks that can be used with Android development. Some popular ones include:

- **Dagger**:
  Dagger is a fully optimized DI framework for Android, maintained by Google. It uses generated code to avoid reflection and provides compile-time validation of dependencies. Dagger is widely used and offers excellent performance.

Figure 6.2: Dagger logo (Source: proandroiddev.com)

- **Hilt**: Hilt is a DI framework for Android that is built on top of Dagger. It simplifies the process of DI by automatically generating Dagger code. Hilt is designed to work seamlessly with Android Jetpack components, such as **ViewModel** and **Fragment**.

- **Koin**:
  Koin is a lightweight DI framework for Kotlin developers. It is written entirely in Kotlin and does not rely on code generation or reflection. Koin offers a simpler and more pragmatic approach to dependency injection, making it easy to get started with.

  Figure 6.3: Koin logo (Source: proandroiddev.com)

- **Toothpick**:
  Toothpick is a runtime DI framework designed to be simple and fast. It offers both, compile-time and runtime DI, giving developers the flexibility to choose their preferred approach. It is less common than Dagger or Koin but is still a viable option for Android DI.

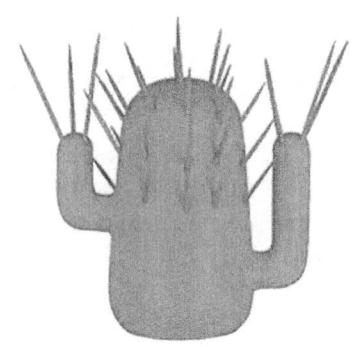

  Figure 6.4: Toothpick logo (Source: github.com/stephanenicolas)

- **Guice**:
  Guice is a DI framework developed by Google, primarily for Java applications. It can also be used with Android, but it is not as common as Dagger for Android development.

  Figure 6.5: Gioce logo (Source: commons.wikimedia.org)

- **RoboGuice**:
  RoboGuice is an extension of Guice specifically tailored for Android. It simplifies DI configuration and reduces the boilerplate code required for DI in Android applications. However, it is not as actively maintained as some other frameworks.

Figure 6.6: RoboGuice logo (Source: github.com/roboguice)

- **Kodein**:
  Kodein is another Kotlin-first DI framework that works well with Android. It provides a DSL for defining dependencies and is designed to be lightweight and easy to use. Kodein also has a version that works with pure Kotlin applications, making it versatile for different Kotlin projects, including Android.

Figure 6.7: Kodein logo (Source proandroiddev.com)

From all these frameworks, this book will only go into detail on Hilt and Koin, as these are the most commonly used by organizations maintaining large code bases.

Hilt injection framework

Hilt, a DI framework for Android developed by Google is built on top of the popular Dagger framework and aims to simplify implementing DI in Android applications.

History of Hilt

To understand the history of Hilt, let us take a look at the evolution of DI in the Android ecosystem:

- **Dagger:** Dagger is a compile-time DI framework for Java and Android. It was initially developed by Square, and its first version, Dagger 1, was released in 2012. Dagger 2, a major update, was released in 2015 and introduced significant improvements in terms of performance, generated code readability, and ease of use. Dagger quickly gained popularity in the Android development community due to its powerful and efficient DI capabilities.
- **Dagger Android:** While Dagger provided robust DI capabilities, it required some additional configuration for Android-specific components, such as Activities and Fragments. To simplify the integration of Dagger into Android applications, the Dagger Android subcomponent was introduced. It provided annotations and classes tailored for Android development, making it easier to inject dependencies into Android components.
- **Hilt:** In 2020, Google introduced Hilt as a part of the Jetpack suite of libraries. Hilt builds on top of Dagger and Dagger Android to provide an opinionated and streamlined approach to DI in Android. It aims to simplify the setup and configuration process, reduce boilerplate code, and integrate well with other Jetpack libraries.

Hilt provides predefined components and annotations that make it easier to configure and use Dagger for Android development.

The introduction of Hilt was driven by the need to provide a more standardized and opinionated approach to DI in Android applications. It offers developers a high-level framework that automates many of the common DI tasks, reduces the learning curve, and ensures best practices are followed.

Since its introduction, Hilt has gained popularity among Android developers due to its integration with the broader Android ecosystem, strong community support, and the backing of Google. It continues to evolve and improve with updates and new features to enhance further the developer experience of implementing DI in Android applications.

Working with Hilt

Here is how Hilt works:

- **Annotating application class**: In an Android application, you start by annotating your `Application` class with the `@HiltAndroidApp` annotation. This annotation informs Hilt that your application will use Hilt for dependency injection.
- **Generated Hilt components**: Hilt automatically generates a set of components based on your `Application` class. These components include the `ApplicationComponent`, `ActivityRetainedComponent`, `ViewModelComponent`, and others. These components form the backbone of Hilt's DI mechanism.
- **Module declarations**: Hilt uses modules to define bindings and dependencies. You can create modules using the `@Module` annotation, where you define the

dependencies and provide implementations for interfaces or abstract classes. These modules can be scoped to specific components to control their lifecycle and visibility.

- **Scoping**: Hilt provides scoping annotations such as **@Singleton**, **@ActivityScoped**, and **@ViewModelScoped** to define the lifecycles and scopes of dependencies. Scoping ensures that dependencies are created and reused appropriately within their designated scopes.
- **Injection annotations**: Hilt provides injection annotations like **@Inject**, **@AssistedInject**, and **@ViewModelInject** to mark the injection points in your code. These annotations indicate where dependencies should be injected.
- **Automatic injection**: Hilt performs automatic injection into Android framework classes, such as **Activity**, **Fragment**, **ViewModel**, and **Service** implementations. You can simply annotate these classes with the appropriate Hilt annotations, such as **@AndroidEntryPoint**, to trigger the automatic injection of dependencies.
- **Gradle plugin**: Hilt utilizes a Gradle plugin that processes your code and generates the necessary Dagger components and injection code during the build process. This code generation eliminates the need for manual Dagger setup and reduces the potential for errors.
- **Integration with Android Jetpack**: Hilt seamlessly integrates with other Android Jetpack libraries, such as **ViewModel**, **WorkManager**, and **Navigation**. It provides special annotations and utilities to simplify the injection of dependencies into these components.

Setting up Hilt

Follow these steps to set up Hilt:

Step 1: Adding dependencies

    a. To use Hilt in your Android project, you need to add the necessary dependencies in your project's **build.gradle** file:

```
1.  buildscript {
2.      repositories {
3.          // other repositories...
4.          mavenCentral()
5.      }
6.      dependencies {
7.          // other plugins...
8.          classpath 'com.google.dagger:hilt-android-gradle-plugin:latest_ver'
9.      }
10. }
```

  b. Also, add the corresponding dependencies in your app's **build.gradle** file:

```
1.  // Add Hilt Android Gradle plugin
2.  plugins {
3.      id 'kotlin-kapt'
4.      id 'dagger.hilt.android.plugin'
5.      // ...
6.  }
7.
8.  android {
9.      // ...
10. }
11.
12. dependencies {
13.     implementation "com.google.dagger:hilt-android:latest_ver"
14.     kapt "com.google.dagger:hilt-android-compiler:latest_ver"
15.     // ...
16. }
```

Step 2: Annotate application class

Annotate your **Application** class with the **@HiltAndroidApp** annotation. This informs Hilt that your application will use Hilt for dependency injection.

```
1.  @HiltAndroidApp
2.  class MyApplication : Application() {
3.      // ...
4.  }
```

Step 3: Using Hilt annotations

  a. Use Hilt annotations in your classes to trigger dependency injection:

```
1.  class UserRepository @Inject constructor() {
2.      // ...
3.  }
4.
5.  class UserService @Inject constructor(
6.      repository: UserRepository
7.  ) {
8.      // ...
9.  }
```

b. In this example, **UserService** takes a **UserRepository** constructor parameter, and both classes are resolved by Hilt using the **@Inject** annotation.

c. In an **Activity** or **Fragment**, you can use the **@AndroidEntryPoint** annotation to enable Hilt's injection for that component.

```
1.  @AndroidEntryPoint
2.  class UserActivity : AppCompatActivity() {
3.      @Inject
4.      lateinit var userRepository: UserRepository
5.
6.      // ...
7.  }
```

d. In this example, the **UserActivity** class is annotated with **@AndroidEntryPoint**, which tells Hilt to enable DI for this activity. The **userRepository** variable is annotated with **@Inject**, indicating that Hilt should provide an instance of **UserRepository** to this variable.

e. This, however, is a prime example of field injection, so this arrangement is no longer encouraged. Instead, given the following definition of **UserViewModel**:

```
1.  @HiltViewModel
2.  class UserViewModel @Inject constructor(
3.      service: UserService
4.  ) : ViewModel() {
5.      // ...
6.  }
```

f. The **@HiltViewModel** annotation tells Hilt to generate an Android **ViewModel** instance, and the **@Inject** annotation to resolve the constructor parameters. All injection is via the constructors mapped by **@Inject**, and all that is left is to inject the **ViewModel** using the existing Android system **viewModels()** delegate:

```
1.  @AndroidEntryPoint
2.  class UserActivity2 : AppCompatActivity() {
3.      private val viewModel: UserViewModel by viewModels()
4.      // ...
5.  }
```

Step 4: Let Hilt do the injection

Hilt generates the necessary components and handles the injection for you. When you create an instance of **UserActivity**, Hilt will automatically inject the **UserService** dependency into the **userRepository** parameter in **UserViewModel** and subsequently, the **viewModel** field into **UserActivity**.

It should be emphasized that Hilt works with annotations. Annotations will auto-generate code, and that generated code is currently Java. One of the biggest arguments for the use of Hilt/Dagger over other injection frameworks is that of compile-time rather than runtime configuration problem identification. Hilt has come a long way since Dagger 1 when this identification came in the form of a compile-time error in nasty, auto-generated Java code that you did not own.

Koin injection framework

Koin is a lightweight DI framework for Kotlin-based applications, including Android. It was developed by *Ekito* and first released in 2017.

History of Koin

Here is an overview of the history of Koin:

- **Inception:** Koin was initially created as a response to the complexity and verbosity of existing DI frameworks for Kotlin. The aim was to provide a simple, lightweight, and easy-to-use DI solution specifically designed for Kotlin developers.
- **Version 1.0:** Koin 1.0 was released in 2017, introducing the core features of the framework. It offered a **Domain-Specific Language (DSL)** approach for declaring and resolving dependencies, using Kotlin's concise syntax and leveraging its language features, such as function literals with the receiver.
- **Growing popularity:** Koin gained popularity within the Kotlin community due to its simplicity and developer-friendly approach. It resonated well with developers who preferred a more straightforward DI framework without requiring extensive configuration or complex setup.
- **Android support:** Koin expanded its focus to include Android development. It provided specific modules and integrations for Android, making it easier to perform DI in Android applications. Koin's lightweight nature and minimal setup aligned well with the Kotlin-first approach in Android development.
- **Evolution and new features:** Koin has continued to evolve with regular updates and new features. Subsequent versions introduced enhancements such as support for named dependencies, support for property injection, and improvements in testability.
- **Koin 2.0:** The major release of Koin 2.0 came in 2020, introducing several significant updates and improvements. It featured increased performance, reduced start-up time, improved compile-time safety, and better integration with **Kotlin Multiplatform (KMP)** projects.
- **Community and adoption:** Koin has built a strong community of developers who actively contribute to the project. It has gained significant adoption, particularly in Kotlin and Android development communities, where its simplicity and Kotlin-centric approach have resonated well.

Today, Koin continues to be actively maintained and updated to meet the evolving needs of Kotlin developers. It offers an alternative DI framework that prioritizes simplicity, ease of use, and a lightweight footprint.

As with any DI framework, Koin provides benefits such as code modularity, testability, and reduced coupling between components. It offers a viable choice for Kotlin developers who prefer a more lightweight and straightforward DI solution for their projects.

Working with Koin

Follow these steps to understand how Koin works:

Step 1: Add dependencies

To use Koin in your Kotlin project, add the necessary dependencies in your app's **build.gradle** file:

```
1. dependencies {
2.     implementation  "org.koin:koin-core:latest_version"
3.     implementation "org.koin:koin-android:latest_version"
4.     // ...
5. }
```

Step 2: Define modules

In Koin, you define modules that encapsulate related dependencies. Modules are typically defined using a DSL approach, leveraging Kotlin's concise syntax.

```
1. val myModule = module {
2.     single { UserRepository() }
3.     factory { UserService(get()) }
4.     viewModel { UserViewModel(get()) }
5. }
```

In this example, a module is defined with three dependencies: **UserRepository**, **UserService,** and **UserViewModel**. The **single** function declares a singleton dependency (only ever one instance), the **factory** function declares a factory dependency (a new instance with each injection) and the **viewModel** function declares a **ViewModel** dependency (subject to Android's rules on **ViewModel** instance creation and destruction).

Step 3: Start Koin

In your application's **Application** class, you need to start Koin by calling the **startKoin** function and passing the modules you have defined.

```
1. class MyApplication : Application() {
2.     override fun onCreate() {
```

```
3.      super.onCreate()
4.      startKoin {
5.          androidContext(this@MyApplication)
6.          modules(myModule)
7.      }
8.  }
9. }
```

In this example, we start Koin in the **onCreate** method of the **MyApplication** class, providing the application context and the **myModule** module.

Step 4: Inject dependencies

To retrieve dependencies, you can use the **get()** function or inject dependencies directly into your code using the by **inject()** syntax. Koin resolves and provides the requested dependency based on its definition in the modules.

```
1. class MyClass {
2.      private val userRepository: UserRepository = get()
3.      private val userService: UserService by inject()
4.
5.      // ...
6. }
```

This, however, is a prime example of field injection so this arrangement is no longer encouraged. Instead, given the following definition of **UserViewModel**:

```
1. class UserViewModel (
2.      service: UserService
3. ): ViewModel() {
4.      // ...
5. }
```

All injection is via the constructors defined in **myModule** and all that is left is to inject is the **ViewModel**:

```
1. class UserActivity : AppCompatActivity() {
2.
3.      private val viewModel by viewModel<UserViewModel>()
4.
5.      // ...
6. }
```

The point of injection can also be written as:

```
1.      private val viewModel: UserViewModel by viewModel()
```

This is due to Kotlin's built-in type inference. Note that the injection delegate is called `viewModel()` (singular) as opposed to Android's built-in `viewModels()`. The `viewModel()` delegate is supplied by Koin.

Pros and cons of Hilt and Koin

Both Koin and Hilt are popular DI frameworks for Kotlin-based Android applications. Each has advantages and disadvantages, and their choice depends on various factors. Here is a comparative analysis of Koin and Hilt:

Hilt pros

Some advantages of Hilt are as follows:

- **Integration with Android**: Hilt is specifically designed for Android and integrates seamlessly with Android components such as activities, fragments, and view models. It simplifies DI setup for Android development.
- **Dagger integration**: Hilt is built on top of Dagger, a robust and widely used DI framework. Hilt leverages Dagger's powerful features and compile-time safety while providing a more opinionated and streamlined approach for Android developers.
- **Officially supported by Google**: Hilt is an official project of the Android team at Google, which means it has strong support and is likely to receive regular updates and improvements.
- **Scoping support**: Hilt provides built-in support for scoping of dependencies, allowing you to manage the lifecycle of objects easily, such as having dependencies tied to the lifecycle of an activity or a view model.

Hilt cons

Some cons for Hilt are as discussed below:

- **Complexity**: Hilt, being built on top of Dagger, inherits some of its complexity. While Hilt provides a more opinionated approach, it may still require more configuration and setup compared to Koin.
- **Code generation**: Hilt relies on code generation during the build process. While this ensures robust compile-time safety, it can lead to longer build times, especially in larger projects.

Koin pros

Some pros for Koin are discussed as follows:

- **Simplicity**: Koin is designed to be simple and easy to use. It offers a straightforward **Domain-Specific Language (DSL)** for declaring dependencies, making it accessible for Kotlin developers, including those new to DI.

- **Lightweight**: Koin is a lightweight DI framework, meaning it introduces minimal overhead to your application. This can be beneficial if you want to keep your app size small and avoid complex setup.
- **No code generation**: Unlike Dagger and Hilt, Koin does not rely on code generation during compilation. This can lead to faster build times and less complexity in the build process.

Koin cons

Some cons for Koin are as follows:

- **Limited compile-time safety**: Since Koin does not use code generation, it may not provide the same level of compile-time safety as Dagger and Hilt. This could lead to runtime errors if dependencies are not properly configured.
- **Smaller community**: While Koin has gained popularity in the Kotlin community, its user base might be smaller compared to the more established frameworks like Dagger and Hilt. This could mean fewer resources and community support.

Conclusion

Many sources will state that Koin is best suited for smaller projects, whilst Hilt is best suited for larger ones, but the opposite is true.

Hilt requires all classes that are part of the injection arrangement to be annotated at their definitions, either with `@Inject`, `@AndroidEntryPoint`, or `@HiltViewModel`. This means that the DI map configuration is scattered throughout the code base.

In contrast, Koin's DI map for all participating classes is (or at least can be) in one place, that is, the Koin `module` object or objects. Due to the clear separation of these concerns, these objects can reside in their own code module (*code module* here referring to an independent code library and not to be confused with a Koin `module` object) and this code module, in turn, can have its own code module dependencies independent of the presentation layer. This is especially convenient for maintaining CCA dependency inversion. There will be examples of this in a later chapter.

There is also the matter of the auto-generated Java code produced by Hilt. Apart from adding to the overall size of your code base, it removes a level of control over how classes are resolved. For these reasons, we would strongly recommend Koin DI for large, multi-module projects.

Having said that, Hilt is extremely popular with many organizations, given its support from Google, and even appears on job specifications from time to time. Therefore, from this point on, all code samples will give examples of both when relevant.

In the next chapter, we will introduce Jetpack Compose with some code examples to get you started with Google's current (at the time of writing) preferred method of creating UI.

Points to remember

- Dependency Injection allows the dependencies of an object to be provided externally rather than being created or managed by the object itself.
- There are three main ways of achieving DI. Dependencies can be set on an object via its constructor (Constructor Injection), with an exposed method (Setter Injection) or directly using a DI framework (Field Injection).
- The fields to be injected can be represented as interfaces in the object, adding further separation of concerns and adding flexibility (Interface Injection).
- Kotlin's default constructor parameter feature makes it a lot easier to manually create your own DI maps. However, we would recommend you pick a DI framework instead. This is especially convenient around the mapping of `ViewModel` objects.

Questions

1. How does DI facilitate Separation of concerns?
2. What are the differences between the three methods of DI?
3. What are the advantages of Interface Injection?
4. What is the main difference between Koin and Hilt DI frameworks?
5. What are the pros and cons of each of Koin and Hilt?

Join our book's Discord space

Join the book's Discord Workspace for Latest updates, Offers, Tech happenings around the world, New Release and Sessions with the Authors:

https://discord.bpbonline.com

CHAPTER 7
Introduction to Jetpack Compose

Introduction

Jetpack Compose is a modern UI toolkit for building native Android apps. It is part of the Android Jetpack library and is designed to simplify and accelerate UI development. With Jetpack Compose, developers can create interactive and dynamic user interfaces using a declarative approach, which means describing the UI elements and their behavior without worrying about the underlying implementation details. It offers a more intuitive and efficient way to build the UIs, with features like live editing, state management, and reusable components. Jetpack Compose is built on Kotlin and is fully integrated with the existing Android ecosystem.

This will by no means be a comprehensive guide to Compose. Such a discussion would require an entire book on its own – and would likely be out of date by the time it was published, given the fluid nature of the technology. Instead, we will just cover the stable basics needed for subsequent chapters.

Structure

This chapter covers the following topics:
- Overview of Jetpack Compose
- Advantages over traditional views

- Getting started with Jetpack Compose
- Some commonly used composables
- Scoped custom composables
- State management primitives

Objectives

Subsequent chapters rely on some rudimentary knowledge of Jetpack Compose. This chapter provides some basic concepts for those unfamiliar with Compose. By the end of this chapter, you will understand the benefits of Compose over traditional Views, know how to create a basic app using Compose, be familiar with some common Composable elements. You will also understand the concepts of modifiers and state management primitives.

Overview of Jetpack Compose

Jetpack Compose is a modern UI toolkit for building native user interfaces in Android applications. It is a declarative UI framework developed by Google, designed to simplify and streamline the process of creating UIs for Android apps. Compose allows developers to build UI components using Kotlin code, providing a more concise, intuitive, and flexible way to describe the app's user interface.

Some key features of Jetpack Compose are as follows:

- **Declarative UI**: Compose uses a declarative approach, where the developers describe what the UI should look like based on the current state. Instead of managing complex UI updates manually, developers define the UI components as composable functions that automatically update when the underlying state changes.
- **Kotlin based**: Compose is fully written in Kotlin, making it the preferred choice for Kotlin developers. It leverages Kotlin's language features and extensions to provide a seamless and idiomatic development experience.
- **UI components as functions**: In Compose, UI components are represented as composable functions. Each composable function describes a small piece of the UI and can be combined to build complex UI hierarchies. Composable functions can be reused and composed to create UI elements dynamically.
- **Reactive updates**: Compose follows a reactive programming model. When the underlying data changes, only the affected UI elements are automatically recomposed and updated. This approach optimizes UI rendering and improves performance.
- **Jetpack integration**: Compose is part of the Android Jetpack library suite, which means it can be used alongside other Jetpack components to create modern and feature-rich Android apps.

- **Android studio integration**: Compose offers strong integration with Android Studio, providing real-time previews of the UI as developers write the code. This visual feedback streamlines the development process.

Jetpack Compose represents a shift in Android UI development, offering a more intuitive and efficient way to create UIs compared to traditional XML-based layouts. It simplifies the process of handling UI state and interactions, reduces boilerplate code, and improves app performance by optimizing UI rendering.

Advantages over traditional views

Jetpack Compose offers several advantages over traditional views or XML-based layouts in Android app development. Some of the key advantages are as follows:

- **Declarative UI**: Compose follows a declarative programming model, where UI components are defined using Kotlin code as composable functions. This approach simplifies UI development by focusing on what the UI should look like based on the current state, rather than how to update it manually. This leads to more concise and intuitive UI code.
- **Less boilerplate code**: Compose reduces boilerplate code significantly compared to XML-based layouts. It eliminates the need for separate XML layout files and associated resource IDs, leading to cleaner and more readable code. Compose's composable functions also encapsulate both UI structure and behavior, reducing the need for separate classes like `ViewHolders`.
- **Improved performance**: Compose introduces a reactive programming model, where UI updates are optimized and triggered only when the underlying data changes. This reactive approach minimizes unnecessary UI rendering, leading to improved performance and smoother user experiences.
- **Kotlin integration**: As Compose is built entirely with Kotlin, it seamlessly integrates with the Kotlin language, leveraging its powerful features such as extension functions, lambda expressions, and DSL capabilities. This makes UI development more natural and enjoyable for Kotlin developers.
- **Real-time previews**: Compose offers real-time previews in Android Studio, enabling developers to see how the UI changes as they write the code. This visual feedback helps developers iterate and experiment with the UI design more efficiently.
- **Enhanced UI reusability**: Composable functions in Compose promote better UI reusability. Developers can create and compose UI elements as functions, making it easier to reuse them across different parts of the app.
- **Easier state management**: Compose introduces state management primitives like `remember` and `mutableStateOf`, making it easier to handle and manage UI state changes without relying on external libraries or complex setup.

- **Unification of UI and logic**: Compose brings UI logic and rendering together in the same code, which can improve code maintainability and readability. Developers do not have to jump between XML layout files, separate activity, or fragment classes.
- **More intuitive learning curve**: For new Android developers or those coming from other UI frameworks, Compose may have a more intuitive learning curve, as it is designed with modern development practices in mind.

Jetpack Compose provides a more modern and efficient way to build UIs for Android apps. While traditional views are still widely used and supported, Jetpack Compose offers a more straightforward and expressive alternative for developers looking to adopt modern UI development practices.

Getting started with Jetpack Compose

In this section, we will often mention scopes. By way of reminder, this means code between the scoping operators **{ ... }**. Scoping is an aspect of Kotlin that is heavily exploited by compose.

The quickest and easiest way to get a taste of Compose is to start a fresh project in Android Studio using the *Empty Compose Activity* wizard or just *Empty Activity* from Flamingo onwards. Doing this will match the compatible version of Kotlin to the latest version of Compose. Note that this is almost never the latest version of Kotlin. Kotlin and compose are not released together. For example, at the time of writing, the latest version of Kotlin was 1.8.20, but the latest version of Compose was written against 1.7.20.

Let us take a look at **MainActivity**. Despite the *Empty* wizard's name, a lot of code has been generated for us:

```
1.  class MainActivity : ComponentActivity() {
2.      override fun onCreate(savedInstanceState: Bundle?) {
3.          super.onCreate(savedInstanceState)
4.          setContent {
5.              // ...
6.              Greeting("Android")
7.              // ...
8.          }
9.      }
10. }
```

The following figure depicts empty activity:

Figure 7.1: Empty Activity

For the purposes of simple illustration, the code above has been stripped down to the essential elements.

Instead of **Activity** or **AppCompatActivity**, **MainActivity** now extends **ComponentActivity**. **ComponentActivity** supplies the **setContent** extension that provides a scope for **Composable** functions that generate the UI. In this case **Greeting**, as seen in the following code:

```
1. @Composable
2. fun Greeting(name: String, modifier: Modifier = Modifier) {
3.     Text(
4.         text = "Hello $name!",
5.         modifier = modifier
6.     )
7. }
```

Whilst it is technically possible to have **Composable** functions as members of a class, they are normally first-order and are always annotated with **@Composable** as above. In this case **Greeting** takes a **name** string parameter and uses the built-in **Text** composable to output **name** prepended with Hello onto the screen.

Modifier supplies a chained interface pattern for setting various attributes on the composable. For example, **Modifier.width(20.dp).height(5.dp)** passed to **Greeting** would set the text size to **20 X 5** device independent pixels (**dp**). Different modifier attributes will be available depending on the scope in which a modifier is created. We will discuss more about this later.

The full **MainActivity** produced by the wizard should look something like this:

```
1.  class MainActivity : ComponentActivity() {
2.      override fun onCreate(savedInstanceState: Bundle?) {
3.          super.onCreate(savedInstanceState)
4.          setContent {
5.              Chapter7Theme {
6.                  Surface(
7.                      modifier = Modifier.fillMaxSize(),
8.                      color = MaterialTheme.colorScheme.background
9.                  ) {
10.                     Greeting("Android")
11.                 }
12.             }
13.         }
14.     }
15. }
```

The custom composable **Greeting** is called within the scope of a **Surface** composable. The Surface composable sets a background color and fills the screen. The **Greeting** composable then draws on that full-screen background. The **Surface** composable is called within the scope of a composable that sets up the various color schemes for everything in its provided scope. The wizard auto-generates this composable and names it in line with the project, in this case, **Chapter7Theme**.

Note that the **MaterialTheme** used by the **Surface** to set the background color is a scoped static (known as *compositional local*) that is set by **Chapter7Theme**. This means that the values in **MaterialTheme** will only be valid within the scope provided by **Chapter7Theme**.

The last function you will see in the same file as **MainActivity** is the preview:

```
1. @Preview(showBackground = true)
2. @Composable
3. fun GreetingPreview() {
4.     Chapter7Theme {
5.         Greeting("Android")
6.     }
7. }
```

The **@Preview** code in Jetpack Compose is used for previewing and testing UI components during the development process. It is not included in the released app. The **@Preview** annotation is used to generate a preview of the UI component in Android Studio's Preview window, allowing developers to visualize and interact with the UI without running the entire app. Once the development and testing are complete, the **@Preview** code is typically removed or ignored before releasing the app. In order to render the preview to the screen, the user should have **Split** or **Design** selected in the top-right corner of the code window:

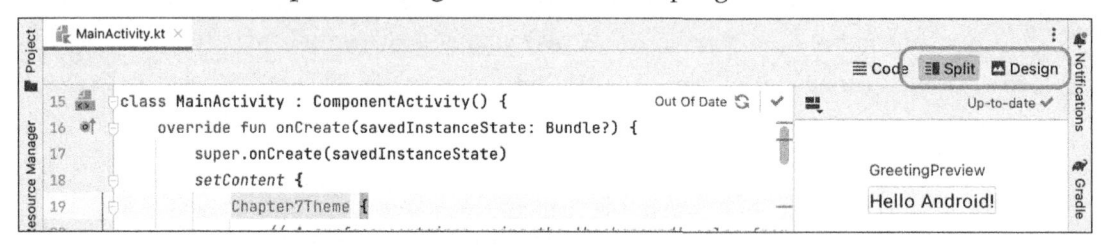

Figure 7.2: Split preview

The **@Preview** arrangement has some limitations, for example, you have to feed the Composable-under-test real data. If your Composable interprets an object of a complex custom data class, you would need to populate every field, or every nested field before you can see a preview. The old XML design view did not have this issue. It would just render the limits of each **View** giving you at least an idea of the relative positioning.

The wizard will make this function public, but it can be private if it is in the same file as the Composable under test. Although, since it will be removed from the binary, it makes no difference.

The `@Preview` code does not need to be in the production code to work. It can just as easily be in test code – so long as the Composable under test has at least `internal` scope.

Some commonly used composables

In Jetpack Compose, the UI hierarchy and its behavior is described using composable functions. Composables are responsible for generating UI elements based on the current state of your application. When the state changes, compose automatically updates the UI to reflect the changes, making it highly reactive. In the previous section we already examined the built-in `Text` and `Surface` composables. The library is always evolving so it is a good plan to check the official Jetpack compose documentation and samples documentation for the latest information.

Some of the other most commonly used composables are as follows:

- **Button:** Represents a clickable button. The `Button` composable is used to create a clickable button. It allows you to define the button's appearance and behavior:

    ```
    1.  @Composable
    2.  fun ButtonExample() {
    3.      Button(
    4.          onClick = {
    5.              // Action to perform when the button is clicked
    6.          }
    7.      ) {
    8.          Text("Click me")
    9.      }
    10. }
    ```

    The following figure depicts the button from the preceding code:

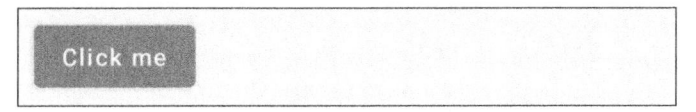

    Figure 7.3: Button

    Here, two scopes are provided. The first scope is for the `onClick` parameter. This will be called when the user clicks the button. The second, or *provided* scope defines the UI content of the button, in this case, a `Text` composable displaying **Click me** on the button.

- **TextField:** An editable text input field. The `TextField` composable is used to accept user input. It allows you to define the input type, hint text, and handle user interactions:

```
1.  @Composable
2.  fun TextFieldExample() {
3.      var text by remember { mutableStateOf("") }
4.
5.      TextField(
6.          value = text,
7.          onValueChange = { text = it }
8.      )
9.  }
```

The following figure depicts the text field from the preceding code:

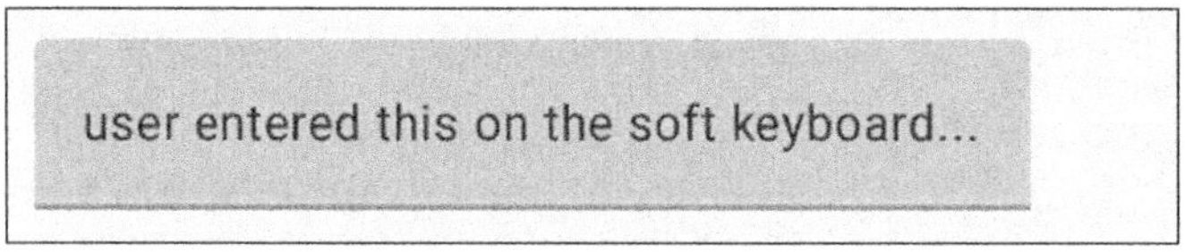

> user entered this on the soft keyboard...

Figure 7.4: TextField

In this example, **TextField** has two compulsory fields configured. There are further fields for hint text and various other decorations. **value** will be the text displayed. The **onValueChanged** scope will be called every time the user taps a button on the keyboard with the latest full entry in it. The **remember**/ **mutableStateOf** arrangement has the effect of changing the **value** of the **TextField** when the user enters text. This will be covered in greater detail in the following sections.

- **Image:** The **Image** composable is used to display images. It can load images from different sources like local resources or network URLs:

```
1.  @Composable
2.  fun ImageExample() {
3.      Image(
4.          painter = painterResource(
5.              id = R.drawable.fig7_5_source
6.          ),
7.          contentDescription = "Sample Image",
8.      )
9.  }
```

The following screenshot is rendered from the preceding code:

Figure 7.5: Image (Emdedded image source: freeiconspng.com)

Image uses the first-class **painterResource** function to render an imported drawable. There are third-party first-class functions available for supplying images from network sources instead. One such library is Coil. In this particular case, a **png** was added to the drawable resource for the **painterResource** to reference.

The **contentDescription** field is set as compulsory and encourages developers to at least think about accessibility for those users with impaired sight.

- **Icon:** Similar to **Image**, **Icon** renders **ImageVector** objects either built-in as in the example below or imported from SVG files into local XML. Unlike **Image** which is designed to work with images from **.jpg** or **.png** sources, **Icon** is designed for the type of simple, small mono-toned images you might see decorating buttons:

```
1. @Composable
2. fun IconExample() {
3.     Icon(
4.         imageVector = Icons.Default.Favorite,
5.         contentDescription = "Favorite Icon",
6.         tint = Color.Red
7.     )
8. }
```

Here, the built-in heart icon will be displayed in red:

Figure 7.6: Icon

- **Column and Row**: These Composables arrange other composables in a vertical or horizontal layout. They are used to arrange other composables horizontally (**Row**) or vertically (**Column**). They help in creating more complex layouts:

    ```
    1.  @Composable
    2.  fun RowColumnExample() {
    3.      Column {
    4.          Row {
    5.              Text("Item A")
    6.              Text("Item B")
    7.              Text("Item C")
    8.          }
    9.          Row {
    10.             Text("Item A")
    11.             Text("Item B")
    12.             Text("Item C")
    13.         }
    14.     }
    15. }
    ```

    The following figure depicts the column and row arrangement from the preceding code :

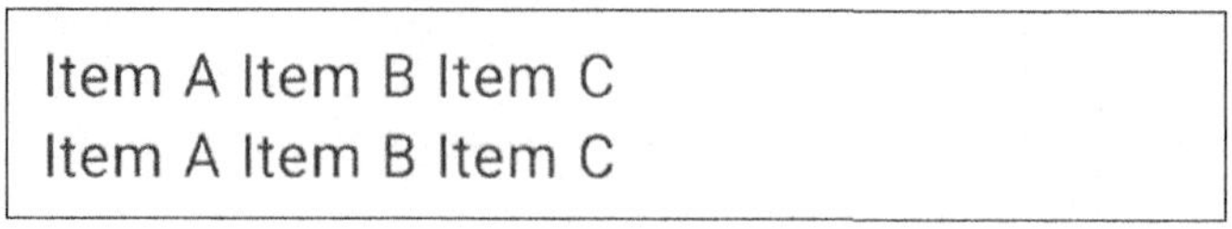

    Item A Item B Item C
    Item A Item B Item C

    Figure 7.7: Column and row

    In this simple example, two rows of three text items each will be displayed, one below the other.

- **Box**: A composable that allows you to stack elements on top of each other:

    ```
    1.  @Composable
    2.  fun BoxExample() {
    3.      Box {
    4.          Text("Hello")
    5.          Text("World")
    6.      }
    7.  }
    ```

In the following figure the word **World** is drawn over the top of **Hello**:

```
Wellod
```

Figure 7.8: Box

This composable is mostly used for formatting more complex arrangements globally in its provided scope.

- **Spacer**: A composable that adds empty space between elements:
    1. `@Composable`
    2. `fun SpacerExample() {`
    3.   `Column {`
    4.   `Text("Item 1")`
    5.   `Spacer(modifier = Modifier.height(16.dp))`
    6.   `Text("Item 2")`
    7.   `}`
    8. `}`

This example will display a 16 device-independent-pixel (**dp**) vertical space between the first and second text items in a column:

```
Item 1

Item 2
```

Figure 7.9: Spacer

- **Card**: A composable that creates a card-like container with a drop shadow. The **Card** composable is used to create a material design card with a shadow. It provides a container for other composables and adds elevation:
    1. `@Composable`
    2. `fun CardExample() {`
    3.   `Card {`
    4.   `Text("This is a card content")`
    5.   `}`
    6. `}`

The following figure depicts the card from the code above:

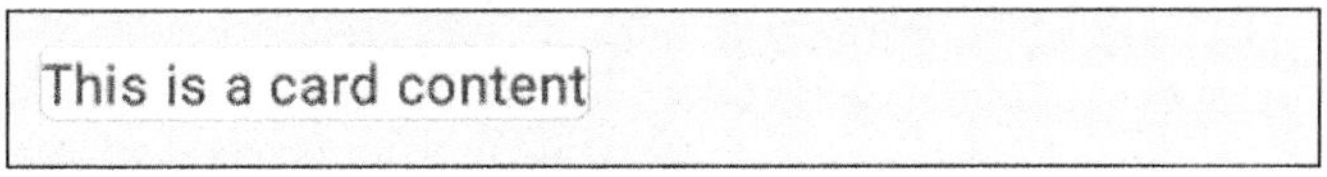

```
This is a card content
```

Figure 7.10: Card

- **LazyColumn:** These composables are used to display lists of items. They efficiently

    ```
    1.  @Composable
    2.  fun LazyListExample() {
    3.      val itemsList = listOf("a", "b", "c")
    4.
    5.      LazyColumn {
    6.          items(itemsList) { item -> Text(item) }
    7.      }
    8.  }
    ```

    The following figure depicts the list from the code above. Had there been enough items to overflow the screen, the list would have been scrollable:

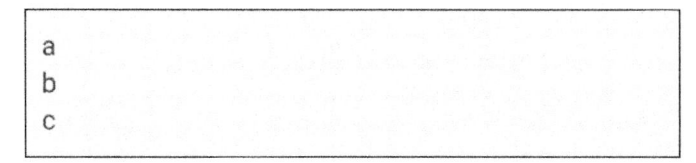

    Figure 7.11: LazyList

    items is an inline function supplied by the lazy list scope that effectively operates like a **for** loop, iterating over the list and rendering each item in turn it according to the provided scope. This is all you need to render a dynamic, scrollable list. This is a massive simplification over the complex XML/ **RecyclerView**/ **Adapter** arrangement that was required to do the same thing with traditional Views.

    There is also **LazyRow** and several lazy grid variants that are configured the same way.

- **Dialog:** The **Dialog** composable is used to display a dialog box on the screen. It allows you to define the dialog's content, title, buttons, and handle user interactions:

    ```
    1.  @Composable
    2.  fun DialogExample() {
    3.      Dialog(
    4.          onDismissRequest = {
    5.              // Dialog dismiss logic
    6.          }
    7.      ) {
    8.          Text(text = "Dialog")
    9.      }
    10. }
    ```

The following figure depicts a partial image rendered from the preceding code:

Figure 7.12: Dialog

In this example, the scope provided by **onDismissRequest** will be called when the dialog is dismissed. The content scope will contain other composables defining the look of the dialog.

This is just a small selection of the many composables available in the material libraries.

Modifiers

Modifiers are functions that are used to apply visual changes or behavior to UI elements. Modifiers are applied in a chained manner, allowing you to modify various aspects of a UI element, such as size, padding, background color, etc.

All built-in composables, such as those discussed in the previous section, can take a modifier parameter available via the **Modifier** factory object. The **SpacerExample** in the previous section demonstrated the **padding** modifier. Some other commonly used modifiers are as follows: -

- **clickable:** Adds a click listener to the composable element:

    ```
    1.  @Composable
    2.  fun ImageExample() {
    3.      Image(
    4.          modifier = Modifier.clickable {
    5.              // on click logic
    6.          },
    7.          // ...
    8.      )
    9.  }
    ```

    In this updated example, the displayed image will now be clickable and the scope provided by the **clickable** modifier will be called when the image is clicked on.

- **border:** Adds a border around the composable element:

    ```
    1.  @Composable
    2.  fun ButtonExample() {
    3.      Button(
    ```

4.   modifier = Modifier.border(2.dp, Color.Black),
5.   // ...
6.   )
7. }

Here, we have added an extra black, **2 dp** thick border around our button:

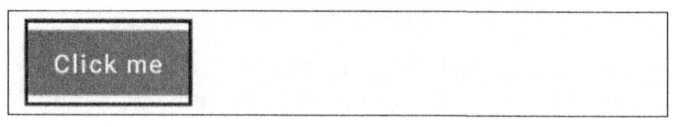

Figure 7.13: Border modifier

- **background:** Sets the background color or drawable for a composable element:
    1. @Composable
    2. fun BoxExample() {
    3.   Box(
    4.   modifier = Modifier.background(Color.Gray)
    5.   ) { /* .. */ }
    6. }

Our **Box** now has a gray background:

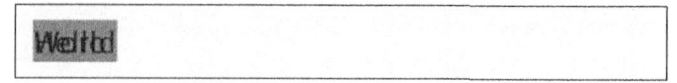

Figure 7.14: Box with background

- **height and width:** They set the height and width resp. of a composable:
    1. @Composable
    2. fun IconExample() {
    3.   Icon(
    4.   modifier = Modifier.height(100.dp).width(50.dp),
    5.   // ...
    6.   )
    7. }

The following depicts a red heart icon proportionally enlarged from the previous example:

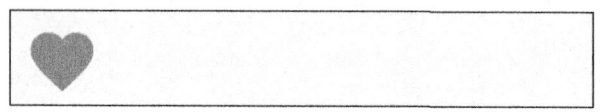

Figure 7.15: Icon with modifier

Here, we have set the height and width of our **Icon** to 100 and 50 dp respectively. One might expect the image to be stretched in height; however, by default, Jetpack Compose uses the intrinsic aspect ratio of the image to maintain its proportions even when different width and height values are set. This is an example of how modifiers can be applied in a chained manner.

- **fillMaxWidth, fillMaxHeight, fillMaxSize:** These mutually-exclusive modifiers will set a composable's size to the limits of the available space:

    ```
    1.  @Composable
    2.  fun BoxExample() {
    3.      Box(
    4.          modifier = Modifier
    5.              .background(Color.Gray)
    6.              .fillMaxSize()
    7.      ) { /* composable content */ }
    8.  }
    ```

The following image depicts a partial screenshot of the modified code above:

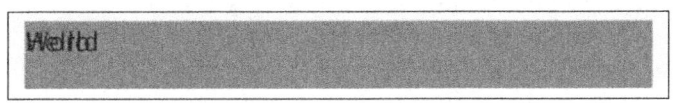

Figure 7.16: Box with fillMaxSize

The gray **Box** now fills the size of the available space determined by the modifier set by the parent (calling) composable. If this was the first composable in **setContent**, that would be the whole screen, but in this case it is not. All of the examples have a Box parent with **5 dp** padding to make them more aesthetically pleasing.

fillMaxHeight would have set the vertical limits to that of the parent and allowed the width to float to the limits of the composable content, or the parent, whichever is smaller. Conversely, **fillMaxWidth** would have set the horizontal limits to that of the parent and allowed the height to float in a similar way. All three of these modifiers can take a **Float** parameter **fraction** that specifies what fraction of the available space to use.

- **weight**: There are modifiers that are only available in certain scopes, for example in the **Row** composable:

    ```
    1.  @Composable
    2.  fun WeightExample() {
    3.      Row {
    4.          Text(
    5.              modifier = Modifier.weight(0.3f),
    ```

```
6.            text = "Item A"
7.        )
8.        // ... sibling composables
9.    }
10. }
```

With one more sibling with the same weight, the preceding code renders to the following:

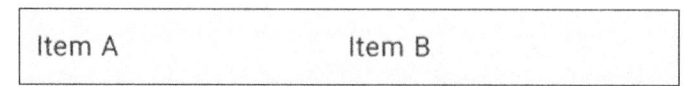

Item A	Item B

Figure 7.17: Weight modifier

In this case, The **Text** element is spaced horizontally in proportion to the **weight** value of its sibling composables against the available width. The **weight** modifier is only available to **Text** because **Text** is inside the scope of a **Row**. There are other modifiers that are specific to the parent composable as well, such as the **Column** composable.

These are just a few examples of the many modifiers available in Jetpack Compose. You can combine them and apply them to different composable elements to create flexible and responsive UIs for your Android application.

Scoped custom composables

It is a common practice to make code more readable and reduce topology by extracting groups of composables out into their own composable. Given the **weight/row** example at the end of the previous section, to still have the **weight** modifier available to the extracted **Text**, the new composable would need to extend **RowScope**. For example:

```
1. @Composable
2. fun WeightExample() {
3.     Row {
4.         ExtractedText("Item A")
5.         ExtractedText("Item B")
6.         ExtractedText("Item C")
7.     }
8. }
9.
10. @Composable
11. private fun RowScope.ExtractedText(text: String) {
12.     Text(
```

```
13.            modifier = Modifier.weight(0.3f),
14.            text = text
15.        )
16. }
```

This arrangement may be applicable in certain circumstances; however, it is usually more flexible to pass the modifier to the extracted composable and then chain it with any modifiers used in the extraction:

```
1.  @Composable
2.  fun WeightExample() {
3.      Row {
4.          ExtractedText(
5.              text = "Item A",
6.              localModifier = Modifier.weight(0.3f)
7.          )
8.          // ... sibling composables
9.      }
10. }
11.
12. @Composable
13. private fun ExtractedText(
14.     localModifier: Modifier = Modifier,
15.     text: String
16. ) {
17.     Text(
18.         modifier = localModifier.padding(start = 10.dp),
19.         text = text
20.     )
21. }
```

Here, the **weight** will be chained with the **padding** modifier in the extracted composable (although it does not necessarily need to chain with anything) and the extracted composable does not need to extend **RowScope**. This is a contrived example showing just one composable in the extraction so does not appear to provide much benefit over the original embedded arrangement. It becomes much more powerful when the extraction contains a grouping of several composables.

The modifier parameter has been named **localModifier** in this example to draw attention to its use, however this is a Lint error and should just me named **modifier**.

State management primitives

In general, state management primitives are tools or techniques used in software development to manage and handle the state of an application. These primitives provide a way to store, update, and retrieve data that affects the behavior and appearance of the user interface. Developers may be familiar with the Observer Pattern and its implementation in Java, the **observable**. The observable object provides a scope that gets called when the state of the observable changes. There are specific mechanisms provided by Jetpack Compose to achieve this for updating UI elements on a data state change. Some of these key state management primitives in Jetpack Compose include:

- **State variables** (`remember` and `mutableStateOf`): Compose provides the `remember` and `mutableStateOf` functions to manage and observe changes in state. `mutableStateOf` creates a mutable state variable that can be updated, and Compose automatically recomposes the UI when the state changes. **Remember** is used to remember a value across recompositions, ensuring that the value is retained and consistent across updates.

    ```
    1. @Composable
    2. fun Counter() {
    3.     var count by remember { mutableStateOf(0) }
    4.
    5.     Button(onClick = { count++ }) {
    6.         Text("Count: $count")
    7.     }
    8. }
    ```

    In this example, the `mutableStateOf` function is used to create a mutable state variable **count**. Whenever the button is clicked, the value of **count** is updated, and Jetpack Compose automatically recomposes the UI to reflect the new value.

    remember is a composable function that can be used to cache expensive operations. It can be thought of as a cache which is local to a composable. The value returned by **remember**'s scope is immutable unless it is wrapped by a `mutableStateOf` function. In fact, a `mutableStateOf` without a wrapping **remember** is flagged as an error in Android Studio. The code above uses the **by** delegate keyword to initialize count. Currently (as of Android Studio Flamingo) you have to manually add the following imports to get this to work:

    ```
    1. import androidx.compose.runtime.getValue
    2. import androidx.compose.runtime.setValue
    ```

    Without these code imports the example would need to be written like this:

    ```
    1. @Composable
    2. fun Counter() {
    ```

```
3.      val count = remember { mutableStateOf(0) }
4.
5.      Button(onClick = { count.value++ }) {
6.          Text("Count: $count")
7.      }
8.  }
```

In this example, the mutable state value **count** has to be incremented against its **value** field on line five.

remember will reset the returned value back to the value in its scope on orientation change. In this case the value of **count** will be reset to zero in that instance. **rememberSaveable** can be used in place of **remember** to retain the current value of the state across orientation changes. Given the example above, the value of **count** will be retained if the screen is refreshed due to a change in a parent or sibling Composable requiring a redraw. However, count will be reset to zero if the device is rotated to a different orientation. Replacing **remember** with **rememberSaveable** will ensure that **count** is also retained with an orientation change.

- **Derived state (derivedStateOf)**: Compose offers the **derivedStateOf** function to create derived state that depends on other state variables. This is useful when you want to compute a value based on existing state variables and have Compose automatically update the UI when any of the dependencies change.

```
1.  @Composable
2.  fun DerivedCounter() {
3.      var count by remember { mutableStateOf(0) }
4.      val doubledCount = remember { derivedStateOf { count * 2 }
        }
5.
6.      Button(onClick = { count++ }) {
7.          Text("Doubled Count: $doubledCount")
8.      }
9.  }
```

Here, **derivedStateOf** is used to create **doubledCount**, which depends on the value of **count**. Any change to **count** will trigger a recomposition of **DerivedCounter**, updating the UI with the new **doubledCount** value.

- **Side effects (LaunchedEffect and DisposableEffect)**: **LaunchedEffect** and **DisposableEffect** are functions that allow you to perform side effects (such as making network requests or updating external resources) based on changes in state. They ensure that the side effect is triggered only when the specified state changes, preventing unnecessary side effects.

```kotlin
1.  @Composable
2.  fun LaunchedEffectExample() {
3.      var count by remember { mutableStateOf(0) }
4.
5.      LaunchedEffect(count) {
6.          println("Count changed: $count")
7.      }
8.
9.      // increment count
10. }
```

In this example, the **LaunchedEffect** function is used to perform a side effect (printing a message) when the **count** state changes. The side effect is launched in a coroutine context, ensuring it runs asynchronously.

DisposableEffect is used to perform a side effect when a component is first composed (similar to **onCreate** in Android components) and when it is no longer needed (similar to **onDestroy**). It allows you to allocate and release resources associated with a composable.

```kotlin
1.  @Composable
2.  fun DisposableEffectExample() {
3.      DisposableEffect(Unit) {
4.          // Perform side effect when the
5.          // composable is first composed
6.          println("Composable created")
7.
8.          onDispose {
9.              // Perform cleanup when the
10.             // composable is no longer needed
11.             println("Composable disposed")
12.         }
13.     }
14. }
```

In this example, the **DisposableEffect** is used to print messages when the composable is created and disposed. The **onDispose** lambda is used to clean up resources when the composable is no longer needed. Note that **onDispose** is only available within the scope provided by **DisposableEffect**.

In summary, **LaunchedEffect** is suitable for performing asynchronous side effects based on changing state, while **DisposableEffect** is used for managing resources associated with a composable's lifecycle.

- **View model (ViewModel and viewModel)**: While View Models are not exclusive to Compose, Jetpack Compose integrates well with the Android **ViewModel** architecture component. You can use **viewModel** to access the View Model from a composable and observe its state changes using **observeAsState**.

  The use of the **ViewModel** is pivotal to the presentation architecture proposed in a later chapter so a full example will be provided there.

- **Collecting Flows (collectAsState)**: Compose can directly work with Kotlin Flows, allowing you to collect and observe Flow emissions using the **collectAsState** function. This is useful for integrating Compose with asynchronous and reactive programming patterns.

  ```
  1. @Composable
  2. fun FlowExample() {
  3.     val countFlow = MutableStateFlow(0)
  4.     val count by countFlow.collectAsState()
  5.
  6.     Button(onClick = { countFlow.value++ }) {
  7.         Text("Count: $count")
  8.     }
  9. }
  ```

  Here, a **MutableStateFlow** is used to represent the **count** state, and **collectAsState** is used to collect the flow emissions and update the UI with the latest value.

- **Local composition (Local)**: Compose introduces the concept of **Local** values, which are scoped values that can be accessed by composable functions within a specific composition hierarchy. Local values enable sharing of state within a specific context.

  ```
  1. val LocalCount = staticCompositionLocalOf<Int> {
  2.     error("No count provided")
  3. }
  4.
  5. @Composable
  6. fun CounterWithLocal() {
  7.     val count = LocalCount.current
  8.
  9.     Button(onClick = { /* Increment count */ }) {
  ```

```
10.            Text("Count: $count")
11.        }
12. }
```

In this example, a **Local** value **LocalCount** is defined to provide the current count. This value can be accessed within any composable function that is within the scope of a **LocalCount** provider.

- collectAsStateWithLifecycle: This is a recent **StateFlow** extension function included with **androidx.lifecycle:lifecycle-runtime-compose** from version 2.6.0-alpha01 onwards. It addresses a memory management issue regarding subscribers being active whilst the app is in the background. Internally, it will start and stop collection with lifecycle **onStart** and **onStop** resp.

```
1. @Composable
2. fun CollectAsStateWithLifecycleExample() {
3.     val countFlow = MutableStateFlow(0)
4.     val count by countFlow.collectAsStateWithLifecycle()
5.
6.     Button(onClick = { countFlow.value++ }) {
7.         Text("Count: $count")
8.     }
9. }
```

- **BackHandler:** This is a state management primitive dedicated to observing the back button. The provided scope will be called if the back button is pressed. It is useful for adding a condition or pre-check when attempting to back out of a screen.

```
1. @Composable
2. fun BackHandlerExample() {
3.     BackHandler {
4.         // do some checks on back pressed
5.     }
6. }
```

- These examples demonstrate how various state management primitives in Jetpack Compose can be used to handle and manage state in your UI components. The choice of which primitive to use depends on the specific requirements of your application and the level of control and reactivity you need for your state updates.

Conclusion

Jetpack Compose is a modern UI toolkit for building native user interfaces in Android applications. It dispenses with traditional XML View definitions that need to be inflated at runtime and allows the UI to be declared directly in Kotlin code.

Using this toolkit, the developer can build all the UI elements provided by the traditional View arrangement as Kotlin functions, unifying the code base and generally improving performance.

This chapter has provided just a taste of what is available in Jetpack Compose, so further reading and experimentation are encouraged, especially since Compose is constantly evolving.

In the next chapter, we chart the evolution of presentation layer design patterns and propose a model that is particularly suited to Jetpack Compose.

Points to remember

- Jetpack Compose composables are first-class functions with names starting with a capital letter by convention and annotated with **@Composable**.
- Composable functions can only be called from other composable functions or from within a composable scope, such as that provided by **setContent** in a **ComponentActivity** derivative.
- Built-in composables take **modifier** parameters which allow manipulation of their characteristics. The characteristics that can be manipulated may depend on the composable scope they are used in.
- Compose provides a set of state management primitives that allow the UI to be updated automatically when displayed data changes.
- Jetpack Compose is constantly evolving so further reading is encouraged.

Questions

1. What is the quickest way to get started with a Jetpack Compose app?
2. How do you configure an **Image** composable to display images from the network?
3. How would you set the horizontal padding of a composable?
4. How do you change the app theme settings in Jetpack Compose?
5. Which compose elements will be updated when a state management primitive changes state?
6. What advantages does Jetpack Compose **LazyList** have over the traditional View arrangement?

Join our book's Discord space

Join the book's Discord Workspace for Latest updates, Offers, Tech happenings around the world, New Release and Sessions with the Authors:

https://discord.bpbonline.com

CHAPTER 8
Presentation Layer Evolution in Compose

Introduction

The design patterns aimed at separating concerns in the presentation layer have evolved over time. The evolution of **separation of concerns** (**SoC**) techniques in the Android presentation layer has seen a shift towards adopting architectural patterns that promote a clear separation between UI logic and business logic. Initially, developers relied heavily on the **Model-View-Controller** (**MVC**) pattern, where activities and fragments acted as both controllers and views. However, this led to tightly coupled code and difficulty in testing. Approaches have come and gone. This chapter charts the evolution from MVC through to the current UDF paradigm, describing how the latter is particularly suitable for Jetpack Compose.

Structure

This chapter covers the following topics:

- Summary of presentation architecture evolution
- Model-View-Controller
- Model-View-Presenter
- Model-View-ViewModel
- Model-View-Intent

- Implementing MVI with Jetpack compose
- Disadvantage of the UDF/MVI pattern

Objectives

This chapter will ultimately present a presentation architecture suited for the latest development paradigms in Android. In doing so, it will chart the journey that led to this arrangement by examining each popular architectures that went before.

Summary of presentation architecture evolution

The following points show how SoC techniques have evolved in the Android presentation layer. Note that all of these architectures were normally applied against a single **app** module. Where the *model* is mentioned, it was not a part of any kind of separate layer:

- **Traditional approach (Pre-MVC/MVP/MVVM)**: In the early days of Android development, the presentation layer was often tightly coupled with the user interface components, namely **Activity** and **Fragment**. Business logic, UI interactions, and data retrieval were all combined within these components. This made the codebase difficult to maintain, as changes in one area could lead to unintended consequences in others.
- **Model-View-Controller**: As Android development evolved, developers started adopting the MVC pattern to separate concerns. In MVC, the model represents data and business logic, the view is responsible for UI rendering, and the controller acts as an intermediary between the model and view. While this provided some separation of concerns, the controller still had to manage both UI updates and business logic, leading to some degree of coupling.
- **Model-View-Presenter (MVP)**: MVP became a popular architectural pattern for Android development. In MVP, the presenter serves as the middleman between the view and model, handling UI updates and reacting to user input. This approach achieved better separation of concerns, making it easier to test the presentation logic independently from the UI.
- **Model-View-ViewModel (MVVM)**: MVVM gained popularity as an evolution of the MVP pattern. In MVVM, the **ViewModel** is responsible for exposing data and presentation logic to the view. It allowed for data binding, reducing the need for manual UI updates. MVVM promotes a more declarative and reactive approach, which aligns well with the Android architecture components like **LiveData** and **ViewModel**.
- **Data binding and LiveData integration**: Android introduced Data binding and **LiveData** as part of the Android architecture components. These technologies

promised to provide more seamless integration of MVVM concepts in Android applications. Data binding allows for direct UI updates from `ViewModel` properties, reducing boilerplate code, while `LiveData` facilitates the observation of data changes and automatic UI updates when data changes.

- **ViewModel and lifecycle-aware components**: With the introduction of `ViewModel` and lifecycle-aware components, Android provided built-in support for managing UI-related data across configuration changes and the `Activity`/`Fragment` lifecycle. `ViewModel` can survive configuration changes, ensuring data continuity without leaking memory.
- **Model-View-Intent (MVI)**: MVI is an evolution of the popular MVVM pattern, designed to provide a more predictable and unidirectional flow of data in the app. In MVI, the Model represents the application state, the View is responsible for rendering the UI, and the Intent represents user actions or events that trigger state changes. The flow starts with the View sending an Intent to the Model, which updates the state accordingly. The updated state is then sent back to the View to reflect the changes in the UI.
- **Uni-directional Data Flow (UDF)**: UDF is MVI fine-tuned for Android, Kotlin, Coroutines and Jetpack Compose. The online documentation for Compose discusses UDF at a high level but only offers the sketchiest of code examples for achieving it. This chapter will present a simple `ViewModel` base class for UDF that has been used successfully across several large projects.

Throughout the evolution of SoC techniques in the Android presentation layer, the Android platform has continued to improve tools and libraries that facilitate clean architecture and modular development. To achieve a greater understanding of where we are now, it is useful to go into more depth at each stage of where we have been.

Model-View-Controller

Model-View-Controller is an architectural pattern commonly used in software development platforms, including web, desktop, and mobile applications. It helped to design applications with a clear separation of concerns. It was a pattern that was built into Apple's iOS, so it was the main reason for its early adoption in Android. The MVC pattern divided the presentation layer into the following three interconnected components:

- **Model**: The Model represents the data and related business logic of the application. It encapsulates the data and the rules for manipulating and processing that data. The Model is responsible for managing the state of the application and responding to requests from the controller. It does not have any knowledge of the UI or how the data is presented to the user.

    In its purest form, a model can be represented by a data class. The following example shows a model list being returned by a repository method:

```
1.  data class User(val id: Int, val name: String, val email:
    String)
2.
3.  class UserRepository {
4.      fun getUsers(): List<User> =
5.          listOf() // Simulate fetching users from a remote API
6.  }
```

The code was similar to what might be found in the modern data layer as previously described, except that it would have resided in the app package with no consideration for cross-platform use.

- **View**: The View is responsible for the presentation and display of data to the user. It represents the **user interface (UI)** and is concerned with how the data is visually rendered. The View receives data from the Model and displays it to the user. It does not contain any business logic or directly interact with the data, and its purpose is purely to show information to the user. The following XML is an example of a recycler-view View:

```
1.  <androidx.recyclerview.widget.RecyclerView
2.      xmlns:android="http://schemas.android.com/apk/res/android"
3.      android:id="@+id/userRecyclerView"
4.      android:layout_width="match_parent"
5.      android:layout_height="match_parent" />
```

- **Controller**: The Controller acts as an intermediary between the Model and the View. It receives user input from the View and processes it to determine the appropriate action to take. The Controller updates the Model based on user interactions and also instructs the View to update its presentation accordingly. It contains the application's business logic and coordinates the flow of data between the Model and the View. In the following example, **MainActivity** is acting as the Controller:

```
1.  class MainActivity : AppCompatActivity() {
2.      private val userRepository = UserRepository()
3.
4.      override fun onCreate(savedInstanceState: Bundle?) {
5.          super.onCreate(savedInstanceState)
6.          setContentView(R.layout.mvc_view)
7.
8.          val recyclerView: RecyclerView =
9.              findViewById(R.id.userRecyclerView)
```

```
10.         // initialize adapter and set on recyclerView
11.         val users = userRepository.getUsers() // fetch from
    model
12.         // add users to adapter
13.     }
14. }
```

As can be seen from the above, the Controller in Android MVC means **Activity** or **Fragment**.

The above example is cut down and simplistic but the business logic required to respond to user input, and update the view, which was normally much more extensive. It is very difficult to unit-test logic in **Activity** and **Fragment** objects (unit-testing is covered in a later chapter) due to the challenge in creating these Android-specific classes in a unit-test environment. Moreover, these controllers became overloaded, difficult to read, and unmanageable.

Model-View-Presenter

In an attempt to address the overloaded controller issues of MVC, the MVP architecture was introduced, whereby the business logic not directly associated with the model, was delegated to a separate object, the Presenter. A popular application of this was to use the Contract arrangement. The following describes contract MVP diagrammatically:

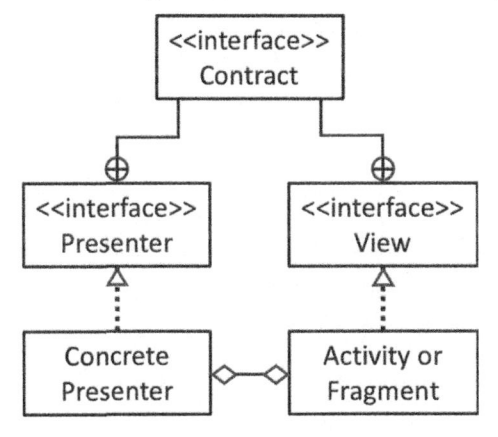

Figure 8.1: Contract MVP

Here, the interfaces **Presenter** and **View** were contained within a parent **Contract**. The parent interface existed purely to add extra scope to the child interfaces and had no direct method signatures. There would be a concrete class implementation of the **Presenter** interface and an **Activity** or **Fragment** would implement the **View**. This way, the **Activity** or **Fragment** changed its role from that of a Controller in MVC to part of the View. Finally, those concrete views and presenters would aggregate each other via their interfaces.

The following example demonstrates a simple implementation of MVP in Android. The Model handles the login logic, the Presenter coordinates the communication between the Model and View, and the View captures user input and displays the UI.

- **Contract**: An extra set of nested interfaces that enforce SoC between the View and the Presenter. This is the direct coding of the contract, presenter and view interfaces from *Figure 8.1*:

```
1.  interface LoginContract {
2.      interface View {
3.          fun showLoading()
4.          fun hideLoading()
5.          fun showError(message: String)
6.          fun navigateToHome()
7.      }
8.
9.      interface Presenter {
10.         fun loginButtonClicked(name: String, pwd: String)
11.     }
12. }
```

The nested interfaces restrict access between the View and the Presenter. Notice that there is a `showLoading` and `hideLoading` methods instead of, say, an `isLoading` attribute. This ensures that the View only handles UI update and does not require any logic.

- **Model**: Much the same as in MVC, the Model represents the data and related business logic of the application, only this time it provides methods to respond to requests from the concrete implementation of the **Presenter** interface. In the following example, the model is supplying the **login** method:

```
1.  class UserModel {
2.      fun login(
3.          user: String, pwd: String,
4.          callback: (Result<Int>) -> Unit
5.      ) { /* Perform login logic, call callback with result */ }
6.  }
```

In this example, the `UserModel` class handles user authentication and data retrieval.

- **View**: The **Activity** or **Fragment** implements the **View** contract, and, by definition *is* the **View**. Continuing our *login* themed example, the following extends the **Activity** with the View contract:

```kotlin
1.  class LoginActivity : AppCompatActivity(), LoginContract.View {
2.      private val presenter by lazy {
3.          LoginPresenter(this, UserModel())
4.      }
5.      override fun onCreate(savedInstanceState: Bundle?) {
6.          super.onCreate(savedInstanceState)
7.          // ...
8.          // Set click listener for login button ...
9.          findViewById<View>(R.id.button1).setOnClickListener {
10.             presenter.loginButtonClicked("user", "pwd")
11.         }
12.     }
13.
14.     override fun showLoading() { /* ... */ }
15.     override fun hideLoading() { /* ... */ }
16.     override fun showError(message: String) { /* .. */ }
17.     override fun navigateToHome() { /* .. */ }
18. }
```

LoginActivity would contain UI elements like **EditText** and **Button** for login. In this cut-down example, the presenter is initialized lazily and aggregated with the View, in this case, when the user clicks the login button on the UI.

LoginActivity implements the UI rendering methods **showLoading**, **hideLoading**, and so on, that are called back by the presenter in response to the presenter's **loginButtonClicked** method.

- **Presenter**: Acts as an intermediary between the Model and View. Handles user interactions, updates the UI, and communicates with the Model. The following class implements the Presenter contract:

```kotlin
1.  class LoginPresenter(
2.      private val view: LoginContract.View,
3.      private val userModel: UserModel
4.  ) : LoginContract.Presenter {
5.
6.      override fun loginButtonClicked(name: String, pwd: String) {
7.          view.showLoading()
8.          userModel.login(name, pwd) { result ->
```

```
9.                  view.hideLoading()
10.                 result.apply {
11.                     onSuccess { view.navigateToHome() }
12.                     onFailure { view.showError(it.message.
    orEmpty()) }
13.                 }
14.             }
15.         }
16. }
```

In summary, the **LoginActivity** implements a contract interface, which defines the methods that the **LoginPresenter** can call to update the UI. The **LoginPresenter** interacts with the **UserModel** to perform login operations and notifies the **LoginActivity** of the result.

The MVP architecture separates logic away from **Activity**s and **Fragment**s. The Contracts arrangement made it even easier to write tests against the logic as the View dependencies were supplied by injected interfaces, much like the use case ports discussed previously.

It was, however, a complicated arrangement, not directly supplied by the Android framework, that had to be repeated for every single UI screen. As projects grew and the UI got more complicated, it became more and more difficult for the developers unfamiliar with the code to follow the flow of control. In addition, Presenter objects' lifespan matched that of the host **Activity** or **Fragment** meaning that any data they held would be lost on orientation change. There are ways around this, of course, leveraging **savedInstanceState** or shared preferences, but these are complex solutions.

Model-View-ViewModel

Google finally addressed the Presenter lifespan issue in 2017 when they introduced the **ViewModel** base class. The **ViewModel** class is part of the MVVM architectural pattern. MVVM is simply MVP replacing the Presenter with a **ViewModel**. It is designed to store and manage UI-related data, surviving configuration changes, such as screen rotations. It helps in separating the UI logic from the UI components, making them more independent and reusable. Just like the Presenter before it, the **ViewModel** derivative acts as an intermediary between the Model and the View.

The initial version used a somewhat convoluted way of resolving the **ViewModel** class, as can be seen in the following example:

```
1. class UserProfileActivity : AppCompatActivity() {
2.     private lateinit var viewModel: UserProfileViewModel
3.
```

```
4.      override fun onCreate(savedInstanceState: Bundle?) {
5.          super.onCreate(savedInstanceState)
6.          // ...
7.          viewModel = ViewModelProvider(this).get(
8.              UserProfileViewModel::class.java
9.          )
10.         // ...
11.     }
12. }
```

This was replaced a year later by an inline extension function that made the arrangement significantly simpler. The following **Activity** class uses that inline function:

```
1. class UserProfileActivity : AppCompatActivity() {
2.     private val viewModel: UserProfileViewModel by viewModels()
3.     // ...
4. }
```

In both cases, **ViewModelProvider** and **viewModels** provided a **ViewModel** instance tied to the lifecycle of the containing **Activity** or **Fragment** that survived orientation change.

LiveData

Initially, the recommended way for the **ViewModel** to communicate with the view controller (**Activity** or **Fragment**) was by using **LiveData**.

LiveData is an observable data holder class provided by the Android architecture components library. It is designed to hold and observe changes to data in a lifecycle-aware manner. The primary purpose of **LiveData** is to provide a way to communicate changes in data from the data source such as a database or network to UI components while ensuring that the updates are only delivered when the component is in a live or active state.

The key features of **LiveData** are as follows:

- **Lifecycle-Aware**: **LiveData** is designed to work seamlessly with the Android lifecycle. It automatically stops sending updates to UI components that are not in an active state, that is, paused or destroyed.
- **Data observation**: UI components can observe changes to **LiveData** objects. This means that when the data held by a **LiveData** object changes, any UI component observing that **LiveData** will be notified and can update itself accordingly.
- **Prevents memory leaks**: **LiveData** helps in preventing memory leaks by automatically removing observers when the lifecycle of the observing UI component is ended.

- **Reactive updates**: `LiveData` is often used in conjunction with data sources, such as databases. When the data in the source changes, `LiveData` automatically updates the UI components observing it.
- **UI update on main thread**: `LiveData` ensures that updates are delivered on the main UI thread, preventing threading issues when updating UI elements.

So, given the previous `UserProfileActivity` example, the corresponding `ViewModel` may look this:

```
1.  class UserProfileViewModel : ViewModel() {
2.      private val _user = MutableLiveData<User>()
3.      val user: LiveData<User> get() = _user
4.
5.      fun loadUserData() {
6.          val user = fetchDataFromDataSource()
7.          _user.value = user
8.      }
9.
10.     private fun fetchDataFromDataSource(): User? {
11.         return null // Simulate loading user data from a data source
12.     }
13. }
```

Given this arrangement, the previous `Activity` example would be updated to observe the `LiveData` exposed by the `ViewModel`:

```
1.  class UserProfileActivity : AppCompatActivity() {
2.      private val viewModel: UserProfileViewModel by viewModels()
3.      private val username: TextView by lazy { findViewById(R.id.username) }
4.
5.      override fun onCreate(savedInstanceState: Bundle?) {
6.          super.onCreate(savedInstanceState)
7.          setContentView(R.layout.user)
8.
9.          viewModel.user.observe(this) { user -> username.text = user.name }
10.         viewModel.loadUserData()
11.     }
12. }
```

In this simple example, only one field from the **User** data class is being displayed. More fields would require more members to be initialized and more assignments made in the observer.

Data binding

Data binding was a feature in Android that allowed the connection of UI components layout files directly to data sources in an app's data model. It provided a declarative way to bind UI elements to data, reducing the amount of boilerplate code needed to update UI components with data changes.

Data binding promised to eliminate much of the manual view manipulation code and instead establish a direct connection between data and UI. The following example demonstrates the use of data binding in XML layouts:

```
1.  <layout xmlns:android="http://schemas.android.com/apk/res/android">
2.      <data>
3.          <variable
4.              name="user"
5.              type="com.example.User" />
6.      </data>
7.
8.      <TextView
9.          android:layout_width="wrap_content"
10.         android:layout_height="wrap_content"
11.         android:text="@{user.name}" />
12. </layout>
```

By way of reminder, **com.example.User**:

```
1. data class User(val id: Int, val name: String, val email: String)
```

The **<data>** entry binds the variable user to the **User** data class directly in the XML layout. The **TextView** object's text is subsequently bound to the **name** field of **User** using that variable. In order to leverage data binding the previous **Activity** example would be updated to resolve the binding from the layout, as can be seen in the following example:

```
1. class UserProfileActivity : AppCompatActivity() {
2.     private val viewModel: UserProfileViewModel by viewModels()
3.     private val binding: UserBinding by lazy {
4.         DataBindingUtil.setContentView(this, R.layout.user)
5.     }
6.
```

```
7.      override fun onCreate(savedInstanceState: Bundle?) {
8.          super.onCreate(savedInstanceState)
9.          viewModel.user.observe(this) { binding.user = it }
10.         viewModel.loadUserData()
11.     }
12. }
```

In order to get this to work a switch needed to be set in the app's **build.gradle** file:

```
1. android {
2.     ...
3.     buildFeatures {
4.         dataBinding true
5.     }
6. }
```

Instead of the traditional **setContentView** from the **Activity**, the layout is now inflated via a similar method provided by the **DataBindingUtil** class. The resulting **binding** field is then updated in one go by the observer. If more fields from **User** were needed to be displayed, the change would be purely in the XML layout file.

Data binding tended to fall out of favor with developers for a number of reasons:

- **Complexity**: Data binding introduced an additional layer of complexity to the development process. Developers need to understand the intricacies of data binding expressions, binding adapters, and other related concepts, which can be overwhelming for newcomers or less experienced developers. With data binding, UI logic can be embedded directly in the layout XML. Not only does this adds to the complexity, but it also violates SoC and made unit-testing of the embedded code impossible.
- **Learning curve**: Learning data binding can take time, especially for developers who are already familiar with traditional Android UI development approaches. The learning curve can deter some developers from adopting it, especially for smaller projects.
- **Documentation and resources**: At various points in time, data binding documentation and resources were lacking or less accessible compared to other libraries or frameworks. This hindered adoption when developers face difficulties finding relevant information.
- **Performance concerns**: Early versions of data binding had some performance concerns, especially when used improperly or with complex layouts.
- **Generated code**: In order for data binding to work, the compiler needed to generate dedicated classes. In the above example, that would be the **UserBinding** class (derived from the layout file name **user.xml** in this case). That generated code

would have been in Java. This could be time-consuming during development as every change to the binding arrangement required a rebuild of the whole project before the changes manifested in the generated class.

The biggest reason, however, why data binding fell out of favor is because Jetpack compose made it obsolete. Compose does not use XML layouts and data binding depends on them.

Model-View-Intent

One issue that neither MVP nor MVVM addressed was that of method proliferation. Every user or view controller event requires a method in the **ViewModel** or Presenter to handle it. Likewise, every UI view update made by the **ViewModel** or Presenter needs its own method to make the change. The more complex the UI got, the more methods were necessary to satisfy the requirements. Consider the previous MVP contract having been updated to accommodate new requirements:

```
1.  interface LoginContract {
2.      interface View {
3.          fun showLoading()
4.          fun hideLoading()
5.          fun showError(message: String)
6.          fun navigateToHome()
7.          fun navigateToHelp()
8.          fun showPwd()
9.          // …
10.     }
11.
12.     interface Presenter {
13.         fun loginButtonClicked(name: String, pwd: String)
14.         fun helpButtonClicked()
15.         fun showPwdButtonClicked()
16.         // ...
17.     }
18. }
```

A similar situation could occur in MVVM with the **ViewModel** providing many methods and hosting many observables for the view controller to subscribe to. This arrangement can be thought of multi-directional data flow. Such an arrangement becomes difficult to maintain and debug as it gets more complex. At least with contract MVP, there is a level of abstraction provided by the contract which is lost with MVVM.

MVI offers a solution to this problem. It is a design pattern used for building user interfaces in a reactive and declarative manner. MVI is a variation of the MVVM pattern, but it places a stronger emphasis on unidirectional data flow and immutability.

In the MVI pattern, the flow of data is organized into three main components:

- **Model**: This represents the state of the application. The model is immutable and holds all the data needed to render the UI. It does not contain any business logic.

  Note: This dedicated presentation layer Model should not be confused with the classes defined in the decoupled model layer specified by clean code architecture.

  Given the example above, the Model or Ui State will be represented as a data class:

  ```
  1. data class LoginUiState(
  2.     val loadState: LoginLoadState,
  3.     val errorMsg: String,
  4.     val showPassword: Boolean
  5. )
  ```

  Given **LoadState**:

  ```
  1. enum class LoginLoadState { IDLE, LOADING, FAILED }
  ```

- **View**: This displays the UI and observes the model's state changes. It does not hold any state or business logic. Instead, it only focuses on rendering the UI based on the received model/state.

- **Intent**: Represents user actions or events that are translated into changes in the model. Intents are emitted by the view and processed by the model, leading to state changes.

Note: This Intent is not to be confused with the Android Intent class used for navigating between activities.

This is typically passed back to the `ViewModel` in the form of an object of a sealed class:

```
1. sealed class LoginEvents {
2.     object OnHelpClicked : LoginEvents()
3.     object OnShowPwdClicked : LoginEvents()
4.     data class OnLoginClicked(
5.         val name: String, val pwd: String
6.     ) : LoginEvents()
7. }
```

Given this arrangement, the view will only ever have to listen to one observable on the `ViewModel`, and the `ViewModel` will only ever need one method to receive events/Intents.

```
1.  class LoginMviViewModelProto: ViewModel() {
2.
3.      val model = MutableStateFlow(
4.          initialState = LoginUiState(
5.              loadState = LoginLoadState.IDLE,
6.              errorMsg = "",
7.              showPassword = false
8.          )
9.      )
10.
11.     fun intent(intent: LoginEvents) {
12.         when(intent){
13.             LoginEvents.OnHelpClicked -> TODO()
14.             is LoginEvents.OnLoginClicked -> TODO()
15.             LoginEvents.OnShowPwdClicked -> TODO()
16.         }
17.     }
18. }
```

In this MVI **ViewModel**, **model** supplies a **StateFlow** with an initial value which can be observed by the view and is triggered on set up. The **intent** function receives events from the view and processes them, most likely with setting **model** to update the view. This is just a rough prototype to illustrate the concept. There is a lot missing that would make this a complete and correct solution. For example, the glaring omission of the navigation commands (**navigateToHome()**, **navigateToHelp()**), will be discussed shortly.

Key concepts and summary of MVI

There are a number of concepts that MVI aims to encapsulate and facilitate. These concepts are as follows:

- **Unidirectional data flow:** MVI enforces a strict one-way flow of data: View | Intent | Model | State | View. This helps to avoid data inconsistencies and makes the application's behavior more predictable.
- **Immutability:** The model's state is represented as an immutable data structure. When an Intent triggers a state change, a new immutable state is created, ensuring that changes are managed in a controlled and predictable manner.
- **Reactive programming:** MVI heavily relies on reactive programming concepts, like Kotlin Flow to handle asynchronous data flows and event handling.

- **Testing:** Because MVI emphasizes separation of concerns and a clear flow of data, testing becomes easier. Each component can be tested in isolation. We will discuss more on this in a later chapter.

Implementing MVI with Jetpack Compose

The reactive element of MVI makes it an ideal architecture to apply to Jetpack Compose UI. In fact, the official online documentation for Jetpack Compose architecture suggests an identical pattern, but there is no mention of MVI. It is simply referred as, **Unidirectional Data Flow** (**UDF**). The following diagrammatically depicts unidirectional flow:

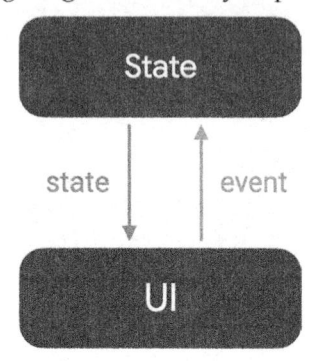

Figure 8.2: Unidirectional data flow (Source: developer.android.com)

This figure was pulled directly from the aforementioned site. In this section, we will propose a general implementation of UDF in the form of a `ViewModel` base class.

UDF base ViewModel: First pass

The goal of creating a base `ViewModel` is to enforce the UDF pattern and introduce consistency among the presentation layer solutions, with all the benefits, such as ease of maintenance and ownership transferability.

Referring back to the previous `LoginMviViewModelProto`, as a first attempt we could extract a templatized abstract class with a state flow and an event method:

```
1. abstract class UdfViewModel<EV : Event, ST : UiState>(
2.     private val initialUiState: ST
3. ) : ViewModel() {
4.
5.     private val _uiState: MutableStateFlow<ST> by lazy {
6.         MutableStateFlow(initialUiState)
7.     }
8.     val uiState: StateFlow<ST> by lazy { _uiState.asStateFlow() }
```

```
 9.
10.        abstract fun handleEvent(event: EV)
11.
12.        protected fun setUiState(reduce: ST.() -> ST) {
13.            _uiState.update { _uiState.value.reduce() }
14.        }
15. }
```

Event and **UiState** are blank interfaces:

```
1. interface UiState
2. interface Event
```

The code above covers the following points:

- Our sealed event and state data classes from the previous example, **LoginEvents** and `LoginLoadState` respectively would extend from the above interfaces.
- Using Jetpack Compose architecture UDF nomenclature, "model" becomes **UiState** and *intent* becomes **Event**.
- The initial state is supplied by the constructor parameter.
- **UiState** is now exposed as an immutable **StateFlow** with a private mutable backing field that can only be set by derived classes via the **setUiState** method. Previously, the **MutableStateFlow** was exposed as public and anything could change it.
- **setUiState** exposes a lambda for setting the backing field of **uiState** instead of setting it directly.. Also, the current state value is supplied as the scope for the lambda. This allows for more familiar Kotlin concise coding arrangement when setting the state from the **ViewModel** implementation.

For example:

```
1. setUiState { copy(loadState = LOADING) }
```

The use of the name **reduce** for the lambda that sets the state, is inspired by functional programming concepts and the behavior of reducing or aggregating values. In functional programming, **reduce** refers to the process of iteratively applying a binary operation to elements in a collection to accumulate a result. In our case, the *reduction* is the copying of the immutable existing state value with an altered member.

Notice that we use the **StateFlow update** method instead of just assigning the result of **reduce** to the states **value** member. This is done for the following reasons:

- **Atomicity and consistency**: The **update** method ensures that the state modification is performed atomically, even if multiple threads or coroutines are concurrently attempting to modify the same **MutableStateFlow**. This helps maintain consistency and avoids race conditions.

- **Thread safety**: The **update** method ensures that the state modification is thread-safe, which is crucial in multi-threaded or concurrent environments. It handles the synchronization required to prevent data races and other threading issues.

In fact, the race condition should never happen since there should only ever be one thread attempting to assign it. However, it is still recommended as a precaution.

Given that **LoginEvents** is made to implement **Event**, and **LoginUiState** implements **UiState**, our new login **ViewModel** could be extended from this templatized abstract class:

```
1. class LoginUdfViewModel : UdfViewModel<LoginEvents, LoginUiState>(
2.     initialUiState = LoginUiState(
3.         loadState = LoginLoadState.IDLE,
4.         errorMsg = "",
5.         showPassword = false
6.     )
7. ) {
8.     override fun handleEvent(event: LoginEvents) {
9.         when(event){
10.             LoginEvents.OnHelpClicked -> TODO()
11.             is LoginEvents.OnLoginClicked -> TODO()
12.             LoginEvents.OnShowPwdClicked -> TODO()
13.         }
14.     }
15. }
```

Implementing view in Jetpack compose

We now have state and event elements that a Composable can hook into directly, exactly as the official Android documentation specifies. The following code is a direct implementation of the UI in *Figure 8.1*:

```
1. @Composable
2. fun LoginUi(
3.     state: LoginUiState,
4.     event: (LoginEvents) -> Unit
5. ) {
6.     // ...
7.     Button(
8.         onClick = { event(LoginEvents.OnLoginClicked("name", "pwd"))
    }
```

```
9.      ) { Text(text = "Login") }
10.     // ...
11.     Text(text = state.errorMsg)
12. }
```

In this cut-down example, the event mechanism is supplied as a lambda that takes a **LoginEvents** and returns nothing, furthermore:

- There is a button labeled Login that when clicked, calls the **event** lambda with a **LoginEvents.OnLoginClicked**. Passing name and pwd are hardcoded in this case for brevity, but it would normally pick up from two **EditText**s.
- There is also a **Text** to display any error message that **state** might provide.

To complete this arrangement, a view controller is required to resolve the **ViewModel** and connect it to the Composable. Here is an example using an **Activity**:

```
1.  class LoginActivity : ComponentActivity() {
2.      private val loginViewModel by viewModels<LoginUdfViewModel>()
3.
4.      override fun onCreate(savedInstanceState: Bundle?) {
5.          super.onCreate(savedInstanceState)
6.          setContent {
7.              val state by loginViewModel.uiState.collectAsStateWithLifecycle()
8.              LoginUi(state = state, event = loginViewModel::handleEvent)
9.          }
10.     }
11. }
```

collectAsStateWithLifecycle requires the following build script entry:

```
1.  dependencies {
2.      implementation("androidx.lifecycle:lifecycle-runtime-compose:$vers")
3.      // ... where vers is the latest version
4.  }
```

Now, every time the **ViewModel** calls **setUiState**, **LoginUi** will be called with a new set of values to display and the **ViewModel** can receive events from **LoginUi** directly on its **handleEvent** method. The unidirectional data flow pattern, as specified by the original official documentation, is now complete.

UDF base ViewModel: Second pass

Unfortunately, there is more to the complete solution than what is specified by that particular diagram from the official documentation. Consider our original MVP contract for the view:

```
1.    interface View {
2.        fun showLoading()
3.        fun hideLoading()
4.        fun showError(message: String)
5.        fun navigateToHome()
6.        fun navigateToHelp()
7.        fun showPwd()
8.        // ...
9.    }
```

We have not done anything with navigation. The **ViewModel** needs some way to tell the view arrangement to navigate to **Home** or **Help**. **navigateToHome()** and **navigateToHelp()** cannot be objects in the **LoginUiState** sealed class as navigation is not a state of **LoginUi**. Furthermore, despite what some online solutions suggest, navigation should not be the responsibility of the **ViewModel** directly. This is something that the view controller, that is, the **Activity** in this case, is designed to do. Clearly, we need another separate data *channel* that connects only to the view controller from the **ViewModel**. Separate official Android documentation refers to this channel as a *side effect*. Therefore, we need to update our diagram as follows:

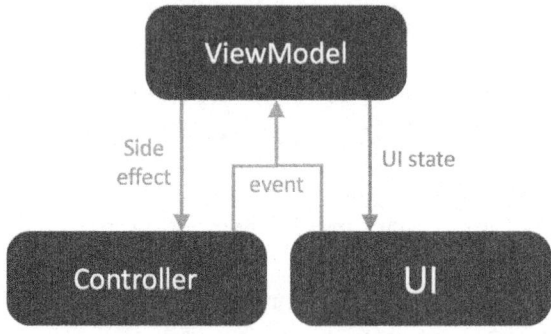

Figure 8.3: Updated UDF

Arguably, this is no longer unidirectional data flow as the flow is now split into two. We could rename it to **Bi-Directional Flow (BDF)** or **Split-Directional Flow (SDF)**, however, we will keep the UDF name as an indication of the concept's origins.

These side effects are usually for navigation but anything that does not directly update the current UI or requires underlying Android OS interaction can be considered a side effect, especially if the resulting call requires an **Activity** or a **Context** reference.

You may notice that an event can come from the Controller as well as the Compose UI. These tend to be captured Android OS events that are not part of the Compose, such as the system back button. There is no reason why such events cannot share the same sealed class as the Composable.

In keeping with the general MVI concept, this new side effect channel can be represented as a collection of objects or data classes in a sealed class, much like the event. The question is, how should we expose this to the Controller? It cannot be a **StateFlow**. As previously discussed, whilst **StateFlows** are hot, they deliver the last known state to the subscriber on subscription, meaning that an effect that is meant to be a one-off will be repeated with every re-subscription which is not desirable here. It cannot be a regular flow as regular flows are cold and will repeat the entire history of effects on re-subscription. What we need is a hot flow that does not have, or deliver, an initial value. On subscription, the subscriber should initially do nothing and just sit and wait for a value. Fortunately, Kotlin coroutines provide just such a mechanism – the **Channel** and our base **ViewModel** class can be updated to include this, as can be seen in the following code sample:

```
1. abstract class UdfViewModel<EV : Event, ST : UiState, EF : SideEffect>(
2.     private val initialUiState: ST
3. ) : ViewModel() {
4.
5.     private val _sideEffect: Channel<EF> = Channel()
6.     val sideEffect: Flow<EF> by lazy { _sideEffect.receiveAsFlow() }
7.
8.     protected fun sendSideEffect(builder: () -> EF) {
9.         viewModelScope.launch {
10.             _sideEffect.send(builder())
11.         }
12.     }
13.
14.     // ...
15. }
```

As before with **Event** and **UiState**, **SideEffect** is a blank interface:

```
1. interface SideEffect
```

UdfViewModel now has the following aspects:

- **sideEffect** is exposed as an immutable **Flow** with a private mutable **Channel** backing field that can only be accessed by derived classes via the **sendSideEffect** method.
- Unlike **UiState**, a state value is not being set. Instead a value is being sent to a subscriber, hence the name **sendSideEffect** as opposed to **setSideEffect**.

- The event to be sent is supplied by a lambda parameter on **sendSideEffect** that returns the event rather than just the event itself. This allows for more familiar Kotlin coding arrangement when sending the event from the **ViewModel** implementation.

For example:

1. sendSideEffect { LoginSideEffect.GotoHome }

The use of the **Channel** provides extra benefits. These benefits are as follows:

- Channels provide a unidirectional communication mechanism. Data sent through a channel is received by a single consumer, and the data flow is unidirectional from sender to receiver.
- Data sent through a channel is typically consumed by a single receiver. Once a value is consumed, it is removed from the channel.

Using the side effect in the controller

Given our login example, we can create a sealed class for our side effects as follows:

1. sealed class LoginSideEffect: SideEffect {
2.   object Close : LoginSideEffect()
3.   object GotoHome: LoginSideEffect()
4.   data class GotoHelp(val search: String) : LoginSideEffect()
5. }

In this new sealed class:

- We have included an extra **Close** side effect. It is good practice to capture any kind of back-press or custom Compose **close** button and refer it to the **ViewModel** for processing, even if it just relays the **Close** directly to the controller. Firstly, this is to maintain our data flow architecture and not have it float at the mercy of the OS and secondly, to allow for any future required checks-on-close, for example, rendering an *Are you sure* dialog.
- We have added a context search parameter for navigating to **Help**. This was not part of the original MVP contract but we have included it just as an example to show what is possible. Such a parameter could be passed to the new screen's **ViewModel** using existing built-in navigation frameworks.

Our new **ViewModel** implementation would be updated to include the new channel, as follows:

1. class LoginUdfViewModel
2.   : UdfViewModel<LoginEvents, LoginUiState, LoginSideEffect>(
3.   // …
4.) {
5.   // ...

6. }
7. The controller could then be updated to collect from this channel to process the side effects from the **ViewModel**:
8. override fun onCreate(savedInstanceState: Bundle?) {
9.   super.onCreate(savedInstanceState)
10.   setContent {
11.   // …
12.   val lifecycle = LocalLifecycleOwner.current
13.   LaunchedEffect(true){
14.   lifecycle.repeatOnLifecycle(Lifecycle.State.STARTED) {
15.   loginViewModel.sideEffect.collect { handleSideEffect(it) }
16.   }
17.   }
18.   }
19. }

In the previous code:

- The **LaunchedEffect** provides a coroutine scope and the code within the scope uses the same **repeatOnLifecycle** method that is used internally by **collectAsStateWithLifecycle**, insuring against memory leakage due to the subscriber being active whilst the app is in background.
- The **LaunchedEffect** is given any constant key, **true** in this case, to effectively disable any unwanted cancelling and relaunching of the coroutine scope.
- **handleSideEffect** is a private custom method in our controller dedicated to handling the specific side effects from our **ViewModel**.

We can reduce these extra lines of code to just one by creating a templatized **Composable** extension function on **Flow**:

1. @Composable
2. fun <T> Flow<T>.collectWithLifecycle(
3.   key: Any? = true,
4.   lifecycleOwner: LifecycleOwner = LocalLifecycleOwner.current,
5.   state: Lifecycle.State = Lifecycle.State.STARTED,
6.   block: (T) -> Unit
7.) = LaunchedEffect(key) {
8.   lifecycleOwner.repeatOnLifecycle(state) {
9.   collect { block(it) }
10.   }
11. }

This is based on the code inside **collectAsStateWithLifecycle** and until recently, **collectAsStateWithLifecycle** had to be manually created in this manner as well. By the time this book is published, there may be an official version of the above code somewhere in an Android library.

Once this is defined in a common infrastructure library, our complete Login controller can be written as in the following example:

```
1.  class LoginActivity : ComponentActivity() {
2.      private val loginViewModel by viewModels<LoginUdfViewModel2>()
3.
4.      override fun onCreate(savedInstanceState: Bundle?) {
5.          super.onCreate(savedInstanceState)
6.          setContent {
7.              val state by loginViewModel.uiState
8.                  .collectAsStateWithLifecycle()
9.              LoginUi(state = state, event = loginViewModel::handleEvent)
10.
11.             BackHandler {
12.                 loginViewModel.handleEvent(LoginEvents.OnClose)
13.             }
14.
15.             loginViewModel.sideEffect
16.                 .collectWithLifecycle { handleSideEffect(it) }
17.         }
18.     }
19.
20.     private fun handleSideEffect(sideEffect: LoginSideEffect) {
21.         when (sideEffect) {
22.             LoginSideEffect.Close -> finish()
23.             is LoginSideEffect.GotoHelp -> startActivity(Intent(/* .. */))
24.             LoginSideEffect.GotoHome -> startActivity(Intent(/* .. */))
25.         }
26.     }
27. }
```

From the preceding above, it can be seen that:

- **BackHandler** has been added to delegate the system back press to the **ViewModel**. This should always be done, even if there is no intermediate logic in the **ViewModel**.
- **handleSideEffect** has been added with a typical implementation for an Activity for completeness.

This arrangement will give a consistent look-and-feel to all controller types and implementations. The UDF **ViewModel** works seamlessly with Activities, Fragments and **Composable** functions acting as controllers.

Here is a similar example of the previous code in a **Fragment**:

```
1.  class LoginFragment : Fragment() {
2.      private val loginViewModel by viewModels<LoginUdfViewModel2>()
3.
4.      override fun onCreateView(
5.          inflater: LayoutInflater,
6.          container: ViewGroup?,
7.          savedInstanceState: Bundle?
8.      ): View = ComposeView(requireContext()).apply {
9.          setViewCompositionStrategy(
10.             ViewCompositionStrategy.DisposeOnViewTreeLifecycleDestroyed
11.         )
12.         setContent { /* same as Activity */ }
13.     }
14. }
```

From the preceding code we can see that:

- The **setViewCompositionStrategy** function is used to configure how the composition of Composables is handled within a particular **Composable** function.
- The **DisposeOnViewTreeLifecycleDestroyed** strategy is often used with Fragments. It automatically disposes of the Composables when the Fragment's view is destroyed. This is useful to ensure that Composables are properly managed and resources are released when the Fragment's view is no longer visible.
- As is often the case, the **viewModels** delegate is provided by a separate library, **androidx.fragment:fragment-ktx** in this case. This will change depending on the DI library used.

The following is an example of a **Composable** used as a controller:

```
1.  @Composable
2.  fun LoginScreen(
```

3.   loginViewModel: LoginUdfViewModel = viewModel(),
4.) { /* same as activity */ }

Here, the **viewModel** delegate is supplied by the **androidx.navigation:navigation-compose** library. Again, this will change depending on the DI library used.

UDF base ViewModel: Third pass

For most organizations, this is enough. There is another consideration however.

In his book, *Effective Java*, Joshua Bloch discusses the importance of programming to interfaces in the item headed *Refer to objects by their interfaces*. The item recommends that you should favor using interface types as method parameters, return types, and fields, rather than using concrete implementation types. This approach promotes flexibility, reusability, and maintainability in your code.

The idea is aligned with the principle of coding to the interface, which encourages the use of the most general interface that provides the necessary functionality. This practice allows the switching of implementations easily, provides better encapsulation, and improves the overall design of the code. A typical example of this is the classic Java List assignment as follows:

1. List<Integer> list = new ArrayList<>();

Unlike contract MVP, our current arrangement does not conform to this principle. The **ViewModel** instance returned by the field injector in the controller is fully accessible as a concrete class. That means there is nothing to stop an inexperienced developer simply adding public methods to the derived **ViewModel**, **LoginUdfViewModel** in our case, and using them in the controller, and breaking the pattern. The **ViewModel** could be cast to its parameterized base class on assignment:

1. private val loginViewModel:
2.   UdfViewModel<LoginEvents, LoginUiState, LoginSideEffect>
3.   by viewModels<LoginUdfViewModel>()

However, not only is this really difficult to read, but it also does not conform to the principle of referring to objects by their interface. It is, in fact, referring to the object by its abstract base class, meaning that public members in the **ViewModel** parent are still accessible.

The first thing to do in order to rectify this is to create an interface that the **ViewModel** can be referenced by. Examining our latest base class, we can extract just the elements that we want to expose, as follows:

1. interface Udf<EV : Event, ST : UiState, EF : SideEffect> {
2.   val uiState: StateFlow<ST>
3.   val sideEffect: Flow<EF>
4.   fun handleEvent(event: EV)
5. }

After that, we update our base class to implement this interface:

1. `abstract class UdfViewModel<EV : Event, ST : UiState, EF : SideEffect>(`
2. `    private val initialUiState: ST`
3. `) : Udf<EV, ST, EF>, ViewModel() {`
4. `    // ...`
5. `    override val uiState: StateFlow<ST> by lazy { /* ... */ }`
6. `    // ...`
7. `    override val sideEffect: Flow<EF> by lazy { /* ... */ }`
8.
9. `    abstract override fun handleEvent(event: EV)`
10. `    // ...`
11. `}`

In order to expose our Login **ViewModel** by the **Udf** interface, we should create a dedicated parameterized interface:

1. `interface LoginUdf : Udf<LoginEvents, LoginUiState, LoginSideEffect>`

The next step is to update the login **ViewModel** to implement this parameterized interface:

1. `class LoginUdfViewModel`
2. `    : LoginUdf, UdfViewModel<LoginEvents, LoginUiState, LoginSideEffect>(`
3. `    // ...`
4. `) { /* ... */ }`

After this, the only thing left to do is to change the way that the **ViewModel** is resolved in the controller. There are a number of ways to do this. It could just be cast at the point of assignment, as following:

1. `private val loginViewModel: LoginUdf by viewModels<LoginUdfViewModel>()`

However, if you are interested in locking the **ViewModel** implementation away from the controller completely, the parameterized interface could be extended with a companion factory function:

1. `interface LoginUdf : Udf<LoginEvents, LoginUiState, LoginSideEffect> {`
2. `    companion object {`
3. `        operator fun invoke(activity: ComponentActivity): Lazy<LoginUdf> =`
4. `            activity.viewModels<LoginUdfViewModel>()`
5.

```
 6.         operator fun invoke(fragment: Fragment): Lazy<LoginUdf> =
 7.             fragment.viewModels<LoginUdfViewModel>()
 8.
 9.         @Composable
10.         operator fun invoke(): LoginUdf =
    viewModel<LoginUdfViewModel>()
11.     }
12. }
```

Here, we have provided examples for factory functions to be used in each of an **Activity**, **Fragment** and **Composable**, but normally only the one that was needed would be defined.

Given this setup, the corresponding assignments in the controllers would look like this:

```
 1. class LoginActivity : ComponentActivity() {
 2.     private val loginViewModel by LoginUdf(this)
 3.     // ...
 4. }
 5.
 6. class LoginFragment: Fragment() {
 7.     private val loginViewModel by LoginUdf(this)
 8.     // ...
 9. }
10.
11. @Composable
12. fun LoginScreen(
13.     loginViewModel: LoginUdf = LoginUdf(),
14. ) { /* ... */ }
```

Our UDF arrangement now conforms to the principle of coding to the interface.

We like the use of the **invoke** operator for the factories because the corresponding assignment in the controller looks like it is from a constructor. However, this may be the exact reason why others may *not* like it, arguing that it is misleading. This, of course, can be changed to be a named function or value, like **factory** or **resolver**.

Also note that the extension functions that the factories call will vary depending on the DI package used, for example, **viewModel** in Koin instead of **viewModels** for the Activities and Fragments and **hiltViewModel** or **koinViewModel** for the Composable. The examples shown above assume no external DI package.

This fully evolved UDF pattern is now available free of charge as a Maven library. See **github.com/aimicor/uniflow**. The library also includes the definition of **collectWithLifecycle** previously described.

Disadvantage of the UDF/MVI pattern

The next chapter will explore the test-driven development. It will show how testing and test coverage is vital to maintain product code. The good thing about contract MVP was that it encouraged the developer to shift logic away from the UI to somewhere it could easily be unit-tested. UI code is notoriously difficult to test-drive so if there is no custom logic in it, then there is nothing to unit test.

By its very nature, MVI pushes custom logic back into the UI, albeit simple **if** statements or **when** switches on a UI state. Android has provided a testing mechanism for Composables, but it is for instrumentation testing and not for unit testing, which means that they require an attached device or emulator in order to run. This presents problems for continuous integration servers that pass a build against unit tests. Since Composables are state-driven, there is no getting away from this, regardless of the presentation architecture behind them.

Conclusion

In this chapter, we explored the evolution of the Android presentation architecture through MVC, MVP, and finally, MVI/ UDF, each time addressing the problems presented by the preceding arrangements and the solutions offered by the subsequent arrangements. Code examples were provided to help illustrate each concept in turn.

This chapter also offered a templatized implementation of UDF that allows the general arrangement of the code deriving from it to become uniform across all app features. It has been proven in the field that such uniformity decreases development time without decreasing code quality. The template used event-driven functionality built into the Kotlin language.

In the next chapter we take a look at Test-driven Development, or TDD. We examine its origins of the concept and provide examples of how it can be used to improve the quality and readability of your code and how it ties in with Dependency Injection. It also includes patterns for testing the UDF arrangement presented in this chapter.

Points to remember

- The recommended presentation layer architecture is constantly evolving.
- Due to the state-driven nature of Jetpack Compose, a state-driven presentation architecture is currently recommended.
- **LiveData** and Data Binding are now obsolete.
- Google recommends the **Unidirectional Flow (UDF)** pattern which is just **Model-View-Intent (MVI)** with different labels.
- Templatized abstract classes and interfaces can be used to impose a uniform presentation layer solution for all features of an app.
- The code for achieving the above is offered in this chapter.

Questions

1. What advantage does MVVM provide over MVP?
2. What issues in MVVM does UDF address?
3. Why is `LiveData` and Data Binding obsolete?
4. Why is UDF an ideal pattern to use with Jetpack Compose?
5. Using the offered UDF pattern, how might you organize your code so that the controller is unable to access or include the concrete implementation of the `ViewModel`?

Join our book's Discord space

Join the book's Discord Workspace for Latest updates, Offers, Tech happenings around the world, New Release and Sessions with the Authors:

https://discord.bpbonline.com

CHAPTER 9
Test-Driven Development with Mocking Libraries for Android

Introduction

Test-driven development (**TDD**) challenged the heart of traditional software techniques when it was first introduced as part of *eXtreme Programming* by *Kent Beck* in the late 1990s. Since then, it has been embraced and promoted by software gurus such as *Martin Fowler* and *Robert C. Martin*. Today, it is at or near the top of almost every Android developer's job specification list. This chapter describes the technique in detail and introduces the popular open-source mocking libraries used in its execution.

Structure

This chapter covers the following topics:
- The TDD cycle
- Advantages of TDD
- Historical obstacles to TDD
- The bowling game example
- Dependency injection and TDD
- Mocking libraries
- Disadvantages of mocking libraries

- Test driving Kotlin flows and StateFlows
- Test driving a UDF ViewModel
- Advanced flow testing scenarios

Objectives

In the previous chapters, we have used phrases such as *facilitates effective testing*, *unit tests*, *testability*, and so on. In this chapter, we delve deeper into these themes. By the end of this chapter, you will have a solid idea as to why dependency injection (externally defined dependencies, see *Chapter 6, Dependency Injection*) is such a useful technique for producing maintainable code.

The TDD cycle

Test-Driven Development (TDD) is a software development methodology that emphasizes writing tests before writing the actual code for a software component. The primary goal of TDD is to ensure the reliability, correctness, and maintainability of the codebase by continuously testing the software as it is being developed. TDD follows a cycle commonly known as the Red-Green-Refactor cycle:

- **Red**: In this phase, you write a failing test for the specific piece of functionality you want to implement. The test essentially defines the expected behavior of the code.
- **Green**: Next, you write the minimum amount of code necessary to make the failing test pass. The goal is to make the test go from failing (red) to passing (green) without adding any unnecessary code.
- **Refactor (Blue)**: After the test passes, you refactor the code to improve its design, readability, and maintainability. This step ensures that the code remains clean and follows best practices.

See the following examples. The cycle is then repeated, with additional tests and functionality being added incrementally. This process helps catch bugs early in the development process, encourages modular and loosely coupled code, and provides a safety net when making changes or refactoring existing code.

Advantages of TDD

Some advantages of TDD include the following:

- **Improved code quality**: By writing tests before code, developers focus on the desired behavior and edge cases, resulting in more robust and reliable code.
- **Faster debugging**: Since issues are caught early by the tests, debugging becomes easier and less time-consuming.

- **Better design**: TDD promotes modular and well-structured code because tests force developers to think about the interfaces and interactions between components.
- **Regression prevention**: As the codebase evolves, the test suite ensures that existing functionality continues to work as expected, preventing regressions.
- **Documentation**: Test cases serve as documentation, illustrating how different parts of the system are intended to work.
- **Confidence for refactoring**: With a comprehensive test suite, developers can refactor the code with confidence, knowing that if they break something, the tests will catch it.

This last point is especially valuable when attempting to write code that is readable by not just yourself but by other developers who are tasked with maintaining your code. It finally dispels the unofficial rule that, *if it is not broken, do not try and fix it*. The unit test code that is a result of TDD is often referred to as a test *harness*. It is a safety harness or net to give the developer confidence to make structural improvements without getting the blame for introducing a regression.

Historical obstacles to TDD

The benefits of TDD are well recognized today, but there was a time when the industry considered it a hindrance. There was a misconception that focusing on writing tests before production code would slow down development. In fact, the opposite is true. TDD is a code development tool. You start writing tests against how you would like the production code to work at a high level. In other words, you write calls in your test code against methods in your product code to get an expected result before those product code methods have been written. This is where the *Design* in TDD comes in. Furthermore, there was a misunderstanding around the phrase *writing tests before production code*. A better phrase might be *developing production code with tests* since the process is iterative.

Another criticism was that it would impact progress in situations where requirements are highly uncertain and subject to frequent changes. This might be true, but a fluid specification will slow down any project. Once the developer is skilled in TDD, they simply add new tests or change existing ones in the process of implementing the new requirement.

Worse, in years gone by, under-informed product owners, who had heard that test harnesses were *a good thing to have*, would insist that developers create them without making sure they understood the TDD process and even assuming that the developers understood it themselves. This inevitably led to tests being written *after* the production code had been developed and manually tested. This really did slow down production as the tests became an afterthought and were difficult to write against tightly-coupled code. No doubt, this malpractice added to the misconception that TDD slows down development.

The best way to describe the technique is via an example.

The bowling game example

The *bowling game* example is a classic demonstration of using TDD to implement a scoring system for a game of bowling. In his series of *Clean Coders* videos, *Robert C. Martin AKA Uncle Bob* describes how he developed this example on location at a C++ conference in the late 1990s, where he and his colleague sketched it out in a hotel room on paper napkins.

Typing *Bowling Game TDD* into any search engine will yield dozens of hits, including step-by-step videos demonstrating TDD in a variety of coding languages using this example. A summary has been included here for completeness. The coding environment for unit testing is included with every new project created in Android Studio. Just look for the `ExampleUnitTest` class.

Ten-pin bowling is a popular bowling game played with ten pins arranged in a triangular formation at the end of a lane. The objective is to knock down as many pins as possible with a bowling ball. The scoring in ten-pin bowling is based on the number of pins knocked down and bonuses earned for strikes and spares. Each pin knocked down is worth one point. The game has the following additional scoring rules:

- **Strike**: If a player knocks down all ten pins with the first roll of a frame, they earn 10 points plus the total number of pins knocked down with their next two rolls. The next frame's rolls will determine the bonus.
- **Spare**: If a player knocks down all ten pins with the two rolls of a frame, they earn 10 points plus the total number of pins knocked down with their next roll. The next frame's first roll will determine the bonus.
- **Open frame**: If a player does not get a strike or spare, their points for that frame are simply the total number of pins knocked down in that frame.
- **Tenth frame**: The tenth frame is special because it allows a player to throw up to three rolls if they get a strike or a spare. If a player gets a strike in the first roll, they will have two more rolls to complete the frame. If a player gets a spare in the first two rolls, they will have one more roll to complete the frame. The maximum score for a game is 300, achieved by getting strikes in all ten frames and additional rolls in the tenth frame if necessary.

With traditional software design, a developer may be inclined to sketch out something like the following:

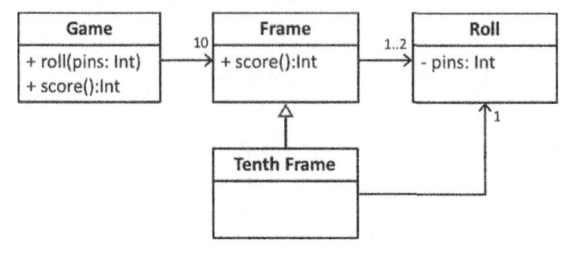

Figure 9.1: Design without TDD

It would seem reasonable to have a game class that has ten instances of frame class. A frame class could have one or two instances of a Roll class, and finally, there is a Frame variant, the *Tenth Frame*, that can have an extra instance of **Roll**.

TDD promises to yield the simplest possible designs when applying the following three rules:

- You are not allowed to write any production code until you have a failing unit test.
- You cannot write more of a test than is sufficient to fail. Not compiling is failing.
- You are not allowed to write more production code than is sufficient to pass the current failing test.

Given the rules of bowling, we can begin writing tests starting with the simplest scenario. The steps are as follows:

1. Write a failing test for rolling a gutter game (Red phase):

```
1. class BowlingGameTest {
2.     @Test
3.     fun 'GIVEN bowling WHEN all gutter balls THEN score 0'() {
4.         // Given
5.         val game = BowlingGame()
6.         // When
7.         repeat(20) { game.roll(0) }
8.         // Then
9.         assertEquals(0, game.score())
10.    }
11. }
```

In the preceding example, we have skipped several iterations of Red-Green-Blue for brevity purposes. A compilation error counts as a failure so, as soon as we attempt to declare an instance of **BowlingGame**, we need to write a basic definition for it to make our test go green.

At that point, we assume if we even need a class at all. In some scenarios, it may become evident from the process that a first-class function would suffice. However, the following calls to **roll()** and then subsequently to **score()**, each requiring their own fix to go green, confirms our choice.

Here are a couple of further things to note here:

- The test function names should describe the test. It has become customary to use the same format for the test function names as is used in **Behavioral-Driven Design (BDD)**. However, it is enough to say that requirement specifications in BDD are broken down and written in the form **given <some pre-condition> when <some event> then <expected result>**.

- It has also become customary to leverage Kotlin's back-ticked function name feature allowing spaces. This makes the resulting reports much easier to read.
2. Write the minimum code to make the test pass (Green phase):

```
1. class BowlingGame {
2.     private var score = 0
3.
4.     // Logic to record the number of pins knocked down
5.     fun roll(pins: Int) {}
6.     fun score(): Int = score
7. }
```

3. Refactor the code (Blue phase):

Since this is just a few lines of code, there is no refactoring required at this point.

Repeat the red-green-blue process for each of increasingly more complex scenarios. For example, the following tests could be:

GIVEN bowling game WHEN all ones THEN score is 20

GIVEN bowling game WHEN one spare THEN next roll added to first frame

GIVEN bowling game WHEN one strike THEN next two rolls added to first frame

…and so on, and each time refactor the production code before moving on to the next test.

During the iterative TDD process, poor design decisions will be flushed out and corrected. For example, until the test for a spare is made, it would be reasonable to have the **roll** method increment the final score each time it is called. Once we try to test drive a spare, we realize that this is misplaced responsibility and that the **score** function should be the method actually calculating the score.

After several red-green-blue iterations we end up with a surprisingly concise solution, as follows:

```
1. class BowlingGame {
2.     private var rolls = IntArray(21)   // max number of possible rolls
3.     private var currentRoll = 0
4.
5.     fun roll(pins: Int) {
6.         rolls[currentRoll++] = pins
7.     }
8.
```

```
9.      fun score(): Int {
10.         var score = 0
11.         var rollIndex = 0
12.
13.         repeat(10) {
14.             if (isStrike(rollIndex)) {
15.                 score += 10 + strikeBonus(rollIndex)
16.                 rollIndex++
17.             } else if (isSpare(rollIndex)) {
18.                 score += 10 + spareBonus(rollIndex)
19.                 rollIndex += 2
20.             } else {
21.                 score += rolls[rollIndex] + rolls[rollIndex + 1]
22.                 rollIndex += 2
23.             }
24.         }
25.
26.         return score
27.     }
28.
29.     private fun isStrike(rollIndex: Int): Boolean = rolls[rollIndex] == 10
30.
31.     private fun isSpare(rollIndex: Int): Boolean =
32.         rolls[rollIndex] + rolls[rollIndex + 1] == 10
33.
34.     private fun strikeBonus(rollIndex: Int): Int =
35.         rolls[rollIndex + 1] + rolls[rollIndex + 2]
36.
37.     private fun spareBonus(rollIndex: Int): Int = rolls[rollIndex + 2]
38. }
```

The original four-class design has been reduced to one and the **score** function is just a loop with two **if** statements. As you can see, the code reads a lot like the rules for scoring in ten-pin bowling. Compare this to the hundreds of lines of code we would have ended up with, had we followed the original design.

The misplaced responsibility issue (code handling functionality that logically belongs elsewhere) highlights the importance of method naming. Had the methods been name `recordRoll` and `getFinalScore` as opposed to `roll` and `score`, this might not have happened. However, it was only the TDD process that revealed this retrospectively.

It is important to refactor your test code at the same time as the production code. Good quality test code will accompany good quality production code and besides, the test code is also meant to act as documentation for the production code.

Dependency injection and TDD

As previously discussed, DI involves providing the necessary dependencies, for example, objects, services, and components to a class rather than having the class create or manage them itself. This separation of concerns can greatly enhance the TDD process in several ways:

- **Test doubles**: Test doubles such as mocks, stubs, and fakes are often used to replace real dependencies during testing. DI makes it easier to inject these test doubles, enabling you to simulate different scenarios and behaviors to thoroughly test the interactions between components.
    - o Mocks focus on verifying interactions and method calls between the unit under test and its dependencies. They set expectations for interactions and fail the test if the interactions do not match expectations. Typically, a mocking library is required to create mock objects in test code (see next section).
    - o Fakes are simplified implementations of dependencies used in testing to reduce complexity and improve testing speed. They aim to provide the required functionality in a simplified manner. Fakes are typically interface implementations local to the test.
    - o Stubs are used to control the behavior of dependencies by providing predefined responses to method calls. They allow you to isolate and simulate different scenarios during testing. Both a fake and a mock, for example, could provide an implementation of a method to return a value that would satisfy the preconditions of a test – often referred as, "stubbing out" a method.
- **Isolation of dependencies**: In TDD, you want to test one unit of code, for example, a class in isolation from its dependencies. By using DI, you can easily provide mock objects or stubs as dependencies during testing, allowing you to control their behavior and isolate the unit under test.
- **Controlled state**: In TDD, you want to ensure that your tests are predictable and reliable. By injecting dependencies, you can initialize the class being tested with specific data and behaviors, ensuring a consistent and controlled state for each test.
- **Behavior verification**: With DI, you can easily verify that the expected interactions between the unit under test and its dependencies are taking place. This helps you write more focused and precise tests that validate the correct interactions.

- **Faster feedback**: TDD emphasizes the importance of quick feedback loops. When you can easily swap out real implementations for test doubles using DI, you can write tests that run faster and provide feedback more quickly.
- **Refactoring confidence**: In TDD, you are encouraged to refactor code with confidence. DI helps ensure that your unit tests remain unaffected by changes to the internal implementations of your class, as long as the public contract (interface) remains the same.
- **Encourages modularity**: By following DI principles, you naturally design your classes to be more modular and loosely coupled. This design makes it easier to replace and inject dependencies, promoting better overall software architecture.
- **Easier integration testing**: While unit tests focus on isolated components, integration tests verify the interactions between various components. DI aids in setting up different configurations for integration testing, allowing you to test the integration points effectively.

Mocking libraries

Mocking libraries are tools used in software testing to create and manage *mock objects* or *test doubles*. They simulate the behavior of real objects or dependencies in a controlled manner during unit testing. These libraries provide an easier and more efficient way to set up, define expectations for, and verify interactions with these mock objects. Using mocking libraries is particularly beneficial when practicing TDD or conducting unit testing in general.

Using a mocking library will considerably reduce the effort of injecting test doubles into your subject-under-test. For example, consider the following use case input port that needs a test-driven implementation:

```
1. interface UserDetailsUseCase {
2.     suspend operator fun invoke(
3.         name: String, pwd: String
4.     ): Result<UserDetails>
5. }
```

Here, the username and password strings are submitted in a coroutine environment. If successful, the user details are returned in a **Result** wrapper.

We know that going in the implementation is going to require a use case input port (see *Chapter 4, Clean Code Architecture*), in the form of a repository interface, for example:

```
1. interface UserDetailsRepository {
2.     suspend fun loginAndGetDetails(
3.         user: String, pwd: String
4.     ): Result<UserDetails>
5. }
```

In our test, we need to create a mock from `UserDetailsRepository` because we need to change its behavior in a controlled manner. Say we then wanted to write a test to drive the failure behavior of the use case without the assistance of a mocking library (using a fake instead):

```
1.  class UserDetailsUseCaseImplTest {
2.      private lateinit var repoMock: UserDetailsRepository
3.
4.      @Test
5.      fun 'GIVEN repo fail WHEN login THEN fail returned'() = runTest {
6.          // Given
7.          val failure = Result.failure(Throwable())
8.          repoFake = object : UserDetailsRepository {
9.              override suspend fun loginAndGetDetails(
10.                 user: String, pwd: String
11.             ): Result<UserDetails> = failure
12.         }
13.         val sut = UserDetailsUseCaseImpl(repoFake)
14.
15.         // When
16.         val result = sut("name", "pwd")
17.
18.         // Then
19.         assertEquals(failure, result)
20.     }
21. }
```

In this example, we have already completed one red-green-blue iteration to create the `UserDetailsUseCaseImpl` class and assign an instance to **Subject-Under-Test** (**SUT**). The fake repository object has been stubbed to always return `failure`. We are testing the coroutine `suspend invoke` operator so the test needs to be in coroutine scope. This is provided by the first-class function `runTest`. This function comes packaged with the coroutines test library and you will need to add the following to your `build.gradle` file:

```
1.  testImplementation 'org.jetbrains.kotlinx:kotlinx-coroutines-
    test:1.7.0'
```

The point of this example is to draw attention to the setup of the injected `repoMock` dependency. In order to force a failure, we need to create a fake implementation of `UserDetailsRepository` and return a failure on its `loginAndGetDetails` method. Even in this example, you can see that the code required for this is verbose. Imagine if

`UserDetailsRepository` specified a dozen different signatures. The mock would need to provide dummy implementations for all of them.

Mockito

Until Kotlin gained popularity, the mocking library of choice for Java was *Mockito*, developed by *Szczepan Faber*. He started working on the framework in 2007 while he was employed at *Google*. Mockito was initially created as an open-source project to provide a simpler and more user-friendly alternative to existing Java mocking frameworks. The project gained popularity rapidly due to its intuitive API, which made it easier for developers to write and understand tests involving mock objects.

Mockito was officially released in 2008, and since then, it has become one of the most widely used and respected mocking frameworks in the Java development community. Its success can be attributed to its focus on simplicity, readability, and ease of use, aligning well with the principles of TDD and encouraging developers to write effective unit tests.

MockK

Mockito could be used to test Kotlin code, but it was not designed for it. A new library was required that could handle Kotlin's specifics. MockK was developed by *Eugene Petrenko*, a software engineer and a Kotlin enthusiast. The project was initiated in 2016 as an open-source effort to provide a Kotlin-focused mocking library. Eugene Petrenko aimed to create a mocking framework that would leverage Kotlin's features and syntax to offer a more natural and expressive way of writing tests involving mock objects.

MockK gained traction quickly in the Kotlin community due to its alignment with Kotlin's philosophy of conciseness and expressiveness. It addressed some of the pain points that Kotlin developers experienced when using existing Java-focused mocking frameworks in Kotlin projects. The keywords and syntax used did not stray far from Mockito making the transition relatively painless.

Key features and concepts of MockK are as follows:

- **Kotlin-focused syntax**: MockK takes advantage of Kotlin's concise syntax, making it feel more natural and idiomatic for Kotlin developers.
- **Mock creation**: MockK allows you to create mock objects using the `mockk()` function. For example, `val myServiceMock = mockk<MyService>()`.
- **Stubbing**: You can define the behavior of mock methods using the `every { ... } returns ...` syntax. This syntax is designed to be expressive and easy to read.
- **Verification**: MockK provides the `verify { ... }` function to verify if the specific methods were called on mock objects. The verification syntax is similarly concise and clear.
- **Argument matchers**: MockK supports argument matchers for flexible argument matching when stubbing or verifying method calls.

- **Partial mocks (spying)**: MockK allows you to create spies, which are partial mock objects that wrap real instances and provide control over specific method behavior.
- **Coroutines support**: MockK provides extensions for working with Kotlin coroutines, making it easy to mock and verify suspending functions.
- **Domain-Specific Language (DSL)**: MockK employs a DSL-style syntax that aims to provide a fluent and intuitive way to work with mock objects.

Applying MockK to our `UserDetailsUseCase` example, the test case can be re-written more succinctly:

```
1.  class UserDetailsUseCaseImplTest {
2.      private val repoMock = mockk<UserDetailsRepository>()
3.      private val sut by lazy { UserDetailsUseCaseImpl(repoMock) }
4.
5.      @Test
6.      fun 'GIVEN repo fail WHEN login THEN fail returned'() = runTest {
7.          // Given
8.          val fail = Result.failure(Throwable())
9.          coEvery { repoMock.loginAndGetDetails(any(), any()) } returns fail
10.
11.         // When
12.         val result = sut("name", "pwd")
13.
14.         // Then
15.         assertEquals(fail, result)
16.     }
17. }
```

This arrangement allows the lazy initialization of **sut** as a field so that it can be reused in subsequent tests. The coroutine variant of **every**, **coEvery**, was used to set up a stubbed failed response from the `loginAndGetDetails` method. We could also have used the coroutine variant of **verify**, **coVerify**, to test that the `loginAndGetDetails` method was used to get the result but, in this case, it was not necessary. The **verify** family should only really be used to test wrappers, that is, when the purpose of the functionality is to call into another library without returning anything. Analytics packages are a good example of this. They tend to require wrappers to allow easier swapping out of analytics providers.

In summary, MockK is specifically tailored to the Kotlin language, which allows it to provide a more Kotlin-like experience for mocking and testing. Its concise syntax, compatibility with Kotlin's features, and support for modern testing practices make it a popular choice among Kotlin developers who want to write effective unit tests while leveraging the strengths of the language.

Disadvantages of mocking libraries

Mockito and especially MockK, provide enormous flexibility with what can be mocked, faked and stubbed. For example, the MockK update to the test above, would have been the same regardless of how many signatures `UserDetailsRepository` has defined. In fact, it did not even need to be an interface. MockK can mock and stub concrete classes just as easily as interfaces. In addition, MockK can be used to stub out calls (provide fake responses) to static functions (scoped or un-scoped first-class functions without containing classes) and Kotlin companion objects.

With all of this flexibility, it becomes much easier to ignore some of the better coding practices while test-driving your code.

It would no longer be necessary to observe the **interface segregation principle (ISP)** for testing purposes. You only need to stub the method you are using. The test would not show up ISP violations when you do not have to provide implementations for methods you are not using.

Apart from injected dependencies, a unit test should not be concerned with how the production code has been internally implemented in order to test it. Being able to mock and stub statics used in internal implementation could lead to the temptation of violating this principle, resulting in fragile tests.

Despite these issues, we would still recommend the use of MockK for unit testing. The benefits outweigh the disadvantages in regard to ease of use and readability. Much of the flexibility that exists in the library is there to support the refactoring of legacy code. In this case, unit tests need to be written retrospectively to provide a safety harness preventing regressions during the refactor. Precautions should be taken to avoid these issues when test driving new code.

Test driving Kotlin flows and StateFlows

In *Chapter 8, Presentation Layer Evolution in Compose*, we discussed the use of Kotlin flows to implement a state-driven unidirectional data flow presentation architecture centered around a `ViewModel`. In this section we discuss how to test-drive a `ViewModel` derived from this pattern.

Problems associated with test-driving flows

Unit testing Kotlin flows, while powerful and beneficial, can present a few challenges due to their asynchronous and reactive nature. Some of the common issues you might encounter when unit testing Kotlin flows include:

- **Asynchronous behavior**: Flows emit values asynchronously, which can make it challenging to write tests that correctly handle the timing of emissions, especially when testing complex sequences of events.
- **Timing dependencies**: Flows that use `delay` or other timing-related operations may lead to timing-dependent tests. Ensuring that tests are stable and not affected by slight timing variations, can be a challenge.
- **Coroutines and dispatchers**: Flows are closely tied to coroutines, and proper management of coroutine scopes, dispatchers, and test execution contexts is crucial to ensure accurate testing.
- **Cancellation handling**: Testing cancellation scenarios, such as cancelling a flow collector, can be complex due to the interaction between coroutines and flows.
- **Verification and assertion**: Verifying the emitted values, error cases, and completion can require custom logic and assertions, particularly for complex flows or flows that emit multiple values.
- **Shared mutable state**: Flows that involve shared mutable state or external dependencies might require additional setup and teardown steps to isolate and manage state changes during testing.
- **Test setup and teardown**: Setting up and tearing down test environments that involve flows and coroutines can be more complex compared to testing synchronous code.

To address these challenges and write effective unit tests for Kotlin flows, you can follow best practices and utilize testing libraries and techniques specifically designed for asynchronous code, such as:

- Using testing frameworks like Turbine (described later in this chapter), MockK (see above), and kotlinx-coroutines-test (see below) to simplify asynchronous testing and provide utilities for coroutine management.
- Isolating flows from external dependencies and using test to control the behavior of external components.
- Managing coroutine contexts and dispatchers (e.g., which dispatcher thread or scope to run your coroutine on) to ensure that your tests execute as expected.
- Properly handling cancellation and completion scenarios to avoid test leaks and ensure tests are properly cleaned up.
- Using assertions and verifications (`assert`, `verify`) to validate the emitted values, errors, and completion states of Flows.

By being aware of these potential challenges and utilizing appropriate testing strategies and libraries, you can overcome these issues and write reliable and maintainable unit tests for Kotlin flows.

kotlinx-coroutines-test and dispatchers

`kotlinx-coroutines-test` is a testing library provided by the Kotlin coroutines project, and is a part of Kotlin's official libraries. It simplifies the testing of code that uses Kotlin coroutines and offers utilities and extensions for testing coroutines and asynchronous code in a controlled and deterministic manner. This library is particularly useful when writing unit tests for functions, methods, or components that involve coroutine-based concurrency.

Here are some of the key features and utilities provided by `kotlinx-coroutines-test`:

- **Test coroutine builders**: `kotlinx-coroutines-test` provides coroutine builders like `runTest`, `TestScope`, and `StandardCoroutineDispatcher` that allow you to create and run coroutines in a controlled testing environment. These builders allow you to write coroutine-based tests that execute synchronously.
- **Advancing time**: You can manually advance the virtual time of coroutines using functions like `advanceTimeBy` and `advanceUntilIdle`. This is particularly useful for testing code that relies on timeouts and delays.
- **Testing suspended functions**: You can test functions that contain **suspend** modifiers by using the provided coroutine builders. This enables you to write tests that verify the behavior of suspend functions in isolation.
- **Testing concurrent and parallel code**: The library allows you to write tests for concurrent and parallel code by creating multiple coroutines and controlling their execution and interaction.
- **Controlled execution**: You have fine-grained control over the execution of coroutines, allowing you to pause, resume, and cancel them as needed for testing purposes.

Here is an example of how `kotlinx-coroutines-test` might be used to write a test for a coroutine function:

```
1.  suspend fun performAsyncOperation(): Int {
2.      delay(100000)
3.      return 42
4.  }
5.
6.  fun main() = runTest {
7.      val deferredResult = async { performAsyncOperation() }
8.      val result = deferredResult.await()
9.      assert(result == 42)
10. }
```

This will run and immediately pass the assertion, despite the large time delay in `performAsyncOperation`. This is because internally, `runTest` uses a special test version of the coroutine task dispatcher that ignores time delays. This also works because the only coroutine scope used is the one that **runTest** creates. If our product code nests its own coroutine scope we need to inject different dispatchers. This is always the case with the previously defined **UdfViewModel** base.

kotlinx-coroutines-test provides two such test dispatchers:

- **StandardTestDispatcher**: Guarantees the order of execution of the coroutine tasks but does not automatically start them. This needs to be done with the **runCurrent** method scoped within **runTest**.
- **UnconfinedTestDispatcher**: Automatically starts the coroutine tasks but does not guarantee the execution order.

In a JUnit environment, the dispatcher can be overridden with **Dispatchers.setMain()** and reset with **Dispatchers.resetMain()**:

```
1. @Before
2. fun 'set up'() {
3.     Dispatchers.setMain(UnconfinedTestDispatcher())
4. }
5.
6. @After
7. fun 'tear down'() {
8.     Dispatchers.resetMain()
9. }
```

Since these lines of code are likely to be repeated for every instance of **UdfViewModel**, the recommended way of doing this, however, is to create a test rule:

```
 1. class MainDispatcherRule(
 2.     private val dispatcher: TestDispatcher = UnconfinedTestDispatcher(),
 3. ) : TestWatcher() {
 4.     override fun starting(description: Description) {
 5.         Dispatchers.setMain(dispatcher)
 6.     }
 7.
 8.     override fun finished(description: Description) {
 9.         Dispatchers.resetMain()
10.     }
11. }
```

This is the formally recommended method and this code was pulled directly from the official Android developer site. Once it has been added to a commonly accessible infrastructure library you need only reference it as a member in your test class:

```
1. @get:Rule
2. val mainDispatcherRule = MainDispatcherRule()
```

Turbine mocking library

Turbine is a testing library for Kotlin's flow and StateFlow APIs. It is designed to simplify and enhance unit testing of asynchronous flows by providing utilities to work with Kotlin's coroutines and flows in a controlled and predictable manner. Turbine aims to make testing asynchronous code, such as flows and StateFlows, more straightforward and less error-prone.

Some key features and concepts of turbine include:

- **Testing coroutines**: Turbine builds upon Kotlin's coroutine testing utilities, such as **runTest**, to provide a familiar and consistent testing experience for asynchronous code.
- **Collectors**: Turbine provides special collectors (logic to capture values emitted by a flow) that allow you to collect values emitted by flows and StateFlows in a synchronous and controlled manner during tests.
- **Sequence-based verification**: Turbine lets you create a sequence of expected values and errors. As the flow emits values, turbine matches them against the sequence to ensure the correct order of emissions.
- **Advanced testing scenarios**: Turbine handles more complex testing scenarios, such as timeouts, exceptions, and suspending functions within flows.
- **Custom collectors**: You can also create your own custom collectors with specific verification logic to fit your testing requirements.

Turbine simplifies the process of testing flows and StateFlows by abstracting away the complexities of dealing with asynchronous behavior, coroutines, and collecting values. This can lead to more focused and maintainable unit tests for your asynchronous code.

For a simple example, here is a unit test of asynchronous code without turbine:

```
1.  @Test
2.  fun 'test synchronous flow emission without Turbine'() = runTest {
3.      val flow = flow {
4.          emit(1)
5.          delay(100)
6.          emit(2)
7.      }
8.
9.      val collectedValues = mutableListOf<Int>()
10.     launch {
```

```
11.            flow.collect { value ->
12.                collectedValues.add(value)
13.            }
14.     }
15.
16.     advanceTimeBy(1)
17.     assertEquals(listOf(1), collectedValues)
18.     advanceTimeBy(101)
19.     assertEquals(listOf(1, 2), collectedValues)
20. }
```

In order to test this flow, we needed to launch a collection of the flow in a separate thread into a list. On the main thread, we use **advanceTimeBy** (part of the **kotlinx-coroutines-test** library) to jump the clock forward and then query the list for the expected collected values.

The following is an equivalent test using Turbine:

```
1. @Test
2. fun 'test synchronous flow emission with Turbine'() = runTest {
3.     val flow = flow {
4.         emit(1)
5.         delay(100)
6.         emit(2)
7.     }
8.
9.     flow.test {
10.        assertEquals(1, expectMostRecentItem())
11.        advanceTimeBy(101)
12.        assertEquals(2, expectMostRecentItem())
13.        awaitComplete()
14.    }
15. }
```

Turbine provides the following extension function:

```
1. public suspend fun <T> Flow<T>.test()
```

The function supplies a **TurbineTestContext** in a lambda scope. This context provides the following methods for accessing the values in a flow:

- **awaitItem()**: Suspends the thread and waits for an item to be emitted. Ignores any delays in the product code and times out and fails after one second if nothing is emitted.

- **awaitComplete()**: Suspend the thread until the flow completes without an exception.
- **awaitError()**: Suspend the thread until the flow completes with a **Throwable**. The **Throwable** is returned for possible further testing.
- **awaitEvent()**: Suspend the thread and wait until the flow returns something. This can be an emitted item, a complete or a **Throwable** wrapped in an **Event** object.
- **expectMostRecentItem()**: Receives the most recently emitted item and ignores any previous ones. Respects any delays in the product code and times out and fails after one second if nothing is emitted.
- **expectNoEvents()**: Assert that there are no unconsumed events which have already been received.
- **skipItems(count: Int)**: Receive count items and ignore them.
- **cancel()**: Terminate any backing coroutines.
- **cancelAndIgnoreRemainingEvents()**: Terminate any backing coroutines and ignores any remaining events.
- **cancelAndConsumeRemainingEvents()**: Terminates any backing coroutines and consumes any remaining events, returning them in a list.
- **ensureAllEventsConsumed()**: Assert all events were consumed.

Test driving a UDF ViewModel

In *Chapter 8, Presentation Layer Evolution in Compose*, we discussed the state-driven UDF/MVI presentation layer pattern for driving composable UIs, and proposed a **ViewModel** base class for achieving this. In this section, we will describe how to test drive a **ViewModel** derived from this base class using Mockk and Turbine.

Given our login example in *Chapter 8, Presentation Layer Evolution in Compose*, we could start writing our test.

As previously described, with TDD you would start with the simplest scenario. In most (but not all) cases, this is the ViewModels response to the back key or close button event as this is usually just a straight-through connection:

```
1. class LoginUdfViewModelTest {
2.
3.     @get:Rule
4.     val mainDispatcherRule = MainDispatcherRule()
5.
6.     @Test
7.     fun 'GIVEN sut WHEN back key event THEN close side effect'() =
8.         runTest {
```

```
 9.          // Given
10.          sut
11.      }
12. }
```

A compilation error is a failure (*red*). Our test has already failed because we have not defined a subject-under-test. To carry on from this point, we could just create a very basic **ViewModel**:

```
1. class LoginUdfViewModel : UdfViewModel<Event, UiState, SideEffect>(
2.     initialUiState = object : UiState {}
3. ) {
4.     override fun handleEvent(event: Event) {}
5. }
```

Our test now compiles and there is no refactoring needed so we can move on. At this point, we have not defined any events, states or side effects. It is just the bare minimum to get our test to pass. We can now continue writing our test:

```
 1. class LoginUdfViewModelTest {
 2.
 3.     private val sut by lazy { LoginUdfViewModel() }
 4.
 5.     @Test
 6.     fun 'GIVEN sut WHEN back key event THEN close side effect'() =
 7.         runTest {
 8.             // Given
 9.             sut.sideEffect.test {
10.                 expectNoEvents()
11.
12.                 // When
13.                 sut.handleEvent(LoginEvent.OnClose)
14.             }
15.         }
16. }
```

Now that we have a basic subject-under-test, we can test its side effect. We expect no effects to be received until we ask it to handle an event, consequently this passes (goes green). The next thing to do is ask the **sut** to handle an event. A compilation error is a failure. Our test has failed because we have not defined **LoginEvent** and associated it with our **sut**. We then write just enough code to make our test go green (compile in this case):

```
1. sealed class LoginEvent: Event {
2.     object OnClose: LoginEvent()
```

```
3. }
4.
5. class LoginUdfViewModel : UdfViewModel<LoginEvent, UiState,
   SideEffect>(
6.     initialUiState = object : UiState {}
7. ) {
8.     override fun handleEvent(event: LoginEvent) {}
9. }
```

Again, no refactoring required at this early stage. We continue with our test and write the code to check that the correct effect was received:

```
1. //...
2. // When
3. sut.handleEvent(LoginEvent.OnClose)
4.
5. // Then
6. assertEquals(LoginEffect.Close, awaitItem())
7. //...
```

Again, our test is red because we have not defined **LoginEffect** (as opposed to **LoginEvent**) and associated it with our **sut**. Again, we write just enough code to get our test to go green:

```
1. sealed class LoginEffect: SideEffect {
2.     object Close: LoginEffect()
3. }
4.
5. class LoginUdfViewModel : UdfViewModel<LoginEvent, UiState,
   LoginEffect>(
6.     initialUiState = object : UiState {}
7. ) {
8.     override fun handleEvent(event: LoginEvent) {}
9. }
```

Our complete test for close now compiles as follows:

```
1. @Test
2. fun 'GIVEN sut WHEN back key event THEN close side effect'() =
   runTest {
3.     // Given
4.     sut.sideEffect.test {
5.         expectNoEvents()
```

```
6.
7.          // When
8.          sut.handleEvent(LoginEvent.OnClose)
9.
10.         // Then
11.         assertEquals(LoginEffect.Close, awaitItem())
12.     }
13. }
```

However, our test still is not green . The test fails with **No value produced in 3s**. This is because we have not written the code to connect the event with the effect. In order to make the test go green, we write the minimum amount of product code:

```
1. // ...
2. override fun handleEvent(event: LoginEvent) {
3.     sendSideEffect { LoginEffect.Close }
4. }
```

We are not bothering to query the **event** parameter at this point since there is currently only one. This, of course is likely to change as we add more events.

This has been the simplest of examples and we are only testing one event and one side effect. There is currently no **uiState**. We need to test drive the addition of a **uiState** by writing a test for the next most interesting scenario. Perhaps this could be:

`'GIVEN invalid credentials WHEN login THEN fail ui state'`

This will likely require a mocked **UserDetailsUseCase** injected into our **LoginViewModel** constructor, a **coEvery** call on this mock to return a failure and a flow test against **sut.uiState**. The TDD process will reveal a new **event** and a new **uiState** as well as the logic for linking them.

Advanced flow testing scenarios

Beyond basic collection and emission verification, here are some advanced testing scenarios for Kotlin flows:

- **Testing error handling:**
    - o Throw exceptions within the flow and assert that downstream collectors receive them correctly.
    - o Verify that specific error types trigger expected fallback mechanisms or error handlers.
    - o Test that cancellation is propagated correctly after encountering errors.

- **Testing timing and scheduling:**
  - Use `advanceTimeBy` or `advanceUntil` to simulate time progression and verify delayed emissions.
  - Test flow behavior with different Dispatchers configurations (for example, immediate, main, IO) and confirm proper scheduling.
  - Verify interaction with time-based operators like `debounce` or `sample` under various timing scenarios.
- **Testing concurrency and context:**
  - Launch multiple collectors concurrently and assert order of received elements or potential race conditions.
  - Test flow behavior with custom `CancellableCoroutineContext` implementations and cancellation propagation.
  - Verify interactions with shared resources or concurrent mutations accessed by multiple flows.
- **Testing flow transformations:**
  - Test operators like `map`, `flatMap`, and `zip` for correct data transformations and emission sequences.
  - Validate filtering and conditional operators like `takeWhile` or `distinctUntilChanged` with various input flows.
  - Verify advanced operators like `conflate`, `collectWhile`, or `buffer` behave as expected under different conditions.
- **Testing side effects and interactions:**
  - Test flows that perform side effects like database access, logging, or UI updates. Use mocks or dependency injection to isolate and verify interactions.
  - Check for resource management (for example, closing files, canceling jobs) triggered by flow completion or cancellation.
  - Verify interactions with external APIs or systems triggered by flow operations.

Conclusion

Test-driven development has become the expected technique for producing code. It improves the code quality, leads to a better design, prevents regressions, and increases confidence for refactoring. We described the TDD process in depth using the classic bowling game example and later applied the same principles to a `UdfViewModel` class. We described the highly regarded mocking library dedicated to Kotlin, Mockk, and explained how it is used to make our tests easier to read and write. We also specifically looked at test driving the kind of state-driven code required by Jetpack compose using the turbine test library in combination with the standard `kotlinx-coroutines-test` library.

In the next chapter we will start to implement the module hierarchy first discussed in *Chapter 3, Feature-Oriented Development in Android* and *Chapter 4, Clean Code Architecture*. The chapter presents a step-by-step practical guide to setting up a feature-based projects with clean-code layering architecture.

Points to remember

- You are not allowed to write any production code until you have a failing unit test.
- You cannot write more of a test than is sufficient to fail. Not compiling is failing.
- You are not allowed to write more production code than is sufficient to pass the current failing test.
- All previous tests in a suite relating to the same code need to pass before moving on, not just the current one.
- Use dependency injection and Mockk to create the injected dependencies for testing.
- In addition to Mockk, use Turbine and `kotlinx-coroutines-test` to test drive asynchronous coroutine code.

Questions

1. Describe the three colored phases of TDD.
2. What functions might you use to stub a method of an object created with Mockk?
3. Why is lazy initialization particularly useful when creating a test subject?
4. What might be considered the disadvantages of Mockk, and how could you avoid these pitfalls?
5. What is the difference between Turbine's `expectMostRecentItem()` and `awaitEvent()`.
6. Given the above `LoginUdfViewModel`, test drive the failed login scenario.

Join our book's Discord space

Join the book's Discord Workspace for Latest updates, Offers, Tech happenings around the world, New Release and Sessions with the Authors:

https://discord.bpbonline.com

CHAPTER 10
Kotlin DSL and Multimodule Apps

Introduction

In *Chapter 7, Introduction to Jetpack Compose*, we briefly examined Jetpack Compose by inspecting the code produced by the **Empty Activity** project creation wizard in Android Studio. The environment created by this wizard had a single **app** module. Traditionally, all the project creation wizards provided by Android Studio, have not been given much thought in setting up a multimodule environment; with **Empty Activity** being no exception.

Furthermore, until the release of Android Studio Giraffe, the Gradle build scripts were produced using the Groovy scripting language, whilst the preferred arrangement was Kotlin DSL. This required manual intervention to unify the languages across the project.

This chapter describes how to create a project from scratch using Kotlin DSL, suggests a strategy for a module hierarchy and examines an approach to maintain consistent dependency versioning across modules.

Structure

This chapter covers the following topics:
- Definition of DSL
- Advantages of Kotlin DSL for build scripting

- Multimodule project creation
- The `buildSrc` module
- Version catalogs
- Updating and adding to the version catalog
- Recommended IDE settings

Objectives

By the end of this chapter, you will understand the benefits of using Kotlin DSL and will be able to create a multimodule-ready project from scratch. This will include setup tips for maintaining the structure through subsequent updates and additions to the code.

Definition of DSL

Domain-Specific Language (DSL) is a specialized programming language or specification language dedicated to a particular problem domain, a particular problem representation technique, and/or a particular solution technique. Unlike general-purpose programming languages, which are designed to be flexible and applicable to a wide range of problems, DSLs are designed for a specific set of tasks within a specific domain.

DSLs are valuable because they allow developers to work at a higher level of abstraction within specific domains, making it easier to express solutions and model problems effectively. This can lead to more maintainable, readable, and efficient code in the targeted problem space.

Advantages of Kotlin DSL for build scripts

The Gradle Kotlin DSL is for configuring and scripting Gradle builds using the Kotlin programming language. While Gradle traditionally uses Groovy as its primary build script language, Gradle Kotlin DSL allows developers to write build scripts in Kotlin.

Key features and aspects of Gradle Kotlin DSL include:

- **Kotlin-based**: Gradle Kotlin DSL is based on the Kotlin programming language, providing benefits from Kotlin's concise and expressive syntax. Kotlin is statically typed, which provides strong type safety and enhances the development experience.
- **Type safety**: One of the significant advantages of the Kotlin DSL is its type safety. Compile-time checks are available, which help prevent many common build script errors. This can lead to more reliable build scripts and faster issue identification.
- **IDE integration**: Gradle Kotlin DSL works exceptionally well with the IntelliJ IDEA IDE (and therefore Android Studio), providing advanced coding assistance,

such as code completion, syntax highlighting, and refactoring support. This tight integration can significantly improve developer productivity.

- **Concise and readable**: Kotlin's syntax allows for concise and readable code. Build scripts written in Kotlin are often easier to understand and maintain. This is especially beneficial for large and complex build configurations.
- **Functional programming**: Kotlin is designed with support for functional programming, which allows build logic to be expressed more elegantly using features like lambdas and higher-order functions.
- **Interoperability**: Gradle Kotlin DSL provides interoperability with Groovy-based Gradle scripts. Groovy scripts and libraries can be used within existing Kotlin scripts and vice versa. This flexibility is helpful when transitioning from Groovy to Kotlin DSL.
- **Community and adoption**: Gradle Kotlin DSL has gained significant adoption in the Gradle community and is widely used for new projects and build scripts. It is actively maintained and receives updates and improvements.

One of the biggest advantages of using Gradle Kotlin DSL, however, is that it makes it much easier to set up and use first-class global constant values for use within build scripts. This is especially useful in multimodule environments for maintaining dependency and plugin versioning across all modules in projects. This will be discussed in detail with examples in the next sections.

Multimodule project creation

Despite Gradle Kotlin DSL being the build script language of choice for several years now, up until the release of Giraffe, Android Studio project creation wizards would only allow creation of new projects with Gradle Groovy build scripts. Following initial project creation, a Kotlin DSL **buildSrc** folder structure had to be manually created, the project, re-synced and then existing build scripts had to be converted or regenerated. Once this **buildSrc** folder structure had been created, it became a convenient location to define the global build constants mentioned in the previous section. There will be more details about the **buildSrc** folder later in this chapter.

Not only do the latest versions of Android Studio wizards allow the creation of projects with Kotlin DSL build scripts by default, they also provide a built-in, IDE-supported arrangement for defining global constants for build scripts. Version catalogs remove *almost* all of the need for the manually created Kotlin DSL. There are still certain elements, such as SDK version references, that version catalogs do not manage. This will be expanded upon in the next section.

Make sure the latest version of Android Studio is installed.

Note: Depending on the current installation, it may become necessary to completely remove Android Studio, along with all associated plugin libraries and SDKs and then

install the latest version from scratch. In one instance, we observed certain problems on a low-spec Windows machine that had Android Studio upgraded from Chipmunk straight to Giraffe. In particular, the newer version prompts for version catalogs (detailed later in this chapter) did not show up.

We recommend creating the project as a multiplatform app. Only Android development will be discussed here but keeping multiplatform in mind while creating modules will reinforce decoupling. As an added benefit, an app created in this way will have the flexibility to be applied to multiplatform at a later date.

The latest versions of Android Studio include a multiplatform app creation wizard. We recommend that you do not use this. At the time of writing, the wizard would force the creation of extensive iOS build files which will be unnecessary for our purposes. Furthermore, if multiplatform was the goal, this wizard will only generate iOS files as well as Android ones. Instead, access the following URL with a web browser:

https://kmp.jetbrains.com/

A dialog similar to the following figure should be seen:

Figure 10.1: Create new project

Fill in the project and package names in the **Project Name** and **Project ID** fields respectively. The dialog will present many platform options, including iOS, Desktop, Web and Server. For our example we will only be examining Android so ensure this is the only option ticked as above in *Figure 10.1*. Other platforms are beyond the scope of this book but can easily be added later.

The new project will be downloaded as a ZIP file. Unzipping the file will create a new folder. Use Android Studio to **Open** the project from this new folder, as shown in the following figure:

Kotlin DSL and Multimodule Apps ■ 195

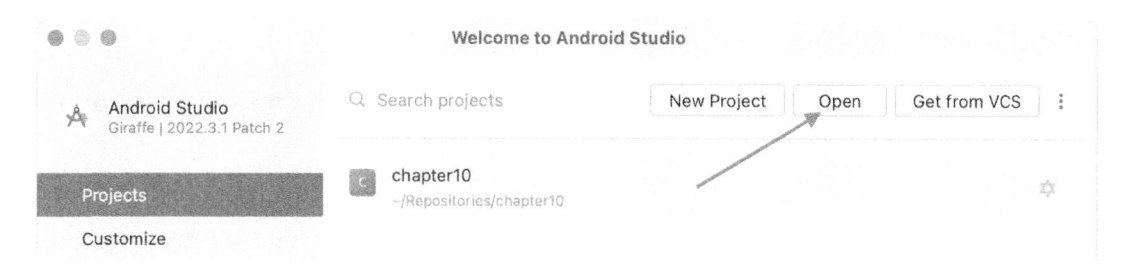

Figure 10.2: *Open the unzipped folder*

Use the system's file browser to locate the root of the unzipped folder and open it. When the project finishes loading, select the **Project Files** view from the drop-down list, as shown in the following figure:

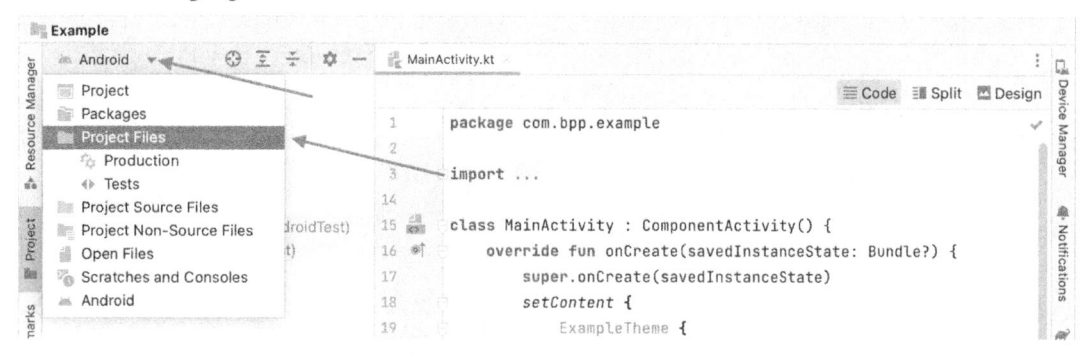

Figure 10.3: *Select the Project Files view*

The buildSrc module

The **buildSrc** module is a special module that serves to centralize and manage build logic and dependencies. It provides a dedicated space for developers to define custom Gradle tasks, plugins, and reusable code snippets that can be shared across the project's build scripts.

Key benefits of using the **buildSrc** module include:

- **Improved code organization**: By keeping build logic and dependencies separate from the main project code, the **buildSrc** module promotes code organization and maintainability, making it easier to manage and understand the project's build process.
- **Code sharing and reusability**: Developers can create reusable code snippets and functions within the **buildSrc** module and easily incorporate them into various build scripts across the project. This promotes code consistency and reduces duplication.
- **Centralized dependency management:** The **buildSrc** module can serve as a central repository for managing project dependencies. This simplifies dependency management and ensures that all components have access to the necessary libraries.

- **Custom build tasks and plugins**: Developers can define custom Gradle tasks and plugins within the `buildSrc` module, allowing for automation of specific build steps and extension of Gradle's functionality. This enhances flexibility and control over the build process.

Typical use cases for the `buildSrc` Module include:

- **Defining custom build tasks**: Developers can create custom tasks to perform specific actions during the build process, such as generating code, running tests, or publishing artifacts.
- **Creating reusable code snippets**: Developers can write common code snippets, such as function definitions or variable declarations, within the `buildSrc` module and share them across various build scripts.
- **Managing project dependencies**: The `buildSrc` module can be used to define and manage project dependencies, ensuring consistent versions across the project and simplifying dependency resolution.
- In fact, all of the functionality of this particular use case can now be handled by Version Catalogs which will be discussed shortly.
- **Developing custom Gradle Plugins**: Developers can create custom Gradle plugins within the `buildSrc` module to extend Gradle's functionality and automate complex build tasks.

Steps for creating the buildSrc module

Regrettably, there are no setup wizards for creating the `buildScrc` module, despite `buildSrc` being a reserved word within the Android Studio IDE. The following file structure needs to be created:

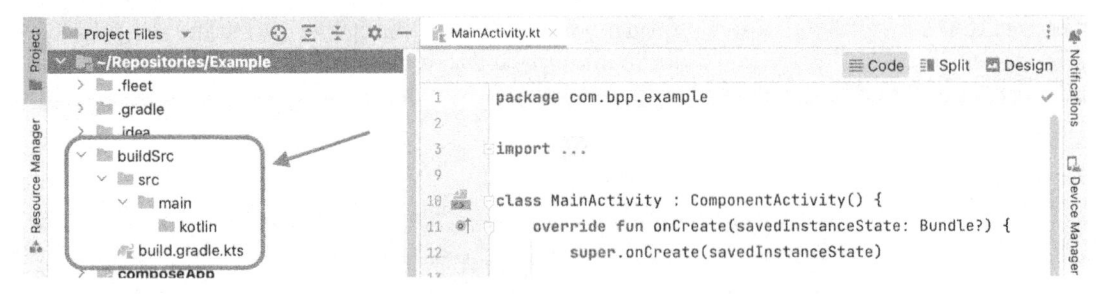

Figure 10.4: Manually created buildSrc file structure

Follow these steps to recreate the arrangement in *Figure 10.4*:

1. Right-click on the project file root and select **New | Directory**
2. Enter `buildSrc/src/main/kotlin` in the resulting dialog:

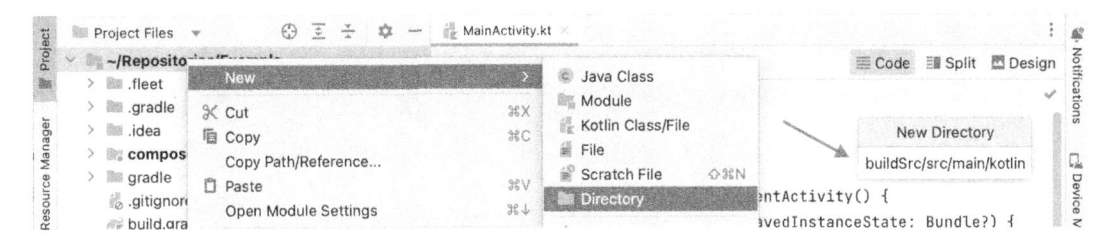

Figure 10.5: Create buildSrc directory

3. Right-click on the new **buildSrc** root and select **New | File** then enter **build.gradle.kts** in the resulting dialog:

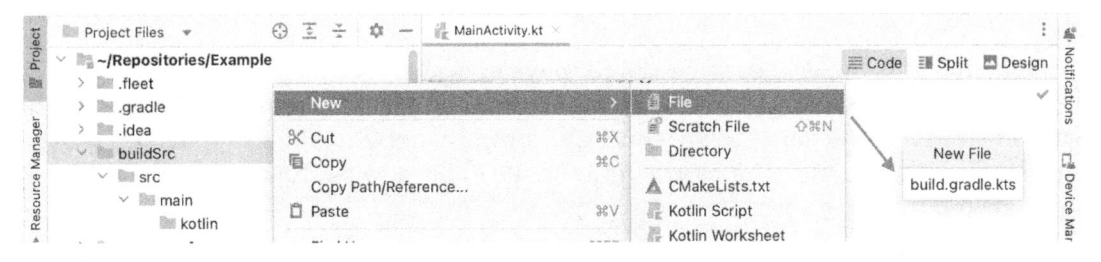

Figure 10.6: Create build.gradle.kts file in buildSrc

4. Edit the newly created **build.gradle.kts** file and add the following lines of code:
   1. plugins { 'kotlin-dsl' }
   2. repositories { mavenCentral() }

5. Finally, sync the project, as shown in the following figure:

Figure 10.7: Sync the project

6. Assuming no problems happened, after sync has finished, the project should look like this (no errors):

Figure 10.8: Integrated buildSrc module

We recommend using **buildSrc** for defining configuration constants, such as that for the JDK versions. This will provide a means of synchronizing all Android modules within the project to the same versions. These values are currently not something handled by version catalogs (see next section). Create a new Kotlin file in the new **buildSrc kotlin** folder. We have called ours **Config**:

Right-click on the **kotlin** director and select **New | Kotlin Class/File** then enter **Config** and select **File** in the resulting dialog, as shown below:

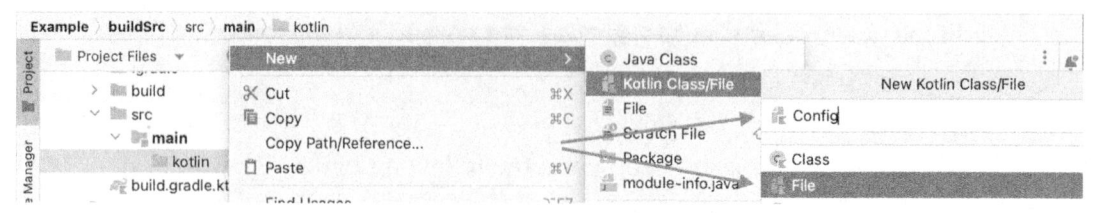

Figure 10.9: Create a buildSrc kotlin file

In this new file, we will create constants to replace the hard-coded values in the generated build scripts, for example, in this abbreviated snippet from the app module **build.gradle.kts**:

```
1.  ...
2.  kotlin {
3.      androidTarget {
4.          compilations.all {
5.              kotlinOptions {
6.                  jvmTarget = "1.8"
7.              }
8.          }
9.      }
10.     ...
```

```
11. }
12.
13. android {
14.     ...
15.     compileOptions {
16.         sourceCompatibility = JavaVersion.VERSION_1_8
17.         targetCompatibility = JavaVersion.VERSION_1_8
18.     }
19.     ...
20. }
```

Add code similar to the following to the recently created **buildrc** Kotlin file (**Config** in our example):

```
1. import org.gradle.api.JavaVersion
2.
3. object Config {
4.     const val jvmTarget = "17"
5.     val javaVersion = JavaVersion.VERSION_17
6. }
```

With this in place the app **build.gradle.kts** can be modified to use these values instead of the hard coded ones:

```
1.  ...
2.  kotlin {
3.      androidTarget {
4.          compilations.all {
5.              kotlinOptions {
6.                  jvmTarget = Config.jvmTarget
7.              }
8.          }
9.      }
10.     ...
11. }
12.
13. android {
14.     ...
15.     compileOptions {
16.         sourceCompatibility = Config.javaVersion
```

```
17.         targetCompatibility = Config.javaVersion
18.     }
19.     ...
20. }
```

The build file for every module added to the project will need the same modification in order to maintain consistent versioning. Doing so will allow the JDK (for example) to be upgraded across all modules with a one-line change.

Version catalogs

Version catalogs in Android projects are a feature of the Gradle build system that allows developers to define and manage dependencies and plugins in a centralized and type-safe manner. They provide a convenient and organized way to specify the versions of libraries and plugins used in the project, ensuring consistency and reducing the risk of errors.

The version catalogs file, `libs.versions.toml` (henceforth referred to as the `toml` file), is auto-generated by the project creation wizard and is located under the `gradle` folder, as shown in the following figure:

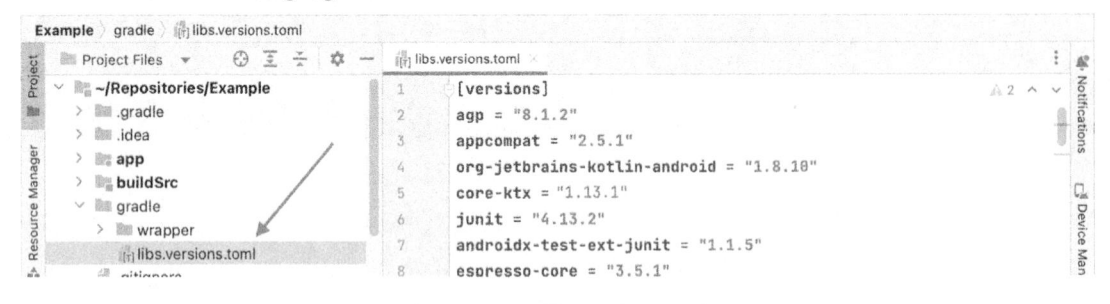

Figure 10.10: libs.versions.toml

Note: Contents of the file shown above may differ with later IDE versions.

Some key benefits of using version catalogs are as follows:

- **Centralized dependency management**: Version catalogs eliminate the need to declare dependencies directly in individual build scripts, instead providing a single, centralized location to define and manage all project dependencies. We will go into further detail on this in the next section.
- **Type-safe dependency access**: Version catalogs offer type-safe access to dependencies, preventing errors caused by typos or incorrect dependency names. This enhances build reliability and reduces the risk of dependency conflicts.

Before using version catalogs, developers would often hardcode dependency versions directly into their build scripts, like this:

```
1. ...
2. dependencies {
```

```
3.    ...
4.        implementation("androidx.appcompat:appcompat:2.5.1")
5. }
```

This approach can lead to errors if the dependency version is changed, as the build script may not be updated accordingly.

Version catalogs eliminate this risk by introducing type-safe accessors that are generated from the version catalog file. These accessors provide a controlled way to reference dependencies, ensuring that the correct versions are always used.

For example, if the version catalog defines a variable for the **appcompat** dependency, the build script would use the accessor to reference it:

```
1. ...
2. dependencies {
3.    ...
4.        implementation(libs.androidx.appcompat)
5. }
```

The **libs** object is generated from the version catalog and provides type-safe access to the defined variables. This means that Gradle will ensure that the correct version of **appcompat** is used, even if the version is changed in the version catalog file.

In addition to preventing errors, type-safe accessors make it easier to understand and maintain build scripts. Developers can easily see which dependencies are being used and their versions, without wading through many hardcoded values.

- **Improved code readability and maintainability**: By centralizing dependency information in version catalogs, build scripts become more concise and readable, making it easier to understand and maintain the project's build process.
- **Simplified dependency sharing**: Version catalogs facilitate sharing dependencies across multiple projects, ensuring consistent dependency versions and simplifying project configuration.

Essential components of a version catalog are as follows:

- **Versions block [versions]**: This block defines variables that hold the versions of dependencies and plugins used in the project, as can be seen in the example below:

```
1. [versions]
2. appcompat = " 2.5.1"
3. ...
```

- **Dependencies block [libraries]**: This block specifies the dependencies required for the project, referencing the version variables defined in the versions block, as can be seen in the following example:

1. [versions]
2. appcompat = "2.5.1"
3. ...
4.
5. [libraries]
6. androidx-appcompat = { module = "androidx.appcompat:appcompat", version.ref = "appcompat" }
7. ...

- **Plugins block [plugins]**: This block declares the plugins required for the project, again referencing the version variables from the versions block, as follows:
  1. [versions]
  2. agp = "8.1.2"
  3. ...
  4.
  5. [plugins]
  6. com-android-application = { id = "com.android.application", version.ref = "agp" }
  7. ...

Additional features of version catalogs are as follows:

- **Aliases**: Version catalogs allow for defining aliases for dependencies and plugins, providing more convenient and memorable names for frequently used components.
- **Publication**: Version catalogs can be published to a repository, enabling developers to consume them from other projects and share dependency configurations.
- **Customizations**: Developers can customize version catalogs to include additional information, such as dependency descriptions or license details. The following code provides a few examples of customizations in the version catalogs file:
  1. [buildInstructions]
  2. appcompat = "To build appcompat..."
  3. ...
  4.
  5. [notes]
  6. appcompat = "This dependency provides ..."
  7. ...
- **Bundles**: Groups of related libraries can be bundled together in this section in a similar way to Google's bill of materials (EOM) build definitions. For example:
  1. ...
  2. [libraries]

Kotlin DSL and Multimodule Apps 203

3. gson = { module = "com.google.code.gson:gson", version.ref = "gson" }
4. nav-android = { module = "com.aimicor:navcompose-android", ... }
5. nav-compose = { module = "androidx.navigation:navigation-compose", ... }
6.
7. [bundles]
8. **navigation** = ["gson", "nav-android", "nav-compose"]

The corresponding dependency declaration in the build file will then require the following single line:

1. implementation (libs.bundles.**navigation**)

Updating and adding to the Version Catalog

Before Version Catalogs were introduced, if centralized dependency management was required, then the **buildSrc** arrangement was required. Typically, string constants has to be created, similar to the SDK constants we created earlier. For example:

```
1. object Versions {
2.     const val appCompat = "2.5.1"
3.     ...
4. }
5. 
6. object Dependencies {
7. 
8.     object AndroidX {
9.         const val AppCompat =
10.             "androidx.appcompat:appcompat:${Versions.appCompat}"
11.         ...
12.     }
13. }
```

The following entry in the build script could then be made:

```
1. ...
2. dependencies {
3.     ...
4.     implementation(Dependencies.AndroidX.AppCompat)
5. }
```

This became difficult to manage. New entries required two new entries in the **buildSrc** files and it could be difficult to find existing entries when adding the same dependency to more than one build script (unless a copy of an existing build script implementation statement could be found). Furthermore, the one advantage from strings directly encoded in the build scripts was lost, that is, the IDE indicating a new version being available by highlighting the out-of-date entry. The following figure depicts an example of this highlighting:

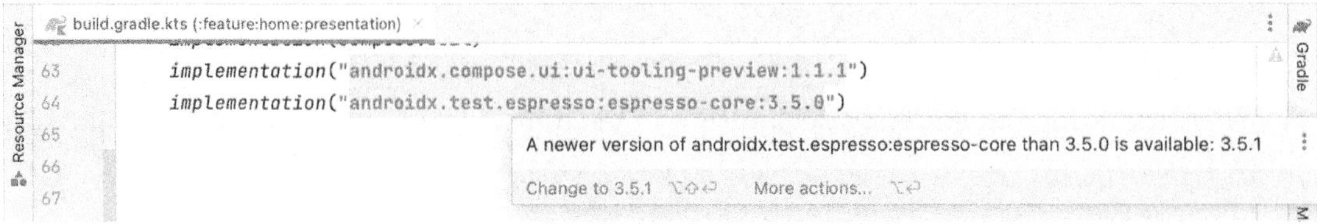

Figure 10.11: "newer version" highlighting

Version Catalogs are integrated with the IDE in much the same way as above so the *newer version* notifications appear in the catalog file, as shown below:

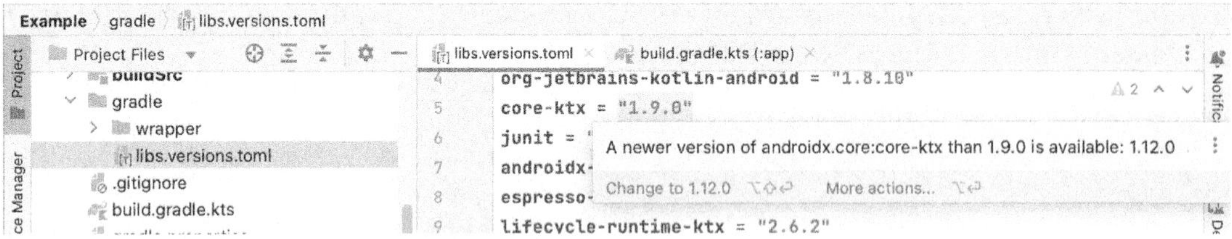

Figure 10.12: Version Catalog "newer version" highlighting

With regards to adding new or existing dependencies, on the surface of it, it appears that matters have been made worse. The developers of Version Catalogs made the decision to use a data meta file instead of a Kotlin DSL for defining dependency constants. Furthermore, they have not even used a familiar metadata format, such as JSON. The obscure data format of choice, **Tom's Obvious Minimal Language (TOML)** for example, has the idiosyncrasy of referring to a previously defined version constant by the string equivalent of that name:

1. [versions]
2. agp = "8.1.2"
3. ...
4.
5. [plugins]
6. com-android-application = { id = "com.android.application", **version.ref = "agp"** }
7. ...

This has the potential of being error-prone if entries need to be added manually. Fortunately, this is not necessary. As mentioned previously, the Version Catalog arrangement is fully integrated into the IDE. New entries can be added automatically simply by adding the traditional entry to the build file. The IDE will offer the option of converting that entry to a Version Catalog addition. This will take care of updating the **toml** file semi-automatically. The following figure depicts an example of the prompt to update the version catalogs **toml** file:

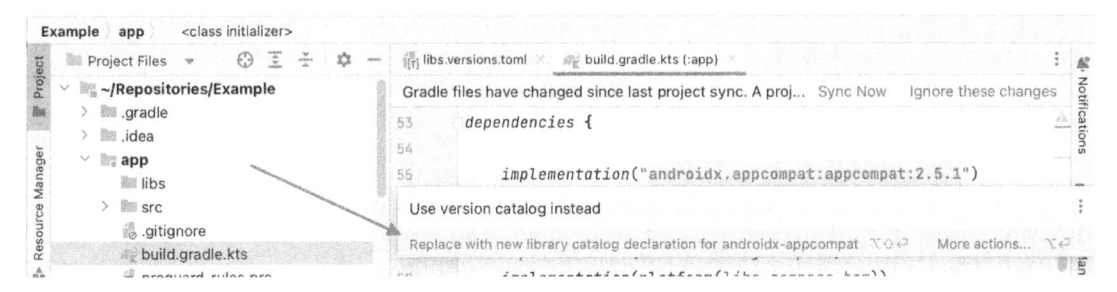

Figure 10.13: Adding dependency to Version Catalogs

Given the preceding scenario, when selecting **Replace with new library...**, a new version and library entry will be added to the **toml** file, an alias created and the literal in the build script replaced by that alias (may require a subsequent **Sync**):

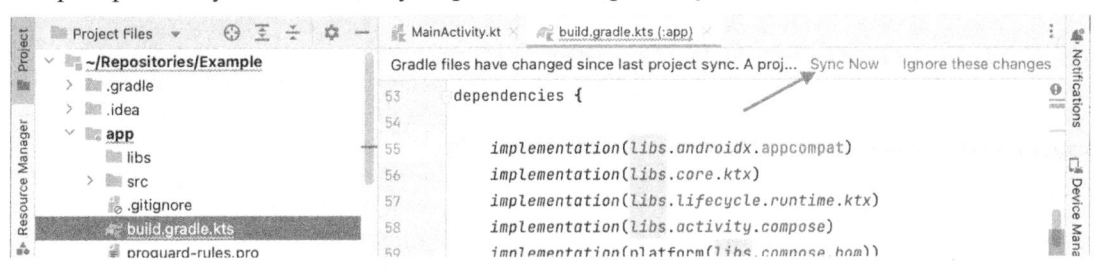

Figure 10.14: Version Catalogs alias created

Similarly, an existing alias can be added to the build scripts of other modules without having to know either the alias name or the version that the alias refers to. In the following example, our **appcompat** library is already defined in the **toml** file but we have attempted to add it again with a different version:

Figure 10.15: Reusing a Version Catalogs alias

The IDE knows that there is an existing entry in the `toml` file and presents options. In this case we want to use the existing entry rather than the default action of replacing it so we select **More Actions** to get that option, as can be seen in the following figure:

Figure 10.16: Reusing a Version Catalogs alias

In summary, version catalogs are a powerful tool for managing dependencies in Android projects. They provide a centralized, type-safe, and shareable approach to versioning dependencies, enhancing build reliability, maintainability, and performance. Adopting version catalogs can significantly improve the organization and management of dependencies in Android development projects.

Version catalogs are utilized in individual builds, which can include multi-project builds, and they can also be shared across multiple builds. For instance, an organization might develop a catalog of dependencies that various projects from different teams can use.

Recommended IDE settings

In this section, we recommend a few workspace settings that make life a little easier during development.

Optimizing imports on-the-fly

One of the most common warnings received from both compilers and continuous integration arrangements is that of unused imports. These occur very easily in the course of development because temporary code may be added that requires an import only for that code to be taken away shortly afterwards. The warning occurs because Android Studio does not automatically remove the unused import in this scenario. The following option under **Settings | General | Editor | Auto Import** needs to be switched on:

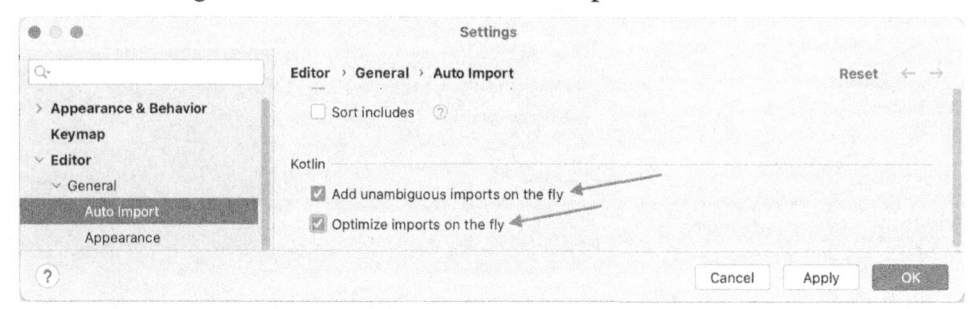

Figure 10.17: Optimize imports on-the-fly

Regrettably, this setting is not something that can be easily shared amongst team members via version control systems, such as Git. The option is recorded in the `workspace.xml` file under the `.idea` folder. This file is automatically added to the `.gitignore` file because it is so easily changed for personal preferences not directly related to code production.

Project structure suggestions

To quickly examine and update outdated library and plugin versions, go to **File | Project Structure | Suggestions**:

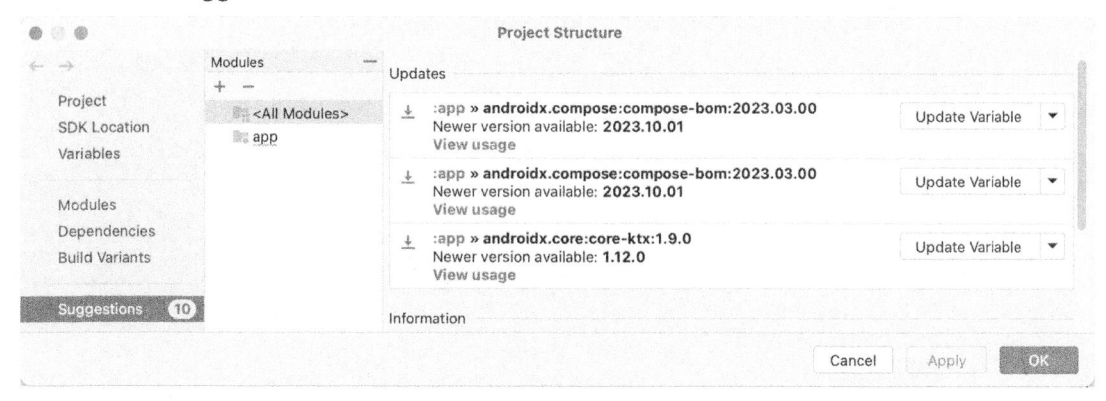

Figure 10.18: Project Structure Suggestions

Conclusion

In this chapter we discussed how to create a multimodule-ready project. We examined the benefits of using Kotlin DSL for the build scripts and how this enables centralized dependency management. We looked at the role that the `buildSrc` module and Version Catalogs play in centralized dependency management. We then described the steps necessary to create the `buildSrc` module and reviewed the Version Catalogs file and how to update it.

In the next chapter, we will describe how to create a multimodule hierarchy in a project that facilitates previously discussed paradigms of clean-code architecture and feature-oriented development.

Points to remember

- Kotlin DSL build scripts are the key to centralized dependency management
- Always use Version Catalogs when creating a new project
- Maintain `buildSrc` code to centralize versioning not handled by Version Catalogs
- Allow the IDE to add new library dependencies via the build scripts as described

- Enable import optimization on-the-fly
- Periodically check Project Structure Suggestions for available dependency updates

Questions

1. What is a Kotlin DSL?
2. How do you create the `buildSrc` module?
3. What is the easiest way to add a new dependency to Version Catalogs?
4. Why should you enable import optimization on-the-fly?

Join our book's Discord space

Join the book's Discord Workspace for Latest updates, Offers, Tech happenings around the world, New Release and Sessions with the Authors:

https://discord.bpbonline.com

Chapter 11
Creating the Module Hierarchy

Introduction

One of the biggest problems faced by developers working on projects with large code bases is finding the correct piece of code that needs to be worked on. This is especially true of bug fixing where a QA engineer, with no knowledge of the code, has reported with, at best, a video capture of the problem or just a list of instructions from a user's point of view to repeat the issue. So often, code is organized with all Activities in one package, all custom Views in another, and so on. Even those that have adopted a modular approach tend to have adopted a flat structure that only marginally helps with readability. This chapter introduces a simple method for creating module hierarchies and suggests an approach in line with solutions highlighted throughout this book, in particular, *Chapter 3, Feature-Oriented Development in Android*, and *Chapter 10, Kotlin DSL and Multimodule Apps*.

Structure

This chapter covers the following topics:
- Creating a feature presentation module
- Creating data and domain modules
- Binding data to domain
- Splitting out UI from presentation
- Creating an infrastructure (common) module

Objectives

By the end of this chapter, you will be able to create a module hierarchy in their project that is consistent with the feature-oriented development and clean code architecture layering discussed in *Chapter 3, Feature Oriented Development* and *Chapter 4, Clean Code Architecture* respectively. The following instructions assume that a multimodule-ready project was previously created as described in *Chapter 10, Kotlin DSL and Multimodule Apps*. Ultimately, we will create a structure that looks like this:

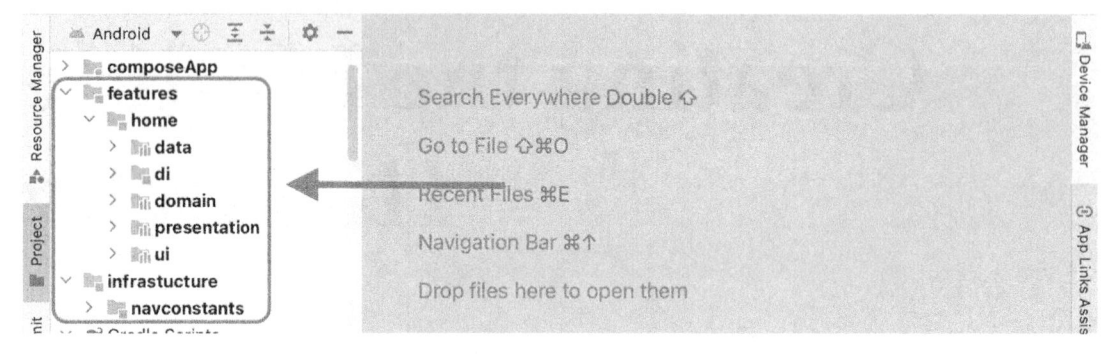

Figure 11.1: Module hierarchy

Creating a feature presentation module

As a key element of SoC, *Chapter 3, Feature-Oriented Development in Android*, we discussed Feature-oriented development. In this chapter we reinforce that concept by separating each feature into its own module and organizing them in a hierarchical structure, as can be seen in *Figure 11.1* above.

First of all, we recommend at least one feature in an app. We suggest the **Home** feature, or main screen. To begin creating the module hierarchy shown in *Figure 11.1*, starting with the **presentation** submodule, complete the following steps:

1. To begin, either right-click on the project's root or, from the top **File** menu, select **New | New Module**, as shown in the following figure:

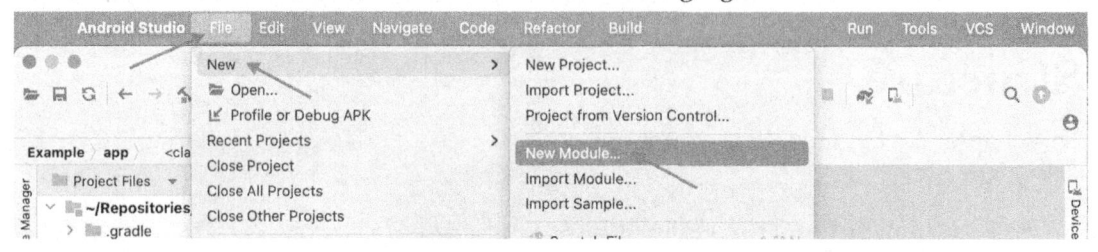

Figure 11.2: Create a module

2. We will group all features under the same heading in order to reduce clutter at the top level of the **Project Files** or **Android** file navigation view in the left panel.

3. In the resulting **Create New Module** dialog, select **Android Library** on the left and then use the **Module name** field to create the module hierarchy.

4. Use a colon (:) to separate each submodule, as shown in the following figure:

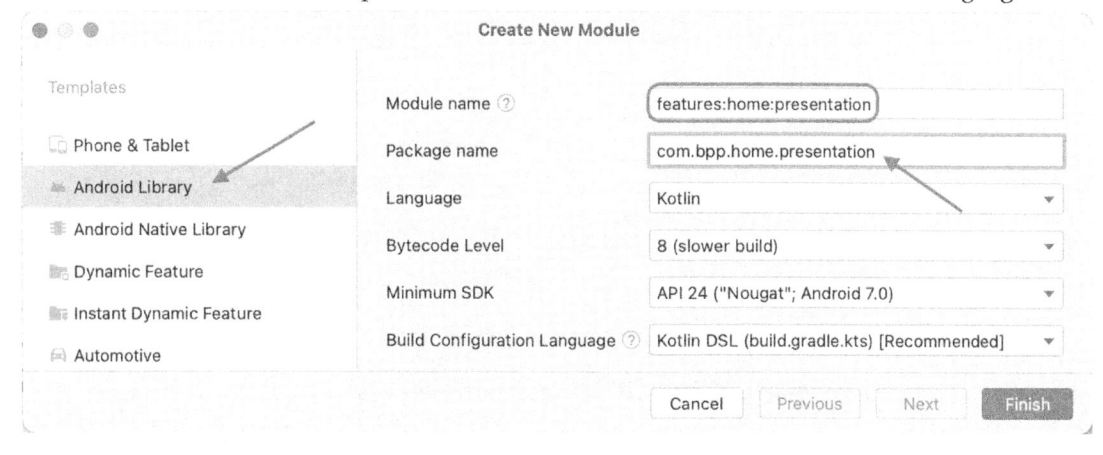

Figure 11.3: Create home presentation feature

5. The `features:home:presentation` will create an Android library module called **presentation** which is a submodule of **home** which in turn is a submodule of **features**.

6. Finally, ensure that the **Package name** field is updated to better identify its purpose. We have gone for **...home.presentation** in our example.

7. This is all that is needed for this dialog so just select **Finish**.

8. Once the resulting re-sync has completed, we will need to update the generated `build.gradle.kts` file with the `buildSrc` constants that we created in *Chapter 10, Kotlin DSL and Multimodule Apps*, and the SDK constants defined in the version catalogs.

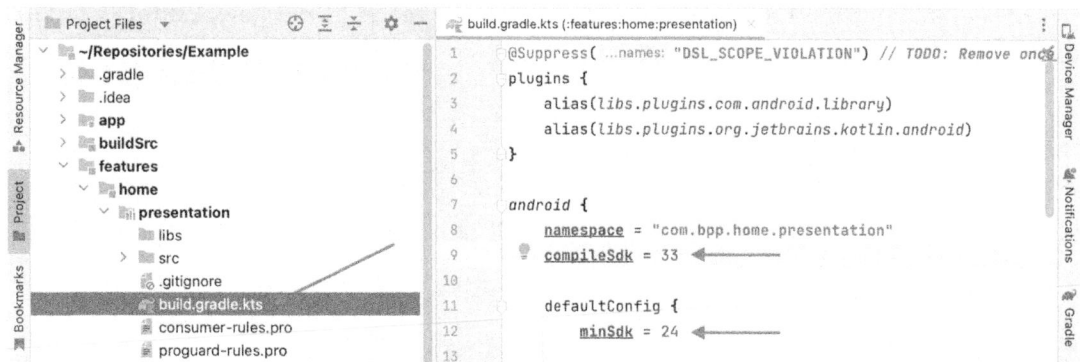

Figure 11.4: Update new build script with buildSrc constants

9. The relevant parts to be changed in the preceding screenshot are highlighted below:

```
1.  ...
2.  android {
3.      namespace = "com.bpp.home.presentation"
4.      compileSdk = 33
5.
6.      defaultConfig {
7.          minSdk = 24
8.          ...
9.      }
10.     ...
11.     compileOptions {
12.         sourceCompatibility = JavaVersion.VERSION_1_8
13.         targetCompatibility = JavaVersion.VERSION_1_8
14.     }
15.     kotlinOptions {
16.         jvmTarget = "1.8"
17.     }
18. }
19. ...
```

10. By way of a reminder, we created **Config** constants for **sourceCompatibility**, **targetCompatibility** and **jvmTarget**.
11. The constants for the SDK can be copied from the app build script that was generated from project creation wizard.
12. Ultimately, the following changes need to be made to the new module's **build.gradle.kts**:

```
1.  ...
2.  android {
3.      namespace = "com.bpp.home.presentation"
4.      compileSdk = libs.versions.android.compileSdk.get().toInt()
5.
6.      defaultConfig {
7.          minSdk = libs.versions.android.minSdk.get().toInt()
8.          ...
9.      }
10.     ...
```

```
11.         compileOptions {
12.             sourceCompatibility = Config.javaVersion
13.             targetCompatibility = Config.javaVersion
14.         }
15.         kotlinOptions {
16.             jvmTarget = Config.jvmTarget
17.         }
18. }
19. ...
```

Note: The highlighted hard-coded version values have been replaced with version catalog and `buildSrc` config references.

13. Following these modifications, re-sync the project as described in *Chapter 10, Kotlin DSL and Multimodule Apps*.

14. Lastly, reference this new module as a dependency in our app. Edit the **build.gradle.kts** file in the app module, scroll to **kotlin sourceSets** and add the following dependency to **androidMain.dependencies**:

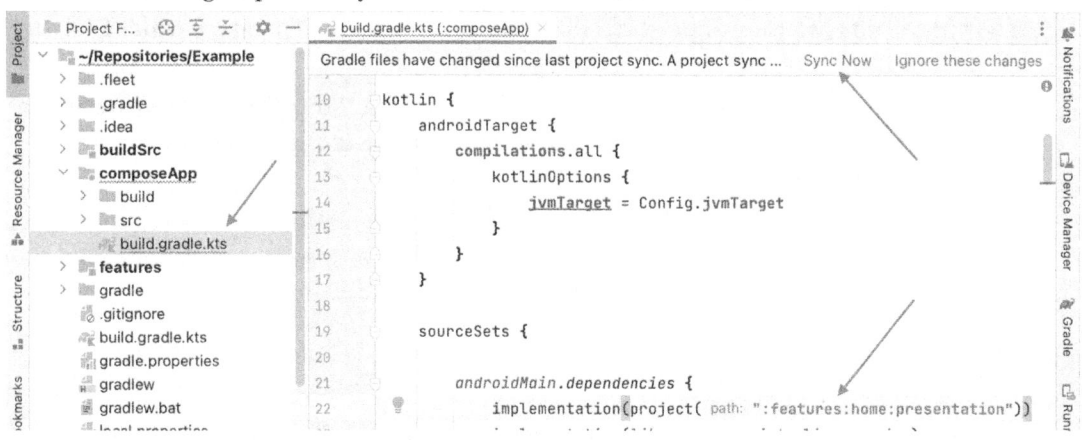

Figure 11.5: Add home presentation feature dependency to the app

15. Add the following line:
    ```
    1. implementation(project(":features:home:presentation"))
    ```

Then, resync the project.

Creating data and domain modules

A similar approach can be used to create corresponding Data and Domain modules for our **home** feature. Furthermore, we can use the dependency configuration in the build scripts to reinforce the layering architecture described in *Chapter 4, Clean Code Architecture*. This will be covered shortly.

We suggest that Android libraries are *not* created for these module layers. They should be platform independent. We suggest creating KMM libraries instead, even if there are no immediate plans to share code between platforms. Doing so will enforce the boundaries between layers. Only data and domain functionalities are offered by the `commonMain` module generated by KMM. To add the data and domain modules to the hierarchy shown in *Figure 11.1*, complete the following steps:

1. Ensure that the KMM plugin is installed in the IDE and enabled. Go to **Settings | Plugins** and search for **kmm** under the **Installed** tab, as shown below:

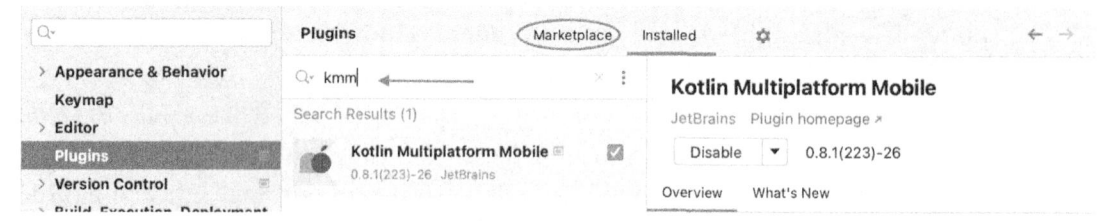

Figure 11.6: Check KMM module is installed

2. If no results are found, perform the same search under the **Marketplace** tab and install it.

3. Follow the instructions in *Figure 11.2* to get to the **Create New Module** dialog. Select **Kotlin Multiplatform Shared Module** on the left and then use the **Module name** field to create the module hierarchy.

4. Depending on the Android Studio version used, the **Kotlin Multiplatform Shared Module** option may not show up in the templates, as shown in *Figure 11.8*. In that case, it needs to be enabled in Studio's **Advanced Settings** first:

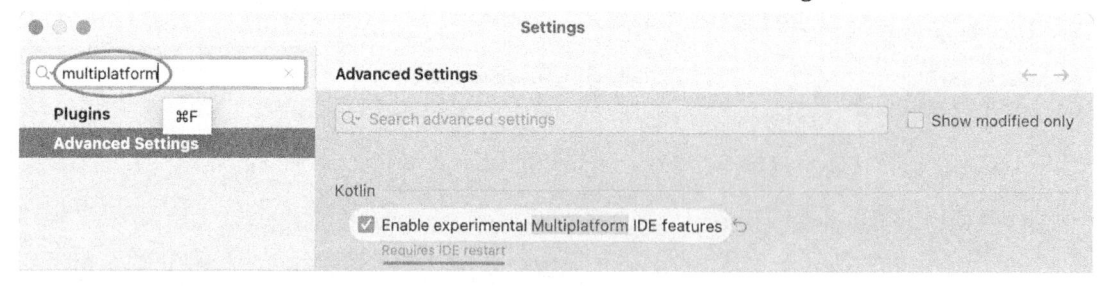

Figure 11.7: Enable multiplatform wizard template.

5. Continuing from step 3, as done earlier, use a colon (`:`) to separate each submodule and make sure the package name is correct:

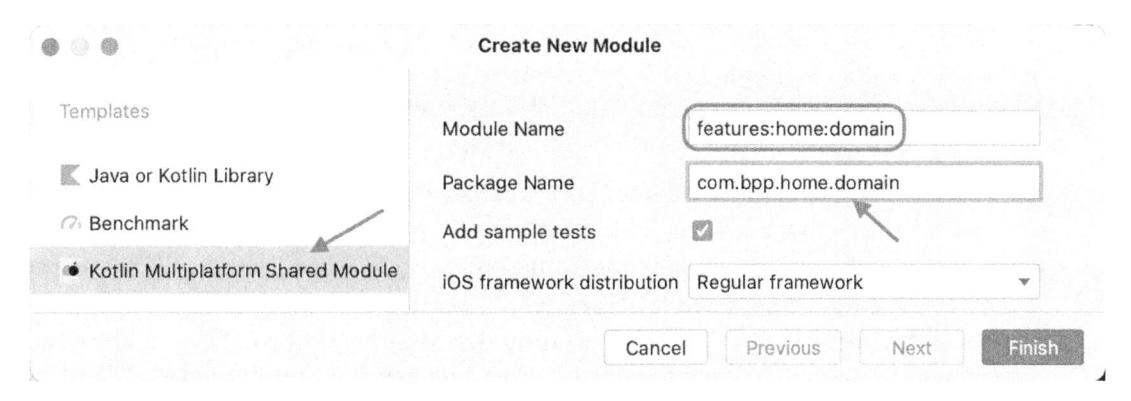

Figure 11.8: Create Domain module

6. We will now need to change the resulting build script and add the Version Catalog constants for the SDK. In addition, as we are only supporting Android for this exercise, we can remove all the iOS configuration. Here is the modified complete script:

```
1.  plugins {
2.      alias(libs.plugins.kotlinMultiplatform)
3.      alias(libs.plugins.androidLibrary)
4.  }
5.
6.  kotlin {
7.      androidTarget()
8.  }
9.
10. android {
11.     namespace = "com.bpp.home.domain"
12.     compileSdk = libs.versions.android.compileSdk.get().toInt()
13.     defaultConfig {
14.         minSdk = libs.versions.android.minSdk.get().toInt()
15.     }
16.     compileOptions {
17.         sourceCompatibility = Config.javaVersion
18.         targetCompatibility = Config.javaVersion
19.     }
20. }
```

216 ■ *Scalable Android Applications in Kotlin*

> Note: If the initial project creation was done via the AS Empty Activity wizard, then resyncing at this point will throw the error unresolved reference: `kotlinMulitplatform`. Ensure that the project was created as described in *Chapter 10, Kotlin DSL and Multimodule Apps.*

7. Notice that there is now one line in the `kotlin` scope. In fact, the `sourceSets` and `listOf` entries that were generated here are deprecated.

8. Now, it is enough to list the platforms directly in the scope. For example, `iosX64()` etc. at the same level as `androidTarget()`. This is because version 1.9.20 of Kotlin uses a default hierarchy template to provide the source sets. However, although the `kotlin` settings automatically pick up that we have upgraded our JVM to version 17 (`jvmTarget`), the `android` setting does not, hence the addition of the `compileOptions`. Without this, in our case, we would get an *Inconsistent JVM-target compatibility* error at build time.

9. We also suggest that the generated `androidMain` and `iosMain` submodules of the `domain` module be removed. We specifically want to enforce platform independent functionality, as shown in the following figure:

Figure 11.9: Delete androidMain and iosMain

10. Repeat all the steps above to create the `data` module (`features:home:data`).

11. At this point, there will be three modules, `data`, `domain` and `presentation`, under the `home` feature. Now is the time to add the dependency rules that reinforce the clean code layering architecture, as depicted in *Figure 4.2*.

12. By way of a reminder, both the presentation and data layers are dependent on the domain layer, and the domain layer is not dependent on anything. Refer to the following figure:

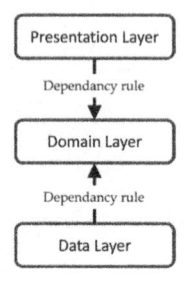

Figure 11.10: CCA layer dependency

13. These dependency rules are easy to set up in the build scripts. Firstly, update the data module's build script, as follows:

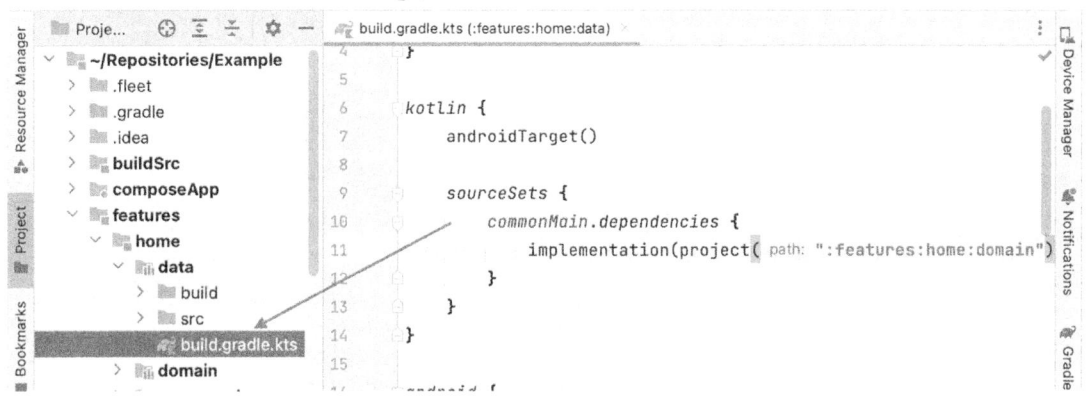

Figure 11.11: Edit the data module's build script

14. Add the domain module dependency:
    1. ...
    2. `kotlin {`
    3. `    androidTarget()`
    4.
    5. `    sourceSets {`
    6. `        commonMain.dependencies {`
    7. `            implementation(project(":features:home:domain"))`
    8. `        }`
    9. `    }`
    10. `}`
    11. ...

15. Secondly, update the **presentation** module's build script, as follows:

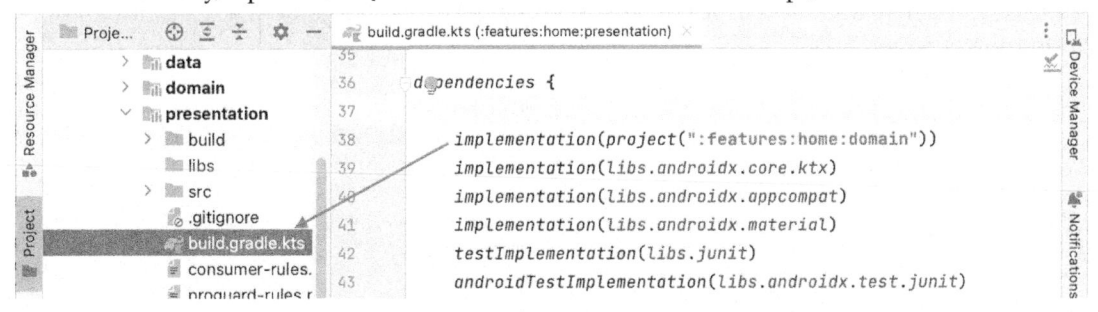

Figure 11.12: Edit the presentation module's build script

16. Add the **domain** module dependency, as shown below:

```
...
dependencies {

    implementation(project(":features:home:domain"))
    ...
}
```

Binding data to domain

There is a practical issue with the dependency rule interpreted by actual build dependencies as detailed above. Some needs access to both data and domain in order to bind use cases in the **domain** module to their dependencies in the **data** module. Regardless of the dependency injection method used, development teams are often tempted to have the presentation layer dependent on both the **domain** and **data** modules, as shown in the following figure:

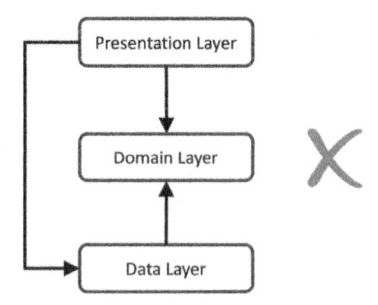

Figure 11.13: Broken architecture layering (Icon source: cleanpng.com)

This defeats the purpose of layering architecture. While the injection arrangement can resolve all dependencies, developers of the presentation module will now have direct access to data layer implementations. There is no longer any hierarchy enforcement. A better approach is to have a module dedicated to resolving dependencies, as shown in the following figure:

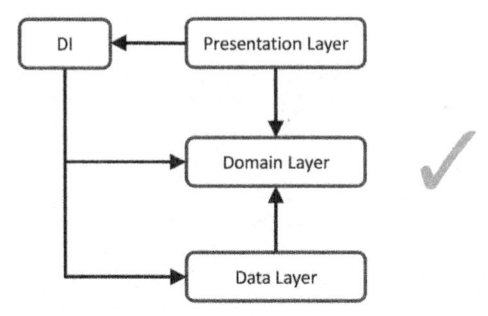

Figure 11.14: Fixed architecture layering (Icon source: cleanpng.com)

The presentation module has dependencies on the domain and **dependency injection** (**DI**) modules. The DI module has dependencies on the domain and data modules. This new module will be dedicated to providing the `@Provides`, `@Binds` methods (in the case of Hilt) or `module` code (in the case of Koin) for concrete implementations of use case interfaces.

Koin DI

If the DI arrangement of choice is Koin, this new module can be created as a KMM module in the same way as the domain and data modules. Since Koin is a pure-Kotlin library, it works well with multiplatform and can be used across iOS and Web, as well as Android.

Repeat steps 1-9 from the previous section, *Creating data and domain modules*, to create the `di` module (`features:home:di`). Add the module dependencies to the new build script as shown in *Figure 11.14* – that is, the **domain** and **data** modules, as can be seen in the following screenshot:

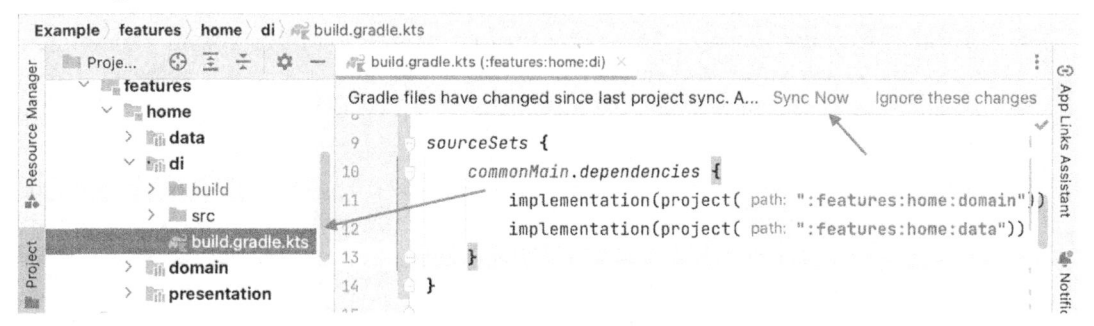

Figure 11.15: Add module dependencies to DI

Update the build script with the following entries:

1. ...
2. `kotlin {`
3. `    androidTarget()`
4.
5. `    sourceSets {`
6. `        commonMain.dependencies {`
7. `            implementation(project(":features:home:domain"))`
8. `            implementation(project(":features:home:data"))`
9. `        }`
10. `    }`
11. `}`
12. ...

The Koin dependency will also need to be added in the same place.

Chapter 10, Kotlin DSL and Multimodule Apps described the Android Studio feature of being able to update the Version Catalogs file automatically via prompts in the IDE (see *Figure 10.12*, *Figure 10.13*, *Figure 10.15*, and *Figure 10.16*). However, this does not always work. Some common causes for this are:

- **Version catalog compatibility**: The new library version might not be compatible with the existing version catalog, leading to potential conflicts or incompatibilities. Android Studio avoids suggesting changes that could introduce issues.
- **Manual dependency management**: If library dependencies in the build scripts are being manually managed, Android Studio might not automatically suggest replacing existing declarations with version catalog entries. This is to avoid disrupting the manual dependency management workflow.
- **Existing version catalog declaration**: If a library is already declared in the version catalog, Android Studio will not prompt to replace it. However, if the version catalog contains an outdated version, Android Studio will suggest updating it.
- **Library upgrade policy**: Android Studio's upgrade policy might not suggest replacing an existing declaration if the new version is a major release. This is because major version changes can introduce breaking changes, and Android Studio assumes that a review of the changes might be required before upgrading.
- **Plugin updates**: Android Studio itself might need to be updated to receive the latest upgrade information for libraries, including when to suggest replacing existing declarations with version catalog entries. Ensure that the latest version of Android Studio is installed.

The issue can be seen in the following screenshot. Only the **newer version** prompt is generated:

Figure 11.16: No Version Catalog prompt

Even when it does work, the mechanism will not know that two libraries share the same version number, as with `koin-core` and `koin-android`, and will generate two version strings in the catalog file with the same value. Instead, make the following manual additions to the `toml` file:

```
1. [versions]
2. ...
3. koin = "3.5.0"
4.
5. [libraries]
6. ...
7. koin-core = {group = "io.insert-koin", name = "koin-core", version.ref = "koin"}
8. koin-android = {group = "io.insert-koin", name = "koin-android", version.ref = "koin"}
```

With this in place and synced, add the version catalog reference to the **di** module's dependencies:

```
1. ...
2. kotlin {
3.     androidTarget()
4.
5.     sourceSets {
6.         commonMain.dependencies {
7.             implementation(project(":features:home:data"))
8.             implementation(project(":features:home:domain"))
9.             implementation(libs.koin.core)
10.        }
11.    }
12. }
13. ...
```

Add the Koin dependency to the main **app** module:

```
1. ...
2. kotlin {
3.     androidTarget()
4.
5.     sourceSets {
6.
7.         androidMain.dependencies {
8.             implementation(project(":features:home:presentation"))
9.             implementation(libs.koin.android)
10.        }
```

11.   ...
12. }
13. ...

To complete the dependency rule as shown in *Figure 11.14*, add the new **di** module dependency to the feature presentation module's build script along with the Koin dependency:

1. ...
2. dependencies {
3.   implementation(project(":features:home:domain"))
4.   implementation(project(":features:home:di"))
5.   implementation(libs.koin.android)
6.   ...
7. }

Hilt DI

Unlike Koin, Hilt is dedicated to Android so when creating the **di** module for Hilt, select the **Android Library** option in the module creation dialog (see *Figure 11.3*), in the same way as the **presentation** module using **features:home:di**. Like the **presentation** module, the new build script needs to be updated to use the version catalog and **Config** constants.

As previously mentioned in the section on Koin, the version catalogs auto-update mechanism cannot tell if two or more libraries have the same version number, as with **hilt-android** and **hilt-compiler**, and so on. Instead, make the following manual additions to the **toml** file:

1. [versions]
2. ...
3. hilt = "<latest>"
4.
5. [libraries]
6. ...
7. dagger-hilt = { group = "com.google.dagger", name = "hilt-android", version.ref = "hilt" }
8. dagger-hilt-compiler = { group = "com.google.dagger", name = "hilt-compiler", version.ref = "hilt" }
9.
10. [plugins]
11. ...
12. hilt = { id = "com.google.dagger.hilt.android", version.ref = "hilt" }

Any change to the **toml** file should be followed by a **gradle resync**. We have not committed to a Hilt version above because, at the time of writing, there were bugs in the Hilt compiler when combined with a multiplatform arrangement. Those bugs were fixed in Hilt's **HEAD-SNAPSHOT** and are likely to be released by the time this book is published. It is a good idea to try and use the latest version of any library regardless.

Edit the top-level build script, as shown in the following figure:

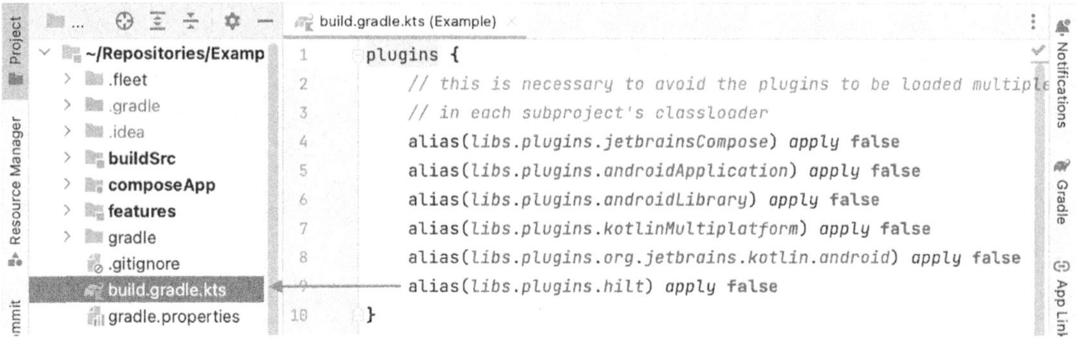

Figure 11.17: Edit top-level build script

Add the Hilt plugin to the list:

1. plugins {
2.   ...
3.   alias(libs.plugins.hilt) apply false
4. }

Hilt uses annotations to auto-generate code at compile time, such as **@HiltAndroidApp**, **@AndroidEntryPoint**, etc. **Kotlin Symbol Processing** (**KSP**) and **Kotlin Annotation Processing Tool** (**KAPT**) are both tools provided by JetBrains for annotation processing in Kotlin, but they have some differences in their architecture and usage. The setup of the Hilt **di** module will depend upon the choice of annotation processor.

KAPT

Kotlin Annotation Processing Tool (KAPT) is a command-line tool and build plugin specifically designed for the Kotlin programming language. Its primary function is to **generate code based on annotations** present in Kotlin source code.

- **Based on Annotation Processors** (**AP**): Kapt uses the standard Java Annotation Processing API. It relies on Java annotation processors to generate code during the compilation process.
- **Java interoperability**: Since it is built on top of Java's annotation processing, Kapt works seamlessly with Java-based annotation processors. Java libraries that utilize annotation processing in a Kotlin project using Kapt can be used.

- Gradle Plugin: Kapt is integrated into the Kotlin Gradle plugin (**kotlin("kapt")**). It is widely used in Android projects and other Kotlin projects where compatibility with existing Java-based annotation processors is essential.
- **Generated code location**: The generated code is typically placed in the **build/generated/source/kapt** directory.

To add the **kapt** plugin, make the following changes to the **toml** file:

1. ...
2. [plugins]
3. ...
4. kapt = {id = "org.jetbrains.kotlin.kapt", version.ref = "kotlin" }

Following the **gradle** resync, add the **kapt** plugin to the list in the top-level build script:

1. plugins {
2.   ...
3.   alias(libs.plugins.kapt) apply false
4. }

Add the Hilt dependencies to the main **app** module, as follows:

1. plugins {
2.   ...
3.   alias(libs.plugins.kapt)
4.   alias(libs.plugins.hilt)
5. }
6. ...
7. android {
8.   dependencies {
9.   implementation(libs.dagger.hilt)
10.   add("kapt", libs.dagger.hilt.compiler)
11.   ...
12.   }
13. }

Add the Hilt dependencies to the new DI build script (note the difference in adding **libs.dagger.hilt.compiler**). Also, add the module dependency rules as depicted in *Figure 11.14*. Refer to the following code:

1. plugins {
2.   ...
3.   alias(libs.plugins.kapt)
4.   alias(libs.plugins.hilt)

```
5.  }
6.  ...
7.  dependencies {
8.      implementation(project(":features:home:domain"))
9.      implementation(project(":features:home:data"))
10.     implementation(libs.dagger.hilt)
11.     kapt(libs.dagger.hilt.compiler)
12.     ...
13. }
```

To complete the dependency rule as shown in *Figure 11.14*, add the new **di** module dependency to the feature **presentation** module's build script along with the same Hilt plugins and dependencies:

```
1.  plugins {
2.      ...
3.      alias(libs.plugins.kapt)
4.      alias(libs.plugins.hilt)
5.  }
6.  ...
7.  dependencies {
8.      implementation(project(":features:home:domain"))
9.      implementation(project(":features:home:di"))
10.     implementation(libs.dagger.hilt)
11.     kapt(libs.dagger.hilt.compiler)
12.     ...
13. }
```

KSP

Kotlin Symbol Processing (KSP) is a relatively new tool introduced alongside Kotlin 1.5. Similar to Kapt, KSP also deals with processing code, but with some key differences:

- **Symbol-based processing**: KSP takes a different approach by directly analyzing the Kotlin symbol information (such as classes, functions, and properties) instead of relying on Java annotation processors. This allows KSP to take advantage of Kotlin-specific features.
- **Kotlin-centric**: KSP is designed specifically for Kotlin and is more tailored to Kotlin's language features. It aims to provide a more natural and efficient way of processing Kotlin code.
- **Gradle plugin**: KSP is a separate Gradle plugin (**com.google.devtools.ksp**) that needs to applied in the build script.

- **Generated code location**: The generated code is typically placed in the **build/ generated/ksp** directory.

To add the **ksp** plugin, make the following changes to the **toml** file:

1. [versions]
2. ...
3. ksp = " 2.0.0-1.0.21"
4.
5. [plugins]
6. ...
7. ksp = {id = "com.google.devtools.ksp", version.ref = "ksp" }

Following the gradle resync, add the ksp plugin to the list in the top-level build script:

1. plugins {
2.   ...
3.   alias(libs.plugins.ksp) apply false
4. }

Add the Hilt dependencies to the main **app** module:

1. plugins {
2.   ...
3.   alias(libs.plugins.ksp)
4.   alias(libs.plugins.hilt)
5. }
6. ...
7. android {
8.   ...
9.   dependencies {
10.   implementation(libs.dagger.hilt)
11.   ksp(libs.dagger.hilt.compiler)
12.   ...
13.   }
14. }

Add the same Hilt dependencies to the new DI build script. Also, add the module dependency rules as depicted in *Figure 11.14:*

1. plugins {
2.   ...
3.   alias(libs.plugins.ksp)

```
4.         alias(libs.plugins.hilt)
5.     }
6.     ...
7.     dependencies {
8.         implementation(project(":features:home:domain"))
9.         implementation(project(":features:home:data"))
10.        implementation(libs.dagger.hilt)
11.        ksp(libs.dagger.hilt.compiler)
12.        ...
13.    }
```

To complete the dependency rule as shown in *Figure 11.14*, add the new **di** module dependency to the feature **presentation** module's build script along with the same Hilt plugins and dependencies:

```
1.     plugins {
2.         ...
3.         alias(libs.plugins.ksp)
4.         alias(libs.plugins.hilt)
5.     }
6.     ...
7.     dependencies {
8.         implementation(project(":features:home:domain"))
9.         implementation(project(":features:home:di"))
10.        implementation(libs.dagger.hilt)
11.        ksp(libs.dagger.hilt.compiler)
12.        ...
13.    }
```

Key considerations

Some key considerations are as follows:

- **Interoperability**: Kapt is more interoperable with existing Java-based annotation processors, making it a suitable choice for projects with a mix of Kotlin and Java.
- **Kotlin-specific features**: If a project heavily relies on Kotlin-specific features and a more Kotlin-centric annotation processing experience is desired, KSP might be a better fit.
- **Tooling and maturity**: Kapt has been around for a longer time and is more mature.

Splitting out UI from presentation

In *Chapter 4, Clean Code Architecture, Figure 4.2* depicts the presentation layer comprising of `ViewModel` ojbects and UI. In fact, the `ViewModel` layer also comprises of Activities, Fragments and all things specifically Android. Since the introduction of Compose Multiplatform, pure Compose UI is no longer peculiar to Android. Optionally, this presents an opportunity to further enforce separation of concerns whilst also offering the possibility of code sharing with other platforms. The layered architecture diagram from *Figure 11.14* can be extended to include a UI module, as shown in the following figure:

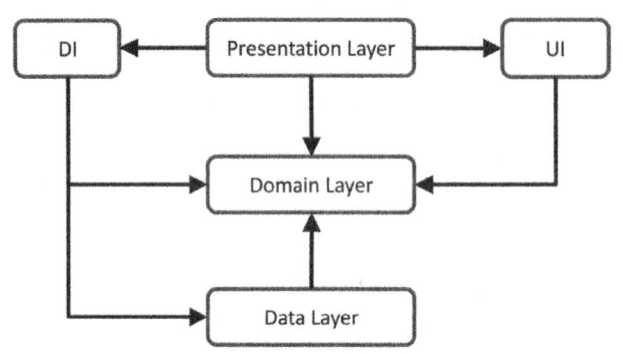

Figure 11.18: Extended layer architecture

The `presentation` module is dependent on the new `ui` module for rendered graphics. Controversially, the new `ui` module is shown as having a dependency on the `domain` module. This is so that data objects supplied by use cases in the `domain` module, invoked by the `presentation` module, can be passed directly to the UI for rendering. This means that the UI module will also have direct access to the `domain` module's use cases, which is arguably undesirable. Putting aside the fact that this would have happened anyway if the UI was integrated with Presentation, there are a couple of solutions to this:

- Having the `ui` module supply its own data classes.
  - **Advantages**: The `ui` module becomes completely independent, like the `domain` module. This can be a significant factor in frictionless team based development.
  - **Disadvantages:** Mapping between `domain` objects and `ui` objects will have to be performed by the `presentation` module. This is an extra layer of processing which will also require unit tests. Furthermore, should the project become truly multiplatform, this mapping will have to be duplicated with every platform's Presentation layer.
- Split the Domain's data classes off into their own module. The `domain` module can supply a transitive dependency on this `data` class module and the UI can have a direct dependency on it.
  - **Advantages**: No need for any extra classes, mapping or unit tests. Also, the `ui` module has direct access to the `domain` module's data classes without having access to its use cases.

o   **Disadvantages**: The **ui** module is yet another module in the system that is not completely independent. However, assuming the Domain's data class module is set up as multiplatform (which it should be), it will be a case of one KMM module being dependent on another.

There is no dedicated module creation wizard for a Compose Multiplatform library. Instead, create a regular **kmm** module and add the Compose Multiplatform plugins to the resulting build script. Follow all the same steps to create the **ui** module as the **domain** module using **features:home:ui** then make the following changes to the **ui** module's build script:

```
1. plugins {
2.     ...
3.     alias(libs.plugins.jetbrainsCompose)
4. }
5.
6. kotlin {
7.     androidTarget()
8.
9.     sourceSets {
10.        commonMain.dependencies {
11.            implementation(compose.runtime)
12.            implementation(compose.foundation)
13.            implementation(compose.material)
14.            @OptIn(ExperimentalComposeLibrary::class)
15.            implementation(compose.components.resources)
16.            implementation(project(":features:home:domain"))
17.        }
18.    }
19. }
20. ...
```

Note: By default, the compiler might raise warnings or errors when you use experimental APIs. The @OptIn(ExperimentalComposeLibrary::class) annotation tells the compiler you're aware of the experimental nature and choose to use the feature at your own risk.

Essentially, the plugin and its subsequent usages in the dependencies block have been copied directly from the main **app** module's build script. Additionally, that **domain** module dependency has also been added.

To complete the dependency rule arrangement from *Figure 11.18*, add the UI dependency to the **presentation** module's build script:

```
1.  dependencies {
2.      implementation(project(":features:home:domain"))
3.      implementation(project(":features:home:di"))
4.      implementation(project(":features:home:ui"))
5.      ...
6.  }
```

It should be pointed out that there are only two modules from *Figure 11.18* that are dedicated to Android libraries if using Hilt. If Koin is used, then the only module that would need translating to other platforms is the Presentation module.

Creating an infrastructure (common) module

Typically, multimodule projects will have common custom code shared between modules. Traditionally, in Android projects, this has been a top-level Android library named **common**. Too often, this module becomes a dumping ground for all shared code. Over time, this too will become unmanageable.

We recommend adopting a hierarchical module approach, similar to that described above, with each submodule being dedicated to a particular function. Also, given the aforementioned notoriety of common, we recommend avoiding that name. For example, we wanted a common module defining constant values for navigation between screens:

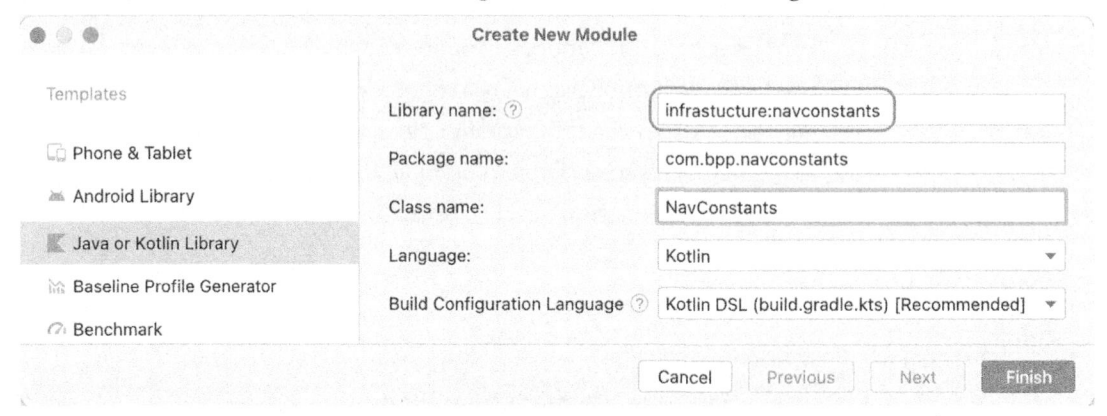

Figure 11.19: Creating a common module

We are arranging all of our common modules under a group called **infrastructure**. In this case, the Kotlin library template has been selected but this will change depending on the common module's purpose. The resulting module structure in this example will look like this:

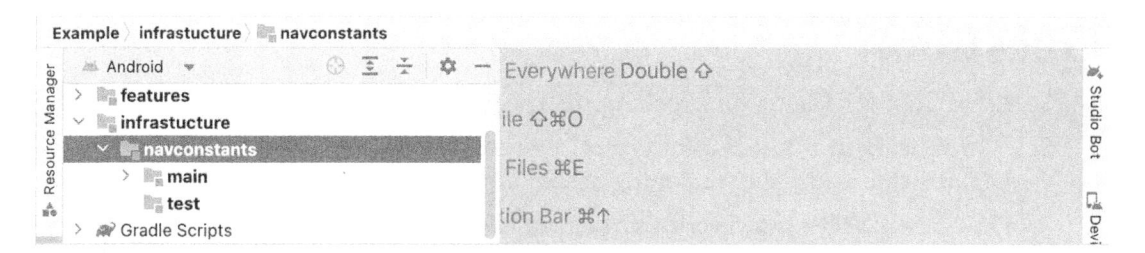

Figure 11.20: Common module structure

Conclusion

This chapter presented the steps required to create a module hierarchy in a project that is consistent with the feature-oriented development and clean code architecture layering discussed in *Chapter 3, Feature Oriented Development,* and *Chapter 4, Clean Code Architecture* respectively. Ultimately, only two types of modules were created: multiplatform and Android-specific. The multiplatform modules were used primarily to reinforce the separation of concerns between the layers defined by CCA layering rather than to provide support for other platforms. However, the latter is an added bonus.

A criticism could be leveled against this approach due to the sheer number of modules that need to be created. The complexity of the build scripts and the time taken to set up modules is a common developer complaint. For that reason, a team at JetBrains is developing an alternative method for defining build scripts. Project **Amper** simplifies build script definition using `yaml` files, similar in syntax to the `toml` Version Catalog file. The project was still in preview at the time of writing, so it has not been documented here. However, Amper is a layer on top of gradle rather than a replacement for it, so this chapter will remain valid.

The next chapter will examine the Data Layer in more detail by reviewing networking and APIs in Kotlin.

Points to remember

- Use a modularization technique to mirror the CCA layering pattern for features.
- Use KMM modules for Data and Domain.
- Create a separate `di` module dedicated to binding `domain` interfaces with Data implementations.
- Consider splitting your UI out of your `presentation` module into a Compose multiplatform module

Questions

1. What are the reasons for breaking up a feature into submodules?
2. Which fields in a build script typically need changing from that generated by the wizards to coordinate versioning across modules.
3. How can a KMM build script be simplified to target just Android?
4. What additions are made in build scripts to affect the CCA dependency rules?
5. How do build scripts using Hilt and Koin differ?
6. How do you create a Compose multiplatform module?
7. What would the build script definitions described in this chapter look like using Amper?

Join our book's Discord space

Join the book's Discord Workspace for Latest updates, Offers, Tech happenings around the world, New Release and Sessions with the Authors:

https://discord.bpbonline.com

CHAPTER 12
Networking and APIs in Kotlin

Introduction

In the dynamic landscape of mobile applications, seamless connectivity and efficient data exchange are fundamental to providing a rich and interactive user experience. Android, as a leading mobile operating system, empowers developers to harness the power of networking and **Application Programming Interfaces** (**APIs**) to connect their applications with external servers, services, and data sources. This connectivity enables a wide range of functionalities, from retrieving real-time information to uploading user-generated content.

Networking in Android involves the exchange of data between a user's device and remote servers over the internet. This communication is crucial for fetching information, sending updates, and synchronizing data. Understanding the intricacies of HTTP requests, asynchronous processing, and secure communication protocols forms the foundation for robust networking in Android.

Structure

This chapter covers the following topics:

- Networking in Android
- Definition of an API
- RESTful APIs

- Networking libraries
- Authentication and security
- Data module setup
- Data classes
- Test-driving the network call
- Caching
- Test-driving the use cases
- DI module binding

Objectives

This chapter examines use cases for aspects of networking in Android. By the end of this chapter, you will understand the concepts of APIs (in particular, RESTful APIs), caching, and authentication. You will also be able to understand various networking libraries in the end.

This chapter will provide a working example of a network call using the clean-code architecture and test-driven development concepts introduced in *Chapter 4, Clean Code Architecture* and *Chapter 9, Test Driven Development* respectively.

Networking in Android

In the context of Android development, networking refers to the communication between an Android application and external servers, services, or other devices over the internet. Networking is a fundamental aspect of mobile app development, enabling apps to send and receive data, interact with web services, and access information from remote servers. This communication allows apps to:

- **Access data**: Download content like images, videos, music, and text from online sources.
- **Transfer data**: Send information like photos, messages, and app data to other devices.
- **Use online services**: Connect to social media platforms, banking apps, streaming services, etc.
- **Sync data**: Keep data (contacts, calendar entries, notes) consistent across different devices.

Here are some specific examples of how networking is used in Android apps:

- **Social media apps**: Send and receive messages, share photos, and access news feeds.
- **Streaming apps**: Play music, watch videos, and listen to podcasts from online sources.

- **Navigation apps**: Download maps, get directions, and find real-time traffic updates.
- **E-commerce apps**: Browse products, add items to carts, and make purchases online.

Here are key aspects of networking in Android:

- **HTTP requests**: Android apps commonly use **Hypertext Transfer Protocol (HTTP)** to communicate with servers. This involves sending requests (for example, `GET`, `POST`) to a server and receiving responses.
- **RESTful APIs**: Many Android apps interact with **Representational State Transfer (RESTful APIs)**. REST is an architectural style that uses standard HTTP methods and status codes for communication. It is widely used for building web services. See the next section for details on APIs.
- **Asynchronous processing**: Networking operations can be time-consuming, so it is crucial to perform them asynchronously to avoid blocking the main (UI) thread. Kotlin's coroutines are commonly used for this purpose.
- **JSON parsing**: The data exchanged between an Android app and a server is often in **JavaScript Object Notation (JSON)** format. Parsing libraries, such as Gson or Moshi, help convert JSON data into usable objects within the app.
- **Background execution**: Networking operations are typically performed in the background to maintain a responsive user interface. Android services or background threads can be used to handle background networking tasks.
- **Error handling**: Robust error handling is critical for a good user experience. Android apps should gracefully handle scenarios like network unavailability, server errors, or unexpected responses.
- **Data caching**: To improve performance and reduce the load on servers, apps may implement caching strategies. Cached data can be used when the device is offline or when retrieving fresh data is unnecessary.
- **WebSockets**: For real-time communication, some apps use WebSockets, a protocol that enables bidirectional communication between a client and a server over a single, long-lived connection.
- **Testing**: Networking code should be thoroughly tested. Unit tests can be written to verify that networking-related functions behave as expected. Mocking frameworks are often used to simulate server responses during testing.

Definition of an API

An API is a set of rules and tools that allow different software applications to communicate with each other. Applications in this context, can refer to mobile apps, web apps, backend services, etc. It defines the methods and data formats that applications can use to request and exchange information. APIs play a fundamental role in modern software development, enabling developers to access the functionality of external services, libraries, or platforms without needing to understand their internal workings.

Here is a simple analogy: Imagine a customer at a restaurant. The customer wants to order food but cannot go directly into the kitchen and start cooking. Instead, they rely on the waiter as an intermediary. The waiter takes the customer's order, communicates it to the kitchen, and brings back the prepared meal. In this scenario:

- The customer is the application making a request.
- The kitchen is the system that holds the data or functionality the customer needs.
- The waiter is the API, acting as the bridge between the customer and the kitchen. Refer to the following figure:

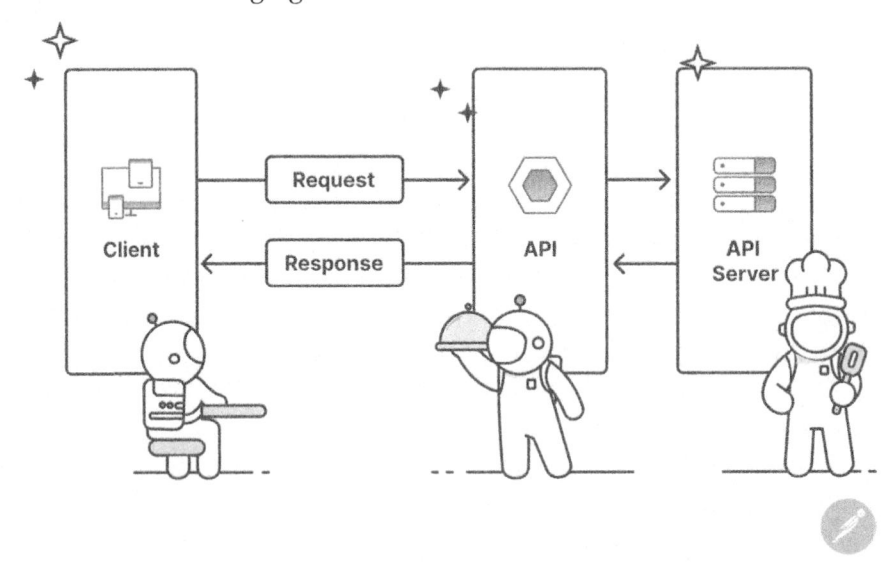

Figure 12.1: API (Source: postman.com)

Key aspects of APIs

Here are some key aspects of APIs:

- **Communication protocol (rules and specifications)**: APIs define a set of rules for how software components should interact. This includes specifying the data formats that should be used in requests and responses.
- **Request-response model**: Typically, applications make requests to an API, and the API sends back responses with the requested data or actions.
- **Abstraction layer**: APIs act as an abstraction layer, allowing developers to use certain features or services without understanding the underlying implementation. This simplifies development by providing a standardized way to interact with external systems.

- **Functionality access**: APIs expose a set of functions or methods that developers can use to perform specific tasks. For example, a weather API might provide methods to retrieve current weather conditions based on location.
- **Data exchange**: APIs facilitate the exchange of data between different software systems. This data exchange can occur in various formats, such as JSON or XML, and is typically sent over HTTP or another communication protocol.
- **Authentication and authorization**: Many APIs require authentication to ensure that only authorized users or applications can access certain features. This is often done using API keys, OAuth tokens, or other authentication mechanisms.
- **Documentation**: API documentation is crucial for developers to understand how to use an API correctly. It provides information about available endpoints, request and response formats, authentication requirements, and usage examples.
- **Versioning**: As software evolves, APIs may be updated to add new features or improve existing ones. API versioning ensures that changes do not break existing applications that rely on the API.

Common types of APIs

Here are some common types of APIs:

- **Web APIs**: These APIs are accessed over the internet using web protocols like HTTP. They are widely used for sharing data and functionality between web services and applications.
- **REST APIs**: REST is a popular architectural style for web APIs that emphasizes simplicity, flexibility, and scalability.
- **SOAP APIs: Simple Object Access Protocol (SOAP)** is another web API approach, often used in enterprise applications for its structured messaging and security features.
- **Mobile app APIs**: These APIs enable mobile apps to interact with backend services and data.
- **Internal APIs**: Organizations often create internal APIs to facilitate communication between different parts of their software systems.
- **Third-party APIs**: Developers often use third-party APIs to integrate existing services into their applications. For example, a mobile app might use a mapping API to display location data.
- **Library APIs**: APIs are not limited to web services. Libraries and frameworks also expose APIs that developers can use to integrate functionality into their applications.

In summary, an API serves as a bridge between different software systems, allowing them to work together by providing a standardized way for them to communicate and share data.

RESTful APIs

Of all of these types of APIs, the most popular – at least with regard to mobile applications – is RESTful APIs. The following figure provides an overview of the RESTful API architecture:

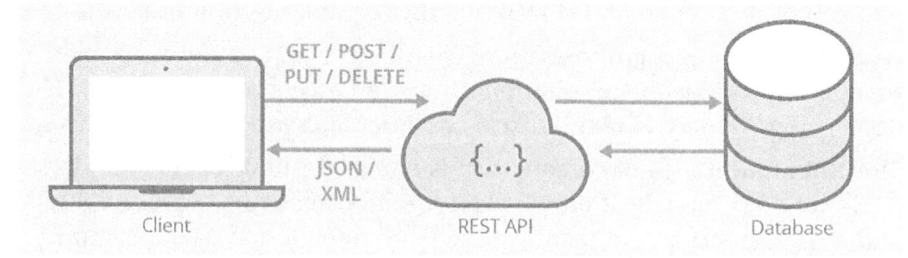

Figure 12.2: RESTful API (Source: interserver.net)

RESTful APIs are a type of architectural style for designing networked applications. They are based on a set of principles that, when followed, make it easier for different systems to communicate with each other. RESTful APIs are widely used for building web services due to their simplicity, scalability, and ease of integration. Here are some key aspects of RESTful APIs:

- **Resource-based**: It models data as resources with **unique identifiers (URIs)** to access and manipulate them.
- **Stateless**: Each request contains all necessary information to understand and process it, without relying on server-side session state.
- **Client-server architecture**: Clients (like web browsers or mobile apps) make requests to servers, which process them and send back responses.
- **Data formats**: Commonly use JSON or XML to exchange data between client and server, offering human-readable and machine-parseable formats.

Here are the essential parts of a RESTful API request:

- **URL**: The URL specifies the address of the API endpoint to interact with and identifies the resource requested or the action to perform. For example:
- `https://api.example.com/users`
- **HTTP method**: Indicates the type of operation requested. Common methods are:
  - `GET`: Retrieves data from the server.
  - `POST`: Creates new data on the server.
  - `PUT`: Updates existing data on the server.
  - `DELETE`: Removes data from the server.
- **Headers**: Provide additional information about the request or client, typically in key/value pairs. Examples are:

o **Content-type**: Specifies the format of the request body (for example, `application/json`).

o **Authorization**: Contains authentication credentials (for example, API keys, tokens).

o **Accept**: Indicates the preferred response format (for example, `application/json`).

- **Body (optional)**: Used for sending data to the server, primarily with `POST`, `PUT`, and sometimes `PATCH` requests. The body can contain various data formats like JSON, XML, or plain text.
- **Parameters (optional)**: Parameters are used to filter or modify the request and can be included in the URL as query parameters or in the body as request parameters. For example: `https://api.example.com/users?page=2&limit=10`

Networking libraries

Android offers several popular libraries to simplify and handle various aspects of networking and fetching data from APIs, each with its own strengths and considerations. In this section we will be fetching data from a simple API and present the alternative approaches with each library. The following libraries will be covered:

- Android framework (java.net)
- OkHttp
- Volley
- Retrofit
- Ktor

The API we will be using is the fictitious Martian real-estate data used by a number of Android beginner's tutorials. Source: **udacity.com**.

https://mars.udacity.com/realestate

We will be assigning this string in our code to a constant called `marsUrl`. Calling this API will yield JSON formatted results similar to the following code:

```
1.  [
2.      {
3.          "price":450000,
4.          "id":"424905",
5.          "type":"buy",
6.          "img_src":"http://mars.jpl.nasa.gov/msl-raw-images/..."
7.      },
8.      ...
9.  ]
```

This will correspond directly to a list of the following **data** class:

```
1.  data class MarsData(
2.      val price: Int, // currency price (in dollars?)
3.      val id: Int, // unique id number for the plot of land
4.      val type: String, // either "buy" or "rent"
5.      val img_src: String // a url of an image
6.  )
```

In each case we will be writing a function with the following signature:

```
1.  suspend fun fetchMarsData(): Result<List<MarsData>>
```

As a **suspend** function, **fetchMarsData** will need to be called on a background coroutine thread, as discussed in previous chapters. **Result** is a built-in Kotlin class designed to wrap an http result with either a success or failure status.

> Note: When attempting to make any network calls in Android, do not forget to add the permission in the app's **AndroidManifest** file just before the application entry:

```
1.  <uses-permission android:name="android.permission.INTERNET" />
```

Android framework (java.net)

In fact, it is not strictly necessary to use a third-party library. Android provides basic classes for network operations like **URL**, **URLConnection**, and **HttpURLConnection** via java.net

They offer low-level control but require more manual work. **fetchMarsData** can be achieved with the following code:

```
1.  suspend fun fetchMarsData(): Result<List<MarsData>> {
2.      val connection = URL(marsUrl).openConnection() as HttpURLConnection
3.
4.      try {
5.          return withContext(Dispatchers.IO) {
6.              connection.connect()
7.              if (connection.responseCode == HttpURLConnection.HTTP_OK) {
8.                  Result.success(
9.                      Gson().fromJson(
10.                         connection.inputStream.bufferedReader().readText(),
11.                         Array<MarsData>::class.java
12.                     ).toList()
13.                 )
14.             } else {
```

```
15.             Result.failure(IOException(connection.responseMessage))
16.         }
17.       }
18.    } catch (e: Throwable) {
19.       return Result.failure(e)
20.    } finally {
21.       connection.disconnect()
22.    }
23. }
```

A **connection** value is created by down-casting the result of **openConnection** on a **URL** object formed from the **marsUrl**. Calling **connect** on the **connection** needs to be done within the scope of a dispatcher context and can throw an exception, hence the try-catch arrangement.

withContext(Dispatchers.IO) {…} provides the coroutine dispatcher context. Anything within the scoping brackets will be run on the thread specified by the dispatcher – the IO thread in this case.

If the connection is successful, **Gson** is used in this case to return a parsed list of **MarsData** objects otherwise a **failure** result is returned instead.

The preceding example is a simple **GET**. The framework supports the other REST commands with methods and attributes on the **connection** object, such as **requestMethod** and **setRequestProperty** to set headers.

OkHttp

OkHttp is a low-level HTTP client library written by Square that provides building blocks for other libraries. As such, it is not intended for direct use by most developers and requires understanding of lower-level networking concepts.

It features powerful customization options and supports various HTTP features like caching, interceptors and timeouts. It is highly flexible and suitable for advanced users with specific needs. The following code is an example usage of **OkHttp**:

```
1. suspend fun fetchMarsData(): Result<List<MarsData>> =
2.    withContext(Dispatchers.IO) {
3.       val client = OkHttpClient()
4.       val request = Request.Builder().url(marsUrl).build()
5.       val response = client.newCall(request).execute()
6.
7.       if (response.isSuccessful) response.body?.run {
```

```
8.              Result.success(
9.                  Gson().fromJson(
10.                     string(),
11.                     Array<MarsData>::class.java
12.                 ).toList()
13.             )
14.         } ?: Result.failure(IOException("Empty response"))
15.         else Result.failure(IOException(response.message))
16.     }
```

Although **OkHttp** is Kotlin under the hood, it does not have embedded support for coroutines. The previous example has been adapted to work with coroutines by using a dispatcher coupled with the **execute** call that runs on the current thread. In fact, **OkHttp** supplies its own background processing arrangement with callbacks, as can be seen in the following example:

```
1.  fun fetchMarsData() {
2.      val client = OkHttpClient()
3.      val request = Request.Builder().url(marsUrl).build()
4.      client.newCall(request).enqueue(
5.          object : Callback {
6.              override fun onFailure(call: Call, e: IOException) {
7.                  TODO("Not yet implemented")
8.              }
9.
10.             override fun onResponse(call: Call, response: Response) {
11.                 TODO("Not yet implemented")
12.             }
13.         }
14.     )
15. }
```

The previous examples can be converted to a **POST** with a chained interface method on the request builder, for example:

```
1.  val content = "some content"
2.
3.  val request: Request = Request.Builder()
4.      .url(marsUrl)
5.      .post(content.toRequestBody())
6.      .build()
```

There is also a method on the builder for setting header values: **addHeader**.

Volley

Volley is a popular networking library for Android, developed by Google. It aimed to simplify network requests and improve performance compared to using the raw `HttpURLConnection` approach.

Volley provides the following features:

- **Automatic request queue management**: Manages concurrent requests on a background thread, preventing UI thread blockage.
- **Prioritization and cancellation**: Supports setting request priorities and cancelling individual or groups of requests.
- **Caching**: Efficiently caches responses to improve performance for subsequent requests with the same data.
- **Image loading**: Offers built-in functionality for loading images asynchronously from URLs.
- **JSON parsing**: Provides basic JSON parsing capabilities, although external libraries like Gson or Moshi are recommended for all but the simplest of responses.
- **Cancellation with coroutines**: Seamless integration with Kotlin coroutines allows for advanced asynchronous control and cancellation.

Here is the volley version of the `Mars` data fetch mechanism:

```
1. suspend fun fetchMarsData(
2.     context: Context
3. ): Result<List<MarsData>> = suspendCoroutine { result ->
4.     val queue = Volley.newRequestQueue(context)
5.
6.     val request = JsonArrayRequest(GET, marsUrl, null, { response ->
7.         result.resume(
8.             Result.success(
9.                 Gson().fromJson(
10.                     response.toString(),
11.                     Array<MarsData>::class.java
12.                 ).toList()
13.             )
14.         )
15.     }, { error -> result.resume(Result.failure(error)) })
16.
17.     queue.add(request)
18. }
```

The first thing to notice is that we needed to change the function signature to take an Android **Context** object. This is because Volley is designed to be called from Activities or Fragments. Volley's internal code will manage lifecycle states via the **Context** reference and will handle request cancellation in the event of an orientation change to avoid memory leaks (allowing Activities to be correctly destroyed and recreated). This is likely to be the reason why Volley has fallen out of favor. Modern apps now make network calls from **ViewModel**s which persist between orientation changes. Furthermore, since Volley is dependent on Android, it cannot be used in cross-platform KMM modules.

Retrofit

Retrofit, another Square product, is a popular type-safe HTTP client library for Android and Java developers. It simplifies sending and receiving data from REST APIs, making it a robust and convenient choice for network communication in apps.

Retrofit offers a powerful and user-friendly approach to interacting with REST APIs in Android and Java development. Its focus on type safety (for example, **Int** objects cannot be overwritten by **String** types), automatic parsing (see JSON parsing above), and asynchronous communication makes it a popular choice for building robust and maintainable network connections in Android apps. Here is the Retrofit version of the **Mars** data fetch mechanism:

```
1.  interface MarsApi {
2.      @GET("realestate")
3.      suspend fun getMarsData(): List<MarsData>
4.  }
5.
6.  suspend fun fetchMarsData(): Result<List<MarsData>> {
7.      val retrofit = Retrofit.Builder()
8.          .baseUrl("https://mars.udacity.com/")
9.          .addConverterFactory(GsonConverterFactory.create())
10.         .build()
11.
12.     val marsApi = retrofit.create(MarsApi::class.java)
13.
14.     return try {
15.         Result.success(marsApi.getMarsData())
16.     } catch (e: Throwable) {
17.         Result.failure(e)
18.     }
19. }
```

We needed to split **marsUrl** into scheme/domain and path for Retrofit. This is useful where a single base URL provides several APIs. In those cases, the **retrofit** object can be extracted as a lazy object or returned by a first-class method which would make this code significantly more concise.

At the time of writing, Retrofit was the most popular network library used in Android apps. The main disadvantage, however, is that it cannot be used in KMM modules. Retrofit's primary design and development focus is on Android, with its core features and dependencies tailored for the Android platform. Retrofit relies on **OkHttp**, which in turn depends on platform-specific classes and APIs for network calls. Furthermore, the code-generation from the annotations that Retrofit also relies on is not supported by KMM.

Ktor

Ktor is a powerful, asynchronous framework for building clients, web applications and APIs using the Kotlin programming language. It offers a comprehensive set of features and a lightweight, modular approach, making it a popular choice for both simple and complex web development projects as well as Android clients.

Ktor includes the following features:

- **Asynchronous**: Leverage Kotlin coroutines for non-blocking, high-performance server and client communication.
- **Lightweight and modular**: Choose only the features needed for a specific project, keeping codebases lean and maintainable.
- **Kotlin-first**: Designed specifically for Kotlin, leveraging its conciseness and functional programming features for a productive development experience.
- **Scalable and robust**: Highly performant and capable of handling high traffic volumes.
- **Comprehensive features**: Covers a wide range of functionalities, including routing, templating, authentication, serialization, and more.
- **Multiplatform**: Build servers and clients for various platforms, including Linux, Windows, macOS, Android, and iOS.

The **Ktor** client for our **Mars** data fetch mechanism would look like this:

```
1.  suspend fun fetchMarsData(): Result<List<MarsData>> = try {
2.      val ktorClient = HttpClient {
3.          install(ContentNegotiation) { json() }
4.      }
5.      val response: HttpResponse = ktorClient.get(marsUrl)
6.
7.      if (response.status.isSuccess()) {
```

```
 8.            Result.success(response.body<List<MarsData>>())
 9.        } else {
10.            Result.failure(IOException(response.status.description))
11.        }
12. } catch (e: Exception) {
13.     Result.failure(e)
14. }
```

In a similar way to Retrofit, the **ktorClient** definition can be extracted as a lazy object or returned by a first-class method. That way it can be reused for other API calls with the same content negotiation.

As with all of the libraries documented here, Ktor provides methods on the client object for setting headers, HTTP method and **POST** data.

Ktor is the network client library of choice for modern, multi-module apps and is the only one recommended to work in KMM modules, given that there are platform versions to compile for Android, iOS, JVM (Linux, Windows, macOS) and JavaScript – all from the same source code. Furthermore, Ktor supplies libraries for backend development so the entire client-server arrangement *could* be written in Kotlin – another reason why Kotlin is a great choice for a coding language!

Authentication and security

Secure communication is paramount. Android apps use HTTPS for encrypted data transfer, and mechanisms like API keys or OAuth tokens ensure authentication and authorization.

API keys

An API key is a code passed in by an app calling an API to identify the calling program. API keys are typically used to control access and monitor usage of an API. They serve as a form of authentication and authorization, allowing the API provider to track and control how their services are being used.

Here is a breakdown of how API keys work:

- **Generation**: API keys are generated by the service or platform providing the API. This is typically done through their developer portal or backend systems. For example, an API provider might require the creation of an account on their website, often including payment details. Once registered the site would provide a unique identifier string to use with the app.
- **Inclusion in requests**: When making a request to an API, the developer includes the API key in the request. This is often done by adding it to the request headers or parameters. For simplicity, the Mars real estate API described in the previous

section does not require any authorization. However, if it did, our fetch may be modified in the following way (using Ktor):

```
1. val apiKey = "your_api_key"
2. ...
3. val resp: HttpResponse = ktorClient.get(marsUrl) {
4.     header("Authorization", "Bearer $apiKey")
5. }
6. ...
```

A less secure but equally valid way would be to include the key as a query parameter in the URL:

```
1. val resp: HttpResponse = ktorClient.
   get("$marsUrl?apiKey=$apiKey")
```

- **Authentication**: The API provider's servers receive the request along with the API key. They check the key to verify the identity of the requester. If the key is valid, the request is processed; otherwise, access is denied.

OAuth tokens

Open Authorization (OAuth) tokens are a type of access token used in the OAuth protocol to grant third-party applications limited access to a user's resources without exposing their credentials. OAuth is a widely adopted open standard for access delegation, commonly used for authorization in scenarios where one application needs to access resources on behalf of a user from another application. In other words, an app can use tokens generated by services that are already installed and authenticated on a device, like Google, Facebook, X, and so on. The use of OAuth is recognizable when a dialog is presented such as Login with Google (or a list of other services).

OAuth services provide the following:

- **Access token**: The primary token in OAuth is the access token. It grants the client limited access to specific resources on behalf of the user. Access tokens are time-limited and need to be refreshed periodically.
- **Refresh token**: A refresh token is an optional component that comes with some OAuth flows. It is used to obtain a new access token once the original access token expires without requiring the user to re-authenticate.

Providing a simple Kotlin code example is difficult due to the complexity of the back-and-forth exchange of data needed to fetch the various tokens and the different requirements of each of the OAuth providers. However, Ktor provides plugins that can be applied to the client object to help achieve it:

```
1. val client = HttpClient {
2.     ...
```

```
3.    install(Auth) {
4.        bearer {
5.            loadTokens { /* BearerTokens object */ }
6.            refreshTokens { /* BearerTokens object */ }
7.        }
8.    }
9. }
```

For example, the Ktor documentation provides the following diagrammatic example of the data exchange required to fetch the tokens and achieve the authorization flow for Google OAuth:

```
(1)  --> Authorization request                    Resource owner
(2)  <-- Authorization grant (code)               Resource owner
(3)  --> Authorization grant (code)               Authorization server
(4)  <-- Access and refresh tokens                Authorization server
(5)  --> Request with valid token                 Resource server
(6)  <-- Protected resource                       Resource server
         Token expired
(7)  --> Request with expired token               Resource server
(8)  <-- 401 Unauthorized response                Resource server
(9)  --> Authorization grant (refresh token)      Authorization server
(10) <-- Access and refresh tokens                Authorization server
(11) --> Request with new token                   Resource server
(12) <-- Protected resource                       Resource server
```

Figure 12.3: OAuth authorization flow (Source: ktor.io)

The initial authorization request will require *secret* key strings allocated by the OAuth providers when an app is registered with them. The next section demonstrates how to set up the feature data module, created in the previous chapter, to use Ktor.

Data module setup

In this section, we will revisit the module hierarchy introduced in *Chapter 11, Creating the Module Hierarchy,* and configuring the home feature KMM data module for the Ktor client. We will use the Mars real estate example from the previous section.

Build script updates

To build script updates, follow these steps:

1. The first thing to do is to add the Ktor library references to the **libs.versions.toml** (**toml**) file:
    1. [versions]
    2. ...

       3. kotlin = "1.9.21" # should already be here
       4. ...
       5. ktor = "2.3.7" # ...or latest
       6.
       7. [libraries]
       8. ...
       9. ktor-serializationJson = { module = "io.ktor:ktor-serialization-kotlinx-json", version.ref = "ktor" }
       10. ktor-android = { module = "io.ktor:ktor-client-android", version.ref = "ktor" }
       11. ktor-contentNegotiation = { module = "io.ktor:ktor-client-content-negotiation", version.ref = "ktor" }
       12.
       13. [plugins]
       14. ...
       15. serialization = { id = "org.jetbrains.kotlin.plugin.serialization", version.ref = "kotlin" }
    2. Remember to re-sync the project directly after changing the **toml** file. Otherwise, the changes will not be automatically picked up when the additions are made to the build scripts.

       Ktor uses Kotlin serialization annotation when parsing responses, hence the addition of the associated plugin, as seen on the last line of the **toml** file above. An example of the serialization annotation in the code will follow shortly. The serialization plugin needs to be referenced in the top-level project build script:
       1. plugins {
       2.   ...
       3.   alias(libs.plugins.serialization) apply false
       4. }
    3. Similarly, the feature data module build script, will be as follows:
       1. plugins {
       2.   ...
       3.   alias(libs.plugins.serialization)
       4. }
       5. ...
    4. The serialization plugin works in tandem with the Ktor JSON serialization library which needs to be referenced in the same data module build script:

```
1.  ...
2.  kotlin {
3.      ...
4.      sourceSets {
5.          androidMain.dependencies {
6.              implementation(libs.ktor.android)
7.          }
8.          commonMain.dependencies {
9.              implementation(project(":features:home:domain"))
10.             implementation(libs.ktor.serializationJson)
11.             implementation(libs.ktor.contentNegotiation)
12.         }
13.     }
14. }
15. ...
```

5. As can be seen, the Ktor Android client library reference has also been added here (line 6). The addition of the content negotiation library at line 11 is optional, depending upon where the Ktor client object is located (`ktorClient` in the `fetchMarsData` code example in the previous section). The client definition is the only code that needs the content negotiation library. If the same client object is shared between several modules, then the client could be defined in a common infrastructure library, as described in *Chapter 11, Creating the Module Hierarchy*. In which case, that common module is the only one that needs the dependency.

Data classes

When parsing the response from an API call in Ktor, typically two data classes are required for each unique JSON response format. One is an annotated class used directly by Ktor to fetch the data and the other is the corresponding Domain layer object used by the Presentation layer to populate the UI, as can be seen in the following example.

As previously mentioned, Ktor uses Kotlin serialization annotation when parsing responses. We would need to add these annotations to our previously defined `MarsData` class:

```
1.  @Serializable
2.  internal data class MarsData(
3.      val price: Int,
4.      val id: Int,
```

```
5.      val type: String,
6.      @SerialName("img_src")
7.      val imgSrc: String
8.  )
```

The updated class has been marked as **internal** to reinforce the fact that this raw data class should not be available outside of the **data** module.

Notice the **@SerialName** annotation on the **imgSrc** field. If the field names match the corresponding JSON response and they are descriptive enough, there is no need for this annotation. However, in this case **img_src** was raising an IDE warning **Property name 'img_src' should not contain underscores**. This annotation allows the assignment of any field name required associated with the corresponding JSON field.

As previously mentioned, this data class is not typically exposed to the UI via the Domain layer for two reasons:

- The raw data is not particularly UI friendly. Consider the string field type for example. This would be better served as an **enum** or even in this case, a **Boolean** since there are only two valid possibilities, **buy** or **rent**. This is a particularly simple example but in real life there are generally only a relatively small number of fields that are useful to the UI.
- The annotations are specifically used by Ktor. It would become awkward if the other layers were dependent on this class and Ktor needed to be replaced at some stage.

For that reason, the data layer will be responsible for mapping the raw data class (**MarsData**) to a UI-friendly **data** class defined by the Domain layer. For example:

```
1. data class MarsEstate(
2.     val price: Int,
3.     val isBuy: Boolean,
4.     val imgSrc: String
5. )
```

The **id** field has been dropped as all our information on the estate is already in the **data** class. This would have to be retained had there been a separate call to retrieve further details on each estate.

Test-driving the network call

Ktor provides an http mocking library so the calls to the repository and the subsequent data mapping can be developed via TDD, as described in *Chapter 9, Test-Driven Development with Mocking Libraries for Android*. The mocking arrangement is achieved by supplying a mock *engine* to the client object.

MockEngine

Ktor needs to know what platform it is running on, to make platform-specific network calls under the hood. This is achieved by passing a platform-specific object to the **HttpClient** constructor. In the **Networking** libraries section, we defined a client this way:

```
1.    val ktorClient = HttpClient {
2.        ...
3.    }
```

In this particular instance, Ktor invokes a factory function with **HttpClient** to return a client object constructed with an engine object. The factory looks up the most appropriate engine for the host client. There are predefined engine objects for Android, Apache, Jetty, and several others. In the case above, the **Android** engine is automatically supplied to the **HttpClient** constructor. If the code was restricted to only work with Android, the above example could just as easily be written like this:

```
1.    val ktorClient = HttpClient(Android) {
2.        ...
3.    }
```

For testing purposes, the engine can be replaced in test code to supplying a predictable result bypassing any actual network calls. For example, say that we wanted to test our original **fetchMarsData** function with a list containing a single result defined like this:

```
1.  val jsonString = """
2.      [
3.          {
4.              "price":450000,
5.              "id":"424905",
6.              "type":"buy",
7.              "img_src":"http://mars.jpl.nasa.gov/msl-raw-images/..."
8.          }
9.      ]"""
```

The preceding **string** could then be used to define the output from the network call in the test engine definition:

```
1.  val mockEngine = MockEngine { request ->
2.      /* test request object to match expected api call */
3.      respond(
4.          content = ByteReadChannel(jsonString),
5.          status = HttpStatusCode.OK,
6.          headers = headersOf(HttpHeaders.ContentType, "application/json")
```

```
7.    )
8. }
```

There are a few things to note here:

- The **MockEngine** lambda presents the opportunity to test whether or not the request is formed correctly, as defined by the API documentation. The **HttpRequestData** object supplied by **request** can be tested for the expected URL, method, headers and body.
- The **content-type** header is important as it is used by Ktor to select the appropriate parser. There exists a different version of this same Mars data API that incorrectly sets the resulting **content-type** to **text/plain** – even if the request header is set to **Accept application/json**. In that case, objects are unable to be extracted directly with **response.body<List<MarsData>>()**. Attempting to do so will throw a **NoTransformationFoundException**. The response must first be extracted as a string using **response.body<String>()**, then a third-party string parser must be used, like **Gson** in the other library examples. This is unlikely to be a problem with properly maintained APIs, however.

Once the engine object is defined similar to the above, it can be used to create the client object, as follows:

```
1. ktorClient = HttpClient(mockEngine) {
2.     install(ContentNegotiation) { json() }
3. }
```

Of course, this code cannot be substituted directly into the existing **fetchMarsData** example. In fact, as it stands, the **fetchMarsData** example is not fit for purpose. The method returns a list of **MarsData**, not **MarsEstate**. Instead, a use-case input port with dependency injection needs to be test-driven.

Use-case input port

Clean code architecture (**CCA**) was discussed in *Chapter 4, Clean Code Architecture*. Specifically, in the section on Flow control, use-case input ports were examined. To comply with CCA, the Mars real estate fetching mechanism must implement a use-case input port interface defined by the Domain layer. This can be test-driven. Firstly, ensure that the data module has the prerequisite test dependencies:

The following is a suggestion for the test dependency entries in the **libs.versions.toml**:

```
1. [versions]
2. ...
3. junit = "4.13.2"
4. ktor = "2.3.7"
5. coTest = "1.7.0"
```

```
6.
7.  [libraries]
8.  ...
9.  junit = { group = "junit", name = "junit", version.ref = "junit" }
10. ktor-mock = { module = "io.ktor:ktor-client-mock", version.ref =
    "ktor" }
11. coTest = { module = "org.jetbrains.kotlinx:kotlinx-coroutines-test",
    version.ref = "coTest" }
12.
13. [plugins]
14. ...
```

With the highlighted additions in place in the version catalog, the following corresponding entries in the build script can be made (**features/home/data/build.gradle.kts**).

```
1.  ...
2.  kotlin {
3.      androidTarget()
4.
5.      sourceSets {
6.          ...
7.          commonTest.dependencies {
8.              implementation(libs.junit)
9.              implementation(libs.coTest)
10.             implementation(libs.ktor.mock)
11.         }
12.     }
13. }
```

Also, ensure that the data and domain modules have the corresponding **commonMain** and **commonTest** packages (so that there is somewhere to put the code).

As previously mentioned, a way of injecting the mock engine is required. This might be driven by the following test code located in the **commonTest** package of the **data** module:

```
1.  class MarsRepositoryTest {
2.
3.      private var jsonString = ""
4.
5.      private val mockEngine = MockEngine { request ->
6.          /* test request object to match expected api call */
```

```
7.          respond(
8.              content = ByteReadChannel(jsonString),
9.              status = HttpStatusCode.OK,
10.             headers = headersOf(ContentType, "application/json")
11.         )
12.     }
13.
14.     private val ktorClient = HttpClient(mockEngine) {
15.         install(ContentNegotiation) { json() }
16.     }
17.
18.     private val sut: MarsRepository = MarsRepositoryImpl(ktorClient)
19. }
```

Much of this code we have seen before, however:

- The **mockEngine** request/response parameter is a lambda that is only called when **get** is called on **ktorClient**. Therefore, **jsonString** can be a var overwritten for each test before calling the fetch.
- We write the code the way we would expect to use it in production and a test that does not compile is a failing test. Adhering to TDD techniques, **MarsRepository** and **MarsRepositoryImpl** are undefined and drive the developer to create them. Initially **MarsRepository** can be a blank interface defined in the **Domain** module and **MarsRepositoryImpl** is a regular class, with just the client injected at the constructor, defined in the **data** module, as can be seen in the following code snippets:

  ```
  1. // Domain module
  2. interface MarsRepository
  3.
  4. // Data module
  5. class MarsRepositoryImpl(
  6.     private val ktorClient: HttpClient
  7. ) : MarsRepository
  ```
- **MarsRepository** is the use case input port in the preceding example.

The first test

With the product repository code, including the use case input port minimally defined, the first test can be added:

```
1.  @Test
2.  fun 'GIVEN a single estate WHEN fetched THEN data parsed'() =
    runTest {
3.      // Given
4.      val price = 450000
5.      val imgSrc = "some/url"
6.      jsonString = """
7.      [
8.          {
9.              "price":$price,
10.             "id":"424905",
11.             "type":"buy",
12.             "img_src":"$imgSrc"
13.         }
14.     ]"""
15.
16.     // When
17.     val result: Result<List<MarsEstate>> = sut.fetchMarsData()
18. }
```

A test that does not compile is a failing test. **fetchMarsdata** is undefined so we need to stop and write just enough code to make the test compile. Hovering over the error in Android Studio will often (but not always) provide a coding suggestion to fix. Either way, a minimal code addition might look like this:

```
1.  // Data module
2.  interface MarsRepository {
3.      suspend fun fetchMarsData(): Result<List<MarsEstate>>
4.  }
5.
6.  // Domain module
7.  class MarsRepositoryImpl(
8.      private val ktorClient: HttpClient
9.  ) : MarsRepository {
10.
11.     override suspend fun fetchMarsData(): Result<List<MarsEstate>>
        =
12.         Result.failure(Throwable())
13. }
```

`fetchMarsData` has to return something so a minimal implementation might be the above, it could also perhaps have been a success with an empty list. It does not matter at this stage.

With the test code now compiling, we are free to complete the first test:

```
1.  @Test
2.  fun 'GIVEN a single estate WHEN fetched THEN data parsed'() =
        runTest {
3.          ...
4.          // Then
5.          assertTrue(result.isSuccess)
6.          result.getOrThrow().first().let {
7.              assertEquals(price, it.price)
8.              assertTrue(it.isBuy)
9.              assertEquals(imgSrc, it.imgSrc)
10.         }
11. }
```

The test checks that the individual fields of the raw data are mapped to `MarEstate` object fields correctly. The test will fail at the first assert. The minimum code required to make the test pass might be:

```
1.  class MarsRepositoryImpl(
2.      private val ktorClient: HttpClient
3.  ) : MarsRepository {
4.
5.      override suspend fun fetchMarsData(): Result<List<MarsEstate>> =
6.          Result.success(
7.              listOf(MarsEstate(450000, true, "some/url"))
8.          )
9.  }
```

This is simply hard-coding the test data into the product code. Further tests would be written with different data, different amounts of data, error conditions, and so on. Eventually after several iterations, the rough use case input port implementation may look like this:

```
1.  class MarsRepositoryImpl(
2.      private val ktorClient: HttpClient = HttpClient {
3.          install(ContentNegotiation) { json() }
4.      }
5.  ) : MarsRepository {
```

```
6.
7.      override suspend fun fetchMarsData(): Result<List<MarsEstate>> =
   try {
8.          val response: HttpResponse = ktorClient.get(marsUrl)
9.
10.         if (response.status.isSuccess()) {
11.             Result.success(
12.                 response.body<List<MarsData>>().map {
13.                     MarsEstate(it.price, it.type == "buy",
   it.imgSrc)
14.                 }
15.             )
16.         } else {
17.             Result.failure(IOException(response.status.description))
18.         }
19.     } catch (e: Exception) {
20.         Result.failure(e)
21.     }
22. }
```

The algorithm is similar to the initial example, except:

- The Ktor client is a constructor parameter with a default production instance overridable by test code.
- The resulting raw data is mapped to domain objects.

There may be other considerations, such as checks for data integrity (duplicate IDs, invalid types, and so on) which can all be test-driven. Furthermore, with a comprehensive set of unit tests, the code can be refactored to be more readable without fear of breaking the logic.

Caching

Caching, in the context of network calls, refers to the practice of storing and reusing previously retrieved data instead of fetching it again from the server. This can significantly improve the performance and efficiency of an application by:

- **Reducing network traffic**: Repeatedly downloading the same data is unnecessary and consumes bandwidth. Caching stores frequently used data locally, minimizing the need for subsequent network requests.
- **Decreasing response times**: Fetching data from the server can take time, depending on network conditions and server load. Cached data is readily available locally, resulting in faster app responsiveness.

- **Improving offline access**: With a local cache, users can access data even when they are offline or have limited internet connectivity. This enhances the user experience and makes an app more reliable.

There are several types of caching, however, the two most important ones, from an app developer's point of view are:

- Server-side
- Client-side

There are various caching techniques, however, there are two methods that are most used by app developers:

- Manual
- Using the networking library

Http caching

Ktor provides a plugin that enables a response to be cached either in-memory or persistent storage, as can be seen in the following example:

```
1. val ktorClient = HttpClient {
2.     install(HttpCache) {
3.         // In-memory cache by default
4.         // For persistent cache:
5.         // diskStorage(File("cacheDir"))
6.     }
7. }
```

This is useful in the circumstance where two or more identical calls are made in quick succession. Only the first call is actually made and the subsequent calls return the cached value. The caching behavior can be customized in many different ways using request headers. For example:

```
1. val response: HttpResponse = ktorClient.get(marsUrl) {
2.     // Cache images for a longer duration
3.     header("Cache-Control", "max-age=3600")
4. }
```

In this case, the cached response will be returned for five minutes.

Custom caching

In some cases, data only needs to be refreshed when specifically requested. In these instances, the result can simply be held in a local variable. For example, the `MarsRepository` code could be test-driven to include a flag `isStale`, that, when true, indicates that the cached data is stale and should be refreshed:

```kotlin
1.  // Domain module
2.  interface MarsRepository {
3.      suspend fun fetchMarsData(
4.          isStale: Boolean = false
5.      ): Result<List<MarsEstate>>
6.  }
7.
8.  // Data module
9.  class MarsRepositoryImpl(
10.     ...
11. ) : MarsRepository {
12.
13.     // local variable where cache will be stored
14.     private var marsCache: List<MarsEstate>? = null // initial value
15.
16.     override suspend fun fetchMarsData(
17.         isStale: Boolean
18.     ): Result<List<MarsEstate>> ...
19.
20.     // ... only fetch if marsCache is null or isStale is true
21. }
```

The **isStale** flag could be set, for example, upstream on pull-to-refresh (a common UI feature whereby attempting to drag a list down when the first item triggers a data refresh).

Test-driving the use cases

The result of the use case input needs to be exposed to the presentation layer via a use case and a use case output port. As previously discussed in *Chapter 4, Clean Code Architecture*, Kotlin provides a generic use case output port with the **Result** class. Arguably, the use case input port could just be exposed directly to the presentation layer, but this would break CCA and separation of concerns. Furthermore, the Domain layer exists to offload as much data processing logic as possible from the Presentation layer.

For example, given the Mars real estate data; the presentation layer may display different page styles and information for each **buy** or **rent**. Filtering for one or the other would require different use cases for each. These use cases can be test-driven. The initial test code for, say, estate purchase may look like this (assuming appropriate dependencies have been applied to the **toml** file and the Domain build script):

```
1. class MarsEstateSaleUseCaseTest {
2.
3.     private val repo = mockk<MarsRepository>()
4.     private val sut: MarsEstateSaleUseCase by lazy {
5.         MarsEstateSaleUseCase(repo)
6.     }
7. }
```

From the preceding example, it can be seen that:

- We write the code the way we would expect to use it in production and a test that does not compile is a failing test. We want a use case called **MarsEstateSaleUseCase** that takes a **MarsRepository** as a constructor parameter so that is what we write in the test. The failing test drives us to create a minimal definition for **MarsEstateSaleUseCase**.

    ```
    1. class MarsEstateSaleUseCase(marsRepository: MarsRepository)
    ```

- As **MarsRepository** is an interface, it is not strictly necessary to use **mockk** to define it. However, it will be more convenient than defining a concrete implementation for each test.

With the code compiling with the minimum use case definition, we can continue writing tests:

```
1.  @Test
2.  fun 'GIVEN two types WHEN invoked THEN only buy returned'() = runTest {
3.      // Given
4.      val expected = MarsEstate(456, isBuy = true, "")
5.      coEvery { repo.fetchMarsData() } returns Result.success(listOf(
6.          MarsEstate(123, isBuy = false, ""),
7.          expected
8.      ))
9.
10.     // When
11.     sut()
12. }
```

We write the code the way we would expect to use it in production. A test that does not compile is a failing test. The previous code is not compiling using parenthesis after **sut**. The IDE suggestion in this case is not helpful as what we want is the standard use case **invoke** operator. The minimal definition for this would be:

```kotlin
class MarsEstateSaleUseCase(marsRepository: MarsRepository) {

    operator fun invoke() {}
}
```
Continuing with the test:
```
        ...
        // When
        sut().onSuccess { }
```
onSuccess is not compiling. This drives us to make the **invoke** operator return a **Result** type – and so on. After several iterations, we end up with the following test:
```
        ...
        // When
        sut()

            // Then
            .onSuccess { result ->
                assertEquals(1, result.size)
                assertEquals(expected, result.first())
            }

            // Else
            .onFailure { throw it } // throw the passed "it" param
```
Given further testing of different scenarios, edge cases and failure conditions we may end up with a rough use case that looks like this:
```kotlin
class MarsEstateSaleUseCase(
    private val marsRepository: MarsRepository
) {

    suspend operator fun invoke(): Result<List<MarsEstate>> =
        marsRepository.fetchMarsData().let { result ->
            result.onSuccess { estates ->
                return Result.success(
                    estates.filter { estate -> estate.isBuy }
                )
            }
            return result
```

```
13.         }
14. }
```

As with the use case input port implementation, with a comprehensive set of unit tests the code can be refactored to be more readable without fear of breaking the logic.

A similar process can be followed to create a `MarsEstateRentUseCase`.

Further test-driven develop will reveal, in this particular example, that the code for *buy* and *rent* differ only by the filter predicate. With unit tests for both the buy and rent scenarios, the code can be safely rationalized to one algorithm with two different inputs. Furthermore, the algorithm implementation can be private and exposed via an interface. Consider the following interface with two companion methods for fetching buy or rent results:

```
1. interface MarsEstateUseCase {
2.     suspend operator fun invoke(): Result<List<MarsEstate>>
3.
4.     companion object {
5.         fun rent(marsRepository: MarsRepository): MarsEstateUseCase =
6.             MarsEstateRentUseCaseImpl(marsRepository) { estate ->
7.                 !estate.isBuy
8.             }
9.
10.        fun buy(marsRepository: MarsRepository): MarsEstateUseCase =
11.            MarsEstateRentUseCaseImpl(marsRepository) { estate ->
12.                estate.isBuy
13.            }
14.    }
15. }
```

The corresponding interface implementation can then be made private (as all `-impl` code should be, where possible):

```
1. private class MarsEstateRentUseCaseImpl(
2.     private val marsRepository: MarsRepository,
3.     private val filter: (MarsEstate) -> Boolean
4. ) : MarsEstateUseCase {
5.
6.     override suspend operator fun invoke(): Result<List<MarsEstate>> =
7.         marsRepository.fetchMarsData().let { result ->
```

```
 8.          result.onSuccess { estates ->
 9.              return Result.success(estates.filter(filter))
10.          }
11.          return result
12.      }
13. }
```

DI module binding

With the use case input ports implemented in the **data** module and the use cases defined in the **domain** module, all that remains to set up the networking and API calls is, binding them together in the DI module. This will be different depending upon the choice of DI library.

Hilt

Create qualifier annotations in the Hilt DI module for each of the buy and rent scenarios. This only needs to be done when the same interface can have multiple implementations, as in our **MarsEstate** example:

```
 1. @Qualifier
 2. @Retention(AnnotationRetention.RUNTIME)
 3. annotation class MarsRent
 4.
 5. @Qualifier
 6. @Retention(AnnotationRetention.RUNTIME)
 7. annotation class MarsBuy
 8. Then, create a class in the Hilt DI module containing the use case bindings:
 9. @Module
10. @InstallIn(SingletonComponent::class)
11. class Module {
12.
13.     @Provides
14.     @MarsRent
15.     fun provideMarsEstateRent(): MarsEstateUseCase =
16.         MarsEstateUseCase.rent(MarsRepo.impl())
17.
18.     @Provides
```

```
19.    @MarsBuy
20.    fun provideMarsEstateBuy(): MarsEstateUseCase =
21.        MarsEstateUseCase.buy(MarsRepo.impl())
22. }
```

Ensure that the main application is setup for Hilt:

```
1. @HiltAndroidApp
2. class HiltApplication: Application()
```

This is all that is necessary from the domain and data modules. In the previous chapter we set up the presentation module's dependency on the DI module. The compiler will process the annotations and apply the injections where necessary.

Koin

Follow these steps to bind the use case input ports implemented in the **data** module and the use cases defined in the **domain** module using Koin:

Create a file in the Koin DI module containing the qualifiers (in this case) and the use case bindings:

```
1.  sealed class Estate : Qualifier {
2.      object Rent : Qualifier {
3.          override val value = "rent"
4.      }
5.
6.      object Buy : Qualifier {
7.          override val value = "buy"
8.      }
9.  }
10.
11. val homeDiModule = module {
12.     single(Estate.Buy) { MarsEstateUseCase.buy(MarsRepo.impl()) }
13.     single(Estate.Rent) { MarsEstateUseCase.rent(MarsRepo.impl()) }
14. }
```

Create a file in the presentation module containing a Koin module referencing the DI module from above:

```
1. val homePresentationModule = module {
2.     includes(homeDiModule)
3. }
```

Finally, add the presentation module to the Koin setup in the main application:

```
1.  class KoinApplication: Application() {
2.
3.      override fun onCreate() {
4.          super.onCreate()
5.
6.          startKoin{
7.              androidLogger()
8.              androidContext(this@KoinApplication)
9.              modules(homePresentationModule)
10.         }
11.     }
12. }
```

Conclusion

There are very few mobile apps that do not require any kind of network connection. Even most games offer the feature of backing up a player's progress in the cloud. Traditionally, the code required to make network calls and to receive and process data has been complex. There have been many attempts to wrap this code with third-party libraries to make the process tidier and more intuitive.

As far as Kotlin development is concerned, there can really only be one choice of networking library. The Ktor library is written by JetBrains, the organization that created Kotlin in the first place. Not only is it created in Kotlin for Kotlin, it can also be compiled to work in multiple environments. This makes it future-proof with the current trend to develop cross-platform applications. In fact, Ktor is split into multiple libraries allowing developers to only include the functionality they need. Ktor also provides a server mocking library making test-driven development of API calls relatively straightforward, as has been demonstrated above.

The next chapter builds on *Chapter 7's Introduction to Jetpack Compose* by presenting more advanced concepts, such as the Scaffold, animated transitions and screen navigation.

Points to remember

- Android apps will always need to make network calls.
- To make network calls, Android apps need the relevant permission entry in the manifest.
- The Ktor library provides everything a developer might need to code network calls.

- Use an API's official documentation to test drive the calls needed.
- For up-to-date information, use **postman.com** to check API responses.
- Adhere to architecture layering (Domain and Data).
- Remember to test-drive edge-case scenarios, such as errors, empty responses, timed-out responses, unexpected data, etc.
- Pay special attention to an API's authentication and security requirements.
- Consider caching arrangements.

Questions

1. Why is networking so important when writing an Android app?
2. What is a RESTful API?
3. Why is Ktor a great choice for a networking library?
4. What build script dependencies are required to use Ktor?
5. What other scenarios could be covered by the test code for the final `fetchMarsData` algorithm in the example?
6. Given a comprehensive set of unit tests, how could the final `fetchMarsData` algorithm be refactored to be more readable?
7. How could the algorithm be test-driven to include custom caching?
8. How can Google OAuth be integrated into Ktor code?

Join our book's Discord space

Join the book's Discord Workspace for Latest updates, Offers, Tech happenings around the world, New Release and Sessions with the Authors:

https://discord.bpbonline.com

CHAPTER 13
Creating UI with Jetpack Compose

Introduction

In the ever-evolving landscape of Android app development, the quest for intuitive, flexible, and efficient user interfaces has taken center stage. With the advent of Jetpack Compose, a modern UI toolkit for building native Android applications, developers are empowered with a declarative approach that simplifies UI development and enhances the overall user experience.

In *Chapter 7, Introduction to Jetpack Compose*, provided the basics of Jetpack Compose, including low-level paradigms such as common composables and state management primitives. This chapter is not intended to be comprehensive Jetpack Compose documentation, rather, it aims to present high-level Compose elements and general techniques to structure and polish an app.

Structure

This chapter covers the following topics:
- Themes
- The Scaffold
- Navigation
- Animation
- Multiplatform considerations

Objectives

This chapter examines four important high-level aspects of Jetpack Compose, namely, themes, the scaffold, navigation, and animation. They help structure the code and provide a smooth experience to the user. By the end of this chapter, you will have a solid foundation in the application of these features and have some ideas for their use in a multiplatform environment.

Themes

In *Chapter 7, Introduction to Jetpack Compose,* we briefly mentioned Themes. In this section, we will cover them in more depth.

Jetpack Compose themes are the core of personalizing an app's visual identity and branding. They act like a paintbrush, allowing control over colors, typography, shapes, and more, across all UI elements. For example, Jetpack Compose Material components such as **Button** and **Checkbox** use values provided by the Theme when retrieving default values. The theme sets the following aspects of an app:

- **Color scheme**: Defines primary, secondary, background, and other colors used throughout an app.
- **Typography**: Specifies font families, sizes, weights, and styles for various text elements.
- **Shapes**: Determines the corner radius, edges, and overall silhouette of UI components.

The **Empty Activity** Android Studio wizard described in *Chapter 7, Introduction to Jetpack Compose,* generates a custom Theme that helps explain this. To set or change a Theme, call the built-in **MaterialTheme** composable method. For example:

```
1. MaterialTheme(
2.     colorScheme = CustomColors,
3.     typography = CustomTypography,
4.     shapes = CustomShapes
5. ){
6.     // app content
7. }
```

While this demonstrates the syntax, it is not the usual way of defining the app theme. It is normal to provide a way of switching the theme. For example:

```
1. @Composable
2. fun ExampleTheme(
3.     isDarkTheme: Boolean,
```

```
4.     content: @Composable () -> Unit
5. ) {
6.     MaterialTheme(
7.         colorScheme =
8.             if (isDarkTheme) DarkColorScheme
9.             else LightColorScheme,
10.        content = content
11.    )
12. }
```

The following simple example demonstrates the code above in action:

```
1. class MainActivity : ComponentActivity() {
2.
3.     override fun onCreate(savedInstanceState: Bundle?) {
4.         super.onCreate(savedInstanceState)
5.         setContent {
6.             var isDarkTheme by remember { mutableStateOf(false) }
7.             ExampleTheme(isDarkTheme) {
8.                 Button(onClick = { isDarkTheme = !isDarkTheme }) {
9.                     Text(text = "Toggle Theme")
10.                }
11.            }
12.        }
13.    }
14. }
```

In this example, tapping the **Toggle Theme** button will toggle the theme between dark and light, as shown in the following figure:

Figure 13.1: Toggle Theme

In fact, the **ExampleTheme** code above is just a simplification of the code generated by the *Empty Activity* wizard. The main difference being that the **isDarkTheme** parameter defaults to `isSystemInDarkTheme()`. This is a built-in method that detects the device-level theme mode, similar to Google Maps. The theme will switch to dark mode when using Google Maps for navigation as day turns into night.

It is common to support dark and light themes in an app, but we are not restricted to this arrangement. For example, UK's global player audio streaming app had a different theme for each of its ten-plus featured radio stations.

Setting a theme via the `MaterialTheme` composable will set the values provided by the `MaterialTheme` object within the content scope of the `MaterialTheme` composable. This will be expanded upon shortly. In the example above, the `Toggle Theme` button is within the content scope of `ExampleTheme` (which wraps `MaterialTheme`).

Color scheme

Color schemes are the backbone of any theme, whether in Jetpack Compose, web design, or any other visual creation. They define the palette of colors used throughout a UI, ensuring visual consistency and coherence. Any composable element with a configurable color aspect can use a color from the `MaterialTheme` object. For example:

```
1. Text(
2.     text = "Hello",
3.     color = MaterialTheme.colors.primary
4. )
```

The `MaterialTheme` object is configured via the `MaterialTheme` composable method, as discussed above. A `Colors` object is passed to the `MaterialTheme` method defining a named set of colors corresponding to those available via the `MaterialTheme` object. The following is a contrived example for setting the primary color of the `Hello` text above to demonstrate how this works:

```
1. MaterialTheme(
2.     colors = MaterialTheme.colors.copy(secondary = Color.Magenta)
3. ) {
4.     Text(
5.         text = "Hello",
6.         color = MaterialTheme.colors.secondary
7.     )
8. }
```

Figure 13.2: Color scheme

The theme colors are only affected within the content scope of the `MaterialTheme` method content, in this case, just the `Text` element. We used `MaterialTheme.colors` to get an instance of `Colors` that had all `Color` members defined by default or by any parent `MaterialTheme` method, and then overwrote the value for `secondary` by making a copy. Subsequently, the Text element color (default `primary` in this case) was overridden with the `secondary` value.

An instance of `Colors` could have been created in the `MaterialTheme` method directly, but in that case, all of the `Color` members would have had to be defined – and there are a lot of them. The following are a few of them. See the accompanying Javadoc for a full list:

- **Primary**: The primary color is displayed most frequently across an app's screens and components.
- **Secondary**: The secondary color provides more ways to accent and distinguish a product. Secondary colors are best for floating action buttons (see below), selection controls, like checkboxes and radio buttons, highlighting selected text, links and headlines

Selecting the right color scheme depends on several factors:

- **Brand identity:** Align the colors with the product brand's personality and message.
- **Target audience:** Consider the demographics and preferences of users.
- **Usability and accessibility**: Ensure sufficient contrast for readability and accessibility.
- **Emotional impact**: Colors evoke different emotions, choose colors that align with the desired mood.

Color schemes are essential for creating visually appealing and cohesive themes. Choosing the right colors and applying them thoughtfully can significantly impact an app's user experience and brand perception. A well-crafted color scheme can elevate themes and create a delightful user experience.

In addition, dynamic color, which was added in Android 12, enables users to personalize their devices to align tonally with the color scheme of their personal wallpaper or through a selected color in the wallpaper picker. This feature can be leveraged by adding the `DynamicColors` API, which applies this theming to an app or activity to make an app more personalized to the user. For full details, see the official documentation at **developer.android.com**.

Typography

Typography plays a crucial role in establishing the look, feel, and accessibility of Jetpack Compose themes. Good typography will provide:

- **Visual hierarchy**: Different font sizes, weights, and styles create a clear hierarchy between headings, body text, labels, and other elements, guiding the user's eye through the content.

- **Brand identity**: The chosen fonts and styles can convey a brand's personality, professionalism, or playfulness.
- **Readability**: Selecting easy-to-read fonts and ensuring appropriate contrast improves user experience and accessibility.

Like the color scheme, the theme typography is set via a parameter on the `MaterialTheme` method. Customizing it, however, can be considerably more complicated. At the top-level, the code can be similar to the color scheme:

```
1.  MaterialTheme(
2.      typography = Typography(h1 = textStyle)
3.  ) {
4.      Text(
5.          text = "Hello",
6.          style = MaterialTheme.typography.h1
7.      )
8.  }
```

Figure 13.3: Typography

Unlike the `Colors` class, `Typography` has all its members defaulted so there is no need to copy from the existing `MaterialTheme.typography` object. The `textStyle` value assigned to `h1`, shown above, is a `TextStyle` object. Like `Colors`, `TextStyle` has a very long list of definable characteristics including font, font weight, color and many others. The example above uses a custom font so this needs to be defined first.

Fonts

A font refers to a set of typefaces or graphical representations of text characters. Fonts determine the visual appearance of text in an Android application, including attributes such as style, weight, size, and spacing. Fonts play a crucial role in defining the overall aesthetic and readability of an app's user interface.

In Android development, there are primarily two types of fonts:

- **System fonts**: These are pre-installed fonts with the Android operating system. System fonts include default typefaces like Roboto, Noto, and Sans Serif, which are commonly used in Android applications. System fonts provide consistency across different Android devices and versions.
- **Custom fonts**: These are fonts that developers can include in their Android applications to achieve specific visual styles or branding. Custom fonts can be

added to an app's resources and referenced programmatically or in XML layout files. Developers can use tools like Android Studio to import custom font files (for example, TrueType Font or TTF files) and apply them to text views or other UI elements.

In recent versions of Android, developers can also use the downloadable fonts feature provided by the Android support library. This feature allows apps to request fonts from the Google Fonts catalog at runtime, reducing the app's APK size and enabling dynamic font loading based on user preferences or locale.

As previously mentioned, the example above uses a custom font, so this must first be defined as a **FontFamily** object.

FontFamily

Outside the fonts catalog feature, fonts can be downloaded free for commercial use from a multitude of third-party sites. *Font family* is a generic phrase for a set of fonts in roughly the same style. For example, there could be different fonts for each of bold, italic and regular under the same family as, say, Sans Serif. In this example we have downloaded two files of type **.ttf** for regular and bold and placed them in the **res/fonts** folder as can be seen in the following screenshot:

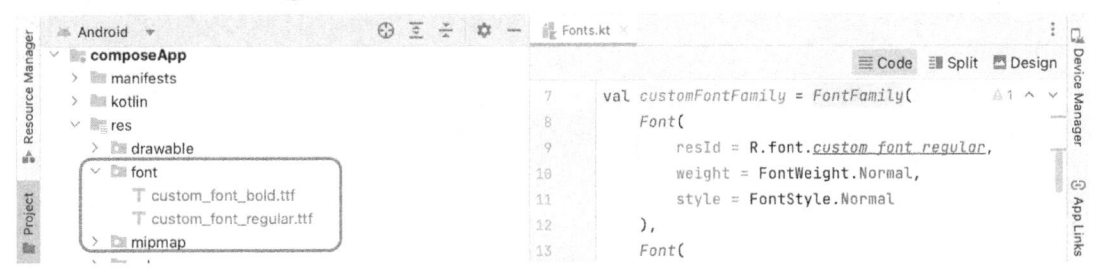

Figure 13.4: Downloaded fonts

The files will likely need to be renamed from their original names to comply with the Android xml rules, that is, lower-case and underscores only. Once these are in place, a **FontFamily** object can be defined, for example:

```
1.  val customFontFamily = FontFamily(
2.      Font(
3.          resId = R.font.custom_font_regular,
4.          weight = FontWeight.Normal,
5.          style = FontStyle.Normal
6.      ),
7.      Font(
8.          resId = R.font.custom_font_bold,
9.          weight = FontWeight.Bold,
```

```
10.         style = FontStyle.Normal
11.     )
12. )
```

The **FontFamily** takes a list of Font objects, each assigning a font file with a particular weight and style. There are only two styles that can be defined, **Normal** and *Italic* but here are *many* different weights apart from **Normal** and **Bold** that *could* be defined, such as **ExtraBold**, **SemiBold**, **Medium**, and so on. A full list can be found in the Javadoc for **FontWeight**.

In the example above, only two font files in the family have been downloaded, i.e., normal and normal-bold, so these are the only two listed in the **FontFamily** example above. With the **FontFamily** object defined, a **TextStyle** object can be created.

TextStyle

A **TextStyle** object defines the appearance and styling of text displayed within a user interface. It encapsulates attributes such as font family, font size, font weight, font style, color, alignment, and other text-related properties. A full list of these properties can be found in the Javadoc for **TextStyle**.

In the **Hello** example previously, we created **textStyle** of type **TextStyle** with a trivial definition:

```
1. val textStyle = TextStyle(
2.     fontFamily = customFontFamily,
3. )
```

All the other possible settings in this case have picked up default values. This is a contrived example. Under normal circumstances, careful attention would be paid to the **TextStyle** font size, weight, and so on to match expectations. For example, this text style was assigned to **h1** in the **Typography**. **h1** should be large and bold, but the rendered text, as seen from the example, was relatively small.

Typography

By way of a reminder, we set up typography for our theme with the following code:

```
1. MaterialTheme(
2.     typography = Typography(h1 = textStyle)
3. ) { ... }
```

Again, this was a contrived example. It is clearer and maintainable when creating typography to have a named value with text style objects declared on-the-fly. Much like the **FontFamily**, **customFontFamily** is a named value with Font objects declared on-the-fly. For example:

```
1.  val customTypography = Typography(
2.      defaultFontFamily = customFontFamily,
3.      h1 = TextStyle(
4.          fontSize = TextUnit(20f, TextUnitType.Sp),
5.          fontWeight = FontWeight.Bold
6.      ),
7.      h2 = TextStyle(
8.          fontSize = TextUnit(18f, TextUnitType.Sp),
9.          fontWeight = FontWeight.Normal,
10.         color = Color.Blue
11.     ),
12.     // ... etc.
13. )
14. ...
15. MaterialTheme(
16.     typography = customTypography
17. ) { ... }
```

The text style for **h1** will pick up the corresponding bold font defined in the default font family and **h2** will pick up the normal via the **fontWeight** parameter. **TextUnitType.Sp** refers to scaled pixels. **TextUnitType.Em** is also available and refers to a unit for specifying text size relative to the current font size.

Like **Colors**, **Typography** has a large number of fields that can be set. The full Javadoc describing each field can be seen in Android Studio by hovering the mouse pointer over **Typography** in code or by jumping to its definition. The following are a few of them:

- defaultFontFamily: The default **FontFamily** to be used for **TextStyles** provided in this constructor. This default will be used if the **FontFamily** on the **TextStyle** is null.
- h1: **h1** is the largest headline, reserved for short, important text or numerals.
- h2: **h2** is the second largest headline, reserved for short, important text or numerals.
- subtitle1: **subtitle1** is the largest subtitle, and is typically reserved for medium-emphasis text that is shorter in length.

Shapes

In the context of **MaterialTheme**, **Shapes** refer to predefined sets of corner shapes that define the appearance of components such as buttons, cards, and other surfaces. **Shapes** help maintain consistency and provide a cohesive visual style throughout an app's user interface. The following code gives an example of setting the **shapes** parameter:

```
1. MaterialTheme(
2.     shapes = Shapes(
3.         small = RoundedCornerShape(4.dp),
4.         medium = RoundedCornerShape(16.dp),
5.         large = RoundedCornerShape(40.dp)
6.     )
7. ) { ... }
```

The **shapes** parameter of **MaterialTheme** provides three shape sets: small, medium, and large. Each set contains predefined shapes for different components, with varying corner radii. These shapes are designed to match the material design guidelines and can be customized or overridden as needed. The following examples show the effects of small, medium and large shapes on composable components:

- **Small shapes**: These shapes are typically used for smaller components such as buttons, icons, and text fields. They have smaller corner radii to create a compact appearance. Refer to the following figure for a depiction of button with a default small corner radii:

Figure 13.5: Button with default small corner radii

- **Medium shapes**: Medium shapes are used for medium-sized components like cards, dialogs, and containers. They have slightly larger corner radii compared to small shapes, providing a balance between compactness and visual appeal, as shown in the following figure:

Figure 13.6: Card with default medium corner radii

- **Large shapes**: Large shapes are designed for larger components such as dialogs, sheets, and panels. They have the largest corner radii among the three sets, creating a softer and more spacious appearance. Refer to the following figure:

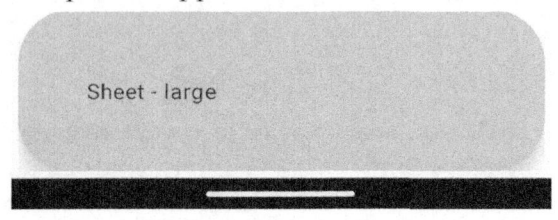

Figure 13.7: Bottom sheet with default large corner radii

If a particular composable element has the shape parameter, then the corners can be overridden with values set on the local **MaterialTheme** object, for example, with the previous button:

```
1. Button(
2.     shape = MaterialTheme.shapes.medium,
3.     onClick = { },
4. ) {
5.     Text(
6.         modifier = Modifier.padding(5.dp),
7.         text = "Button - medium override"
8.     )
9. }
```

The preceding code has the effect of changing the normally small corners of a button to medium:

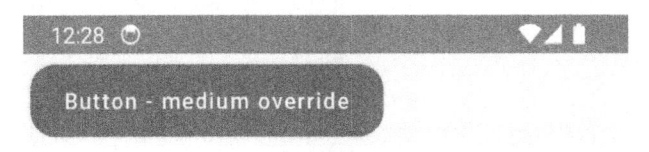

Figure 13.8: Button with overridden medium corner radii

By using the predefined shapes provided by **MaterialTheme**, developers can ensure that their app's UI elements adhere to material design principles and guidelines. Additionally, shapes can be customized or extended to match specific design requirements or branding preferences, offering flexibility and control over the app's visual appearance.

The Scaffold

The Jetpack Compose Scaffold is a fundamental composable that provides the structural foundation of an app. It adheres to material design principles, ensuring a consistent and user-friendly experience across different screens. It is the scaffolding for UI, holding together key elements like app bars, floating action buttons, and the content area.

It provides a standardized structure by predefining slots for essential UI elements like:

- **Top app bar**: Holds titles, navigation menu, actions, etc.
- **Bottom bar**: Provides secondary navigation or persistent actions.
- **Floating action button**: A prominent button for key actions.
- **Snack bar**: A simple pop-up dialog.
- **Drawer**: An optional side panel for navigation or settings.
- **Content area**: The custom UI elements take center stage here.

Figure 13.9 shows the typical elements of a **Scaffold**:

Figure 13.9: Scaffold UI

The scaffold simplifies UI implementation as there is no need to manually manage the placement and interaction between these elements. Scaffold takes care of that, saving time and code. Simply pass the desired composables for each slot (for example, a custom **TopAppBar**) and focus on building the content area. For example:

```
1.  @Composable
2.  fun Scaffolder(
3.      content: @Composable () -> Unit
4.  ) {
5.      val scaffoldState: ScaffoldState = rememberScaffoldState()
6.      Scaffold(
7.          scaffoldState = scaffoldState,
8.          topBar = { TopBar() },
9.          bottomBar = { BottomBar() },
10.         drawerContent = { DrawerContent() },
11.         floatingActionButton = {
12.             val coScope: CoroutineScope = rememberCoroutineScope()
```

```
13.             Fab { coScope.showSnackBar(scaffoldState.
    snackbarHostState) }
14.         },
15.         snackbarHost = { SnackHost(scaffoldState.snackbarHostState) }
16.     ) { scaffoldPadding ->
17.         Box(modifier = Modifier.padding(scaffoldPadding)) { content() }
18.     }
19. }
```

The previous example is a custom wrapper for the **Scaffold** element allowing its details to be separated from that of the contents (screens). It can be called from within the **setContent** scope of an **Activity** or from another composable:

```
1. Scaffolder {
2.     // screen content details here
3. }
```

Things to note about the **Scaffolder** code are as follows:

- The **scaffoldState** defined in line 5 contains two state values, **drawerState** and **snackbarHostState**. These values are used to control the visibility of the drawer and the snack bar respectively. This will be discussed shortly.
- **TopBar()**, **BottomBar()**, **DrawerContent()**, **Fab()**, and **SnackHost()** are all custom composables that will be discussed in the following subsections.
- The floating action button composable (**Fab**) takes a parameter of the **snackbarHostState**. This is because, in this example and this example only, the floating action button is used to invoke the snack bar.
- The **Scaffold** composable supplies a padding value to its content that must be used by that content. In this case, it is applied to a **Box** composable that wraps the content in line 14.

There are a lot of actions that can be performed by the scaffold and many ways in which the visual state could be updated as a result. For that reason, it is advisable to deploy a UDF **ViewModel** arrangement (see *Chapter 8, Presentation Layer Evolution in Compose*) to centralize the state management. In that case the preceding code could be updated:

```
1. @Composable
2. fun Scaffolder(
3.     state: ScaffoldState,
4.     event: (ScaffoldEvent) -> Unit,
5.     content: @Composable () -> Unit
6. ) { /* ... */}
```

This would have a corresponding upstream call similar to the following:

```
1. val scaffoldState by scaffoldViewModel
2.     .uiState.collectAsStateWithLifecycle()
3. // ...
4. Scaffolder (
5.     state = scaffoldState,
6.     event = scaffoldViewModel::handleEvent
7. ) {
8.     // screen content details here
9. }
```

TopAppBar()

As can be seen from *Figure 13.9*, the top app bar sits near the top of the screen below the status bar and can contain a title and several icon buttons. A typical implementation may look like this:

```
1. @Composable
2. fun TopBar(
3.     state: ScaffoldState,
4.     event: (ScaffoldEvent) -> Unit,
5.     drawerState: DrawerState
6. ) {
7.     TopAppBar(
8.         title = { Text(state.topBarTitle) },
9.         navigationIcon = { OpenDrawer(drawerState) },
10.        actions = { TopBarDropdown(event) }
11.    )
12. }
```

In this particular implementation, the title is set by the scaffold state from the **ViewModel**. The **navigationIcon** is the icon to the left of the title, and **actions** define a list of icons to the right of the title justified against the right-edge of the screen, as can be seen in *Figure 13.9*.

Again, in this particular case, the drawer state is passed in from the scaffold and is used to open the drawer. Typically, this may look like this:

```
1. @Composable
2. fun OpenDrawer(drawerState: DrawerState) {
3.     val coroutineScope: CoroutineScope = rememberCoroutineScope()
```

```
4.     IconButton(
5.         onClick = {
6.             coroutineScope.launch { drawerState.open() }
7.         }
8.     ) { Icon(Icons.Filled.Menu, contentDescription = null) }
9. }
```

drawerState.open() is a **suspend** function and must be called on a background thread. A **CoroutineScope** has been used for this in the above example. **contentDescription** on the **Icon** has been set to null in this case (and all cases in this chapter) for brevity. In real-life scenarios, it is important to set this to a meaningful, translatable string as it will be used for the audio description of the button's function via the **Accessibility** setting on the device.

A common implementation of the **action** items to the right of the title is to display a drop-down menu. The **TopBarDropdown** composable used in the **TopBar** example above could be defined like this:

```
1.  @Composable
2.  internal fun TopBarDropdown(
3.      event: (ScaffoldEvent) -> Unit
4.  ) {
5.      var expanded by remember { mutableStateOf(false) }
6.      Box {
7.          IconButton(
8.              onClick = { expanded = !expanded }
9.          ) { Icon(Icons.Default.Add, contentDescription = null) }
10.         DropdownMenu(
11.             expanded = expanded,
12.             onDismissRequest = { expanded = !expanded }
13.         ) {
14.             DropdownMenuItem(
15.                 onClick = { event(ScaffoldEvent.Item1Clicked) }
16.             ) { Text(text = "Item 1") }
17.             DropdownMenuItem(
18.                 onClick = { event(ScaffoldEvent.Item2Clicked) }
19.             ) { Text(text = "Item 2") }
20.         }
21.     }
22. }
```

For the drop-down menu to be displayed in the following line with the action icon, both the icon and dropdown menu need to be defined in a **Box** in the following way:

Figure 13.10: Drop-down menu

BottomAppBar()

The **BottomAppBar** should be used for changing the content within the scaffold or navigating to another page within the scaffold. In *Figure 13.9*, **BottomBar** was implemented this way:

```
1.  @Composable
2.  internal fun BottomBar(
3.      state: ScaffoldState,
4.      event: (ScaffoldEvent) -> Unit
5.  ) {
6.      BottomAppBar(
7.          content = {
8.              BottomNavigation {
9.                  BottomNavigationItem(
10.                     icon = { Icon(Icons.Default.Home, null) },
11.                     label = { Text("Home") },
12.                     selected = state.barSelect == BarSelect.Home,
13.                     onClick = { event(ScaffoldEvent.HomeClicked) }
14.                 )
15.                 BottomNavigationItem(
16.                     icon = { Icon(Icons.Default.Favorite, null) },
17.                     label = { Text("Favorites") },
18.                     selected = state.barSelect == BarSelect.Fav,
19.                     onClick = { event(ScaffoldEvent.FavClicked) }
20.                 )
21.             }
22.         }
23.     )
24. }
```

BarSelect is an **enum** held as part of the **state**. It is used by the **BottomNavigationItem** to highlight whichever icon has been selected.

DrawerContent()

There is no special **Composable** for defining the drawer content. In *Figure 13.9*, a simple **Column** was used:

```
1.  @Composable
2.  internal fun DrawerContent(
3.      event: (ScaffoldEvent) -> Unit
4.  ) {
5.      Column {
6.          Button(
7.              onClick = { event(ScaffoldEvent.GoSomeWhere) }
8.          ) { Text("navigate") }
9.          // ...
10.     }
11. }
```

Any content defined in the scope of the **drawerContent** parameter of the **Scaffold** will be rendered inside a fixed slide-out window, as seen in *Figure 13.9*. The only way to change the look of this window, such as width and height, has to be done by passing a custom **Shape** object to the **drawerShape** parameter of the **Scaffold**. This can be problematic, however, as this **Shape** will not take its content into account, resulting in ugly truncation in some cases. The **Scaffold** provides some other attributes for changing the look of the drawer, such as **drawerBackgroundColor**, **drawerContentColor**, and so on.

Fab()

Floating action button or **Fab()** is a material design component used to represent the primary action in a screen or application. It is typically a circular button with an icon that floats above the content. It is used to trigger a primary action, such as adding a new item, creating a new task, or initiating a main interaction. The Scaffold provides three parameters for setting the FAB:

- **floatingActionButton**: The Main action button of the screen (see the following code).
- **floatingActionButtonPosition**: Position of the FAB on the screen. At the time of writing, there were only two positions available via **FabPosition**, **FabPosition.Center** and **FabPosition.End** with **FabPosition.End** being the default.
- **isFloatingActionButtonDocked**: Whether floatingActionButton should overlap with **bottomBar** for half a height, if **bottomBar** exists. Ignored if there is no **bottomBar** or no **floatingActionButton**. The default for this parameter if **false**.

The following figure shows a floating action button centered and docked with a bottom bar:

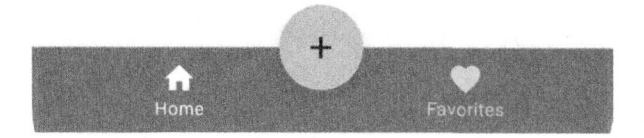

Figure 13.11: FAB centered and docked

floatingActionButton from *Figure 13.9* was set to the custom **Fab** Composable, which was implemented simply by:

```
1. @Composable
2. internal fun Fab(
3.     onClick: () -> Unit,
4. ) = FloatingActionButton(onClick) {
5.     Icon(Icons.Default.Add, null)
6. }
```

SnackHost()

A **Snackbar** is a material design component used to display brief messages or notifications to the user. It typically appears at the bottom of the screen and provides feedback or prompts for actions. **Snackbar** objects are commonly used to inform users about the success or failure of an operation, provide feedback on user actions, or request confirmation for an action.

The **snackbarHost** parameter of the **Scaffold** provides a means of setting the snack bar UI template. In the *Figure 13.9* example, a custom composable **SnackHost** was used:

```
1.  @Composable
2.  fun SnackHost(state: SnackbarHostState) {
3.      SnackbarHost(state) { data ->
4.          Snackbar(
5.              shape = MaterialTheme.shapes.medium,
6.              backgroundColor = MaterialTheme.colors.primary,
7.              snackbarData = data
8.          )
9.      }
10. }
```

There are various parameters for adjusting the look-and-feel of the **Snackbar**. In this case, shape and **backgroundColor** have been set to match the general **Scaffold** more closely. The only required parameter for **Snackbar** is **snackbarData**. This object contains all the raw data required for displaying a particular snack bar and comes from the **showSnackbar** method of the **snackbarHostState** object. Like **drawerState.open()**, the **showSnackbar()** method of **snackbarHostState** is a **suspend** method so for brevity, a **CoroutineScope** extension was created to show the action of setting the **snackbarData** and dealing with the result:

```
1.  fun CoroutineScope.showSnackBar(
2.      snackState: SnackbarHostState,
3.      event: (ScaffoldEvent) -> Unit
4.  ) = launch {
5.      snackState.showSnackbar(
6.          message = "Snack Bar",
7.          actionLabel = "Navigate",
8.          duration = SnackbarDuration.Indefinite
9.      ).let { result ->
10.         when (result) {
11.             SnackbarResult.Dismissed -> event(ScaffoldEvent.SnackDismiss)
12.             SnackbarResult.ActionPerformed -> event(ScaffoldEvent.SnackGo)
13.         }
14.     }
15. }
```

The **message**, **actionLabel** and **duration** parameters are packaged up into a **SnackbarData** object and are received by the **SnackbarHost** and used to populate the **Snackbar**, as can be seen above in the code for **SnackHost**. The subsequent action result from the **Snackbar** is returned back on the **showSnackbar** method for further processing.

Scaffold()

Overall, the Scaffold provides consistent theming and behavior. It automatically applies theme-based colors and padding to its elements, ensuring visual harmony across the app. Furthermore, it manages interactions between elements, like scrolling content behind the **TopAppBar** or hiding the **BottomBar** during scrolling. The **Scaffold** provides complete control over its individual elements (for example, hiding the **Drawer**, customizing the **FloatingActionButton**).

In summary, the Jetpack Compose Scaffold is a powerful tool for building efficient and consistent UIs. It reduces boilerplate code, enforces material design principles, and lets the developer focus on creating the unique elements of an app. Whether a simple list app is being built or a complex multi-screen experience, the Scaffold provides a solid foundation for a delightful user experience.

Navigation

Navigation in Android refers to the process of moving between different screens or destinations within an app. Effective navigation is crucial for providing a smooth and intuitive user experience. Over the years, Android has evolved its navigation patterns and provided various tools and components to facilitate navigation within apps.

Still popular today is the navigation component provided by the Android Jetpack suite (not to be confused with Jetpack **Compose**).

The Navigation component (legacy)

The Navigation component is designed to simplify navigation in Android apps and provide a more structured and declarative approach to handling navigation. The foundation proposes that apps should have a single **Activity** with many **Fragment** objects representing screens to navigate between.

The library would inflate a navigation map defined in XML into a **NavController** object, an instance of which would be available via built-in **Activity** and **Fragment** methods. This is best explained by an example. Given **FragmentA** navigates to **FragmentB** and passes an instance of **User** as a parameter to be used by **FragmentB** (where **User** is some **data** class with a number of fields), the navigation graph XML would look like this:

```
1.  <navigation xmlns:android="http://schemas.android.com/apk/res/android"
2.      xmlns:app="http://schemas.android.com/apk/res-auto"
3.      android:id="@+id/nav_graph"
4.      app:startDestination="@id/fragmentA">
5.
6.      <fragment
7.          android:id="@+id/fragmentA"
8.          android:name="com.example.FragmentA"
9.          android:label="Fragment A"
10.         tools:layout="@layout/fragment_a" >
11.
12.         <!-- Define action to navigate to Fragment B -->
13.         <action
14.             android:id="@+id/action_fragmentA_to_fragmentB"
15.             app:destination="@id/fragmentB" />
16.     </fragment>
17.
```

```xml
18.     <fragment
19.         android:id="@+id/fragmentB"
20.         android:name="com.example.FragmentB"
21.         android:label="Fragment B"
22.         tools:layout="@layout/fragment_b">
23.
24.         <!-- Define argument for passing the User object -->
25.         <argument
26.             android:name="user"
27.             app:argType="com.example.User"
28.             app:defaultValue="@null" />
29.
30.     </fragment>
31. </navigation>
```

Assuming **FragmentA** and **FragmentB** both exist, building the project with this file located in the **res/navigation** folder would generate code to allow **FragmentA** to launch **FragmentB** and the latter to receive the **User** data:

```kotlin
1. class FragmentA : Fragment() {
2.     // Navigate to Fragment B and pass the User object as an argument
3.     fun navigateToFragmentB(user: User) {
4.         val action = FragmentADirections.actionFragmentAToFragmentB(user)
5.         findNavController().navigate(action)
6.     }
7. }
```

In the preceding code:

- **FragmentADirections.actionFragmentAToFragmentB(user)** is code generated from the XML.
- **findNavController()** is the built-in method for fetching the **NavController** object inflated from the XML.

The user data is subsequently picked up in the newly launched **FragmentB**:

```kotlin
1. class FragmentB : Fragment() {
2.     // Retrieve the User object from the arguments
3.     private val args: FragmentBArgs by navArgs()
4.
```

```
5.     override fun onCreate(savedInstanceState: Bundle?) {
6.         super.onCreate(savedInstanceState)
7.
8.         // Access the User object
9.         val user: User = args.user
10.    }
11. }
```

FragmentBArgs is the code generated from the XML, and **navArgs()** is a built-in method. If Hilt or Koin DI is used in the project (see *Chapter 6, Dependency Injection*), then it is just as easy to receive the **User** data directly into a **ViewModel** Associated with **FragmentA**:

```
1. class ViewModelForFragmentB(
2.     savedStateHandle: SavedStateHandle,
3.     private val user: User = savedStateHandle.get<User>("user")
4. ) : ViewModel() { /* ... */ }
```

This arrangement allows any type of data to be passed between screens with default values (**null** in this case) with relative ease. Furthermore, the map can be maintained graphically with Android Studio's Design editor, much like the following screenshot:

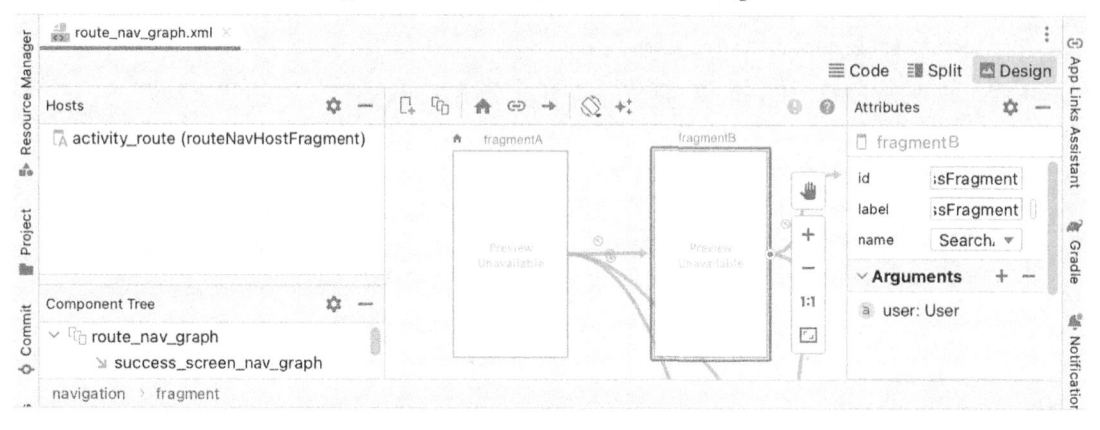

Figure 13.12: Navigation map in design editor.

Navigation Compose

With the launch of Jetpack Compose, the new philosophy is that screens or pages be defined as composables instead of **Fragments**, that is, an app should consist of one **Activity** and everything else is defined in Jetpack Compose. With this philosophy in place, a new navigation library dedicated to navigating between composable screen was required - Navigation Compose:

```
1. dependencies {
2.     // or version catalogs equivalent ...
```

3.   implementation("androidx.navigation:navigation-compose:$vers")
4. }

The library provides methods and objects for associating a unique ID (a **String**) with a composable function representing a screen – essentially, a map of key-value pairs. The unique ID would be used to navigate to another screen. The arrangement is best described with an example. The following code describes two Composable screen stubs, **ScreenA** and **ScreenB**:

```
1. @Composable
2. fun ScreenA(
3.     gotoB: () -> Unit
4. ) {
5.     // ...
6.     gotoB()
7. }
8.
9. @Composable
10. fun ScreenB() { /* ... */ }
```

The following code defines two key strings to be associated with **ScreenA** and **ScreenB**:

```
1. object ScreenKeys {
2.     const val screenA = "screenA"
3.     const val screenB = "screenB"
4. }
```

The keys above can be mapped to **ScreenA** and **ScreenB**, and navigation setup between them using the code from the Navigation Compose library. The following example approximates that of the legacy Navigation component in the last subsection, importantly, *not* attempting to pass the **User** data:

```
1. override fun onCreate(savedInstanceState: Bundle?) {
2.     super.onCreate(savedInstanceState)
3.
4.     setContent {
5.         val navController = rememberNavController()
6.         val gotoB = { navController.navigate(ScreenKeys.screenB) }
7.
8.         NavHost(
9.             navController,
10.            startDestination = ScreenKeys.screenA
11.        ) {
```

```
12.            composable(ScreenKeys.screenA) { ScreenA(gotoB) }
13.            composable(ScreenKeys.screenB) { ScreenB() }
14.        }
15.    }
16. }
```

In the preceding code:

- **rememberNavController()** creates a **NavHostController** object and remembers that instance through compose updates. The resulting **navController** is used to navigate between screens.
- **NavHost** is the composable function that sets up the mapping of the keys to the screens in the **navController**. The function takes as parameters the **navController** that needs to be set up and **startDestination,** the key of the screen that should be displayed first.
- The **composable** method, called within the scope of **NavHost**, maps the keys to the screens. There is also available the navigation method called at a peer-level to **composable**. Similar to **NavHost**, this creates a subgraph of screens, inheriting the **navController** from the parent **NavHost**:

```
1. NavHost(
2.     navController,
3.     startDestination = ScreenKeys.group
4. ) {
5.     navigation(
6.         startDestination = ScreenKeys.screenA,
7.         route = ScreenKeys.group
8.     ) {
9.         composable(ScreenKeys.screenA) { ScreenA(gotoB) }
10.        composable(ScreenKeys.screenB) { ScreenB() }
11.    }
12. }
```

This is useful for better organization of large and complex navigation maps.

- Finally, **navigate**, called on the fully set-up **navController**, will navigate to the screen mapped to the key passed to it.

Navigation Compose with parameters

The previous code looks straightforward, logical and easy to set up, and this is true, until there is a requirement to pass a parameter to the destination screen. At this point, the key

String used to map the screen becomes a URI that also needs to hold information about the parameter passed to the screen, for example:

1. composable("screenB/{userId}") { backStackEntry ->
2.   ScreenB(backStackEntry.arguments?.getString("userId"))
3. }

This would have a corresponding **navigate** call:

1. navController.navigate("screenB/user123")

In this example, the value **user123** is assigned to the parameter key **userId**. It is then picked up from the **backStackEntry** and passed to **ScreenB** as a parameter.

The key is no longer just a key. It is now a combined key and a parameter specification in URI format. This is difficult to manage and error-prone. Things get much worse, however, when there is a requirement to make the parameter optional, or set a default similar to the previous legacy **Navigation** component example:

1. composable(
2.   "screenB?userId={userId}",
3.   arguments = listOf(navArgument("userId") { defaultValue = "user123" })
4.) { backStackEntry ->
5.   ScreenB(backStackEntry.arguments?.getString("userId"))
6. }

Now, not only is there a requirement to formulate a URI string (formatted differently to the previous example), but we now need to create a separate list of objects that specify the default values. Furthermore, the type of data that can be passed from one screen to another is extremely limited to primitives (**String**, **Int**, **Float**, and so on) or an array of primitives. With this arrangement, it is not possible to implement the same arrangement as the previous **Fragment**-based one. Indeed, Google recommends passing just an ID **String** to the destination screen and having a use case in an associated **ViewModel** look up the full details of the actual required object. This will add further complications.

One can only speculate why Google decided to implement navigation compose in this way. However, this awkward, error-prone approach, coupled with a lack of a graphical design interface is likely the reason that the legacy Navigation component is still so popular. Consequently, developers wishing to embrace Jetpack Compose end up creating a hybrid View/Compose affair where each **Fragment** wraps a composable screen, adding an unnecessary layer of legacy code.

Fortunately, there are many third-party libraries available that wrap Navigation Compose and manage its internal complexities, providing the capability to easily pass parameters of any type and with default values. A recent (at the time of writing) addition is the **navcompose-android** library:

```
1. dependencies {
2.     // or version catalogs equivalent ...
3.     implementation("androidx.navigation:navigation-compose:$vers")
4.     implementation("com.google.code.gson:gson:$gsonVer")
5.     implementation("com.aimicor:navcompose-android:$navComposeVer")
6. }
```

Given the dependency declarations above:

- **navcompose-android** works alongside **navigation-compose** so both need to be included.
- **navcompose-android** uses **gson** internally and is not bundled with it so, this also needs to be a dependency.

At the time of writing this book, the library versions were as follows:

- **navigation-compose**: 2.7.7
- **gson**: 2.10.1
- **navcompose-android**: 0.1.3

With this in place, the legacy example can be achieved, allowing some logical refactoring. The screens themselves can be reworked as follows:

```
1.  @Composable
2.  internal fun ScreenA(
3.      gotoB: (User?) -> Unit
4.  ) {
5.      // ...
6.      gotoB(User("user123"))
7.  }
8.
9.  @Composable
10. internal fun ScreenB(user: User?) { /* ... */ }
```

Now, **ScreenA** sends a **User** value via its lambda parameter to **ScreenB** and **ScreenB** receives that **User** value via its own parameter. The **User** type is nullable because, in this case, we want to be able to set a default to **null**, as in the legacy example.

We will define an intelligent parameter key that holds information about the data to be passed, as follows:

```
1. object ParamKeys {
2.     val screenB = navParamSpec<User>()
3. }
```

This parameter key is then used to update the list of screen keys:

```
1.   object ScreenKeys {
2.       const val screenA = "screenA"
3.       val screenB = navComposableSpec(ParamKeys.screenB with null)
4.   }
```

Here, the default is being set with **null**, like the legacy example. However, the syntax does not require it to be null. The syntax allows for an actual **User** instance or nothing at all:

```
1.       val screenB = navComposableSpec(ParamKeys.screenB)
```

In which case, a value *must* be sent when **ScreenB** is navigated to. To complete the arrangement, the **NavHost** graph code can be modified, as follows:

```
1.   setContent {
2.       val navController = rememberNavController()
3.       val gotoB: (User?) -> Unit = { user ->
4.           navController.navigate(
5.               composable = ScreenKeys.screenB,
6.               ParamKeys.screenB with user
7.           )
8.       }
9.
10.      NavHost(
11.          navController,
12.          startDestination = ScreenKeys.screenA
13.      ) {
14.          composable(ScreenKeys.screenA) { ScreenA(gotoB) }
15.          composable(ScreenKeys.screenB) { backStackEntry ->
16.              ScreenB(backStackEntry.getNavParamOrNull(ParamKeys.screenB))
17.          }
18.      }
19.  }
```

The **navController** uses a **navigate** overload that takes the new intelligent screen key and a list of assigned parameters (in this case, just the one) as a **vararg**. Finally, the value is picked up and passed to **ScreenB** with the **getNavParamOrNull** extension of the **backStackEntry**. There is also a stricter **getNavParam** extension which will throw an exception if the value is missing or **null**.

Like the legacy example, the parameter can also be injected directly into a **ViewModel** associated with **ScreenB** instead:

```
1. class ViewModelForScreenB(
2.     savedStateHandle: SavedStateHandle,
3.     private val user: User? = savedStateHandle
4.         .getNavParamOrNull(ParamKeys.screenB)
5. ) : ViewModel() { /* ... */ }
```

As hinted by the **vararg** arrangement above, **navcompose-android** allows multiple parameters to be passed simply by passing a comma-delimited list of **navParamSpecs** to the **navComposableSpec** and subsequently assigning values to them in a comma-delimited list in the **navigate** overload.

Despite providing overloads for all the pertinent methods in Navigation Compose, **navcompose-android** is designed to complement, rather than replace it. This means that there is no need to rip out any existing implementation, and the functionality can be used only where it is needed, as in the example above. It is multimodule-friendly and does not require any annotation auto-generated code. It is open-source and completely free to use by businesses and individuals alike. For more information, see **https://github.com/aimicor/navcompose**.

Navigation Compose with Scaffold

Navigation Compose can be used inside a **Scaffold**, in which case any navigation transition animations will take place inside the scaffold without affecting the **Scaffold** elements. Combining some of the previous examples:

```
1.  @Composable
2.  fun MainNav(
3.      // replace viewModel() with koinViewModel() or hiltViewModel()
4.      scaffoldViewModel: ScaffoldViewModel = viewModel()
5.  ) {
6.      val navController = rememberNavController()
7.      val scaffoldState by scaffoldViewModel
8.          .uiState.collectAsStateWithLifecycle()
9.
10.     Scaffolder(
11.         state = scaffoldState,
12.         event = scaffoldViewModel::handleEvent
13.     ) {
14.         NavHost(
15.             navController,
16.             startDestination = ScreenKeys.screenA
```

```
17.          ) {
18.              composable(ScreenKeys.home) { HomeScreen() }
19.              composable(ScreenKeys.favorites) { FavoritesScreen() }
20.          }
21.     }
22.
23.     scaffoldViewModel.sideEffect.collectWithLifecycle { effect ->
24.         // do navigation
25.     }
26. }
```

This example uses the UDF **ViewModel** pattern described in *Chapter 8, Presentation Layer Evolution in Compose*. However, the thing to note here is that the **NavHost** definition is embedded in the **Scaffold** content. Navigating between **HomeScreen** and **FavoriteScreen** will happen without necessarily triggering an update to the scaffold elements. In practice, the scaffold elements will probably be updated, depending on how the code is written, to show new values for the top bar title and the bottom bar selection. However, any transition animation (more on this later) between screens will only affect the screens in the **NavHost**.

Navigating in and out of the Scaffold

There will almost certainly be requirements to navigate to or from a screen in the **Scaffold** that should not logically be part of that **Scaffold**. For example, navigating from a login screen to a home screen in the **Scaffold** or navigating from any screen to a settings screen. Depending on the requirements, there are at least two valid ways of doing this:

- The first and most straightforward is to hide the individual elements of the Scaffold in response to a UDF state update from the **ViewModel**. For example:

```
1.  @Composable
2.  internal fun Scaffolder(
3.      state: ScaffoldUiState,
4.      event: (ScaffoldEvent) -> Unit,
5.      content: @Composable () -> Unit
6.  ) {
7.      val scaffoldState: ScaffoldState = rememberScaffoldState()
8.      Scaffold(
9.          // ...
10.         bottomBar = {
11.             if (state.isBottomBarVisible) { BottomBar(state, event) }
```

```
12.            },
13.            // ...
14.       )
15. }
```

Animations can be added to make the hiding and showing of the element smoother. This will be covered later in this chapter.

- The second way is to configure two or more **NavHost** objects. This is particularly useful if the feature being navigated has its journey of screens and needs to maintain its own back stack. Similar to Fragments and Activities, the **navController** instance keeps track of the composable screen navigation history in a back stack so that by pressing **back** the current screen will be popped off of the stack, and the previously visited screen will reappear.

Typically, **NavHost**s are nested to achieve this:

```
1.  NavHost( // outer NavHost
2.      fullScreenNavController,
3.      startDestination = scaffoldComposable
4.  ) {
5.      composable(fullscreen1) { Fullscreen1(navViewModel::handleEvent) }
6.      composable(fullscreen2) { Fullscreen2(navViewModel::handleEvent) }
7.      composable(fullscreen3) { Fullscreen3(navViewModel::handleEvent) }
8.      composable(scaffoldComposable) {
9.          Scaffolder(state, navViewModel::handleEvent) {
10.             NavHost( // inner NavHost
11.                 scaffoldNavController,
12.                 startDestination = screenInScaffold1
13.             ) {
14.                 composable(screenInScaffold1) { ScreenInScaffold1() }
15.                 composable(screenInScaffold2) { ScreenInScaffold2() }
16.                 composable(screenInScaffold3) { ScreenInScaffold3() }
17.             }
18.         }
```

```
19.     }
20. }
```

In this simplest of examples, there are three screens inside the **Scaffold** and three outside or **fullscreen**. In this case, on start-up **screenInScaffold1** is the first screen to appear and requests to navigate are handled by **navViewModel**.

fullscreen1, **fullscreen2** and **fullscreen3** will appear without the **Scaffold** and **screenInScaffold1**, **screenInScaffold2** and **screenInScaffold3** will appear inside the **Scaffold**.

Each **NavHost** *must* have its own, dedicated **navController** and each of those **navController** objects maintain their own back-stacks; in the preceding case, **fullScreenNavController** and **scaffoldNavController**. If the same **navController** is used in more than one **NavHost** then the app will crash.

It is possible to navigate from a screen in one **NavHost** to a screen in another by using the destination **NavHost** objects **navController**, for example:

```
1. fullScreenNavController.navigate(fullscreen1)
```

or

```
1. scaffoldNavController.navigate(screenInScaffold2)
```

However, either the destination **NavHost** object's stack must be empty, or the origin's stack must be emptied first, for example:

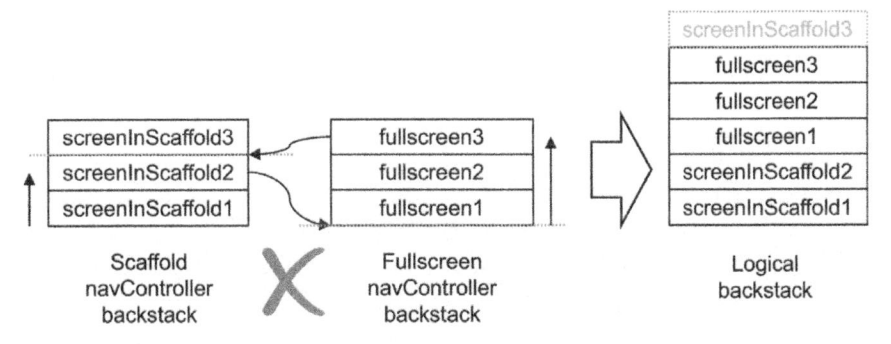

Figure 13.13: Failed navigation attempt

In the previous example, the system can maintain a logical back stack from one **NavHost** to the next until an attempt is made to add a third screen from the first **NavHost** by navigating from **fullscreen3** to **screenInScaffold3**, at which point the navigation fails. This is likely due to the fact that the underlying back-stack-of-back-stacks functionality is limited. In this instance, the app will not crash, and no error is outputted to the logs; it just fails to navigate.

In this example, in order to effectively navigate from **fullscreen3** to **screenInScaffold3**, the full-screen back stack must be cleared first:

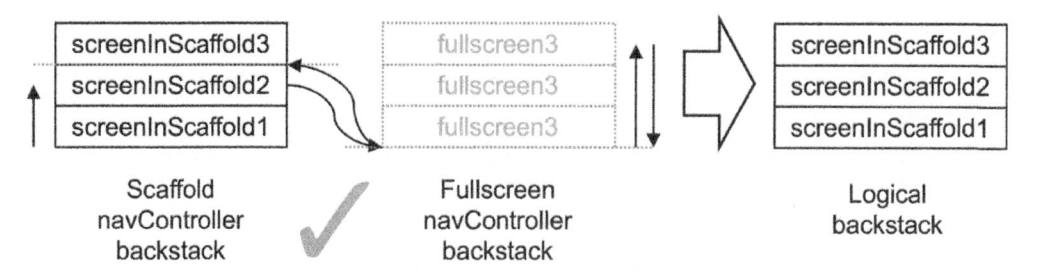

Figure 13.14: Successful navigation attempt

Fortunately, there is a useful line of code to pop all stack entries without manually finding the first screen in the stack entry:

```
1.  navController.apply {
2.      popBackStack(graph.findStartDestination().id, inclusive = false)
3.  }
```

navController.graph.findStartDestination().id finds the ID of the first screen in the stack and **navController.popBackStack** pops down to it.

Animation

Animations play a crucial role in enhancing the user experience of a Jetpack Compose app. They can make transitions between UI elements smoother, add visual interest, and provide feedback to users about their interactions. This section covers a few of the most commonly used animations.

AnimationSpec

An **AnimationSpec** in Jetpack Compose defines the characteristics of an animation, dictating its timing, easing, and behavior. It acts as the blueprint for how a value or property will animate over time. The following example applies an **AnimationSpec** to the size of a **Box** so that it is first displayed at size 100dp then animates to 200dp over 1 second:

```
1.  fun AnimatedBox() {
2.      // Define an Animatable for the size property
3.      val size = remember { Animatable(initialValue = 100f) }
4.
5.      // Define an AnimationSpec for the animation
6.      val animationSpec: AnimationSpec<Float> = tween(
7.          durationMillis = 1000, // Animation duration
8.          easing = LinearEasing // Animation easing
9.      )
```

```
10.
11.     // Trigger the animation
12.     LaunchedEffect(true) {
13.         size.animateTo(
14.             targetValue = 200f, // Target size
15.             animationSpec = animationSpec
16.         )
17.     }
18.
19.     // Composable that animates the size of the box
20.     Box(
21.         modifier = Modifier
22.             .size(size.value.dp) // Size is animated
23.             .background(Color.Blue)
24.     )
25. }
```

The preceding example uses the **tween AnimationSpec**. The following is a list of built-in **AnimationSpec** objects and their function:

- **Tween**: The **tween** spec animates smoothly between values with a specified duration and easing function (linear, ease-in, and so on).
- **Spring**: The **spring** spec creates a spring-like animation with configurable damping and stiffness, simulating natural bouncing behavior.
- **Keyframes**: The **keyframes** animation spec defines keyframes for animating a value. It specifies the value of the property at different keyframes along with their respective timestamps and interpolation methods.
- **Repeatable**: The **repeatable** animation spec creates repeatable animations that loop a specified number of times or indefinitely. It can specify the animation to repeat with a specific duration and easing function.
- **InfiniteRepeatable**: Similar to **repeatable**, the **infiniteRepeatable** animation spec creates an animation that repeats indefinitely. It is useful for creating continuous animations like spinners or blinking effects.
- **Elasticity**: The **elasticity** animation spec creates an animation with an elastic effect, simulating a bouncing motion. It can specify the elasticity factor to control the bounciness of the animation.
- **Decay**: The **decay** animation spec creates a decay animation that gradually slows down to a stop. It is useful for simulating natural motion, such as scrolling or flinging gestures.

These built-in animation specs provide a range of options for creating different types of animations in a Jetpack Compose app, and their parameters can be customized to achieve the desired effect. In a similar way to the previous example, these animations can be applied to several attributes of a composable element:

- **Size**: Animating the size of a composable creates effects like scaling or resizing animations.
- **Position**: Animating the position of a composable creates effects like moving or translating animations.
- **Alpha**: Animating the alpha (opacity) of a composable creates fading in or out animations.
- **Rotation**: Animating the rotation of a composable creates rotating animations.
- **Color**: Animating the color of a composable creates color-changing or tinting animations.
- **Content size**: Animating the content size of a composable creates animations that adjust dynamically based on the content.
- **Shape**: Animating the shape of a composable creates effects like morphing or transforming animations.
- **Elevation**: Animating the elevation of a composable creates effects like lifting or dropping animations.

These are just a few examples of attributes that can be animated using animation specs in Jetpack Compose. The key is to experiment with different animation specs and apply them to the attributes that best suit the individual design and interaction requirements.

AnimatedVisibility

`AnimatedVisibility` is a composable function in Jetpack Compose that allows the animation of the appearance and disappearance of content based on a visibility state. It provides a simple, efficient way to create smooth transitions between showing and hiding UI elements. The following code demonstrates the use of `AnimatedVisibility`:

```
1.  val isVisible = remember { mutableStateOf(false) }
2.
3.  AnimatedVisibility(
4.      visible = isVisible,
5.      enter = fadeIn() + expandVertically(),
6.      exit = fadeOut() + shrinkVertically()
7.  ) {
8.      Text("This content will appear and disappear with animation.")
9.  }
```

```
10.
11. Button(onClick = { isVisible.value = !isVisible.value }) {
12.     Text("Toggle Visibility")
13. }
```

In the preceding example, the content will fade in and expand vertically when shown and fade out and shrink vertically when hidden. Given the code above:

- A **visible** parameter can be added to **AnimatedVisibility**, indicating whether the content should be visible.
- The composable within **AnimatedVisibility** will only be composed and rendered if the **visible** parameter is true.
- When the visibility state changes, **AnimatedVisibility** will animate the transition between showing and hiding the content using the default **EnterTransition** and **ExitTransition**.

By default, **EnterTransition** fades in the content and expands it slightly, and **ExitTransition** fades out the content and shrinks it slightly. The transitions are applied based on the container type of **AnimatedVisibility** (for example, row, column).

The transitions can be customized using the **enter** and **exit** parameters of **AnimatedVisibility**. Each parameter accepts an **EnterTransition** or **ExitTransition** builder, allowing the definition of custom animations or the use of pre-built transitions like **fade**, **expand**, **scale**, or **slide**. Multiple transitions can be also combined using the **+** operator.

Transition animations

Transition animations are used to create smooth and visually appealing transitions between different states of a UI. These animations allow definition of how the UI should change when transitioning from one state to another, such as when showing or hiding a component, changing its size or position, or updating its content. Generally, however, transition animations commonly refer to the animation of moving from one screen to another.

Transition animations in Navigation Compose are now built directly into the library, providing a more seamless and integrated experience compared to previous approaches like the accompanist third-party library:

```
1. import androidx.compose.animation...SlideDirection.Companion.Left
2. import androidx.compose.animation...SlideDirection.Companion.Right
3.
4. NavHost(
5.     navController = navController,
6.     startDestination = homescreen,
```

```
7.     enterTransition = {
8.         if (targetState.destination.route == detailScreen.route)
9.             slideIntoContainer(Left)
10.         else EnterTransition.None
11.    },
12.    popEnterTransition = { EnterTransition.None },
13.    exitTransition = { ExitTransition.None },
14.    popExitTransition = {
15.        if (targetState.destination.route == homescreen.route)
16.            slideOutOfContainer(Right)
17.        else ExitTransition.None
18.    }
19. ) {
20.     // populated by composable and navigation calls
21. }
```

The **NavHost**, **composable** and **navigation** methods of the library all provide the following parameters for transition animation:

- **enterTransition**: This property defines the transition animation that occurs when a new destination is entering the screen, typically when navigating forward to a new destination. It specifies how the new destination appears on the screen.

- **exitTransition**: This property defines the transition animation that occurs when the current destination is exiting the screen, typically when navigating away from the current destination. It specifies how the current destination disappears from the screen.

- **popEnterTransition**: This property defines the transition animation that occurs when a destination is entering the screen as a result of the back navigation (pop operation). It specifies how the destination appears when navigating back to it.

- **popExitTransition**: This property defines the transition animation that occurs when the current destination is exiting the screen as a result of the back navigation (pop operation). It specifies how the current destination disappears from the screen when navigating back.

The lambda scope provided by these parameters allows access to information about the current transition. For example, as can be seen in the preceding code, the **enterTransition** is conditionally set to **slideIntoContainer** when the destination is **detailScreen** and the **popEnterTransition** is conditionally set to **slideOutOfContainer** when the destination is **homeScreen**. The example is there just to show that it can be done. It would have been easier in this scenario to set **enterTransition** and **popEnterTransition** in the respective **composable** calls for each of **detailScreen** and **homeScreen** instead.

The following transitions are available in the **androidx.compose.animation** package:

- **fadeIn()**: This transition animates the opacity of a composable from 0 to 1, creating a fade-in effect when the composable enters the screen.
- **fadeOut()**: This transition animates the opacity of a composable from 1 to 0, creating a fade-out effect when the composable exits the screen.
- **slideInHorizontally()**: This transition animates the position of a composable from outside the screen to its original position, creating a slide-in effect when the composable enters the screen.
- **slideOutHorizontally()**: This transition animates the position of a composable from its original position to outside the screen, creating a slide-out effect when the composable exits the screen.
- **expandVertically()**: This transition animates the height of a composable from 0 to its original height, creating an expand effect when the composable enters the screen.
- **shrinkVertically()**: This transition animates the height of a composable from its original height to 0, creating a shrink effect when the composable exits the screen.
- **expandIn()**: This transition combines a fade-in and expand effect, animating both the opacity and height of a composable when it enters the screen.
- **shrinkOut()**: This transition combines a fade-out and shrink effect, animating both the opacity and height of a composable when it exits the screen.

Animations are powerful tools but use them thoughtfully to enhance the user experience without overwhelming users. By following these guidelines and exploring the resources provided, animations can be incorporated effectively into a Jetpack Compose app and create a truly engaging experience.

Multiplatform considerations

When choosing UI elements for a Jetpack Compose Multiplatform project, it is essential to be aware of which elements are currently available and supported across all target platforms (Android, iOS, desktop, web). Here is a breakdown of the key points:

- **Foundation**
  - **Compose core**: The core building blocks of Compose, including basic UI elements like **Text**, **Button**, **Image**, **Row**, **Column**, **Modifier**, and more, are fully supported across all platforms.
  - **Material design**: Most of the Material Design components from material-components are available, providing a consistent look and feel across platforms. This includes elements like **Card**, **TextField**, **AppBar**, **BottomAppBar**, etc.
- **Additional libraries**
  - **Accompanist**: While some Accompanist libraries are platform-specific, many core libraries like *coil-ktx* for image loading, **insets** for handling screen insets, and **navigation-animation** for animations are Multiplatform-compatible.

- o **Third-party libraries**: The availability of third-party libraries depends on their implementation and support for different platforms. Check the specific library documentation for Multiplatform compatibility information.
- **Areas with limited support**
  - o **Android-specific APIs**: Elements directly tied to Android features, like `Snackbar`, `Toast`, and platform-specific widgets, are naturally not available on other platforms. Alternative solutions or platform-specific implementations will be needed.
  - o **Desktop extensions**: Jetpack Compose Desktop extends Compose with specific components like `Window`, `MenuBar`, and `ContextMenu`, but these are restricted to desktop targets.
  - o **Web limitations**: While Compose for Web is still experimental, some limitations exist. Web-specific libraries or alternative approaches might be necessary for functionalities not yet well-supported.
- **Tips for selecting multiplatform elements**
  - o Prioritize core Compose and material design components for broad platform support.
  - o Carefully evaluate third-party libraries and their multiplatform compatibility.
  - o Be prepared to implement platform-specific alternatives or workarounds when needed.
  - o Leverage accompanist libraries for useful multiplatform functionalities.
  - o Stay updated on Compose multiplatform development and library progress for expanding possibilities.

Remember, Jetpack Compose Multiplatform is an evolving platform. Explore the available elements, stay updated on new developments, and embrace creative solutions to achieve the desired Multiplatform UI experience.

Conclusion

Jetpack Compose provides a vast array of features, far too many to comprehensively document here. Instead, this chapter examined a few of the more salient aspects for organizing and polishing an application. We looked at Themes which are the core of personalizing an app's visual identity and branding. They act like a paintbrush, allowing control over colors, typography, shapes, and more, across all UI elements.

We also examined the Scaffold, a fundamental composable that provides the structural foundation of an app, holding together key elements like app bars, floating action buttons, and the content area. In addition, we studied the evolution of screen navigation from the legacy `Fragment` map arrangement to the Compose-only solution supplied by the Navigation Compose library. Next, we covered some of the techniques in Jetpack Compose for animating content that play a crucial role in enhancing the user experience. Finally, considerations for multiplatform compose were explored.

The next chapter will document the steps required to build an app for distribution.

Points to remember

- Use Themes to standardize colors, fonts and the shape of controls across an app.
- Custom fonts can be imported from standard font file types and used in an app.
- Leverage the **Scaffold** composable to coordinate key elements like app bars, floating action buttons, and the content area.
- To open the **Drawer** or to show the **Snackbar** in a Scaffold, use `scaffoldState.drawerState.open()` and `scaffoldState.snackState.showSnackbar()` methods launched within a coroutine.
- Use the standard `navigation-compose` library to navigate between composable screen content.
- Use the third-party `navcompose-android` library with `navigation-compose` to pass complex data types between composable screen content.
- `AnimationSpec`, `AnimatedVisibility`, and transition animations are some features provided to animate composables.
- Use animations thoughtfully to enhance the user experience without overwhelming users.

Questions

1. How do themes personalize an app's visual identity and branding?
2. How do you leverage dynamic colors in app theming?
3. What is the **Scaffold**?
4. What features are invoked via the **ScaffoldState**?
5. In what ways is legacy fragment-based navigation more flexible than Navigation Compose?
6. What are the pitfalls of using multiple **NavHost** objects?
7. What features can be animated in Jetpack Compose?
8. What other methods of animation other than those documented can be used?
9. What should be considered when using Jetpack Compose for multiplatform development?

Join our book's Discord space

Join the book's Discord Workspace for Latest updates, Offers, Tech happenings around the world, New Release and Sessions with the Authors:

https://discord.bpbonline.com

CHAPTER 14
Debugging in Kotlin

Introduction

In the dynamic world of mobile app development, ensuring that your applications run smoothly and efficiently is paramount. Despite the best coding practices, bugs, and issues are an inevitable part of the development process. Effective debugging is crucial to identify, diagnose, and resolve these problems, ensuring a seamless user experience.

This chapter delves into the essential techniques and tools for debugging Kotlin-based Android applications. Kotlin, with its concise syntax and robust features, simplifies many aspects of Android development. However, the complexity of mobile environments necessitates a thorough understanding of debugging methodologies to tackle runtime errors, crashes, performance bottlenecks, and logical errors.

Structure

This chapter covers the following topics:

- Android device bridge
- Breakpoints
- Watch expressions
- Evaluate expression

- Profiling tools
- Logcat logging
- Timber
- Other considerations

Objectives

This chapter will explore the powerful debugging capabilities integrated within Android Studio. It will demonstrate how to utilize breakpoints, watch variables, and logcat to monitor application behavior and identify issues. By the end of this chapter, you will understand advanced topics such as memory profiling, analyzing thread performance, and leveraging Kotlin-specific debugging tools.

Android device bridge

While it is entirely possible to develop and debug an application purely on the emulator provided by Android Studio, it is advisable instead to do so on an actual device. Android Studio provides the ADB tool to allow synchronization with actual devices. To enable this, devices need to be put into developer mode. To enable this setting, the following sequence of actions need to be performed:

1. Go to **Settings** | **About Device**. See *Figure 14.1*:

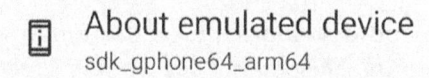

   About emulated device
   sdk_gphone64_arm64

   Figure 14.1: About emulated device

2. Scroll down to the **Build number** and click on the **Build number** seven times. S+ee *Figure 14.2*:

   Build number
   sdk_gphone64_arm64-userdebug 14
   UE1A.230829.036.A1 11228894 dev-keys

   Figure 14.2: Build Number

3. Go back to **Settings** and click on **System**. See *Figure 14.3*:

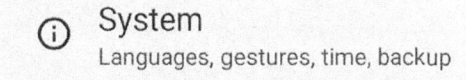

   System
   Languages, gestures, time, backup

   Figure 14.3: System

4. Select **Developer options**. See *Figure 14.4:*

{ }   Developer options

Figure 14.4: Developer Options

5. Scroll down in **Developer options** and enable debugging. See the following *Figure 14.5:*

Debugging

USB debugging
Debug mode when USB is connected

Wireless debugging
Debug mode when Wi-Fi is connected

Figure 14.5 Enable debugging

Breakpoints

Breakpoints are markers in code execution where the program halts for debugging. They are invaluable for debugging and troubleshooting software because they enable developers to:

- **Inspect program state**: Developers can examine the values of variables and objects at the point where the breakpoint is set, helping to identify bugs and understand program behavior.
- **Analyze control flow**: Breakpoints help developers understand the flow of execution through the program, enabling them to track how the program behaves as it runs.
- **Isolate issues**: By stopping execution at specific points in the code, developers can isolate problematic sections of code or identify unexpected behaviors.
- **Modify behavior**: In some debugging environments, developers can modify the values of variables and objects while the program is paused at a breakpoint, allowing them to experiment with different scenarios and test potential fixes.

Breakpoints can be set at various locations in the code, including specific lines of code, function/method declarations, and conditional statements. Android Studio provides advanced breakpoint features such as conditional breakpoints (break when a certain condition is met) and remote breakpoints (debugging across networked environments).

The following describes the usage of Breakpoints:

- **Set breakpoints**: Navigate to the line of code to set a breakpoint. Click on the left margin/gutter of the code editor next to the line number. This action sets a breakpoint at that point. Refer to the following figure:

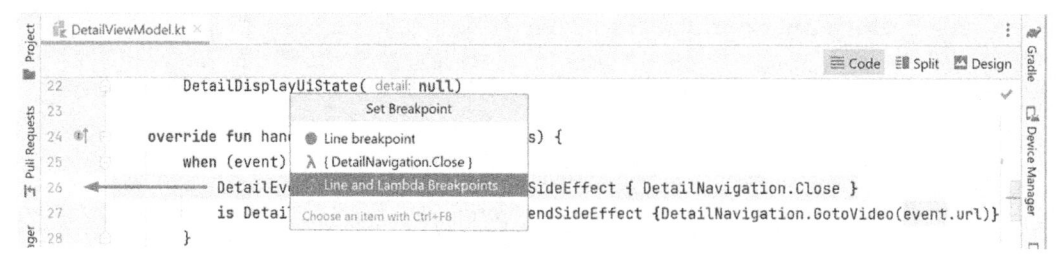

Figure 14.6: Set Breakpoint

If the breakpoint is ambiguous, as shown in the preceding figure, a dialog will appear to select exactly where the breakpoint is required.

- **Debug mode**: Run the test or application in debug mode. This can be done by selecting the **Debug** option instead of **Run** in the IDE. Simply click on the debug button at the top of the IDE window, as shown in the following figure, to run in Debug mode:

Figure 14.7: Run in Debug Mode

- **Attach debugger to process**: Debug mode can also be invoked on an app that is already running by selecting the Attached Debugger to Process button as show in the following figure:

Figure 14.8: Attach Debugger to Process

- **Debugger controls**: Once the program execution reaches the breakpoint, the debugger pauses, and the current state of variables and call stack are displayed. **Step into**, **Step Over** and **Resume** navigation controls are presented throughout the code. When the program execution reaches the breakpoint, the condition is evaluated. If the condition is true, the debugger pauses, and an inspection of the program completed. Conditional breakpoints can significantly improve debugging efficiency by focusing on specific situations or scenarios where issues arise. Allowing effective debugging to be implemented. See *Figure 14.9:*

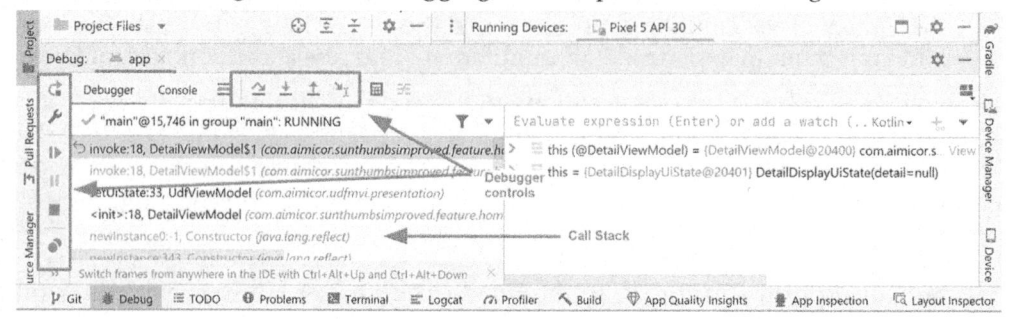

Figure 14.9: Debugger controls

- **Inspect and fix**: Examine variables, evaluate expressions, and identify any issues in the code. Variables can be examined at each layer of the call stack by clicking on the stack call (stack call listings under **Debugger** and **Console** menu options) in the left-hand panel as in *Figure 14.9*. This makes necessary adjustments to fix bugs or unexpected behavior.
- **Continue execution**: After resolving code issues, removing the breakpoint and running the program normally or by using the debugger controls will resume execution.

Conditional breakpoints

Conditional breakpoints are a type of breakpoint that allows the developer to pause the execution of the program only when a specific condition is met. Instead of stopping the program every time the breakpoint is reached, a conditional breakpoint introduces a condition that must be evaluated to be true for the program to pause.

Android Studio breakpoints are set when specific conditions are met, for example:

1. Click on the location in the code to set a breakpoint first, as shown in *Figure 14.6*. Then, right-click on that breakpoint.
2. Then, enter a condition into the resulting dialog box, as shown in *Figure 14.10*:

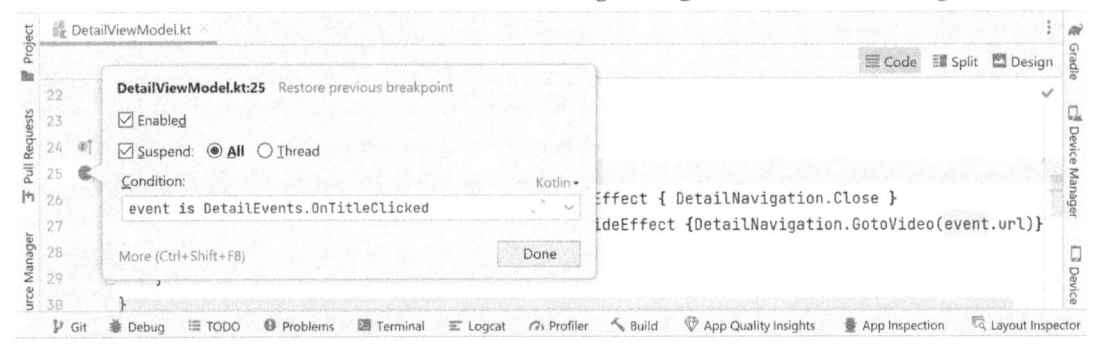

Figure 14.10: Conditional breakpoints

3. The breakpoint will pause code execution when the specified condition is evaluated as true.

Exception breakpoints

Exception breakpoints are a powerful debugging feature found in Android Studio. Breakpoints are useful when a specific exception is thrown, providing a convenient way to catch and investigate exceptions during debugging as follows.

Set an exception breakpoint

Follow these steps to set an exception breakpoint:

1. Having paused on a breakpoint while debugging an app, click on the **View Breakpoints**. See *Figure 14.11:*

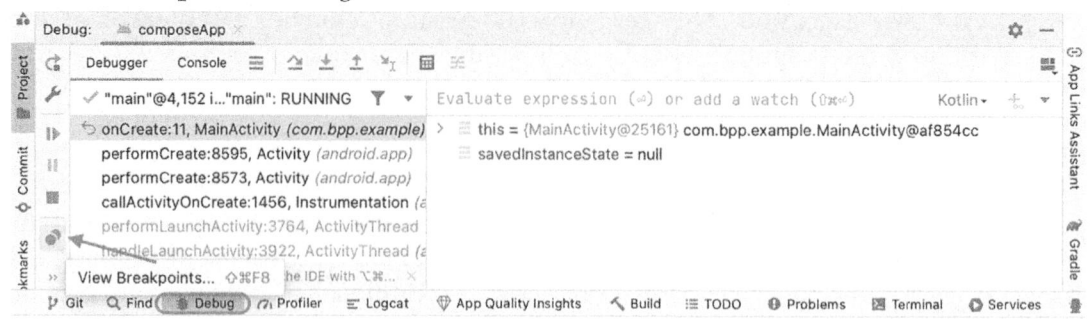

Figure 14.11: Setting an exception breakpoint

2. Click on the + button to add **Java Exception Breakpoints**. See *Figure 14.12*. (Using **Java Exception Breakpoints** instead of just **Exception breakpoints** provides the ability to filter breakpoints for a specific exception class.).

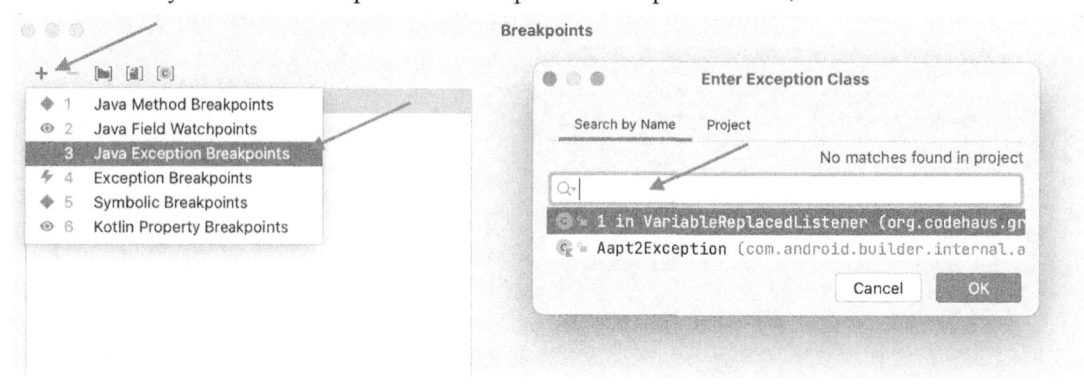

Figure 14.12: Java Exception Breakpoints

Click on **Java Exception Breakpoints,** and the dialog **Enter Exception Class** will be displayed, as shown in *Figure 14.12.*

3. If custom exceptions have been created within the project, these will be displayed under **Enter Exception Class**. A check box will be displayed for **Include non-project items**. See *Figure 14.13:*

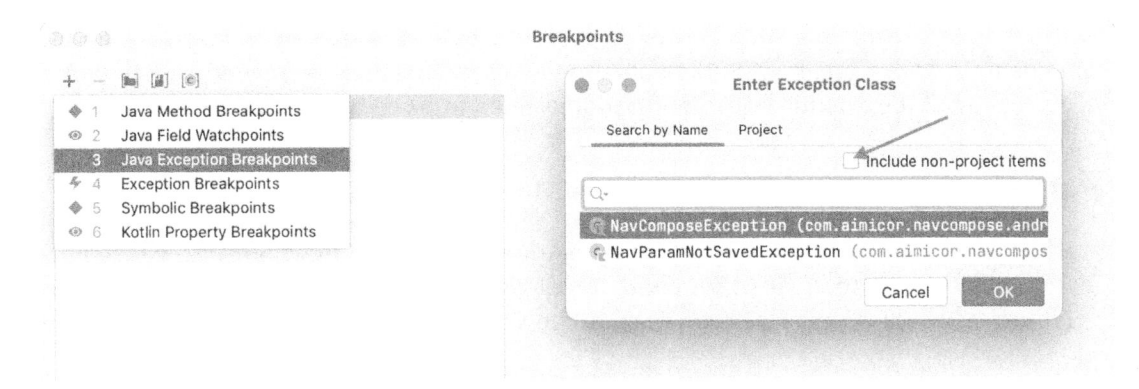

Figure 14.13: Enter Exception Class

4. If no custom exceptions have been created, the message, **No matches found in project** will be displayed.
5. Select the exception class required to break on.
6. **Debugger pauses on exception**: When a specific exception is thrown during the execution of code, the debugger will automatically pause the program where the exception occurred as in *Figure 14.14*. In this instance, it is a `ClassNotFoundException`.

Figure 14.14: ClassNotFoundException

Exception breakpoints are particularly useful for catching and diagnosing unexpected errors during debugging. Allowing focus on specific types of exceptions without having to manually search through code. This feature is valuable for troubleshooting issues related to unexpected runtime errors and improving reliability of Kotlin applications.

Watch expressions

Use a watch expression to monitor the value of a variable, expression, or property during program execution. The debugger displays its current value whenever it changes.

In Android Studio, watch expressions may be added by right-clicking on a variable or expression in the code editor or debugger window and selecting an option like **Add Watch** or **Add Watch Expression**. After this, the required variable or expression may be added. The debugger will display its current value and update it as the program executes.

Android Studio provides this; however, it does not add much in the way of added functionality. At any breakpoint, the value of all available data is displayed. Watch points create a copy of the existing value being monitored and put it at the top of the list.

Evaluate expression

Evaluate expression is another debugging feature found in Android Studio. This feature allows developers to manually input and execute expressions during a debugging session, providing a way to inspect variables, calculate values, or evaluate complex expressions on-the-fly.

Figure 14.15 shows how to use the *Evaluate Expression* feature:

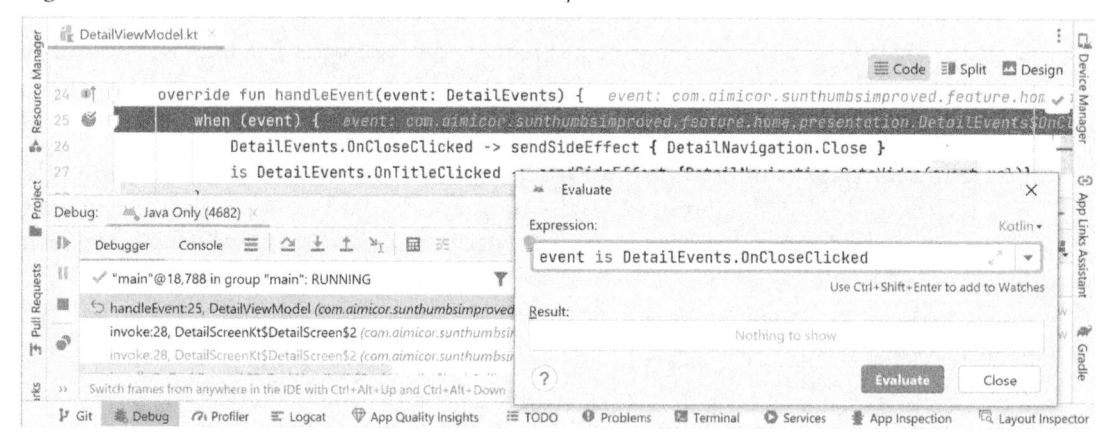

Figure 14.15: Evaluate expression

- **Run to breakpoint:** Insert a Breakpoint and Run in Debug (see section on *Breakpoints*). When execution halts at the breakpoint, click on the **Evaluate** icon (*Figure 14.15*). Clicking on the **Evaluate** icon displays an evaluate expression menu.
- **Evaluate expression menu:** Enter the expression to be evaluated and click **Evaluate**. The result will then be displayed.

The Evaluate Expression feature is a useful tool for dynamic and interactive debugging. It allows developers to gain insights into the state of their code without modifying the source or adding temporary print statements. This can be especially useful when dealing with complex algorithms, mathematical calculations, or situations where there is a need to inspect values on-the-fly.

Profiling tools

Profiling tools in Android Studio are essential for analyzing the performance of Android applications. They help developers identify bottlenecks, memory leaks, and other performance issues, allowing for optimization and improvement. Android Studio provides a set of powerful profiling tools that can be accessed from the Android Profiler window. Here are some key profiling tools available in Android Studio:

- **CPU profiler**: The CPU Profiler helps to understand how an application utilizes the device and CPU resources over time. It displays a timeline showing CPU usage, thread activity, and method traces, allowing identification of performance hotspots.
- **Memory profiler**: The memory profiler provides monitoring and analysis of the memory usage of an application. It provides information about heap memory, memory allocations, and garbage collection events, assisting in identifying memory leaks and optimizing memory usage.
- **Systems trace**: The system trace profiler provides a detailed timeline of system-level events, including CPU, memory, network activities, and system processes. It helps identify correlations between different system components and an application's behavior.

To start a new Profiler or Memory Session follow these steps:

1. Click on **View** | **Tool Windows** | **Profiler**, as shown in *Figure 14.16*:

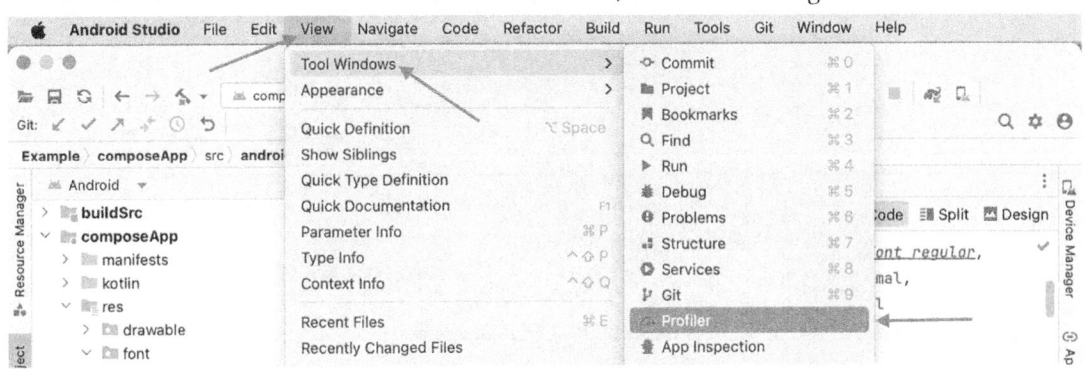

Figure 14.16: Profiler Menu Options

2. Alternatively, the **CPU** or **Memory** by clicking on the **Profiler** button is displayed, as shown in *Figure 14.17*:

Figure 14.17: Profiler Tab

318   ■   *Scalable Android Applications in Kotlin*

3. Click + in the **Sessions** menu, as shown in *Figure 14.18*:

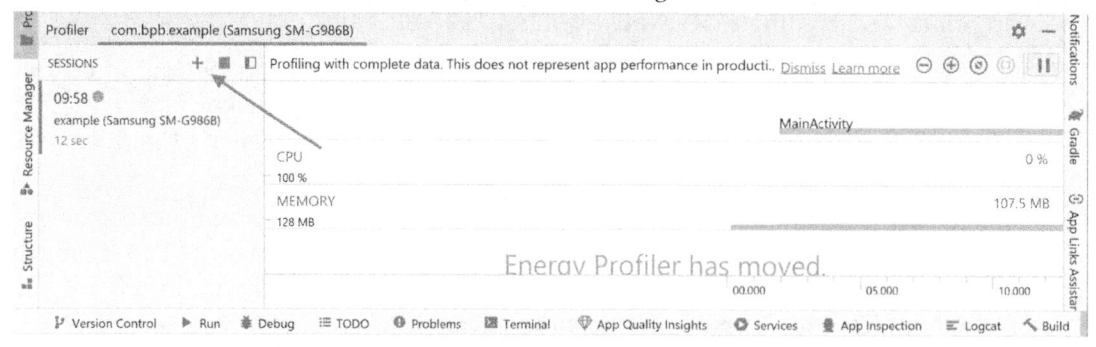

Figure 14.18: *Profiler Memory and CPU*

4. Then, select either **Load from File** or the running process from the drop-down menus, as shown in *Figure 14.17*. The profiler will run and display both the CPU Profiler and memory information, as shown in *Figure 14.18*.

CPU profiler information is shown in *Figure 14.19*:

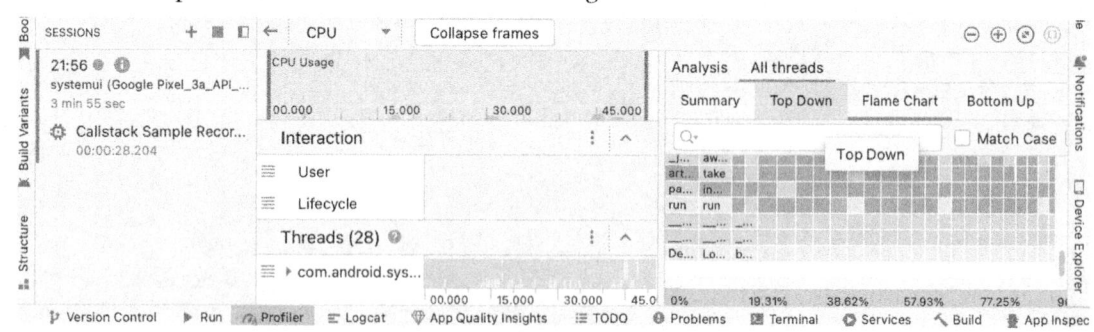

Figure 14.19: *CPU Flame chart*

Memory Profiler information is shown in *Figure 14.20*:

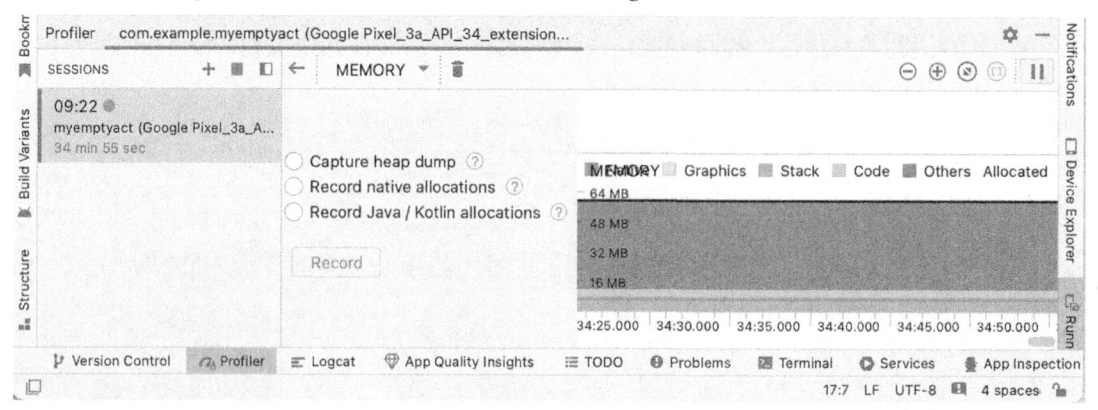

Figure 14.20: *Memory Profiler*

Logcat logging

The name **Logcat** comes from the fact that it primarily deals with log messages categorized by a tag and a priority level. Logcat is used to monitor the output of log calls in an app, helping debug issues, track the flow of an application, and monitor system activities. See *Figure 14.21:*

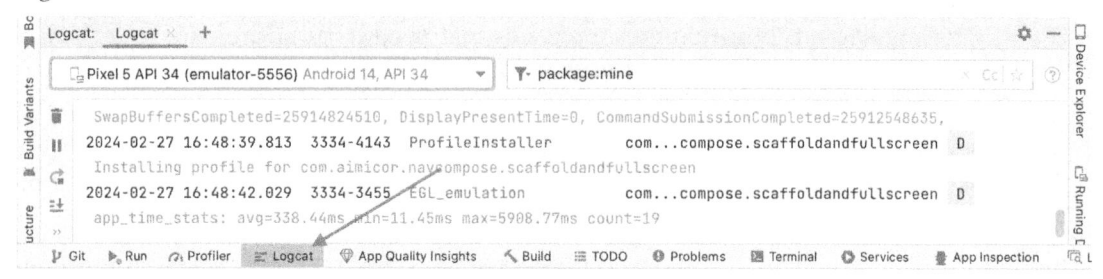

Figure 14.21: Logcat window

The following is a brief overview of Logcat functionality:

- **Logging levels**: Logcat provides several logging levels, including *debug* (`Log.d`), *info* (`Log.i`), *warn* (`Log.w`), and *error* (`Log.e`). Each level corresponds to a priority and can be filtered via **Logcat** output based on these priorities.
- **Tagging**: Logcat messages are associated with a tag, which is typically a string identifier that is specified in a logging statement. This allows filtering and identifying messages from specific parts of the code.
- **Viewing Logcat output**: In Android Studio, access Logcat from the bottom panel. It displays a scrolling window of log messages, and a filter message based on tags, log levels, and other criteria (*Figure 14.21*).
- **Logging messages**: In the app's code, the Log class can be used to output messages to Logcat. For example, `Log.d(TAG, "Message")` can be used to log a debug message with a specific tag.

The Logcat hierarchy represents different priority/severity levels of log messages that can be generated by the system or an application. These levels categorize log messages based on their importance or severity. The Android logging system defines several priority levels, each represented by a single character. The priority levels, in descending order of severity, are:

- **Verbose (V)**: This is the least severe priority level. These messages are typically used for providing detailed information during development, such as variable values or method calls.
- **Debug (D)**: This is used for debugging purposes. Debug messages provide information about the application's behavior at runtime. These messages are typically removed from production code.

- **Info (I)**: This is used for informational messages that highlight the progress of the application. Info messages are typically used to log important events or milestones.
- **Warning (W)**: This indicates potential issues or situations that might need attention. Warnings do not necessarily indicate errors but may suggest areas for improvement.
- **Error (E)**: This indicates errors that occurred during the execution of the application. Error messages typically represent issues that need to be addressed, as they may impact the functionality or stability of the application.
- **Assert (A)**: This is the most severe priority level. Assert messages are used to indicate critical errors that should never occur during normal operation. These messages are typically used to assert conditions that must be true for the application to function correctly.

These priority levels help developers categorize and filter log messages effectively, allowing them to focus on relevant information during debugging and troubleshooting. Developers can specify the priority level when logging messages within their code such as `Log.v()`, `Log.d()`, `Log.i()`, `Log.w()`, `Log.e()`, and `Log.wtf()`. Additionally, Logcat in Android Studio provides options to filter log messages based on their priority level, making it easier to identify and analyze issues in the application. The logcat messages are hierarchical.

The following figure shows how to navigate the **Logcat** option. After pressing the **logcat** button, the following screen is displayed. After selecting the **Formatting Options** indicated by the first arrow, in *Figure 14.22* and selecting **Modify Views** from the menu, the following screen is displayed:

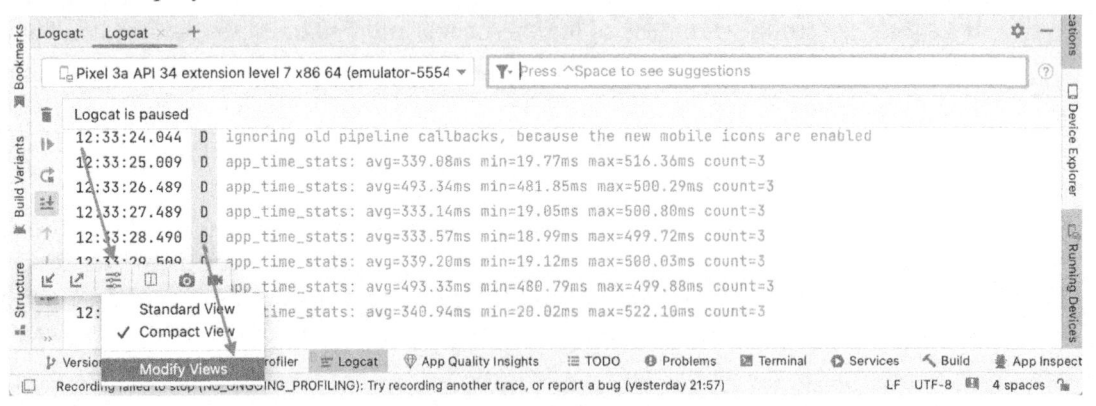

Figure 14.22: Logcat Compact View

The **Logcat Format** screen is displayed in *Figure 14.23*:

Figure 14.23: Configure Logcat formatting options

Figure 14.24 demonstrates the previously mentioned priority levels of error, debug, and so on. These can be used as filters.

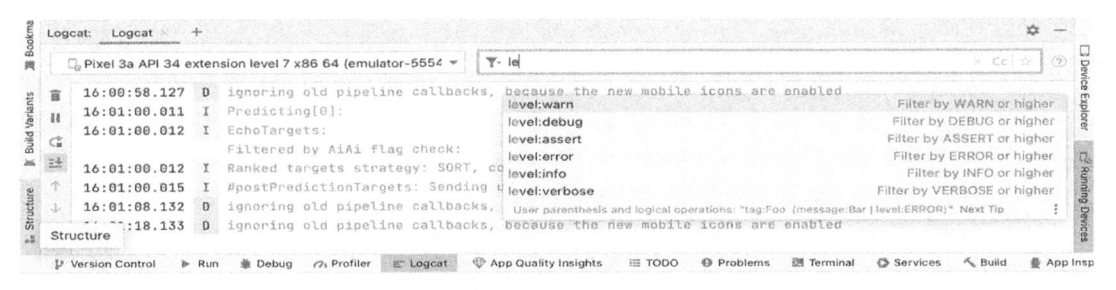

Figure 14.24: Logcat Filters

Timber

Timber is a popular logging library for Android, which provides a simple API for logging messages in an Android application. It is often used as a replacement for the default Android logging mechanism (Logcat) because it offers several advantages, such as:

- Cleaner syntax for logging messages.
- Easy integration and configuration.

- Built-in support for logging levels.
- Ability to customize log output and formatting.

To integrate Timber into an Android project in Android Studio, follow these steps:

1. Add the Timber dependency to an app's **build.gradle.kts** file:

    ```
    1.  dependencies {
    2.      // or version catalogs equivalent ...
    3.      implementation("com.jakewharton.timber:timber:$vers")
    4.  }
    ```

    Where **vers** is the latest version.

2. Initialize Timber in the application class or in the main activity's **onCreate()** method:

    ```
    1.  class MyApplication : Application() {
    2.      override fun onCreate() {
    3.          super.onCreate()
    4.          if (BuildConfig.DEBUG) {
    5.              Timber.plant(Timber.DebugTree())
    6.          } else {
    7.              // For production, might want
    8.              // to plant a different tree. For example,
    9.              // Crashlytics or another logging service.
    10.         }
    11.     }
    12. }
    ```

3. Now, use Timber to log messages throughout an application:

    ```
    1.  class MyActivity : AppCompatActivity() {
    2.      override fun onCreate(savedInstanceState: Bundle?) {
    3.          super.onCreate(savedInstanceState)
    4.          setContentView(R.layout.activity_main)
    5.
    6.          Timber.d("Activity created") // Example logging
    7.      }
    8.  }
    ```

This code will log a debug message **Activity created** with the tag **MyActivity**. By following these steps, integrate Timber into an Android project using Kotlin and Kotlin DSL for the build scripts. The hierarchy is the same as logcat.

Other considerations

Apart from the techniques described above, there are other things to consider when debugging code:

- **Remote/USB debugging**: For mobile app development, consider using remote debugging for issues that occur on physical devices.
- **Code reviews**: Regularly conduct code reviews with the work team to catch potential issues early on.
- **Version control**: Use version control effectively. Tag important releases and use branches for experimental features or bug fixes.

Conclusion

Debugging Kotlin Android apps is an indispensable skill that bridges the gap between a functional prototype and a polished, user-ready product. This chapter has explored a comprehensive suite of tools and techniques essential for identifying and resolving issues in Kotlin-based Android applications. From setting up and utilizing breakpoints to harnessing the full potential of Android Studio's debugging features, a solid foundation to effectively troubleshoot your code has been provided.

This chapter also discussed advanced debugging practices, such as memory profiling and performance analysis, which are crucial for optimizing an app's efficiency and reliability. Understanding how to interpret logcat output and leverage Kotlin-specific tools further enhances the ability to diagnose and fix a wide range of issues.

Remember, the process of debugging is not merely about fixing errors but also about understanding an application's behavior under different conditions. By adopting a systematic approach to debugging, development time can be significantly reduced, code quality can be improved and the overall user experience can be enhanced.

The next chapter continues this theme of maintenance by examining automation testing.

Points to remember

- Use breakpoints to inspect program state, analyze control flow, isolate issues, and modify code behavior.
- At a breakpoint, use the Evaluate Expression feature to check complex algorithms without modifying the source.
- Identify bottlenecks and performance issues using the Profiling tools in Android Studio.
- Leverage Logcat to filter priority levels and allow accurate categorization and filtering of log messages during debugging.

Questions

1. Name the priority levels for Logcat in order.
2. What are breakpoints good for?
3. How do you set a breakpoint?
4. How do you run the Profiler?

Join our book's Discord space

Join the book's Discord Workspace for Latest updates, Offers, Tech happenings around the world, New Release and Sessions with the Authors:

https://discord.bpbonline.com

CHAPTER 15
Test Automation

Introduction

In the ever-evolving landscape of Android development, maintaining high-quality applications requires robust and efficient testing strategies. Automation testing emerges as a pivotal practice, enabling developers to ensure that their applications function correctly across various scenarios and updates without the need for time-consuming manual testing. With the advent of Jetpack Compose, Android's modern toolkit for building native UIs, the landscape of UI testing has also transformed, offering new opportunities and challenges.

This chapter focuses on automation testing in Kotlin with Jetpack Compose, providing the essential knowledge and tools to create reliable and maintainable test suites for applications. A range of topics will be covered, from setting up a testing environment and writing basic UI tests to more advanced techniques such as testing state management, handling asynchronous operations, and integrating testing into a continuous integration pipeline.

Structure

This chapter covers the following topics:

- Espresso
- Compose tree

- ComposeTestRule
- Finders, Matchers and Asserters
- The Robot Pattern
- Code coverage
- Continuous integration

Objectives

Testing is a crucial aspect of Android app development to ensure reliability, functionality, and user satisfaction. This chapter will concentrate on the type of testing that can be automated, and was not already covered in *Chapter 9, Test-Driven Development with Mocking Libraries for Android*. By the end of this chapter, you will gain knowledge of the Espresso framework, the Robot Pattern, Code Coverage and Continuous Integration as well as those aspects specific to Jetpack Compose, including, the Compose Tree and the `ComposeTestRule`.

Espresso

Espresso is a popular testing framework for Android app development. It is designed to make UI testing smoother and more efficient by providing a fluent, easy-to-use API that interacts with an app's UI components. Espresso tests are written in Kotlin and allow developers to simulate user interactions, such as button clicks, text input, and gestures, and verify the expected behavior of the app in response to these actions.

Espresso tests run directly on the device or emulator, allowing it to interact with the app's UI in the same way a user would. This ensures that the app behaves correctly from the user's perspective, catching any UI-related bugs or issues early in the development process. Espresso tests can be integrated into continuous integration workflows, helping maintain the quality and reliability of the app across different releases and device configurations.

To start using Espresso for UI testing in an Android project, ensure that the necessary dependencies and configurations are entered in the build script. These entries are normally included by the **New Project** wizards. Espresso is a part of the Android Testing Support Library. Check that the build script has the following entries:

```
1.  android {
2.      //...
3.      defaultConfig {
4.          //...
5.          testInstrumentationRunner =
6.              "androidx.test.runner.AndroidJUnitRunner"
7.      }
```

```
 8. }
 9. //...
10. dependencies {
11.     // or version catalogs equivalent ...
12.     androidTestImplementation(
13.         "androidx.test.espresso:espresso-core:$vers"
14.     )
15.
16.     // optional
17.     testOptions {
18.         animationsDisabled = true
19.     }
20. }
```

Here, **vers** is the latest version.

Configuring **testOptions**, such as disabling animations, makes Espresso tests more reliable. See the official documentation: **https://developer.android.com/reference/tools/gradle-api** (search for **TestOptions**).

Espresso is designed to interact with UI components and simulate user interactions within an Android app. It enables automation of actions like clicking buttons, entering text into input fields and scrolling through lists. This is followed by asserting the expected outcomes based on these interactions. It merges with the UI elements defined in the Compose tree, allowing the validation of the behavior and functionality of Compose-based UIs.

Compose tree

In Jetpack Compose, the term Compose tree refers to the hierarchical structure of composables that make up the user interface of an app. It represents the layout and arrangement of UI elements as a tree data structure, with each node in the tree representing a composable function.

The Compose tree is a fundamental concept in Compose development and testing. It allows visualization and understanding of the structure of a UI, helping design, build, and test UI components effectively.

Espresso provides APIs to traverse the Compose tree, locating specific composables, and interacting with them programmatically.

The Compose tree also plays a crucial role in accessibility testing. It exposes accessibility information such as content descriptions, labels, and roles associated with UI elements, ensuring that an app is accessible to users with disabilities.

Accessing the Compose tree for a page will provide information about the components used to render that screen. This information can be used to access the individual controls to automate UI interaction for testing purposes. For example, refer to the following basic layout code:

```
1.  MyApplicationTheme {
2.      Surface(
3.          modifier = Modifier.fillMaxSize(),
4.          color = MaterialTheme.colorScheme.background
5.      ) {
6.          Column {
7.              Greeting("Android")
8.              Button(onClick = { /*TODO*/ }) {
9.                  Text(text = "Click me")
10.             }
11.         }
12.     }
13. }
```

The **Compose** tree can be viewed for a current page by accessing the **Layout Inspector**, by following **Tools | Layout Inspector**. See *Figure 15.1*:

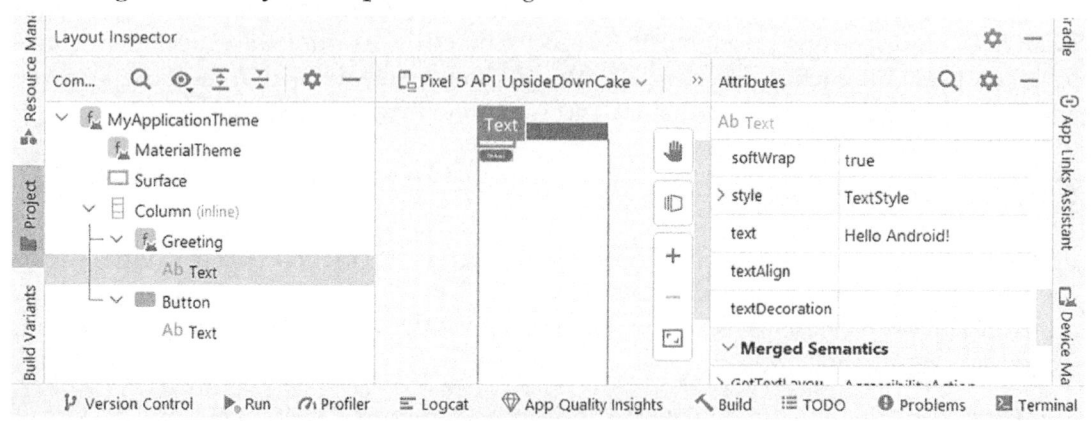

Figure 15.1: Compose Tree

To see the Compose Tree, the running app must be a debug build. The device that it is running on must have **Enable View Attribute Inspection** switched on in the **Developer** options (For instructions on accessing Developer options, see *Chapter 14, Debugging in Kotlin, Figures 14.1-14.5*).

In **Developer options**, scroll down and switch on **Enable view attribute inspection**. See *Figure 15.2*:

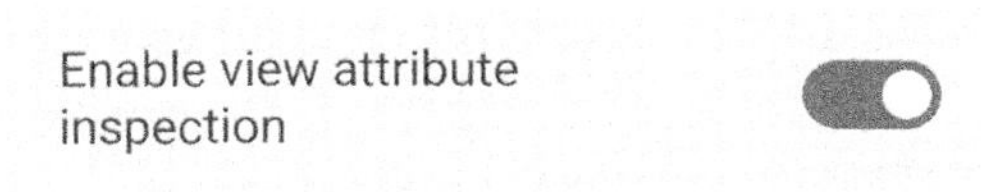

Enable view attribute inspection

Figure 15.2: Enable view attribute inspection

As previously mentioned, accessing the Compose tree for a page will provide information about the components used to render that screen. This information will be used by a test component, `ComposeTestRule`, to access the individual controls to automate UI interaction for testing purposes.

ComposeTestRule

The ComposeTestRule is a part of the Jetpack Compose UI testing framework for Android applications. It provides a convenient way to set up and manage the testing environment for Jetpack Compose UI tests. The following example demonstrates the use of `ComposeTestRule` to access a button control embedded in the test:

```
1.  @RunWith(AndroidJUnit4::class)
2.  class CustomButtonTest {
3.
4.      @Rule
5.      @JvmField
6.      val composeTestRule = createComposeRule()
7.
8.      @Test
9.      fun testButtonIsDisplayedAndClickable() {
10.         composeTestRule.setContent {
11.             // Your composable with a button
12.             // (replace with production code)
13.             Button(onClick = {}, text = "Click me")
14.         }
15.
16.         // Find the button
17.         // Assert that the button is displayed and clickable
18.         composeTestRule.onNode(withText("Click me"))
19.             .assertIsDisplayed()
20.             .isClickable()
21.             .performClick() // Simulate a click
22.     }
23. }
```

To use the `ComposeTestRule`, add the following dependencies to the build script:

```
1.  dependencies {
2.      // or version catalogs equivalent ...
3.      debugImplementation(
4.          "androidx.compose.ui:ui-test-manifest:$vers1"
5.      )
6.      androidTestImplementation(
7.          "androidx.compose.ui:ui-test-junit4:$vers2"
8.      )
9.  }
```

Here, `vers` and `vers2` are the latest respective versions.

Finders, Matchers and Asserters

In the example discussed in the previous section, `withText` is a finder, `isClickable` is a matcher, and `assertIsDisplayed` is an assertion. Assertions, matchers, and finders are fundamental components of the `ComposeTestRule`. They serve different purposes but are all essential for writing effective and comprehensive UI tests. Finders, matchers, and asserters work together to effectively test composables.

Finders

Finders are the starting point for interacting with composables in tests. They act to locate specific composables within the UI hierarchy. The `ComposableTestRule` offers various finders to identify elements based on different criteria, as follows:

- `byText(text: String)`: Finds composables with the specified text content.
- `byContentDescription(description: String)`: Finds composables with the given content description.
- `withId(id: Int)`: Finds composables with the specified resource ID.
- `findByType<T>()`: Finds composables of a specific type (`T`).

Matchers

Matchers are used in conjunction with finders to refine the search and ensure targeting the intended composable. They allow additional conditions to the finder's search criteria. Some common matchers include:

- `hasText(text: String)`: Checks if a component's text matches a specific value.
- `isClickable()`: Checks if a component is clickable.

- **isEnabled()**: Checks if a component is enabled.
- **isAssignableFrom<T>()**: Checks if a component is of a specific type.

Asserters

A finder and potentially a matcher are used to identify a composable. Asserters allow verification of a composables state or behavior against expectations. The **ComposableTestRule** provides various built-in asserters:

- **assertIsDisplayed()**: Verifies that the composable is visible on the screen.
- **assertExists()**: Checks if the composable exists in the UI hierarchy, regardless of visibility.
- **assertTextContains(text: String)**: Confirms that the composable text contains the specified string.
- **performClick()**: Clicks on the identified composable, allowing testing of interactions.

By combining finders, matchers, and asserters, clear, concise, and maintainable tests can be written for Jetpack Compose UI's.

The Robot Pattern

The Robot Pattern, (Page Object Pattern or Screenplay pattern) is a design pattern commonly used in UI automation testing, including instrumentation testing in Android. This pattern aims to improve the maintainability, readability, and reusability and abstraction of UI tests by encapsulating the details of UI components and interactions within reusable objects.

The Robot Pattern involves organizing test code into separate classes or objects that represent different screens or UI components of the application under test. Each of these classes, known as **Robot** or **Page Objects**, encapsulates the details and interactions specific to that particular screen or component. These tests are written in a more human-readable and domain-specific language, resembling a screenplay or a script. The pattern abstracts the interactions with the UI elements into reusable and self-describing components called **robots** or **actors**. The Robot Pattern UI test architecture is displayed in *Figure 15.3*:

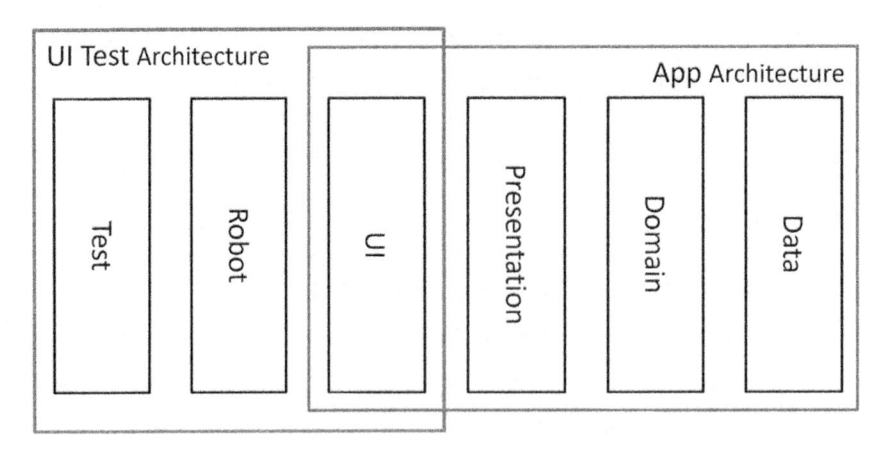

Figure 15.3: UI Test Architecture

The following example demonstrates a basic login screen built with Jetpack Compose and tested with Espresso using the robot pattern and `ComposeTestRule`:

1. @Composable
2. fun LoginContent(
3.   state: LoginState,
4.   event: (LoginEvent) -> Unit,
5.) {
6.   Column {
7.   var username: String by rememberSaveable { mutableStateOf("") }
8.   var password by rememberSaveable { mutableStateOf("") }
9.
10.   TextField(
11.   value = username,
12.   onValueChange = { username = it },
13.   label = { Text("Username") }
14.   )
15.   TextField(
16.   value = password,
17.   onValueChange = { password = it },
18.   label = { Text("Enter password") },
19.   )
20.   Button(
21.   onClick = {
22.   event(LoginEvent.OnLoginTapped(username, password))

```
23.            }
24.        ) { Text("Login") }
25.        if (state.isLoginFailed) Text(text = "Login Failed")
26.    }
27. }
```

LoginScreen (UI from *Figure 15.3*) defines a simple login screen with username, password fields, and a login button. Hard coded strings have been used instead of resource file references for clarity. The code uses the **Uni Directional Flow** (**UDF**) pattern (see *Chapter 8, Presentation Layer Evolution in Compose* and *Chapter 9, Test-Driven Development with Mocking Libraries for Android*) to respond to user input and to update its state:

```
1.  sealed class LoginEvent : Event {
2.      data class OnLoginTapped(
3.          val username: String,
4.          val password: String
5.      ) : LoginEvent()
6.  }
7.
8.  data class LoginState(
9.      val isLoginFailed: Boolean
10. ): UiState
```

LoginContent will render the following:

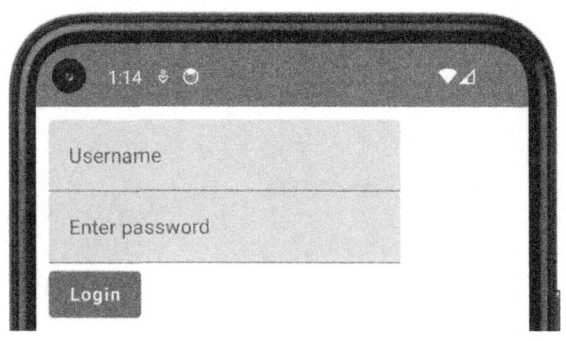

Figure 15.4: LoginContent

For this screen, it is expected that the values entered into the **Username** and **Password** fields will be sent as an event to an upstream controller or **ViewModel** when the button is clicked. The corresponding test Robot, therefore, requires methods for:

- Entering values in the **Username** and **Password** fields
- Clicking on the button
- Testing the resulting event

A typical implementation of these methods can be seen in the following code:

```kotlin
1.  class LoginRobot(
2.      private val rule: ComposeTestRule,
3.  ) {
4.      private var lastEvent: LoginEvent? = null
5.      fun handleEvent(event: LoginEvent) {
6.          lastEvent = event
7.      }
8.
9.      fun enterUsername(username: String): LoginRobot {
10.         rule.onNode(hasText("Username"))
11.             .performTextInput(username)
12.         return this
13.     }
14.
15.     fun enterPassword(password: String): LoginRobot {
16.         rule.onNode(hasText("Enter password"))
17.             .performTextInput(password)
18.         return this
19.     }
20.
21.     fun clickLoginButton(): LoginRobot {
22.         rule.onNodeWithText("Login").performClick()
23.         return this
24.     }
25.
26.     fun assertCredentialsSent(testUser: String, testPass: String) {
27.         (lastEvent!! as LoginEvent.OnLoginTapped).apply {
28.             assertEquals(testUser, username)
29.             assertEquals(testPass, password)
30.         }
31.     }
32. }
```

The somewhat unusual thing to note here is the integration of the Robot with the UDF pattern. The Robot supplies an event handler to record the last event sent to the controller. The **assertCredentialsSent** method then compares the values in the event with the expected ones. Note the use of the !! operator which is normally discouraged. In test code, it is *encouraged* as a cheap test for non-null.

To tidy up the use of the Robot in test code, a convenience factory function can be defined as follows:

```
1. fun login(
2.     rule: ComposeContentTestRule,
3.     state: LoginState,
4.     test: LoginRobot.() -> Unit
5. ) {
6.     LoginRobot(rule).apply {
7.         rule.setContent { LoginContent(state, ::handleEvent) }
8.         rule.onRoot().printToLog("LoginContent") // optional
9.         test()
10.     }
11. }
```

Given the previous arrangement, the actual test can be as neat as the following:

```
1. class LoginContentTest {
2.
3.     @Rule
4.     @JvmField
5.     val composeTestRule = createComposeRule()
6.
7.     private val username = "test_user"
8.     private val password = "test_password"
9.
10.    @Test
11.    fun 'GIVEN credentials WHEN login THEN credentials sent'() = login(
12.        rule = composeTestRule,
13.        state = LoginState(isLoginFailed = false)
14.    ) {
15.        enterUsername(username)
16.        enterPassword(password)
17.        clickLoginButton()
18.        assertCredentialsSent(username, password)
19.    }
20. }
```

Note the use of `ComposeContentTestRule` in the factory function `login`. This `ComposeTestRule` extension has the `setContent` method vital for rendering the screen. In addition to the `ComposeTestRule`, the factory receives the required state to render and a scoped callback for running the actual tests. The factory creates the Robot, binds the state and the Robot's state handler to the screen, and then runs the tests.

Also, the `printToLog` statement in the same function is optional and is used as a Robot development tool. This statement will output the `ComposeTree` to the **Test Logs** window when you run any test, as can be seen in the following figure:

Figure 15.5: composeRule.onRoot().printToLog

To clarify, the output will be near the top of the logs window and will look like this (for this example):

1. ...LoginContent: printToLog:
2. ...LoginContent: Printing with useUnmergedTree = 'false'
3. ...LoginContent: Node #1 at (l=0.0, t=136.0, r=770.0, b=576.0)px
4. ...LoginContent: |-Node #3 at (l=0.0, t=136.0, r=770.0, b=290.0)px
5. ...LoginContent: | EditableText = ''
6. ...LoginContent: | TextSelectionRange = 'TextRange(0, 0)'
7. ...LoginContent: | ImeAction = 'Default'
8. ...LoginContent: | Focused = 'false'
9. ...LoginContent: | Text = '[Username]'
10. ...LoginContent: | Actions = [GetTextLayoutResult, SetText, ...]
11. ...LoginContent: | MergeDescendants = 'true'
12. ...LoginContent: |-Node #10 at (l=0.0, t=290.0, r=770.0, b=444.0)px
13. ...LoginContent: | EditableText = ''
14. ...LoginContent: | TextSelectionRange = 'TextRange(0, 0)'
15. ...LoginContent: | ImeAction = 'Default'
16. ...LoginContent: | Focused = 'false'
17. ...LoginContent: | Text = '[Enter password]'

```
18. …LoginContent:   | Actions = [GetTextLayoutResult, SetText, ...]
19. …
```

This is a text representation of what is produced graphically in the Layout Inspector, as shown in *Figure 15.1*.

There are a few things to note about the **LoginContentTest** example:

- The test function name uses **GIVEN**... **WHEN**... **THEN**... format with back-ticks and spaces that were discussed in *Chapter 9, Test-Driven Development with Mocking Libraries for Android*, for unit tests. In fact, this will only compile for instrumentation tests such as these if the minimum SDK is set to 30. Alternatives might be to delete the back-ticks and replace the spaces with underscores (in which case, the errors would be replaced with warnings about starting function names with a capital) or to have all instrumentation tests in an independent module with the minimum SDK set to 30. Obviously, there are pros and cons with each approach, not least that an independent module would only be able to test public content for devices running SDK 30 or above.
- This is a simple example dedicated to testing standalone content in a UDF arrangement. The Robot pattern could, however, be extended to include presentation, domain, and data layer elements for full integration testing. In these circumstances, it would likely be necessary to mock repository responses using third-party libraries such as WireMock (**wiremock.org**).

Advantages of the Robot pattern

Use of the Robot pattern offers the following advantages when developing instrumentation tests:

- **Page Objects (Robots)**: Each screen or UI component of the Android application is represented by a separate **Robot** class.
- **Test scripts**: The robot pattern abstracts away the details of interacting with UI elements via test scripts.
- **Separation of concerns**: The Robot Pattern promotes a clear separation of concerns by separating the UI interaction logic (robots) and interactions from the test scripts.
- **Reusable components:** Actions and verifications on the UI are encapsulated within reusable robot page objects (for example, the Search text box on the Amazon home page menu can be used to display multiple pages).
- **Improved readability**: By abstracting the details of UI interactions into Page Objects, the test code becomes more readable.
- **Ease of maintenance**: The Robot Pattern centralizes the UI-related logic within Page Objects. By maintaining a layered architecture, the Robot pattern separates tests, robot and UI automation frameworks. This makes maintenance of each layer simpler.

Code coverage

Code coverage is a metric used to measure the amount of code that is executed by the tests. It is valuable because it helps developers understand how much of their codebase is being exercised by their test suite. This understanding can aid in identifying untested or poorly tested areas of code, potentially reducing the number of bugs and increasing the overall quality of the software.

Just like in Java, code coverage tools such as JaCoCo, Kover or IntelliJ IDEA's built-in coverage tool can be used to measure code coverage in Kotlin projects. These tools can generate reports showing which lines of Kotlin code are executed during tests.

Since Jetpack Compose is written in Kotlin, use the same code coverage tools mentioned above to measure code coverage in Compose-based projects. It's important to ensure that the UI code is adequately tested to maintain a high level of code coverage, as UI bugs can have a significant impact on user experience.

Android Studio provides built-in support for running and analyzing tests, including code coverage. Viewable code coverage reports directly within Android Studio can help quickly identify areas of the codebase that require additional testing.

After running the tests, the code coverage report in Android Studio can be seen by going to **Run | Run with Coverage**:

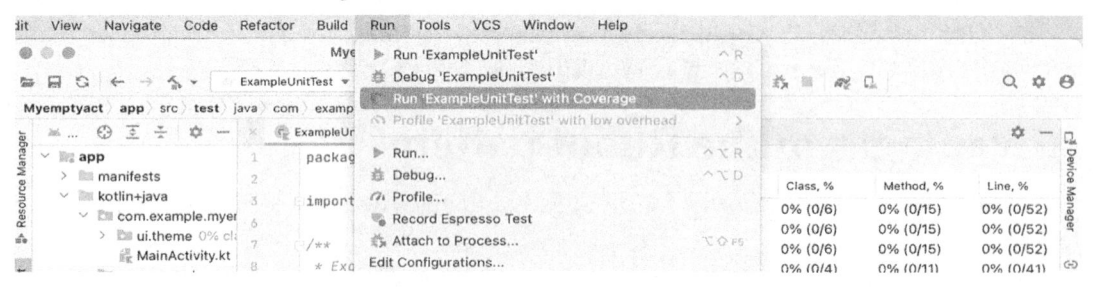

Figure 15.6: Running UnitTest with Coverage

After the tests finish running, they are viewable in the code coverage report by going to **View | Tool Windows | Coverage**:

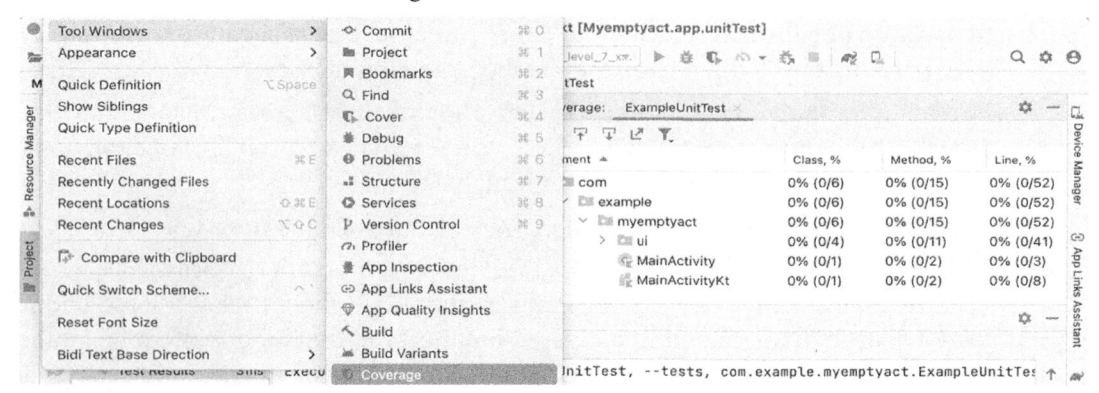

Figure 15.7: Coverage

In the **Coverage** tool window, there is a summary of the code coverage, as well as detailed information about which lines of code were covered by the tests and which lines were not, as shown in the following figure:

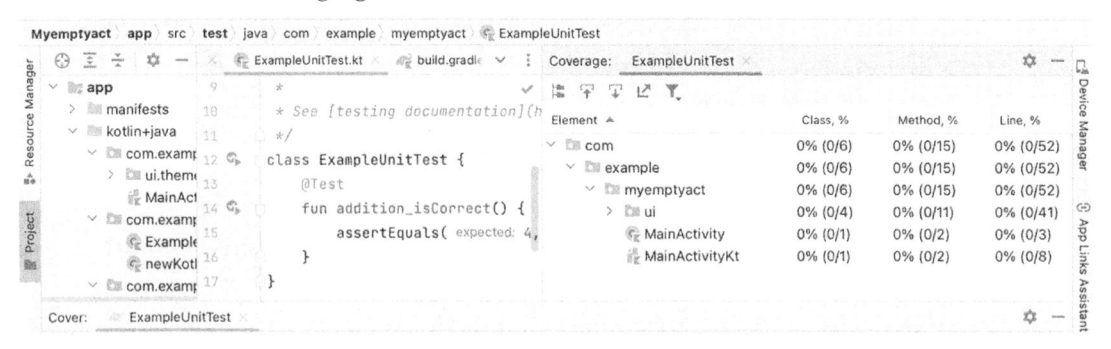

Figure 15.8: Code Coverage

Achieving high code coverage in projects utilizing Kotlin and Jetpack Compose can be challenging due to several inherent characteristics:

- **Dynamic UI generation**: Jetpack Compose allows for UI elements to be constructed dynamically based on state changes. This dynamism poses difficulties for code coverage tools like JaCoCo and Kover, which struggle to track coverage accurately in such scenarios.
- **Lambda expressions**: Jetpack Compose heavily relies on lambda expressions for defining UI components and event handlers. These anonymous functions might not be fully covered by traditional unit tests, leading to lower coverage metrics.
- **Coverage exclusions**: Consider excluding certain portions of code related to Jetpack Compose internals or boilerplate from coverage reports. This helps focus the metrics on custom logic and improves overall reporting accuracy.

Since Android Studio has a built-in coverage support, JaCoCo and Kover is most useful when integrated with **Continuous Integration (CI)**. Kover is Kotlin first and gaining traction in the developer community over JaCoCo.

Continuous integration

Continuous integration is a software development practice where members of a team integrate their code changes into a shared repository frequently and often multiple times a day. Each integration is verified by an automated build process, including tests and code quality checks. The primary goal of CI is to detect and resolve integration errors as quickly as possible, ensuring that the software remains in a working state at all times.

Some key aspects of CI are as follows:

- **Frequent integration**: Developers integrate their code changes into the main codebase frequently, rather than waiting for long before merging their work. This reduces the risk of large integration issues and conflicts.

- **Automated builds**: CI systems automatically build the software whenever a new code change is committed to the repository. This includes compiling the code, running tests, and performing other checks to ensure the integrity of the build.
- **Automated testing**: CI processes typically include automated testing, such as unit tests, integration tests, and sometimes even end-to-end tests (testing a feature's journey from start to finish, see *Chapter 3, Feature-Oriented Development in Android*). These tests help verify that the code changes haven't introduced any regressions or bugs.
- **Continuous feedback:** CI systems provide immediate feedback to developers about the status of their code changes. This feedback may include build success or failure, test results, and code quality metrics.
- **Early detection of issues:** By integrating code changes frequently and running automated tests, CI helps identify integration issues, bugs, and other problems early in the development process. This allows developers to address issues quickly, reducing the time and effort required for debugging and fixing problems.
- **Improved collaboration:** CI encourages collaboration among team members by promoting a shared codebase and ensuring that everyone's changes are integrated smoothly. It also helps enforce coding standards and best practices across the team.

Popular CI tools include Jenkins, Travis CI, CircleCI, GitLab CI/CD, and GitHub Actions. These tools automate the CI process and integrate seamlessly with version control systems like Git, enabling teams to implement CI practices effectively. For the specific setup details see the chosen CI provider's official documentation.

Conclusion

Automation testing in Kotlin with Jetpack Compose is a game-changer for modern Android development. It provides a streamlined and efficient approach to ensuring the quality and reliability of applications.

Throughout this chapter, the fundamentals and advanced techniques necessary to implement robust automation testing strategies for Jetpack Compose applications have been explored. These included the Espresso framework, the Robot Pattern, Code Coverage and Continuous Integration as well as aspects specific to Jetpack Compose, including The Compose Tree and the `ComposeTestRule`.

In the next and final chapter, we will examine the processes required for building and releasing an application.

Points to remember

- Espresso provides easy-to-use efficient APIs traversing the Compose tree to locate specific composables and interact programmatically with app UI components.

- The Compose Tree allows developers to visualize and understand the structure of a UI enabling the effectual design, building and testing of UI components effectively.
- The Compose Test Rule sets up and manages the testing environment for Jetpack Compose UI tests using Finders, Asserters and Matchers for Compose UI's.
- The Robot Pattern organizes test code into separate re-usable, encapsulated readable classes/objects that represent different screens or UI's that are more maintainable.
- Code coverage provides feedback for developers by identifying untested/poorly tested areas of code, reducing the number of bugs.
- Continuous Integration detects and resolves integration errors fast, ensuring that the software remains in a working state at all times.

Questions

1. The Robot Pattern centralizes the UI-related logic within what?
2. What are the various finders for the `ComposeTestRule`?
3. What is the Compose Tree?
4. What is functional testing?
5. What is Espresso?
6. How does the Robot pattern improve the test structure?
7. How would you update the test code for *Figure 14.26* to test for a login failure?
8. How might Code Coverage improve code quality?
9. What project development improvements does CI offer?

Join our book's Discord space

Join the book's Discord Workspace for Latest updates, Offers, Tech happenings around the world, New Release and Sessions with the Authors:

https://discord.bpbonline.com

CHAPTER 16
Building and Distributing Applications

Introduction

In this chapter, we will discuss the process of building and distributing Android apps, exploring the essential steps and best practices to bring ideas to life and share them with the world. Whether you are a seasoned developer looking to refine skills or a newcomer eager to embark on an Android development journey, this chapter provides valuable insights and practical advice to help you succeed in building and distributing Android apps.

The preparation section discusses how to release and distribute an Android app after development, testing, and packaging the app in Google Play Store or other app distribution platforms.

The distribution section looks at creating a developer account for a business on either Google Play Store or Amazon App Store. The specific details and information required by each of the sites to publish an app and set up a store listing is examined in fine detail.

Structure

This chapter covers the following topics:
- Preparing to release an Android app
- Distribution portals

- Google Play store
- Releasing an app on Google Play store
- Releasing an app on Amazon app store
- Amazon App store

Objectives

By the end of this chapter, you will have gained insight into creating and uploading an APK to the Google Play or Amazon App store. In addition, the methods used to achieve a successful app release are examined and compared. You will also learn about all the elements required for preparation, besides uploading the APK or bundle, to create a store listing.

Preparing to release an Android app

Preparing to release an Android app involves finalizing development, testing, and packaging the application for distribution on the Google Play store or other app distribution platforms. This process includes ensuring that the app meets quality standards, optimizing performance, creating promotional materials, generating release builds, and adhering to platform-specific guidelines for publishing.

Setting version information

Updating the versioning for an Android app release involves changing the version code and name in an Android project. Both version code and version name identify different app releases but serve different purposes.

The following is how to update versioning for an Android app:

```
1.  ...
2.  android {
3.      ...
4.      defaultConfig {
5.          ...
6.          versionCode = 1
7.          versionName = "1.0"
8.      }
9.  }
10. ...
```

Modifying the version values involves changing:

- **Version name**: This is a user-friendly version, often displayed in app stores and on the device. Example: *1.2.3* or *Version 1.2*.

- **Version code**: This is an internal integer value for tracking updates and compatibility. It should always increase for new releases. Example: *123*. This version code must be incremented every time a new version is released, even if it is a rollback to an older version.

  The version code serves several purposes:
  - **App updates**: When an update is released for an app on Google Play Store or any other distribution platform, the system uses the version code to determine whether the new version is more recent than the one currently installed on a user's device. If the version code is higher, the system knows that it should replace the old version with the new one.
  - **Identifying builds**: The version code helps developers and system administrators identify and track different builds of the app. This can be useful for troubleshooting, debugging, and managing multiple versions during development.
  - **Compatibility**: Some Android features, such as the Android App Bundle format, rely on version codes to ensure that the right versions of the app components are distributed to devices.

Android Application Package

Android Application Package (APK) is the file format used to distribute and install applications on devices running the Android operating system. An APK file contains all the necessary components of an Android application, including the code (compiled bytecode), resources, assets, manifest file, and digital signature. It is essentially a packaged version of an Android app that can be distributed and installed on Android devices. These .apk files can be distributed through various channels, including app stores like the Amazon App Store, third-party app stores, or directly from the developer's website.

In summary, an APK is the package file format used to distribute and install Android applications. It contains all the necessary components of the application and is digitally signed to ensure its integrity and authenticity. Users can install .apk files on their Android devices to access and use the applications.

Android app bundle

Android App Bundle (.aab) file is a publishing format for Android applications introduced by Google. It is a new way of packaging and distributing Android apps, replacing the traditional APK format. **.aab** files contain compiled code, resources, and assets necessary to run an Android application on a device.

The **.aab** files enable dynamic delivery of Android apps. Instead of a single monolithic **.apk**, **.aab** files contain multiple optimized APKs for different device configurations (such as screen density, CPU architecture, and language). This allows Google Play to deliver only the necessary resources to each user's device, reducing app size and improving download and installation times.

They include an app's compiled code and resources but do not contain every possible combination of resources for every device configuration. Instead, developers upload a .aab file to Google Play, and Google Play generates optimized APKs based on the device configuration of each user's device.

> Note: Google Play Store now only accepts .aab files. At the time of writing, apps created before August 2021 can still submit APK updates.

Keystore

The signing key file or keystore is a cryptographic key used to sign APKs or AABs (henceforth referred to as a bundle) for Android app distribution. It is essential to securely manage and protect the signing key file to maintain the integrity and authenticity of Android apps.

When building an app, using *keystores* to protect the app development process is important. A keystore is a secure file that stores sensitive cryptographic keys and certificates essential for app identity and security. Keystores are used by distribution platforms such as Google Play store to make updates and distributions, link to developer accounts, and enable platforms to verify app updates and ownership. Distribution platforms such as Google Play store require an app to be signed using a keystore file before it can be uploaded and distributed. Keystores encrypt and password-protect the bundle, preventing unauthorized access.

When preparing a bundle file for distribution, the signing key or keystore refers to the cryptographic key file used to sign the bundle. The signing key file contains the private key used to sign the bundle. It is crucial to keep this key file secure because it serves as the proof that the bundle comes from a trusted source and has not been tampered with since it was signed.

A signing key file can be created using key generation tools provided by Android SDK or third-party tools. Android Studio provides a tool called **apksigner** or **jarsigner** to sign bundles using a signing key file. The keystore file consists of the following parts:

- **Key alias**: When generating a signing key file, a specific key alias must be provided. This is a unique identifier for the key within the key store. This allows developers to manage multiple keys within the same key store.
- **Key store**: The signing key file is often stored in a key store file (`.jks` or `.keystore`), which is a binary file that securely stores cryptographic keys. The key store can also contain multiple key entries, each with its alias.

Losing access to the signing key file can have severe consequences, such as being unable to release updates for an app or being unable to prove the authenticity of an app.

Creating a keystore with Android Studio

Generating an upload key and then signing an app with that key is the first step unless the app has previously been signed and published to Google play store. If this is the case, the same upload key used to sign the existing published app must be used. Follow these steps to create a keystore with Android Studio:

1. To use Android Studio to sign into an app click **Build | Generate Signed Bundle / APK** as shown in the following figure:

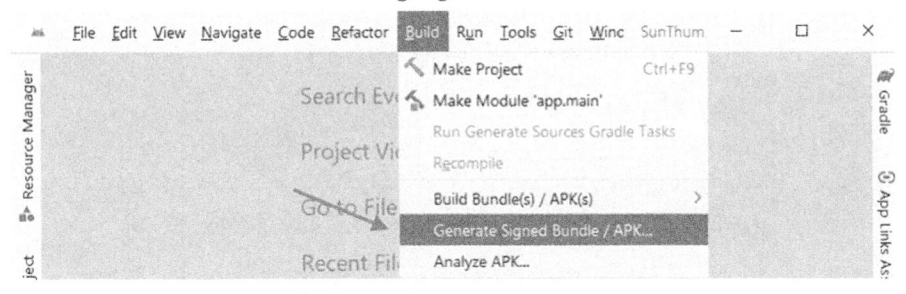

Figure 16.1: Generate Signed Bundle / APK

2. In the resulting **Generate Signed Bundle / APK** dialog (shown in *Figure 16.2*), select **Android App Bundle** or **APK** and click **Next**:

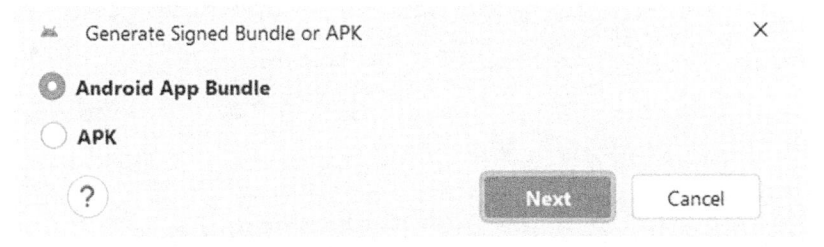

Figure 16.2: Generate Signed Bundle or APK

3. On the following **Generate Signed Bundle or APK** dialog, select the **Key store path**, then click **Create new…** as shown in the following figure:

348 ■ Scalable Android Applications in Kotlin

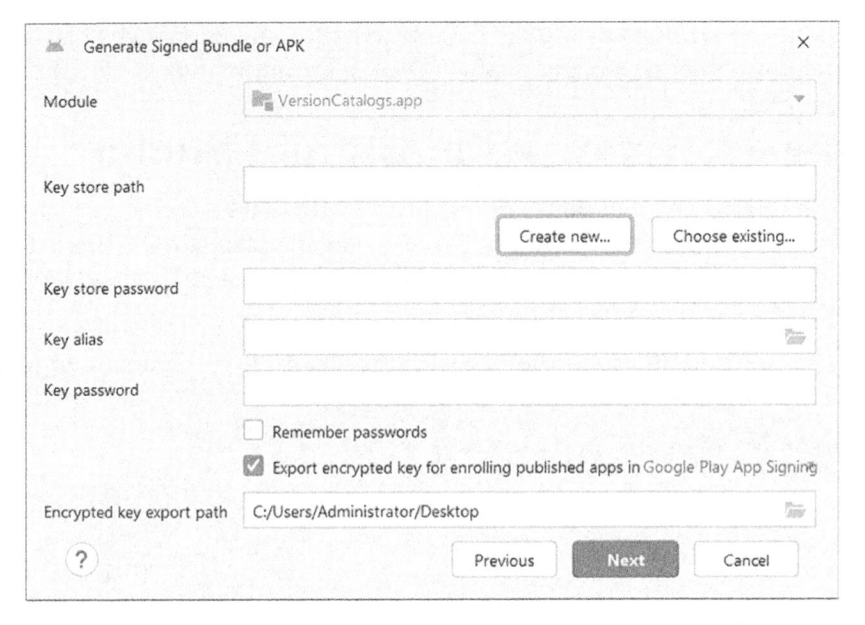

Figure 16.3: Generate Signed Bundle or APK, Key store password

4. Fill in the resulting **New Key Store** window with details for the **Key store path** and **Password**. Be sure to use memorable passwords, as the key store will be used for subsequent projects and updates:

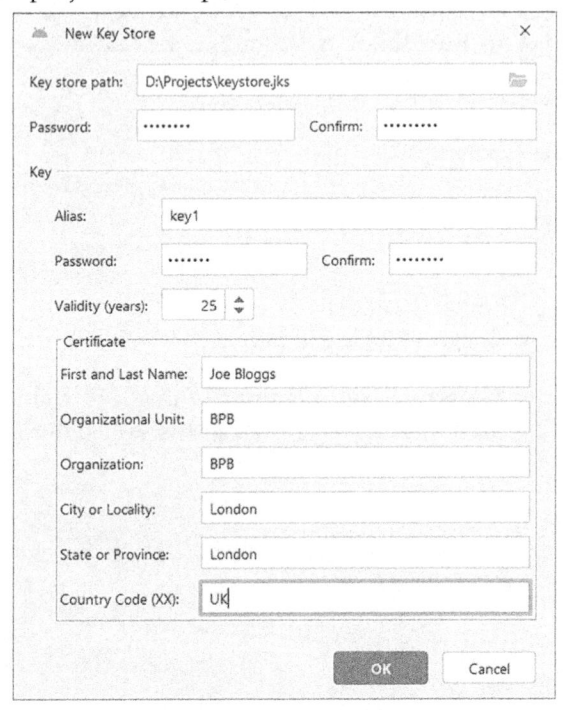

Figure 16.4: Creating a new Key store

5. When creating the key store, select **Validity (years)** of **25** years for the keystore maximum time. The following dialog confirms the keystore details, and pressing **Next** will generate the signed APK:

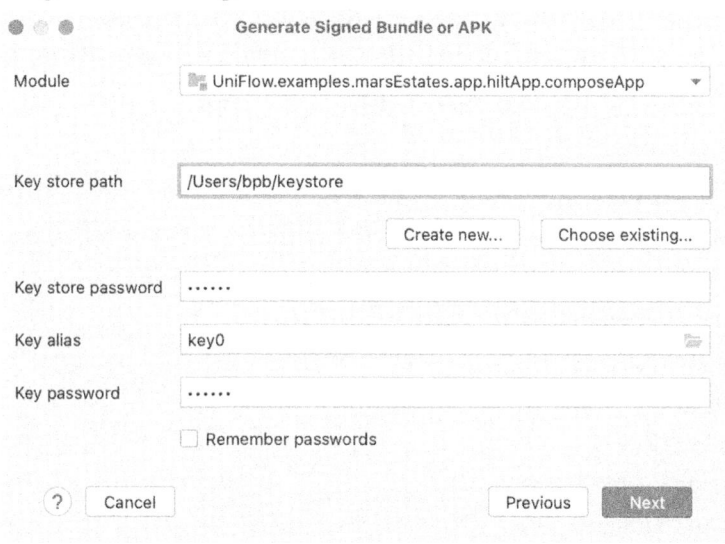

Figure 16.5: Generate signed APK

6. Using this manual generation method, the signed APK will be created in the following folder (*Figure 16.6*):

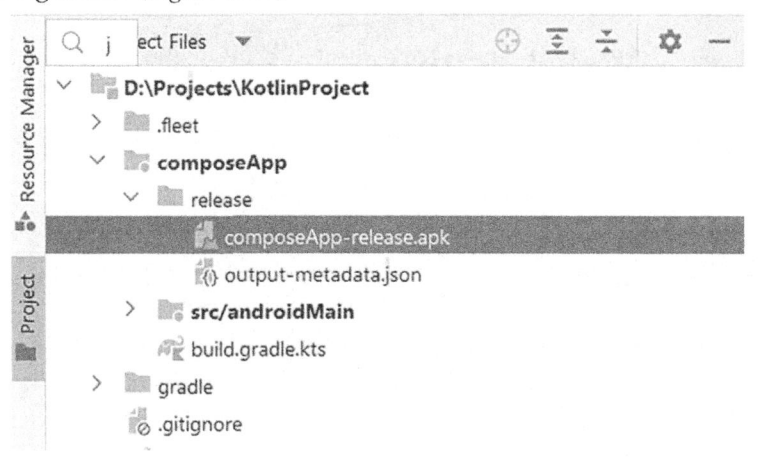

Figure 16.6: Signed APK file

Creating a keystore on the Command Line

In the previous section, a new keystore file was created at the same time as generating the signed bundle. In fact, the same keystore file can be used for subsequent bundle creation. The keystore file can also be created on the command-line using **keytool**.

keytool is a command-line utility provided by the **Java Development Kit (JDK)** for managing cryptographic keys and certificates. It is primarily used for generating, importing, exporting, and managing keys and certificates for various purposes, such as SSL/TLS encryption, code signing, and authentication. For **keytool** to work in any location in a file system, the JDK installation **bin** directory must be referenced in the system **path**.

keytool commands are typically executed from the command line using the following syntax:

keytool [command] [options]

For example, to generate the same keystore file as that created in the previous section, the following command and options would be used:

1. keytool -genkeypair \
2.   -keystore "D:\Projects\keystore.jks" \
3.   -storepass "********" \
4.   -alias "key1" \
5.   -keypass "********" \
6.   -validity 9125 \
7.   -dname "CN=Joe Bloggs, OU=BPB, O=BPB, L=London, ST=London, C=UK"

In this command:

- **-genkeypair**: Specifies the command to generate a new key pair and a self-signed certificate.
- **-keystore "D:\Projects\keystore.jks"**: Specifies the path and filename of the keystore file to be created.
- **-storepass "********"**: Specifies the password for the keystore.
- **-alias "key1"**: Specifies the alias for the key pair entry in the keystore.
- **-keypass "********"**: Specifies the password for the key pair entry.
- **-validity 9125**: Specifies the validity period of the certificate in days (25 years = 9125 days).
- **-dname "CN=Joe Bloggs, OU=BPB, O=BPB, L=London, ST=London, C=UK"**: Specifies the Distinguished Name (**DN**) for the certificate, including the common name (**CN**), organizational unit (**OU**), organization (**O**), locality (**L**), state (**ST**), and country code (**C**).

After executing this command, the specified keystore file (**keystore.jks**) will be generated at the specified location (**D:\Projects**) with the provided parameters.

keytool is a utility for manipulating keystores, not just creating them. Amongst other things, **keytool** can list certificates and export keys. For a full list of commands, see the **keytool** help (**keytool -h**).

Configuring building and signing in Gradle

Configuring the build script enables Gradle to automatically sign APKs during the build process based on the specified configuration. The following Kotlin DSL script demonstrates a build script configuration for this purpose:

```
1.  android {
2.      ...
3.      signingConfigs {
4.          create("release") {
5.              storeFile = file(System.getenv("KEYSTOREFILE") ?: "")
6.              storePassword = System.getenv("KEYSTOREPASS") ?: ""
7.              keyAlias = System.getenv("KEYSTOREALIAS") ?: ""
8.              keyPassword = System.getenv("KEYSTOREPASS") ?: ""
9.          }
10.     }
11.     buildTypes {
12.         getByName("release") {
13.             ...
14.             signingConfig = signingConfigs.getByName("release")
15.         }
16.     }
17. }
```

1. Use environment variables for references to the Key Store in the Gradle script, leveraging Kotlin's syntax for accessing environment variables. In the preceding code:

2. `System.getenv("<ENV_NAME>") ?: ""` retrieves the value of the environment variable specified by `<ENV_NAME>`. If the environment variable is not set, it defaults to an empty string.

3. Ensure the environment variables have been set, according to the host OS before running the Gradle `build` command. This approach allows sensitive information like passwords to be kept outside the source code repository. It provides flexibility in managing the signing configuration based on the environment in which the APKs are built. See the OS documentation for setting environment variables on the computer that builds the APK.

4. With this in place, a release `.aab` bundle file can be produced with a few clicks via the Gradle scripts, as seen in the following screenshot:

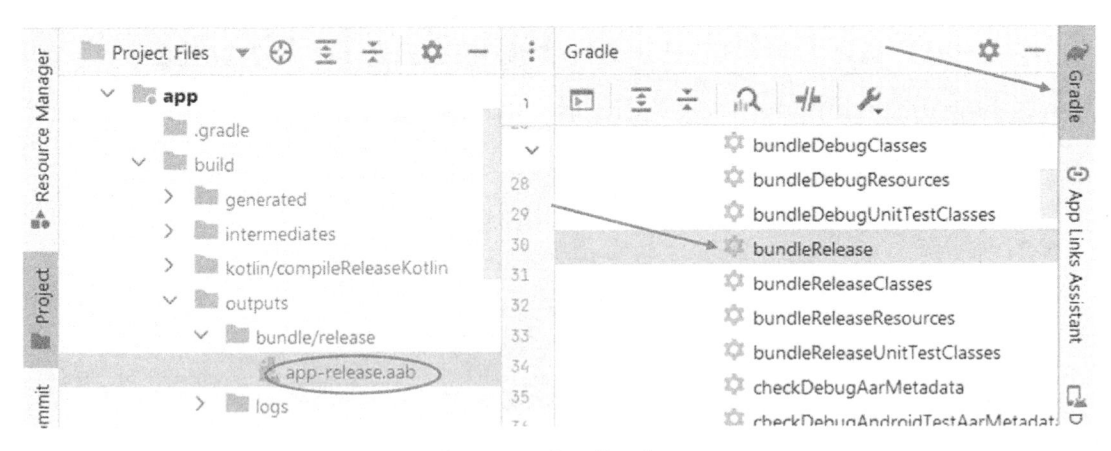

Figure 16.7: Bundle release

5. Select the following sequence in Android Studio to generate an **.abb** file (as can be seen in *Figure 16.7*): **Gradle | Application name | app | Tasks | other | bundleRelease**.

A release **.apk** can be produced in the same way by selecting **assembleRelease** at the same level. Assuming all the steps above have been followed, a signed release **.aab** file should appear in the **app/build/outputs/bundle/release** folder as can be seen in *Figure 16.7*. The release **.apk** should appear in the **app/build/intermediates/apk/release** folder.

The next stage is to upload the **.apk** or **.aab** file to one or more distribution portals from where users can download and install the app.

Building and signing on CI

The problem with the setup above is that a build can only be run on the machine that hosts the keystore and passwords. In *Chapter 15, Test Automation*, **continuous integration** (**CI**) was mentioned. This section will present a simple CI example using GitHub to create release builds remotely. Other CI providers will have similar arrangements. The reader should have some knowledge of Git and repositories, specifically, what it means to commit, push or check-in changes and create branches.

GitHub provides a facility for securely storing strings such as passwords. Known as **secrets**, only repository owners or admins can set them, and once set, are hidden. Only the build process can read them, and their values are obfuscated in the logs. *Figure 16.8* shows how to set them:

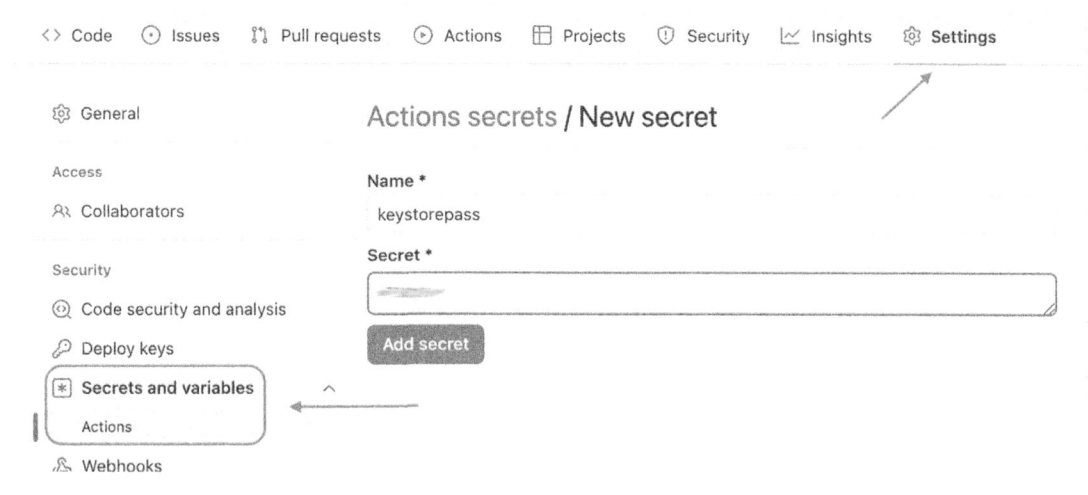

Figure 16.8: Add GitHub secret

From the repository home page, select **Settings | Secrets and Variables | Actions**. Note that secret names are not case sensitive.

The secrets arrangement can only store string values, whereas, the **keystore** file is binary. The workaround for this is to convert the keystore file to a **base64** string, store it as a secret, and then decode it back to a binary file as part of the build process:

1. base64 -w 0 keystore.jks > keystore.jks.base64

base64 is a utility in Linux-based systems for converting binary content to strings. There are free add-ons available for Windows that will do the same thing. Copy the contents of the resulting file to a secret value. The size limit for secret values is 48KB, which is more than enough for keystore contents – typically around 3KB.

The scripts that instruct GitHub to perform builds are called **workflow** files. These YAML scripts are checked into a repository and read by GitHub from the **.github/workflows** folder.

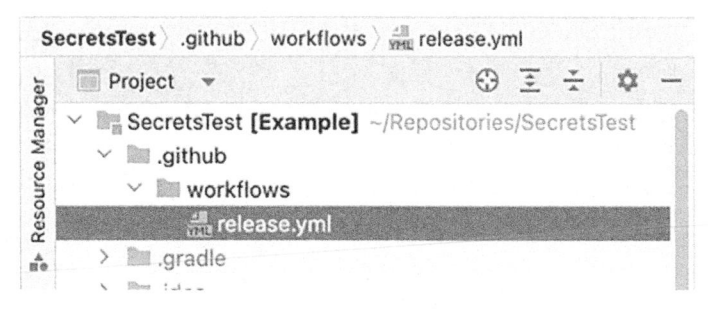

Figure 16.9: Workflow file location in project

The following **release.yaml** example will set up the environment variables to match the **signingConfigs** settings in the build file from the previous example:

```yaml
1.  name: Release Build
2.
3.  on:
4.    push:
5.      branches: [ main ]
6.    workflow_dispatch:
7.
8.  jobs:
9.    build:
10.     runs-on: ubuntu-latest
11.
12.     env:
13.       KEYSTOREPASS: ${{ secrets.KEYSTOREPASS }}
14.       KEYSTOREALIAS: ${{ secrets.KEYSTORE_ALIAS }}
15.       KEYSTOREPATH: ./keystore.jks
16.
17.     steps:
18.       - name: Checkout code
19.         uses: actions/checkout@v2
20.
21.       - name: Set up JDK
22.         uses: actions/setup-java@v2
23.         with:
24.           distribution: 'adopt'
25.           java-version: '17'
26.
27.       - name: Decode Keystore and set env variable
28.         run: |
29.           echo "${{ secrets.KEYSTORE }}" | base64 -decode > ${{ env.KEYSTOREPATH }}
30.           echo "KEYSTOREFILE=$(realpath ${{ env.KEYSTOREPATH }})" >> $GITHUB_ENV
31.
32.       - name: Build Release
33.         run: gradle assembleRelease
34.
35.       - name: Upload APK
```

```
36.          uses: actions/upload-artifact@v2
37.          with:
38.            name: app-release
39.            path: app/build/outputs/apk/release/app-release.apk
```

The preceding workflow script accomplishes the following:

- A workflow entry called **Release Build** will be created under the **Actions** tab in the GitHub repository when this file is first checked in.
- Every subsequent push to the main branch will execute the jobs specified; in this case, just the build job. The job can also be executed manually using the **workflow_dispatch** option on the repository site.
- The build job will create a **virtual machine** (**VM**) in the cloud running Ubuntu.
- Environment variables will be set up on the VM from the secret values.
- The repository code will be checked out on the VM and subsequently, JDK v17 will be installed there.
- The **keystore** secret value is decoded and saved as a temporary file on the VM. An environment variable is then set to the location of that file.
- The **.apk** / **.abb** file is built and (assuming success) is saved in an accessible location in GitHub.
- The VM is then deleted.

Note that the name of the temporary keystore file (**./keystore.jks**) is not set as a secret in the preceding example. This is because the file only exists for the lifetime of the job, after which the VM containing it is deleted. However, there is no reason why this cannot be set as a secret for consistency.

The title of the workflow run will be taken from the message set against the push. The resulting **.apk** / **.abb** file will be stored against that title entry. For example, given the sequence of git commands:

1. `$ git commit -am "workflow build 8"`
2. `$ git push origin main`

Any resulting **.apk** / **.abb** file will be found by navigating from the repository home page via **Actions** | **workflow** run title (workflow build 8 in this case). The artifact will be available to download as shown in the following figure:

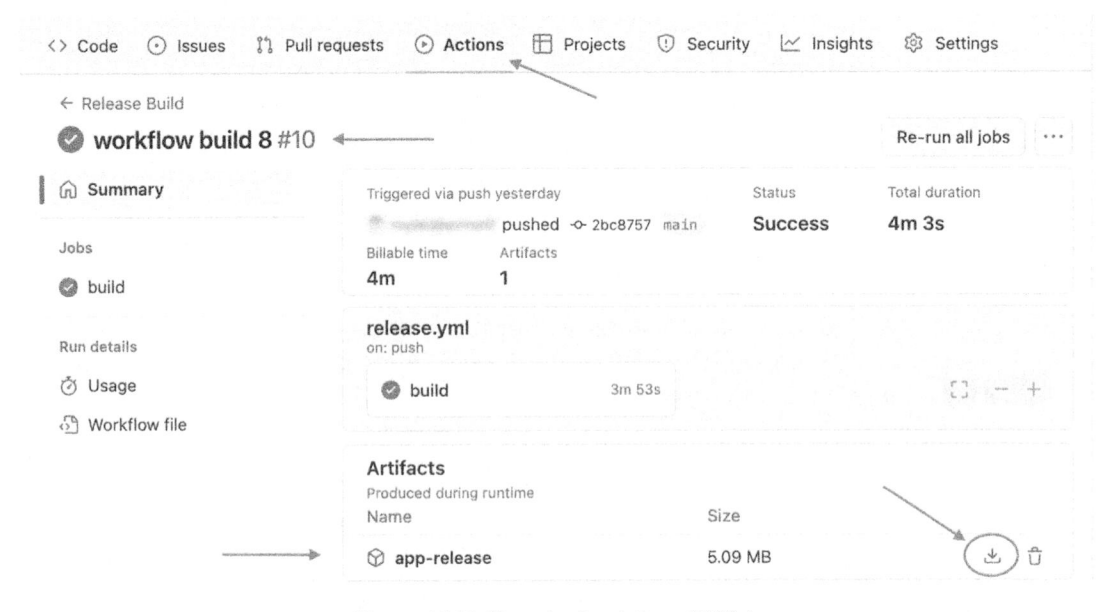

Figure 16.10: Download .apk from GitHub

As hinted at in *Chapter 15, Test Automation*, steps can be added to the job prior to the actual build that run unit and automation tests. If any step fails, the job stops and the repository owner is informed automatically via email.

Build flavors

Build flavors are a feature of the build system that allows different versions of an app to be created from a single codebase. This is useful for creating variations of an app for different markets, customer requirements, or stages of development (like a free version vs. a paid version, or a debug vs. release build). Each flavor can have its own source code, resources, and configuration settings. The following additions to the app build script will produce two `.apk` / `.aab` files when built for release; one for the Google market and another for Amazon:

```
1.  android {
2.      ...
3.      flavorDimensions += "distribution"
4.      productFlavors {
5.          create("google") {
6.              dimension = "distribution"
7.              applicationId = "com.bpp.example.google"
8.              resValue ("string", "greeting", "My Google App")
9.          }
```

```
10.         create("amazon") {
11.             dimension = "distribution"
12.             applicationId = "com.bpp.example.amazon"
13.             resValue ("string", "greeting", "My Amazon App")
14.         }
15.     }
16.     ....
```

In this simple example, each flavor will have its application ID and different settings for the resource value **greeting**. The following is an example of the resource value in the common code base:

```
1. @Composable
2. fun Greeting(modifier: Modifier = Modifier) {
3.     Text(
4.         text = stringResource(R.string.greeting),
5.         modifier = modifier
6.     )
7. }
```

The CI workflow **Build Release** step will now output two **.apk** / **.aab** files, each with different resource string values, as shown in *Figure 16.11*:

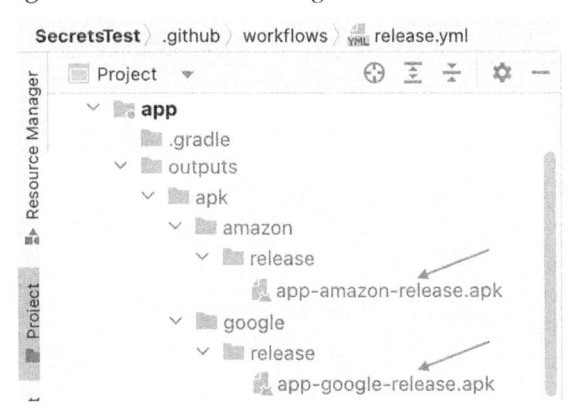

Figure 16.11: Build flavor outputs

This is just a taste of what can be done with build flavors. For example, each flavor could have extra dimensions, such as paid or free, producing further variations.

Distribution portals

There are several distribution portals where an APK can be uploaded and distributed depending upon the device manufacturer. For example, Samsung Galaxy and Huawei have their own store and processes. This can be a significant factor when distributing apps in other territories. For brevity, the following sections will only provide an overview of the steps required to release an app through the Google Play and Amazon App store.

Note: These steps are subject to change; however, they still provide a high-level baseline for the requirements.

Google Play store

Distributing an Android app through the Google Play store involves several steps. Here is a general overview of the process.

Create Developer account

Setting up a Google developer account is a lengthy process and is different depending on whether you are a business or an individual. At the time of writing, the following URL was the starting point:

https://play.google.com/console/signup

Alternatively, go to the Google Play Store website and Select the Play Console, as shown in *Figure 16.12*:

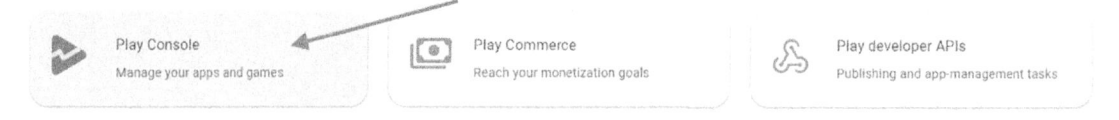

Figure 16.12: Play Console (Source google.com)

The process of creating a developer account is constantly changing and evolving, so it will be up to the reader to navigate the current process. However, the following pieces of information are likely to be required:

- D-U-N-S number (business accounts only)
- Payment details
- Your play console and Android experience
- Other google accounts
- Customer website
- Number of apps
- Earning money on Google Play
- App categories
- Google customers' contact details

Releasing an app on Google Play store

Log in to Google Console or Create Account as above. The Google Play console will be displayed as shown in *Figure 16.13*:

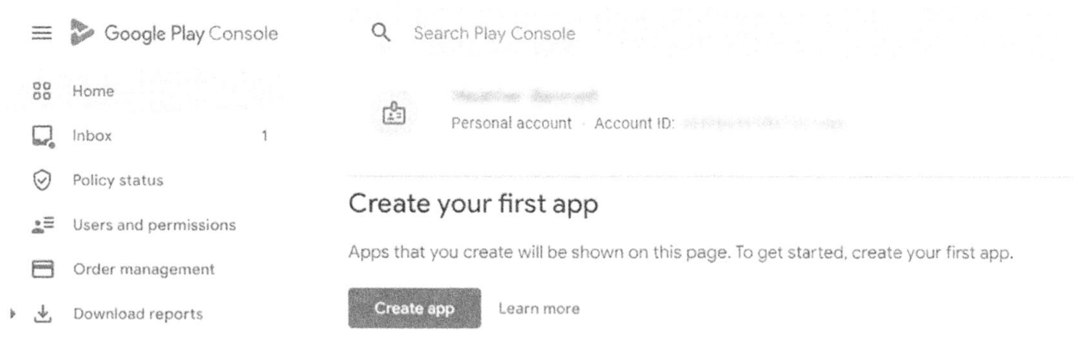

Figure 16.13: Create your first app

Releasing an app on Google Play store is a multi-step process:

1. Internal testing
2. Finish setting up your app
3. Closed testing
4. Apply for access to production

The final step, **applying for access to production**, requires that the app has completed **Closed testing**. Closed testing requires that the forms under **Finish setting up your app** be submitted. Internal testing is optional but useful for checking if the app bundle has been correctly signed and meets initial digital requirements.

To start the process, follow these steps:

1. Select **Create app from the account developer console** account screen.
2. In the subsequent dialog, enter the **App name,** then select **Default language**, **App or game, Free or paid**.
3. Confirm the checkboxes for **Developer Programme Policies and US export laws**.
4. Once this has been completed the **Create app** button is enabled.

Finish setting up your application

In this section, information about the app needs to be provided and a store listing must be created. The interface provides the following subsections to be completed:

- **Set privacy policy**: A privacy policy is a document that explains how an app or website collects, uses, and protects a user's data. It is like a promise about how a user's information is handled. Google will fail approval if the Privacy Policy is not included.

The entry here needs to point to a URL with the policy document. Privacy policy documents can be generated free of charge by third-party websites, and the resulting HTML file can be uploaded to any public space (such as GitHub) and referred to here.

- **App access:** App access refers to the permissions and app requests to use features on a specific device, that is, a camera, microphone, location, storage, or other installed apps.
- **Ads**: Confirm whether the app contains ads. Permissions and Ads can be dependent on third-party apps inside the Bundle/APK. The user should be aware of their usage before uploading for submission.
- **Content rating**: This requires completing a somewhat lengthy form. Ultimately, it will provide a label that indicates how appropriate an app or media is for certain age groups. It considers factors like violence, language, or mature themes.
- **Target audience**: The selected users for an app within the selected criteria, i.e., a certain age range if it is an educational app for children.
- **News apps**: A news app is like a portable newspaper on a phone or tablet. It delivers current events and stories from various sources, keeping customers informed on the go.
- **COVID-19 contact tracing and status apps**: COVID-19 contact tracing apps use Bluetooth to anonymously alert users if they have been near someone who tested positive. Status apps show a customer's own vaccination or test results.
- **Data safety**: Data safety is all about protecting a user's information. It refers to practices that keep customers' data secure from unauthorized access, use, or disclosure.
- **Government apps**: Government apps are official tools created by government agencies. They can help customers to access services: renew licenses (pay taxes, or report issues, be informed) view official news (safety alerts, or voting information) and interact (report crimes, track public transport, or find government benefits).
- **Financial features**: Financial features in apps refer to functionalities that involve real money. This could include banking (managing accounts, transferring money, or paying bills), investing (buying and selling stocks, bonds, or other financial products), payments (making purchases within the app or using it as a mobile wallet), and cryptocurrency (buying, selling, or storing cryptocurrency).
- **Select an app category and provide contact details**: Selecting an app category is like sorting an app on a shelf in a digital store. It helps users find an app by placing it with similar apps (for example, games, news, finance). Contact details are a way for developers to connect with users, typically through an email address.
- **Setting up a store listing:** This is where a developer can showcase their app on Google Play with app name, short description and a long description (grabbing users' attention and explaining what an app does), graphics and video (visually showing off a developer's app's features and user experience) and category and

tags (helping users discover your app by placing it alongside similar ones).

Setting up the images for the feature is a 16 by 9 landscape promotional banner not a screenshot. Alternatively, a YouTube video can be referenced to play in this space on the store listing. Additionally, screenshots are required for phones, tablets (7-inch and 10-inch), and chrome books. This is particularly challenging as the resolutions vary and an emulator is useful for creating each device's screenshots and uploading successfully.

Internal/closed testing

Before the app is released, it needs to be uploaded and tested. This can be achieved through two steps within the create app dialogs: internal and closed testing. The following subsections break down the common and unique steps of each of these stages.

Adding countries (closed only)

In the Closed testing section, countries can be selected from a list to be targeted in the *App Release*. One or more countries can be selected at one time during each stage of the process. Once an app has been approved via *Closed testing*, the app will be accessible from the allocated countries and other countries can be added as required. Choose **Set up your closed test track** and select countries and regions. See the *Apply for Production* section for further information on how to change countries post app production release.

Adding testers

Testers should have a Gmail/Play Store account and an Android phone.

When adding testers in *Closed testing*, select **Testers | Email lists | Create Email list** and add at least 20 and up to 100 testers' email addresses. Email addresses can be organized here in groups with the option to enable or disable each group. In addition, to keep the developers informed about app test feedback the *Feedback URL* or *email address* of the developer needs to be added.

Testers can participate in testing via a link shared in an email. The link is available under *Testers* on the same screen. The testers can then click on the link in that email and activate the app within Google Play to install on their Android phone.

Creating new release

Selecting **Create new release** under **Internal or Closed testing** will display the following *Figure 16.14* dialog:

Create testing release

testing releases are available to up to 100 testers that you choose

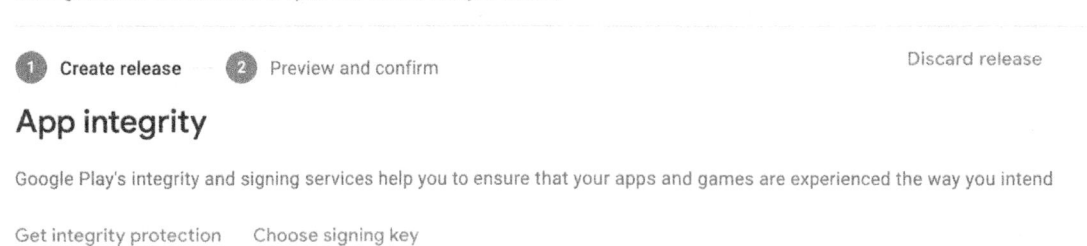

Figure 16.14: Create testing release

On this page, there is an option titled **App Integrity**. If your app has embedded app integrity checks, use this option to link the app to a Google Cloud project. This tool lets your app check if it is running on a genuine device and has not been modified. It requires the app to access an API during key events, such as button presses, to compare the app binary with the one distributed on Google Play store. For more information, see

https://developer.android.com/google/play/integrity

A signing key must be chosen before the signed app bundle can be uploaded, as in *Figure 16.15*:

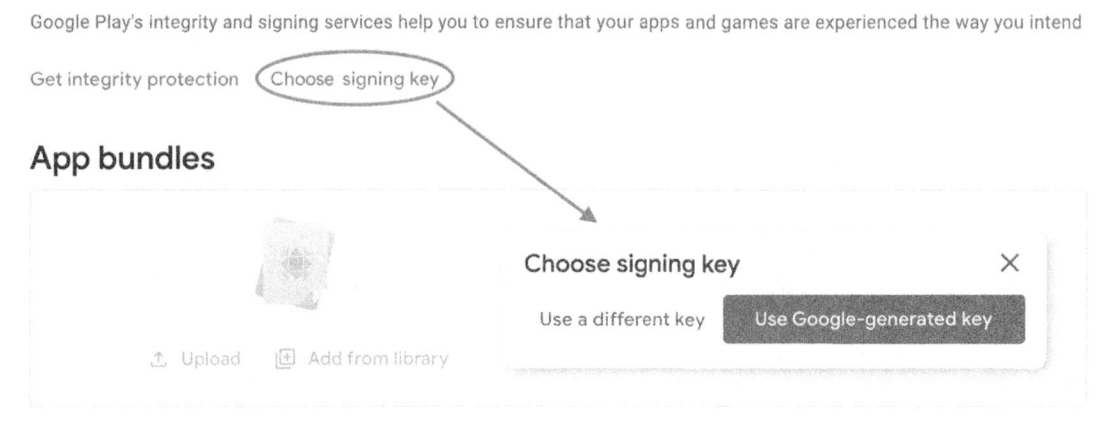

Figure 16.15: Choose signing key

To avoid confusion, this should probably say **Choose private key**. Earlier in this chapter, we discussed the need to build a signed release bundle, and created a keystore file for this purpose. When we built the bundle, the keystore used a locally stored private and public key file, along with the `keystore` file, to sign the app. The public key is then embedded in the bundle signature.

The option to **Use Google-generated key** above offers the chance to allow Google to re-sign the bundle with a private key that Google holds on their servers. If this option is chosen, when the bundle is uploaded, the public key is extracted from the bundle and then re-signed with the remotely held private key. In this instance, it does not matter what private key was used to originally sign the bundle, so long as the public key is the same as the one used to upload the app for the first time. In this way, the developer need never worry about losing the never-to-be-shared private key file.

This will work as long as the public key has not been used to sign any other app anywhere else on Google Play store. If this is the case, a misleading error message, **Bundle is unsigned**, is shown on attempting to upload the bundle. It is not unreasonable to want to use the same keystore to sign several apps. In this instance, select **Use a different key** from the dialog above (shown in *Figure 16.15*) and pick the following option/dialog, as shown in *Figure 16.16*:

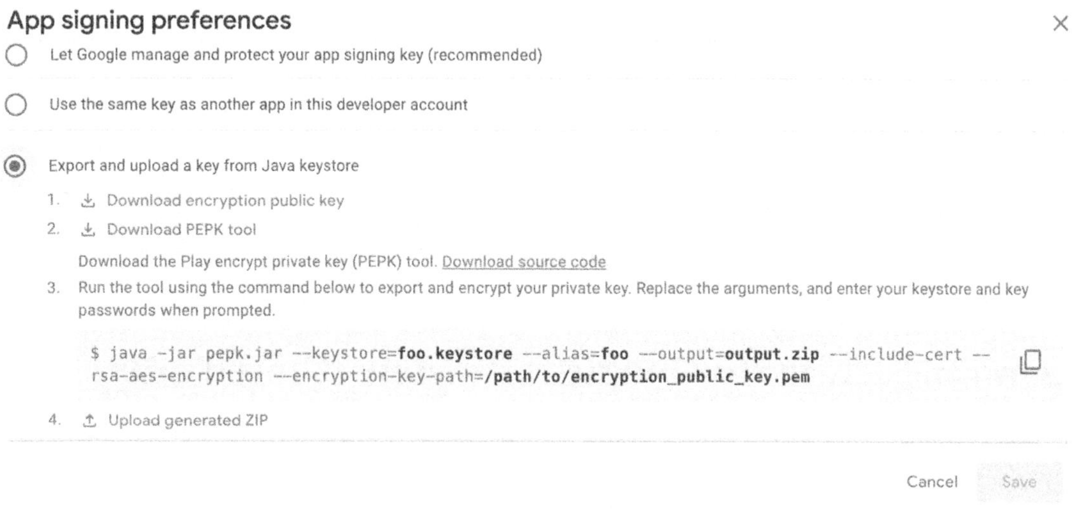

App signing preferences

○ Let Google manage and protect your app signing key (recommended)

○ Use the same key as another app in this developer account

◉ Export and upload a key from Java keystore

1. ⬇ Download encryption public key
2. ⬇ Download PEPK tool

   Download the Play encrypt private key (PEPK) tool. Download source code

3. Run the tool using the command below to export and encrypt your private key. Replace the arguments, and enter your keystore and key passwords when prompted.

   $ java -jar pepk.jar --keystore=**foo.keystore** --alias=**foo** --output=**output.zip** --include-cert --rsa-aes-encryption --encryption-key-path=**/path/to/encryption_public_key.pem**

4. ⬆ Upload generated ZIP

Cancel   Save

Figure 16.16: App signing preferences

Select **Export and upload key from Java keystore.** Then, follow these steps:

1. **Download encryption public key**: Clicking on this will download the file **encryption_public_key.pem**.
2. **Download PEPK tool**: This will download the file **pepk.jar**.
3. Run the PEPK tool from the command line:

   $ java -jar **pepk.jar** --keystore=**foo.keystore** --alias=**foo** --output=**output.zip** --include-cert --rsa-aes-encryption --encryption-key-path=/path/to/**encryption_public_key.pem**

   o java: This needs to be the Java executable from Open JDK (**openjdk.org**), *not* the Oracle version that normally ships with most desktop OSs and is invariably system pathed.

   o pepk.jar: Previously downloaded file.

- `--keystore`: This should reference the keystore file we created earlier in this chapter (`keystore.jks`).
      - `--alias`: This should reference the alias in the keystore we created earlier in this chapter (`key0`).
      - `--encryption-key-path`: This should reference the previously downloaded `encryption_public_key.pem` file.

      Assuming all files are correctly pathed and referenced, the correct version of java is used, and all other entries are correct, the file `output.zip` should be created local to where the command was run.
   4. **Upload generated zip**: Clicking on this will present a dialog for uploading the `output.zip` file created in the last step.

      Selecting **Save** after uploading the ZIP file will return to the **Create testing release** screen, and the option to upload a bundle will be available. Assuming the bundle was signed with the same keystore and alias as was referenced in the steps above, dragging or selecting the bundle in the dialog should upload it without any problems.

Note: If the bundle has not been changed between Internal and Closed testing, there is no need to upload it again at the Closed testing stage. Clicking on Add from library in the same dialog will allow the selection of the existing uploaded bundle.

Send the release to Google for review (Closed only)

To send an app for release, click on **Send the release to Google for review**.

Pre-registration

During pre-registration, a store listing can be published before launching, and users can register interest and receive a notification to download the app onto their devices. From this screen, click on **Go to Dashboard**.

Dashboard shows inbox messages for pre-launch report results. **Apply for access to production** is shown under **Production**.

Apply for production

Apply for production may be selected once closed testing has been completed by a group of testers who have reviewed and approved the app. Preview questions asked as a part of *Apply for production* are:

- Part 1: Tell us about your closed test
- Part 2: Tell us about your app/game
- Part 3: Tell us about your production readiness

The app review usually takes seven days. Once the application has undergone successful review, and access to *Production*, *Release* will make the app available to billions of users on Google Play. Open Testing can be used to test an app extensively before publishing it to production and testing any app updates in future.

To change app release countries post-production, follow these steps:

1. Go to the **Production** page under **Google Play Console | Closed Testing** and select the **Countries/regions** tab.
2. Select from the list of **Countries/regions**.
3. To add, click on the relevant country.
4. To remove, click on **Discard**, then click **Save**.

Production application process

Google will test the release on various devices and form factors, the ones which are enabled during submission. Screenshots and reports of the testing are made available which can be useful to identify UI issues.

For updates, rollout percentage can be enabled to gradually introduce a new release then ramp up the rollout if all goes well. With this option it is also possible to revert the update process if a showstopper issue is found.

It can take 24-48 hours for a new or updated app to appear on a user's device.

Amazon App store

Distributing an Android app through the Amazon App store requires significantly less steps than through Google Play store. Here is a general overview of the process.

Creating Developer Account

Sign up at **https://developer.amazon.com/** by clicking on **Developer Console** and then click on **Create Developer Account** as shown in *Figure 16.17* (the **Create Developer Account** button may be at the bottom of the site):

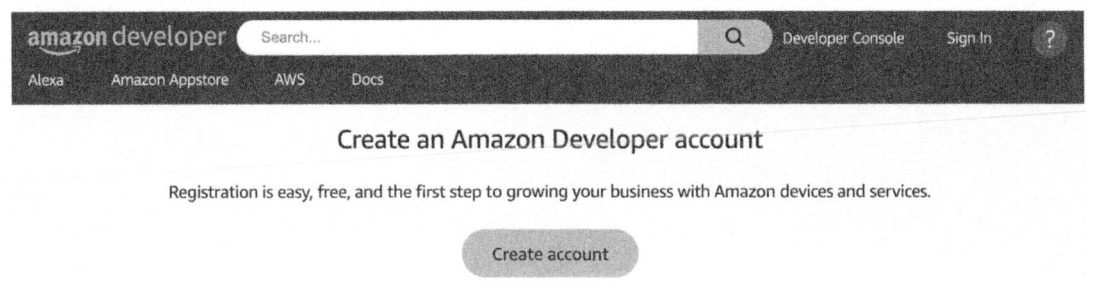

Figure 16.17: *Amazon Developer*

Releasing an app on Amazon App Store

To release an APK on the Amazon App Store, follow these steps:

1. Sign in to an Amazon developer account or **Create Account** (see above).
2. **Prepare an APK for Release**: As with Google Play Store, ensure the APK is properly signed and tested and meets Amazon App Store's guidelines and requirements. Make any necessary adjustments to ensure compatibility with Amazon devices and services as relevant.
3. Click on the **Add a New App** button as indicated in *Figure 16.18*:

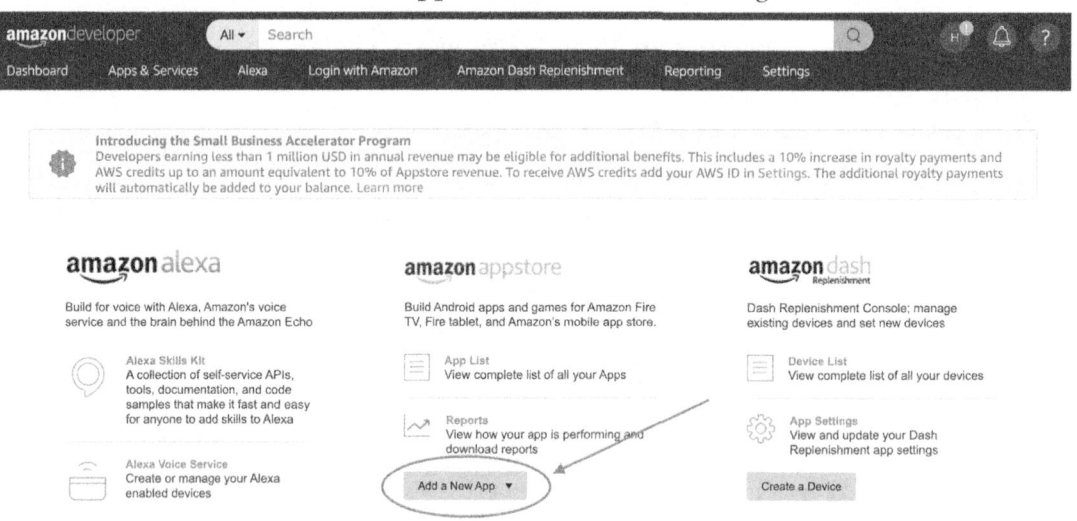

Figure 16.18: Create a new App

4. **Enter app information**: As prompted, enter the app's details, including the app title, app SKU (a unique product identifier. This is optional), app category, customer support email address, customer support phone and customer support website, and click **Save** as shown in *Figure 16.19*:

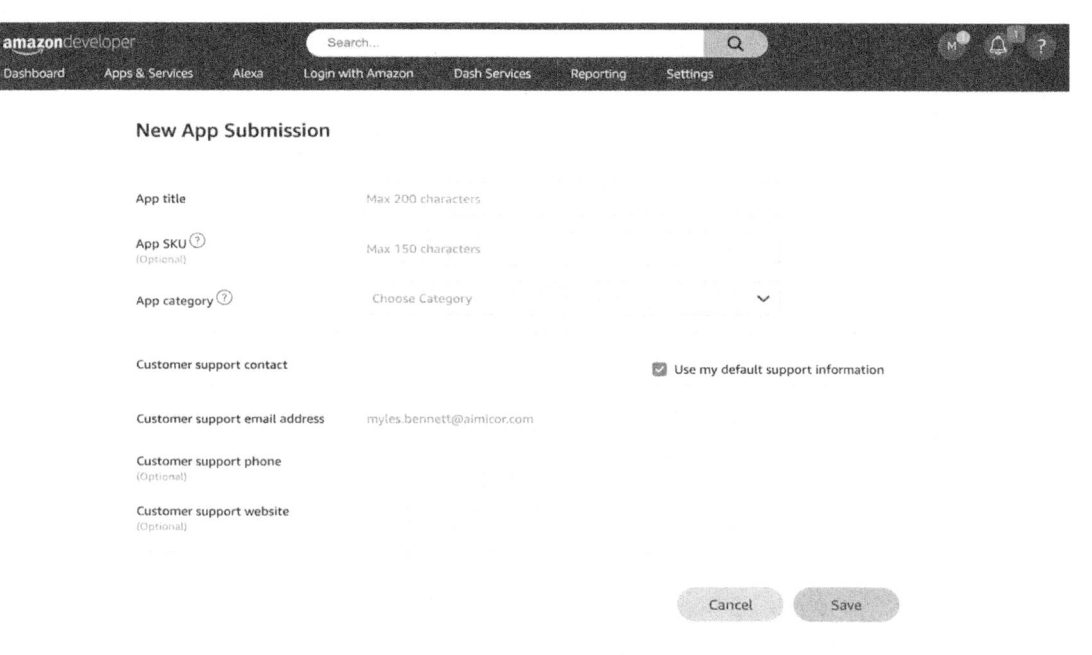

Figure 16.19: New App submission

5. **Upload an app file**: Upload the app APK file as in *Figure 16.20* and click **Next**:

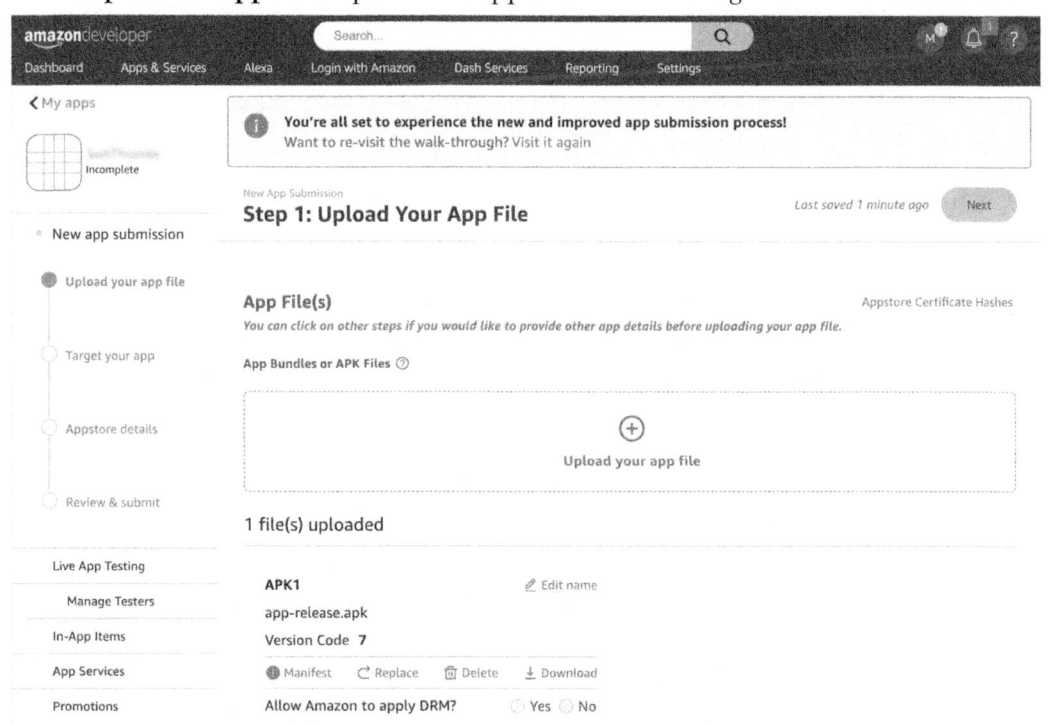

Figure 16.20: Upload the APK file

6. **Target an app:** Fill in the details as shown in *Figure 16.21*. Select the check boxes whether the app collects user data or transfers it to third parties. Add any **Privacy policy URL** as relevant and click **Next**:

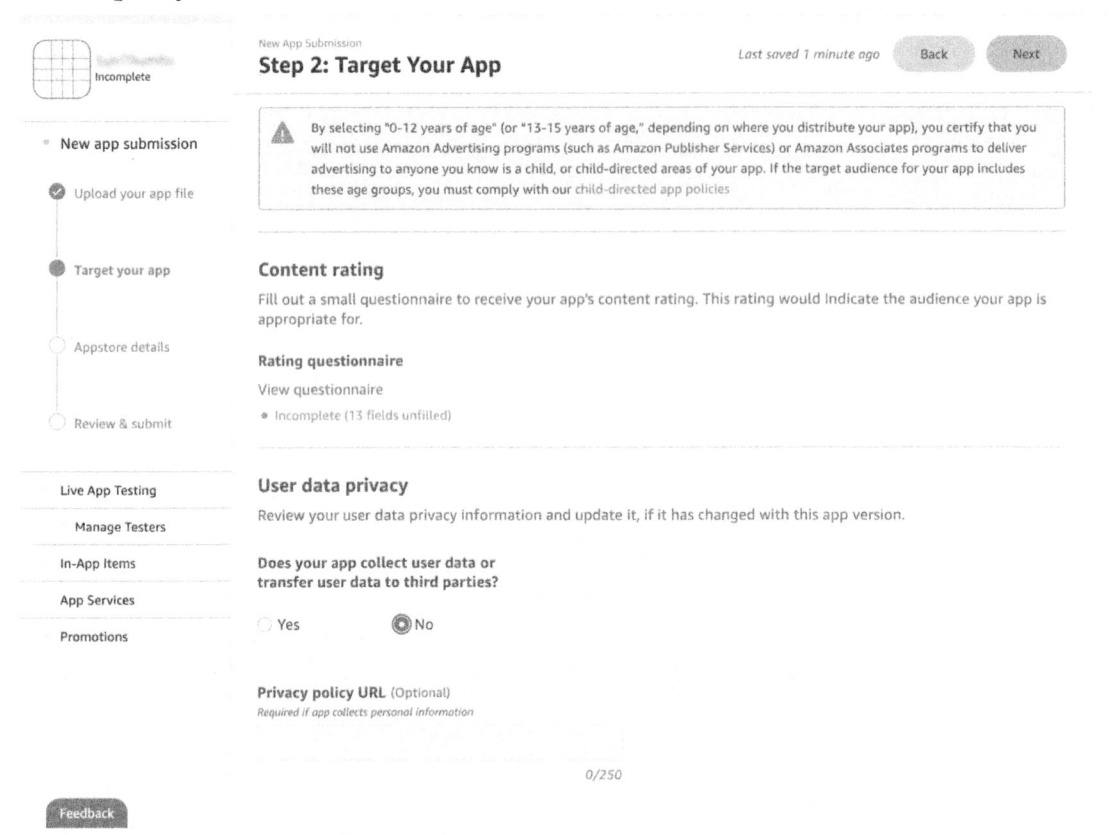

Figure 16.21: Target an app

7. **Set up pricing and availability in appstore details**: Select free app release or paid pricing information for an app release. Click on the countries or regions where the app is available, and add its description, as shown in *Figure 16.22*:

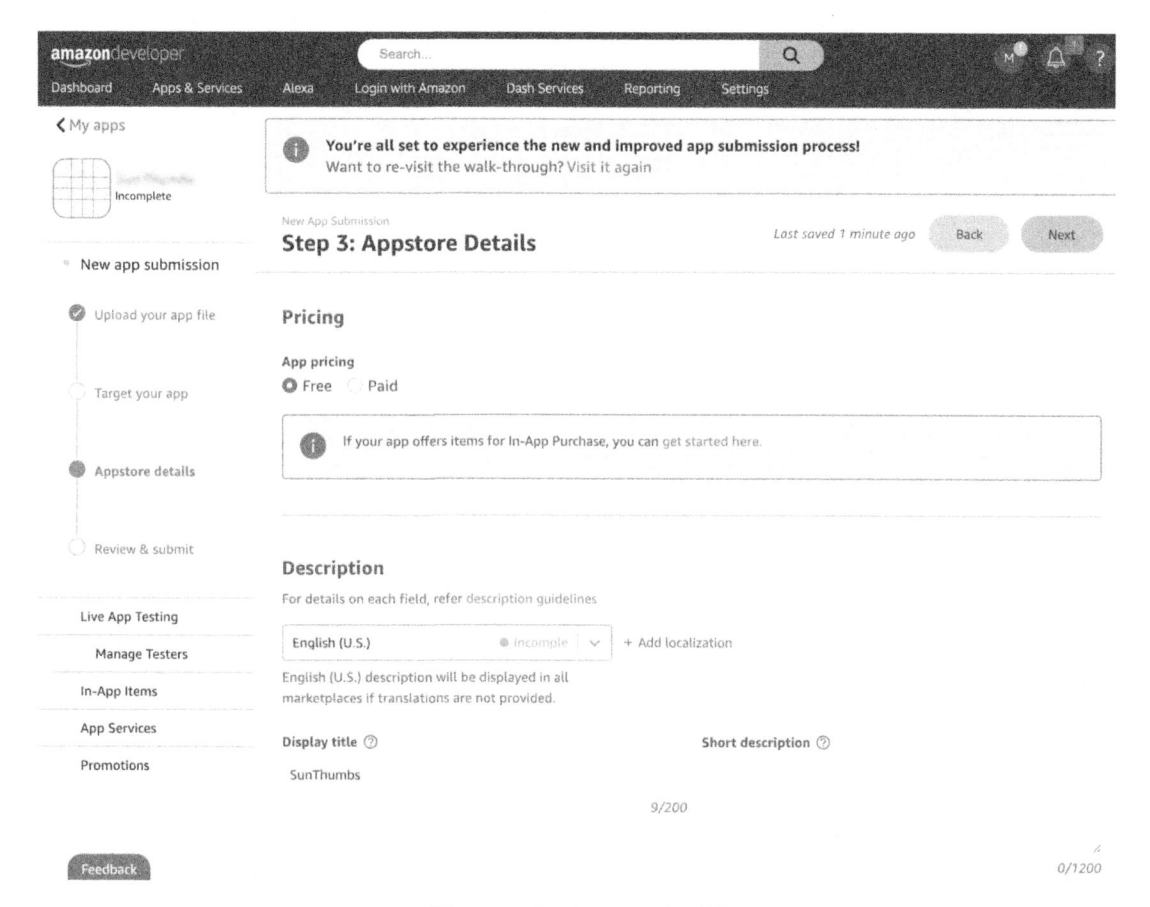

Figure 16.22: *Appstore details*[1]

8. **Add images, videos, and icons**: These elements are required for app approval and release, as shown in *Figure 16.23*:

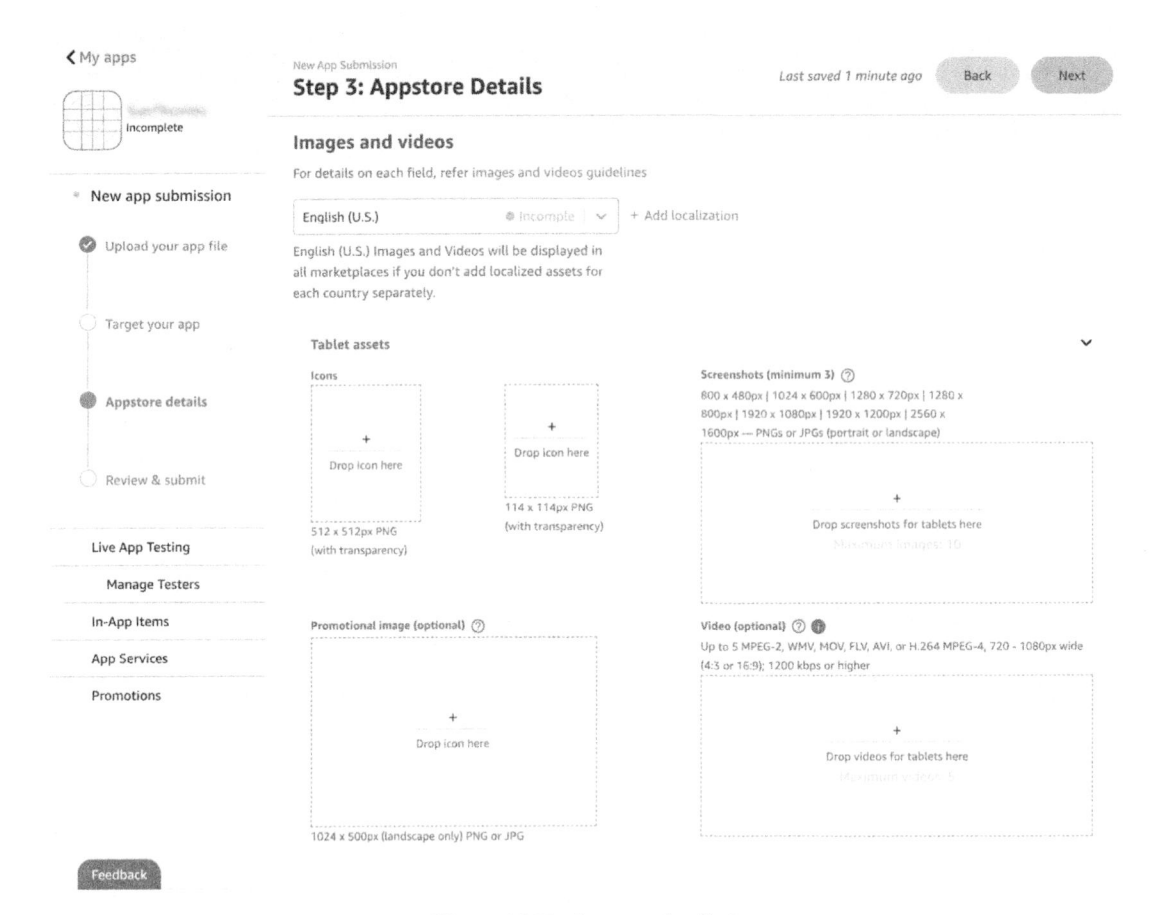

Figure 16.23: Appstore details 2

9. **Content rating questionnaire 1**: Select the check button options for the relevant violence, drug, nudity, or sexual content as shown in *Figure 16.24*:

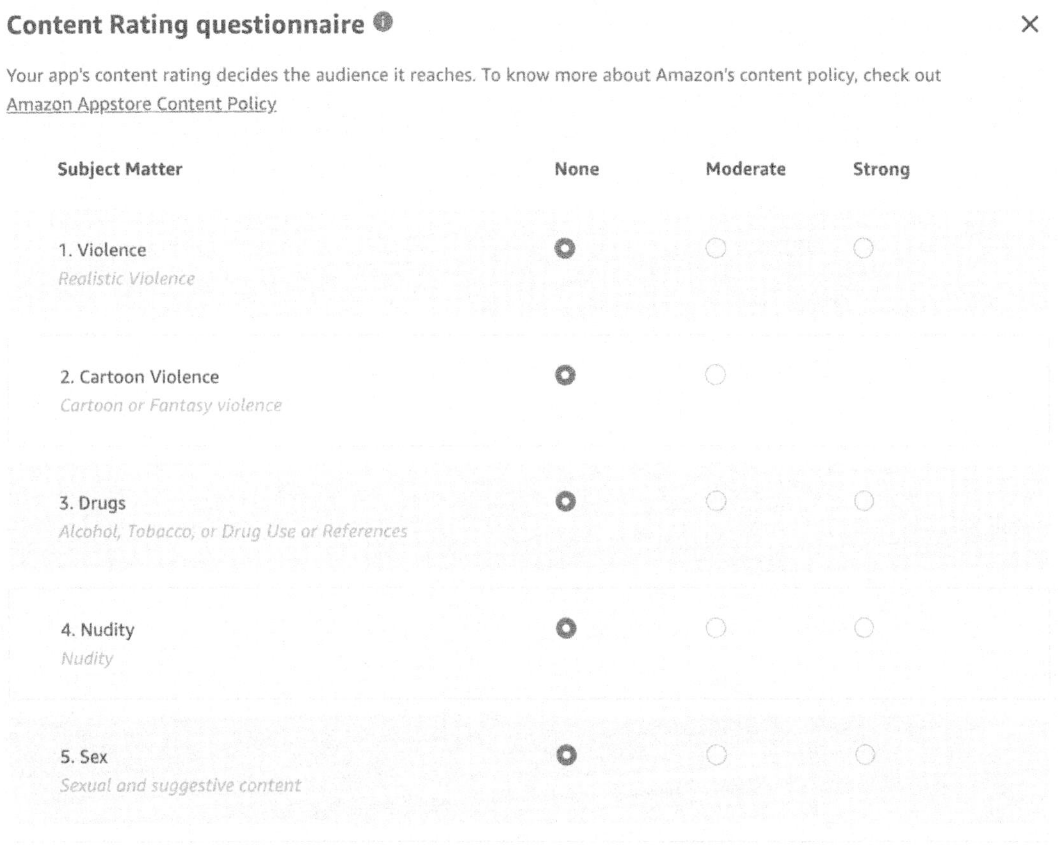

Content Rating questionnaire

Your app's content rating decides the audience it reaches. To know more about Amazon's content policy, check out Amazon Appstore Content Policy

Subject Matter	None	Moderate	Strong
1. Violence *Realistic Violence*	●	○	○
2. Cartoon Violence *Cartoon or Fantasy violence*	●	○	
3. Drugs *Alcohol, Tobacco, or Drug Use or References*	●	○	○
4. Nudity *Nudity*	●	○	○
5. Sex *Sexual and suggestive content*	●	○	○

Figure 16.24: Content Rating questionnaire 1

10. **Content rating questionnaire 2**: Select the check buttons for the relevant options in *Figure 16.25* for account creation/personal information, advertisements, gambling, location detections or location-based services, user-generated content, or user-to-user communication.

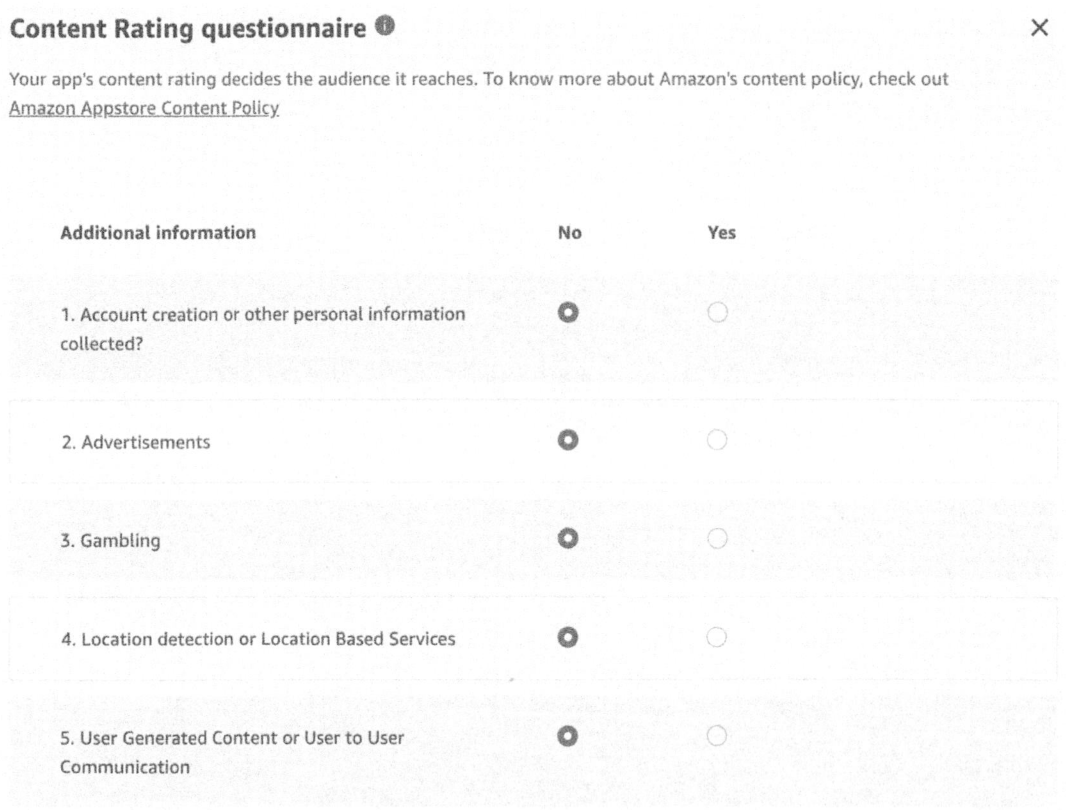

Content Rating questionnaire

Your app's content rating decides the audience it reaches. To know more about Amazon's content policy, check out Amazon Appstore Content Policy

Additional information	No	Yes
1. Account creation or other personal information collected?	●	○
2. Advertisements	●	○
3. Gambling	●	○
4. Location detection or Location Based Services	●	○
5. User Generated Content or User to User Communication	●	○

Figure 16.25: Content Rating questionnaire 2

11. **Submit an app for review**: Submit the app for review as shown in *Figure 16.26*. Amazon will review the app to ensure it meets their guidelines and standards. After approval, the app will be available on the Amazon Appstore for users to download and install.

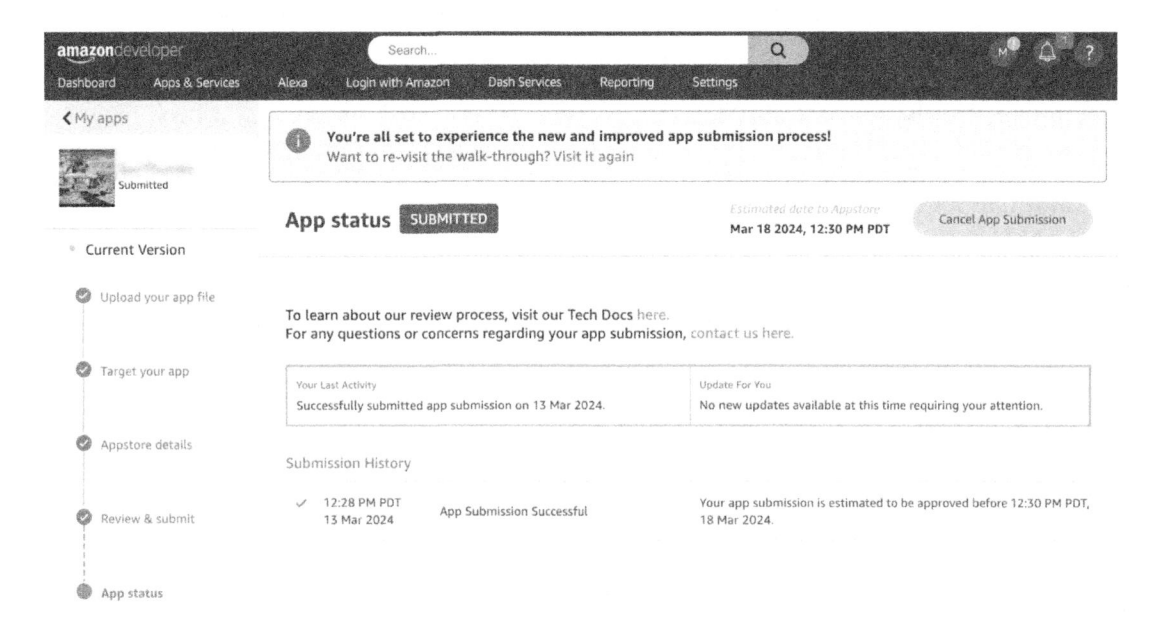

Figure 16.26: App status Submitted

12. **Manage an app**: After the app is live, the Developer Console may be used to monitor its performance, manage updates, and respond to user reviews and feedback.

Conclusion

Applications must be built for Release and signed with a keystore to produce a **.apk** or **.abb** (bundle) file.

Google Play is making it increasingly difficult to navigate through the process of field testing and releasing an app for individuals or small organizations. Domain ownership is mandatory for each app, and whilst a website is not necessary on the domain, if one does not exist, a reason is required. Furthermore, more legal documents are required, such as the privacy policy, etc. Amazon App Store, in contrast, has made this process easier than Google Play Store currently, but is subject to software changes and updates.

It is important to fill in all the current fields requested when uploading a bundle for app review and release. Not correctly preparing the bundle or filling in any of the plethora of forms suitably will quickly result in app submission failure.

This book has presented established paradigms and practical methods for organizing and developing large code bases, concentrating on the Kotlin programming language and mobile apps. It argued why Kotlin is a great choice, not only for Android development but increasingly for multi-platform and full-stack.

It focused on good programming practices, such as test-driven development, clean code architecture and module hierarchy arrangement with practical examples and little-documented techniques. It also presented a way of breaking up code at a high level by splitting requirements out into *features* and then those features into layers.

We are confident that following the techniques and disciplines expressed in this book will increase the chances of any app project's success.

Points to remember

- Sign the distributable bundle with a keystore file.
- Keep the bundle's keystore file secure.
- Avoid storing unsecured keystores or passwords in a public repository.
- Consider using action secrets to secure keystores and passwords in repositories to allow remote release building.
- Make sure that any images or videos that are uploaded to the distribution portals are of the correct size and resolution before submission.
- Do not forget to click all the relevant information boxes on the distribution portals Content rating Questionnaire to submit. This includes creating a Privacy policy.

Questions

1. What is a signing key file or keystore?
2. How would you generate a signing key in Android Studio?
3. What command code would you use to create a keystore on the Command Line?
4. What is the purpose of the `keyalg <alg>: Key algorithm name` parameter in the command line `keytool`?
5. Describe how to set up secrets in one repository provider other than GitHub.
6. How would you Upload the App bundle file to Amazon?
7. Name two additional app stores you could use to upload a mobile app that are not Amazon App Store or Google Play Store and compare them for ease of use and pricing.
8. Name four Google Play policies and discuss why they are required.
9. What information do you need to add to upload a bundle on Amazon?

Index

Symbols

<data> 147

A

Amazon App Store 365

Amazon App Store Account, creating 365

Amazon App Store, concepts 366-373

Android App, concepts
  APK, utilizing 345
  App Bundle 345
  CI, building 352-355
  command line, optimizing 349, 350
  Gradle, configuring 351, 352
  keystore 346
  setting, versioning 344, 345
  studio, generating 347, 348

Android, apps
  e-commerce 235
  navigation 235
  social media 234
  streaming 234

Android, aspects
  asynchronous, processing 235
  background, executing 235
  data, caching 235
  error, handling 235
  HTTP, request 235
  JSON, parsing 235
  RESTful APIs 235
  testing 235
  WebSockets 235

Android, servers
  access data 234

online services 234
sync data 234
transfer data 234
Android Studio 310
Android Studio, sequences 310, 311
Animation 300
Animation, sections
  AnimatedVisibility 302, 303
  AnimationSpec 300-302
  Transition Animations 303-305
API 235
API, key aspects
  abstraction, layer 236
  authentication/authorization 237
  data, exchanging 237
  documentation 237
  functionality, accessing 237
  protocol, communicating 236
  request-response, model 236
  versioning 237
API Keys, breakdown
  authentication 247
  generation 246
  inclusion, request 246
API, types
  Internal APIs 237
  Library APIs 237
  Mobile App APIs 237
  REST APIs 237
  SOAP APIs 237
  Third-Party APIs 237
  Web APIs 237
area() 34
Asserters 331

Authentication, keys
  API Keys 246
  OAuth Tokens 247, 248

B

bowling game 170
Breakpoints 311
Breakpoints, services
  behavior, modifying 311
  control flow, analyzing 311
  issues, isolating 311
  program state, inspect 311
Breakpoints, types
  Conditional 313
  Exception 313
Breakpoints, usage 311-313
Build Flavors 356
buildSrc Module 195
buildSrc Module, creating steps 196-200
buildSrc Module, key benefits
  code organization, improving 195
  code, reusability 195
  dependency, centralizing 195
  task, plugins 196
buildSrc Module, use cases 196

C

Caching 258
Caching, features 258
Caching, methods 259
Caching, techniques
  custom, caching 259
  Http, caching 259
Caching, types 259
calculateArea() 34

Index

CCA, elements
 controllers 55
 entities 55
 external, interfaces 55
 frameworks, drivers 55
 gateways 55
 presenters 55
 use cases 55
CCA, use cases 260-263
CI, aspects
 automated, building 340
 automated, testing 340
 collaboration, improving 340
 continuous, feedback 340
 frequent, integrating 339
 issues, detection 340
class extensions, advantages
 concise/readable, code 13
 functional programe, enhancing 13
 immutable, collections 13
 inference, improving 13
 null, safety 13
class extensions, types
 filter 12
 map 12
 sorted 12
Code Coverage 338, 339
Code Coverage, characteristics
 coverage, exclusion 339
 Dynamic UI, generation 339
 Lambda, expressions 339
Color Scheme, factors 273
Compose Multiplatform 85

Compose Multiplatform, aspects
 composable, functions 86
 ecosystem, tooling 86
 Gradle, plugin 86
 interoperability 86
 platform, adaptations 85
 UI Code, sharing 85
Compose Multiplatform, disadvantages
 curve, learning 86
 developer, tooling 87
 ecosystem, maturity 87
 interoperability, challenges 87
 performance, considering 87
 platform, adjustments 87
 platform, supporting 86
ComposeTestRule 329, 330
Compose Tree 327-329
Continuous Integration (CI) 339
cross-platform development 72
cross-platform development, disadvantages
 challenges, customizing 74
 curve, learning 74
 debugging 75
 framework, limitations 74
 performance 74
 platform, features 74
 third-party, frameworks 75
cross-platform development, aspects
 codebase, sharing 73
 code, deploying 73
 code, reusability 73
 development, efficiency 73
 iteration, prototyping 74
 platform, abstraction 73
 user experience 73

D

Data Binding 147, 148
Data Binding, reasons
  code, generating 148
  complexity 148
  curve, learning 148
  documentation, resources 148
  performance, concerns 148
Data Classes 250
data layer 61
data layer, key points
  abstraction 63
  dependency, inversion 63
  interface, segregation 63
  persistence, retrieval 63
  synchronization, caching 63
data layer, repositories
  data, abstraction 62
  data access, encapsulation 62
  data retrieval, persistence 62
  query, filtering 62
  work, unit 62
Data Module, setup 248-250
Dependency Injection (DI) 94
DI, approaches
  constructor, injection 96
  field, injection 98, 99
  interface, injection 96, 97
  Setter/Method, injection 95
DI, benefits
  decoupling 94
  flexibility 94
  reusability 94
  scalability 95
  testability 94
DI, module
  Hilt 264, 265
  Koin 265
DI, ways
  behavior, verification 174
  confidence, refactoring 175
  dependencies, isolation 174
  encourages, modularity 175
  faster, feedback 175
  integration, testing 175
  state, controlling 174
  test doubles 174
domain entities 57
domain entities, characteristics
  business-centric 58
  business rules, invariants 58
  encapsulate, state 58
  independent, technical 58
  testable, isolation 58
domain layer 57
domain layer, use cases
  encapsulates business, logic 60
  external, details 60
  input/output 60
  testable, isolating 60
  user goal, representing 59
domain modules 213, 214
domain modules, building 218, 219
domain modules, categories
  Hilt DI 222, 223
  Koin DI 219-221
domain modules, steps 214-217
Domain-Specific Language (DSL) 192

Index   379

E

Espresso 326, 327

Evaluate Expression 316

Exception Breakpoint,
   setup 314, 315

F

Feature-Oriented Development (FOD)
  about 42
  case study 45-51
  concept 42, 43
  granularity, features 43
  structures 45

Finders 330

Flutter 83

Flutter, disadvantages
  accessibility, supporting 85
  app, size 84
  curve, learning 85
  limited, community 85
  native, functionality 84
  packages, maturity 84
  platform, interface 84

Flutter, key aspects
  cross-platform,
     developing 83
  dart program, language 83
  ecosystem, community 84
  Hot, reloading 83
  material, designing 83
  native, performance 83
  tools, developing 84
  Widget-based UI,
     developing 83

FOD, aspects
  completion, results 45
  entry point 45
  feedback, notifications 45
  interaction 45
  navigation 45

FOD, concepts 210-213

FOD, features
  break down, functionality 44
  business goals, considering 44
  complexity, evaluating 44
  iterative, approach 44
  prioritize 44
  user requirements,
     identifying 44

functional programming, parameters
  first-class functions 7
  immutability 6, 7
  lambda 7, 8

G

get() 108

getProductById 64

Google Play Store 358

Google Play Store,
   account creating 358

Google Play Store, concepts
  application,
     setting up 359, 360
  app, process 365
  internal/closed, testing 361
  productions 364
  testers, adding 361, 362

Gradle Kotlin DSL 192

Gradle Kotlin DSL,
   concepts 193-195

Gradle Kotlin DSL,
   key features
  community,
     adoption 193

functional, programming 193
IDE, integrating 192
interoperability 193
Kotlin-Based 192
readable, concise 193
safety 192
Greeting 118

H

hashCode() 30
Hilt 101
Hilt, cons
  code, generating 109
  complexity 109
Hilt DI, components
  KAPT 223-225
  KSP 225-227
Hilt DI, concepts 228, 229
Hilt DI, key considerations
  interoperability 227
  Kotlin, features 227
  tool, maturity 227
Hilt, history 101, 102
Hilt, pros
  android, integrating 109
  Dagger, integrating 109
  Google, supporting 109
  scope, supporting 109
Hilt, setting up 103-105
Hilt, workflow 102, 103

I

IDE, workspace
  on-the-fly, optimizing 206
  structure, versioning 207
infrastructure layer 69

infrastructure layer, key aspects
  cross-cutting 70
  external, interfaces 69
  external, services 69
  framework, libraries 69
  platform, interaction 69
  utilities, testing 70
inject() 108
Injection, frameworks
  Dagger 99
  Guice 100
  Hilt 99
  Kodein 101
  Koin 100
  RoboGuice 101
  Toothpick 100
Integer 5
invoke 61
Ionic 78
Ionic, disadvantages
  app store, approving 80
  Device APIs, accessing 80
  ecosystem, community 80
  native, functionality 79
  performance 79
  UI, customizing 80
  web technologies, dependency 80
Ionic, key aspects
  angular, integrating 78
  cordova, integrating 78
  cross-platform, compatibility 78
  Ionic Appflow 79
  Ionic Capacitor 79
  performance, optimizing 78
  UI, components 78

web technologies 78

J
Jetpack Compose 114
Jetpack Compose, advantages
  boilerplate, code 115
  Declarative UI 115
  intuitive curve, learning 116
  Kotlin, integrating 115
  performance, improving 115
  real-time, previews 115
  state, managing 115
  UI Logic, unification 116
  UI Reusability 115
Jetpack Compose, aspects
  android studio, integrating 115
  Declarative UI 114
  Jetpack, integrating 114
  Kotlin 114
  reactives, updates 114
  UI, functions 114
Jetpack Compose, composables
  Box 122
  Button 119
  Card 123
  Dialog 124, 125
  Icon 121
  Image 120, 121
  LazyColumn 124
Jetpack Compose, elements
  areas, supporting 306
  elements, tips 306
  foundation 305
  libraries 305
Jetpack Compose Scaffold 279-281
Jetpack Compose Scaffold, elements 279
Jetpack Compose Scaffold, methods
  BottomAppBar() 284
  DrawerContent() 285
  Fab() 285, 286
  Scaffold() 287
  SnackHost() 286, 287
  TopAppBar() 282, 283
Jetpack Compose Themes 270-272
Jetpack Compose Themes, aspects
  Color Scheme 272
  Shapes 277-279
  Typography 273, 274
Jetpack Compose, workflow 116-118

K
keytool 350
KMM, benefits
  code quality, improving 90
  code reviews, improving 91
  communicate, collaborating 91
  continuous, feedback 91
  knowledge, reducing 91
  knowledge, sharing 90
  problem solve, reducing 91
  skill, enhancing 91
  team morale, bonding 91
  time/effort, reducing 91
KMM, disadvantages
  curve, learning 90
  ecosystem, maturity 90
  iOS Framework, access 89
  maintenance 90
  platform, dependencies 89

team skills, expertise 90
workflow, debugging 90
KMM, key aspects
  API, surface 89
  code, sharing 88
  ecosystem, tooling 89
  Gradle, plugin 89
  interoperability 89
  platform, code 88
Koin 106
Koin, cons
  compile-time, safety 110
  smaller, community 110
Koin DI, causes 220
Koin, history
  android, supporting 106
  community, adoption 106
  features, evolution 106
  inception 106
  Koin 2.0 106
  popularity, growing 106
  version 1.0 106
Koin, pros
  lightweight 110
  no code, generating 110
  simplicity 109
Koin, workflow 107, 108
Kotlin 2
Kotlin, code constructs
  classes, objects 29
  coroutines 29
  data, classes 29
  extension, functions 29
  functional, programming 30
  functions, methods 29

  interfaces 30
  modularization 30
  null, safety 29
  packages 29
  property, delegation 30
Kotlin/Java, key differences
  class extensions 12
  companion, objects 21, 22
  coroutines 23
  Delegation 15-17
  erasure 19, 20
  extension functions 9, 10
  Flows 24
  functional, programming 6
  getters/setters 13, 14
  inference 5, 6
  internal, scope 22
  lazy initialization 18, 19
  named/default, parameters 20, 21
  null safety 3-5
  one-line, functions 15
  scoping functions 10
  StateFlows 24, 25
Kotlin, reasons
  android studio, supporting 3
  code safety, improving 3
  coroutines 3
  expressive syntax 2
  functions, properties 3
  java, interoperability 2
  performance, enhancing 3
  productivity, increasing 2
Kotlin, scenarios
  concurrency, testing 189
  flow transformation, testing 189

side effects, interactions 189
test error, handling 188
time, scheduling 189
kotlinx-coroutines-test 181
kotlinx-coroutines-test,
    key features 181
Ktor, features 245

L

lambda parameter,
    key differences
  API, streaming 8
  inference 8
  nullability, handling 8
  syntax 8
LiveData 145
LiveData, key features
  data, observation 145
  lifecycle-aware 145
  prevents memory, leaks 145
  reactive, updates 146
  UI, update 146
Logcat 319
Logcat, concepts 319
Logcat, levels 319, 320

M

Matchers 330
Mocking Libraries 175, 176
Mocking Libraries, aspects
  Mockito 177
  Mockk 177
Mocking Libraries,
    disadvantages 179
MockK 177
MockK, key features
  argument, matchers 177
  coroutines, supporting 178

DSL 178
Kotlin-Focused, syntax 177
mock, creating 177
partial mocks 178
stubbing 177
verification 177
Model-View-Controller
    (MVC) 139
Model-View-Intent (MVI) 149
Model-View-Presenter
    (MVP) 141
Model-View-ViewModel
    (MVVM) 144, 145
Modifiers 125
Modifiers, types
  background 126
  border 125
  clickable 125
  fillMaxWidth/fillMaxHeight 127
  height/width 126
  weight 127, 128
MVC, components
  Controlller 140, 141
  Model 139
  View 140
MVI, components
  Intent 150
  Model 150
  View 150
MVI, concepts
  immutability 151
  reactive, programming 151
  testing 152
  unidirectional data, flow 151
MVP, components
  Contract 142
  Model 142

Presenter 143, 144
View 142, 143
MVVM, components
   Data Binding 147
   LiveData 145

N

Navigation 288
Navigation, aspects
   component 288-290
   compose 290-292
   parameters 292-296
   scaffold 296, 297
Network, libraries
   android framework 240, 241
   Ktor 245, 246
   OkHttp 241, 242
   Retrofit 244
   Volley 243, 244
NullPointerException 5

O

OAuth Tokens, services
   access, token 247
   refresh, token 247

P

paradigm 55
paradigm, control flow 65-68
paradigm, layers
   data layer 56
   domain layer 56
   presentation layer 56
presentation layer 64
presentation layer, characteristics
   presentation, logic 65
   User Experience (UX) 64
   user input, handling 64
   user interface 64
Profiling Tools 316, 317
Profiling Tools, setup 317, 318

R

React Native 80
React Native, aspects
   code, reusability 81
   community, supporting 81
   developer, efficiency 81
   hot, reloading 81
   JavaScript/React 81
   Native API, accessing 81
   native, components 81
   performance 81
React Native, disadvantages
   curve, learning 82
   ecosystem, community 82
   native modules, dependency 82
   performance 82
   platform, limitations 82
   tool, debugging 82
   UI, customization 82
remember function 130
RESTful APIs 238
RESTful APIs, key aspects
   client-server,
      architecture 238
   data formats 238
   resource-based 238
   stateless 238
RESTful APIs, parts
   Body 239
   Headers 238
   HTTP 238
   Parameters 239
   URL 238

Robot Pattern 331-336
Robot Pattern, advantages
  components, reusable 337
  concerns, separation 337
  maintenance 337
  page objects 337
  readability, improving 337
  test scripts 337
roll() 171

S

scoping functions, types
  also 11
  apply 11
  let 10
  run 10
  with 11
score() 171
Shapes, components
  large 278
  medium 278
  small 278
SoC, benefits
  extensibility, flexibility 28
  modularity, organization 28
  parallel, collaborating 28
  readability, maintaining 28
  reusability 28
  test, debugging 28
SoC, techniques
  lifecycle-aware 139
  LiveData, integrating 138
  Model-View-Controller 138
  Model-View-Intent (MVI) 139

Model-View-Presenter (MVP) 138
Model-View-ViewModel (MVVM) 138
Traditional, approach 138
Uni-directional Data Flow (UDF) 139
SOLID Principles 30
SOLID Principles, categories
  Dependency Inversion 37, 38
  Interface Segregation 35-37
  Liskov Substitution 34, 35
  Open/Closed 32-34
  Single Responsibility 30-32
state management primitives 130
state management primitives, key point
  BackHandler 134
  collecting flows 133
  derived state 131
  local composition 133
  side effects 131, 132
  state variables 130, 131
  state with lifecycle 134
  view model 133
stream() 8
String 4
suspend keyword 23

T

TDD, advantages
  code quality, improving 168
  confidence, refactoring 169
  designing 169
  Documentation 169
  faster, debugging 168
  regression, preventing 169

TDD, concepts
  CCA, optimizing 253, 254
  MockEngine 252, 253
  repository, visualizing 255-258
TDD, history 169
TDD, key points
  Green 168
  Red 168
  Refactor 168
TDD, rules 171-173
ten-pin bowling 170
ten-pin bowling, points
  frame 170
  spare 170
  strike 170
  tenth frame 170
Test-Driven Development (TDD) 168
Timber 321
Timber, advantages 321
Timber, steps 322
Turbine 183
Turbine, features 183
Turbine, methods 184
Typography, key points
  FontFamily 275, 276
  fonts 274, 275
  TestStyle 276

U
UDF/MVI, disadvantage 165

V
val keyword 6
var keyword 6
version catalogs 200
version catalogs, components
  dependencies, block 201
  plugins, block 202
  versions block 201
version catalogs, evolutions 203-206
version catalogs, features
  Aliases 202
  Bundles 202
  customizations 202
  publication 202
version catalogs, key benefits
  code readability, improving 201
  dependency, managing 200
  dependency, simplifying 201
  safe dependency access 200
Volley, features 243

W
watch expressions 315, 316

X
Xamarin 75
Xamarin, disadvantages 77
Xamarin, key aspects 75, 76

Printed in Great Britain
by Amazon

47917400R00229